T0311564

# Financialisation in the European Periphery

In many European countries, the process of financialisation has been exacerbated by the project of closer EU integration and accelerated as a result of austerity policies introduced after the Euro crisis of 2010–2012. However, the impact has been felt differently in core and peripheral countries. This book examines the case of Portugal, and in particular the impact on its economy, work and social reproduction.

The book examines the recent evolution of the Portuguese economy, of particular sectors and systems of social provision (including finance, housing and water), labour relations and income distribution. In doing so, it offers a comprehensive critical analysis of varied aspects of capital accumulation and social reproduction in the country, which are crucial to understand the effects of the official 'bail-out' of 2011 and associated austerity adjustment program. The book shows how these have increasingly relied on deteriorating pay and working conditions and households' direct and indirect engagement with the global financial system in new domains of social reproduction. Through its exploration of the Portuguese case, the book presents a general theoretical and methodological framework for the analysis of financialisation processes in peripheral countries.

This text is essential reading for students and scholars of political economy, development, geography, international relations and sociology with an interest in examining the uneven mechanisms and impacts of global finance.

**Ana Cordeiro Santos** is researcher at the Centre for Social Studies (CES), University of Coimbra, Portugal.

**Nuno Teles** is lecturer at the Faculty of Economics at the Federal University of Bahia, Brazil.

**Routledge Critical Studies in Finance and Stability**
Edited by Jan Toporowski, *School of Oriental and African Studies, University of London, UK*

The 2007–2008 Banking Crash has induced a major and wide-ranging discussion on the subject of financial (in)stability and a need to revaluate theory and policy. The response of policy-makers to the crisis has been to refocus fiscal and monetary policy on financial stabilisation and reconstruction. However, this has been done with only vague ideas of bank recapitalisation and 'Keynesian' reflation aroused by the exigencies of the crisis, rather than the application of any systematic theory or theories of financial instability.

*Routledge Critical Studies in Finance and Stability* covers a range of issues in the area of finance including instability, systemic failure, financial macroeconomics in the vein of Hyman P. Minsky, Ben Bernanke and Mark Gertler, central bank operations, financial regulation, developing countries and financial crises, new portfolio theory and New International Monetary and Financial Architecture.

For more information about this series, please visit: www.routledge.com/series/RCSFS

# Financialisation in the European Periphery

Work and Social Reproduction in Portugal

**Edited by Ana Cordeiro Santos and Nuno Teles**

LONDON AND NEW YORK

First published 2021
by Routledge
2 Park Square, Milton Park, Abingdon, Oxon OX14 4RN

and by Routledge
605 Third Avenue, New York, NY 10017

First issued in paperback 2022

*Routledge is an imprint of the Taylor & Francis Group, an Informa business*

© 2021 selection and editorial matter, Ana Cordeiro Santos and Nuno Teles; individual chapters, the contributors

Publisher's Note
The publisher has gone to great lengths to ensure the quality of this reprint but points out that some imperfections in the original copies may be apparent.

*British Library Cataloguing-in-Publication Data*
A catalogue record for this book is available from the British Library

*Library of Congress Cataloging-in-Publication Data*
A catalog record has been requested for this book

ISBN 13: 978−0−367−54000−5 (pbk)
ISBN 13: 978−1−138−34194−4 (hbk)
ISBN 13: 978−0−429−43990−2 (ebk)

DOI: 10.4324/9780429439902

Typeset in Bembo
by Newgen Publishing UK

# Contents

# Figures

# Tables

# Contributors

**Manuel B. Aalbers** is Professor of Human Geography at KU Leuven/ University of Leuven (Belgium) where he leads a research group on the intersection of real estate, finance and states, spearheaded by a grant from the European Research Council. He is the author of the books *Place, Exclusion, and Mortgage Markets* and *The Financialization of Housing: A Political Economy Approach*, editor of *Subprime Cities: The Political Economy of Mortgage Markets* and associate editor of *Encyclopedia of Urban Studies*. He has also published on redlining, social exclusion, neoliberalism, the privatisation of social housing, neighborhood decline and gentrification.

**Ricardo Barradas** obtained a PhD in Economics on the topic of financialisation and its deleterious effects on the Portuguese economy since the mid-eighties. Currently, he is an assistant professor at Lisbon Accounting and Business School (Polytechnic Institute of Lisbon) and integrated researcher at Center for Research on Socioeconomic Change and Territory, University Institute of Lisbon (DINÂMIA'CET-ISCTE). His main research interests are in the fields of political economy, post-Keynesian economics, financialisation, macroeconometrics and other related areas.

**Maria da Paz Campos Lima**, sociologist, is a senior researcher at the Center for Research on Socioeconomic Change and Territory, University Institute of Lisbon (DINÂMIA'CET-ISCTE), having been a professor at ISCTE-IUL for many years. She is also a senior researcher at the research centre CESIS. She has been a correspondent of Eurofound network, first for EIRO and subsequently for EurWORK. She has participated in several European comparative projects on labour market reforms, social dialogue and collective bargaining. Her research interests include comparative industrial relations, collective bargaining, tripartite concertation, trade unionism and social movements. She is a member of the Editorial Committee of *Transfer: European Review of Labour and Research Quarterly*.

**José Castro Caldas** is currently a researcher at the Collaborative Laboratoty for Work, Employment and Social Protection (CoLABOR) and the Center for Social Studies (CES) of Coimbra University, Portugal. Previously he lectured at the University Institute of Lisbon (ISCTE-IUL), mostly on the history and philosophy of economics. He holds a PhD in Economics.

**Ben Fine** is Emeritus Professor of Economics at the School of Oriental and African Studies, University of London, UK, and Visiting Professor, Wits School of Governance, University of Witwatersrand, South Africa. He is Chair of the International Initiative for Promoting Political Economy and has been elected a Fellow of the Royal Society of Arts.

**Sérgio Lagoa** is Assistant Professor at the University Institute of Lisbon (ISCTE) and researcher at the Center for Research on Socioeconomic Change and Territory (DINÂMIA'CET-ISCTE). His research interests are in monetary and financial economics, financialisation and labour economics. He has participated in research projects on those subjects and published in several journals, notably in the *Journal of Post-Keynesian Economics*, *Journal of Economic Issues*, *Open Economies Review* and *Quantitative Finance*.

**Helena Lopes** holds a PhD in Economics from Paris I, Sorbonne. She is Associate Professor in Political Economy at the University Institute of Lisbon (ISCTE-IUL). Her research interests include labour economics, quality of work and theory of the firm. She has led several multidisciplinary European-funded research projects, and published in *Journal of Institutional Economics*, *Journal of Economic Issues* and *Economic and Industrial Democracy*.

**Ricardo Paes Mamede** is Professor of Political Economy at ISCTE (University Institute of Lisbon) and member of the Center for Research on Socioeconomic Change and Territory (DINÂMIA'CET-ISCTE). He holds a PhD in Economics from Bocconi University (Italy). His main research interests are in the fields of structural change and public policy.

**Diogo Martins** is a PhD student of Economics at the University of Massachusetts Amherst, USA. He obtained an MSc degree in Monetary and Financial Economics and a BSc degree in Economics from Lisbon School of Economics and Management, University of Lisbon (ISEG-UL), Portugal.

**Catarina Príncipe** is a PhD student of the Interdisciplinary Programme on Political Economy at the University Institute of Lisbon (ISCTE-IUL) in Lisbon, Portugal. Her research project aims at studying the mechanisms of state transformation and class recomposition in Portugal throughout the process of European integration. She has also been a contributing editor for *Jacobin Magazine* for several years, where she writes about the European Left and the relation between European states and the European Union.

**José Reis** is a full professor at the Faculty of Economics of the University of Coimbra, and a senior researcher at the Center for Social Studies (CES) of the same university. His main fields of work are institutional economics and political economy, economic thought, territorial dynamics and Portuguese and European economies. He is currently the President of the Portuguese Association of Political Economy (EcPol).

**João Rodrigues** is Assistant Professor at the Faculty of Economics and Researcher at the Centre for Social Studies (CES), both at the University of Coimbra, Portugal. His research interests range from the history of neo-liberalism to the financialisation of capitalism in Portugal. He has published on these topics in journals such as *Cambridge Journal of Economics*, *Review of International Political Economy* and *New Political Economy*.

**Ana Cordeiro Santos** is a researcher at the Centre for Social Studies (CES), University of Coimbra, Portugal. Her research interests include the topics of semi-peripheral financialisation, debt and housing. She has led research projects on those subjects and has published books and articles on these topics in journals such as *Development and Change, Global Social Policy, New Political Economy* and *Review of International Political Economy*.

**Nuno Teles** is a lecturer at the Faculty of Economics of the Federal University of Bahia, Brazil. He obtained his PhD from the School of Oriental and African Studies, University of London, UK. He worked as a post-doc researcher (2012–2016) in the FESSUD project at the Centre of Social Studies (CES) of the University of Coimbra, Portugal.

# Acknowledgements

This book is the outcome of a collective endeavour devoted to the analysis of the financialised trajectory of the Portuguese political economy and subsequent post-crisis developments. The systematic account offered here could not have been provided without the joint reflections of many of those who have studied the subject: Catarina Príncipe, Diogo Martins, Helena Lopes, João Rodrigues, José Castro Caldas, José Reis, Maria da Paz Campos Lima, Ricardo Barradas, Ricardo Paes Mamede and Sérgio Lagoa. The editors thank them for joining this venture.

This work traces back, perhaps in a more fundamental way, to previous collaborations. The FESSUD project (Financialisation, Economy, Society and Sustainable Development, http://fessud.eu), led by Malcolm Sawyer from 2011 to 2016, which pioneered the study of the variegated nature of financialisation comprising 15 core, semi-peripheral and peripheral countries, is a case in point. The editors began such a study for the Portuguese semi-periphery then. Thus, they would like to express their thankfulness to Malcolm Sawyer and the colleagues with whom they have worked closest – Andrew Brown, Daniela Gabor, David Spencer, Eric Clark, Kate Bayliss, Magda Tancau, Mary Robertson, Sigrid Betzelt, Wlodzimierz Dymarski – and the FESSUD team with whom they have learned about the historical-geographical context-specificity of financialisation processes.

It was within the FESSUD project that the editors have begun an enduring collaboration and friendship with Ben Fine. This book is just one token of this relationship, and a much better accomplished one due to almost endless discussions. For this the editors are most grateful (and also relieved that the book is completed). Throughout this journey they have also made new acquaintances. Manuel Aalbers was a most fortunate one, helping them to better understand the utmost relevance of core and peripheral geographies. In addition to commenting on various chapters of this book, Ben and Manuel also agreed to contribute with their reflections on the notions of social reproduction and semi-periphery, which are pivotal in this book. The editors are grateful for this as well.

They would like to extend their appreciation to Jan Toporowski for challenging them to write this book for the Routledge Critical Studies in Finance and

Stability, and to the Routledge team for all the support given prior and during the production process, especially to Andy Humphries, Anna Cuthbert, Emma Morley, Damien Love and Kawiya Bakthavatchalam.

Finally, the editors acknowledge the financial support received from the Portuguese Foundation for Science and Technology (FCT/MEC), through national funds and the European Regional Development Fund (ERDF) through the Competitiveness and Innovation Operational Program COMPETE 2020 (Project FINHABIT-PTDC/ATP-GEO/2362/2014-POCI-01-0145-FEDER-016869).

# 1 Post-crisis financialisation in the Southern European periphery

## Introduction

*Ana Cordeiro Santos and Nuno Teles*

### The context-specificity of the Southern European periphery

This book examines the context-specific attributes of financialisation processes in Portugal and their impact on the economy, labour relations and social reproduction more generally, providing a wide-ranging account of the recent evolution of this Southern European (SE) country in its embedding in the global financial markets. Even though the main focus will be on the Portuguese political economy, the analysis proceeds by placing it in the broader context of the SE region with which it shares many characteristics. This allows us to bring the concepts of semi-periphery and periphery into the analysis, and further elaborate on that concept, as well as the twin concept of the core, and thereby the political and economic power relations at the European level. Even though the book underlines the commonalities of a fairly homogeneous region, shaped by similar socioeconomic structures and trajectories, including the processes of European integration that took place at the same time and at the same pace, it will point to the variegated nature of financialisation itself and the more general processes to which it is attached.

A first premise of this book is, then, that financialisation must be understood as a process that interacts with others in historically given circumstances and in geographically specific contexts. This requires considering how economies are embedded within the international political economy and the multiple and differentiated ways finance penetrates and expands in various realms of economic and social restructuring.

A second premise of this book is that such analyses must address the domain of economic reproduction and its embedding within social reproduction. This allows us to incorporate the economy, at macro and sectoral levels, labour relations and the broad activities required for society to be reproduced. This means that the reproduction of labour force and accompanying ideological relations that are vital in such reproduction are included, as well as underlying power relations despite the conflicts that inevitably arise in contemporary capitalist societies.

Such considerations demonstrate that the reach of finance in particular territories is variegated because national institutional frameworks that shape economic and social reproduction affect the financialisation of the various sectors and systems of social provision, producing differentiated impacts at the national, regional and local levels, as well as at the sectoral composition of the economy, labour relations, housing and water provision on which we focus in some detail in this book.

Indeed, there is a growing body of literature devoted to the context-specific modalities of financialisation in SE countries (Barradas et al., 2018; Gambarotto & Solari, 2015; Orsi & Solari, 2010; Rodrigues, Santos & Teles, 2016) as well as the harsh impacts of the financial crisis of 2008–2009 (Leahy, Healy & Murphy, 2014; Kantola & Lombardo, 2017; Oxfam, 2013) that have resulted in a growing divergence from the EU core, giving rise to further institutional variegation and socioeconomic unevenness (Gambarotto, Rangone & Solari, 2019; Johnston & Regan, 2016; Lains, 2018; Rodrigues, Santos & Teles, 2018; Santos, Rodrigues & Teles; 2018; Weeks, 2019). On the other hand, less attention has as yet been given to the novel ways in which finance continues to pervade economic and social reproduction in SE peripheries. More than a decade since the outburst of the Global Financial Crisis (GFC) these new ways are ever more blatant. Through comparative analysis of recent changes with Portugal as focal point, this book devotes particular attention to the recent transformations of financialisation across Southern Europe.

While SE countries share the same peripheral position with Eastern European (EE) countries within Europe, the focus of this book is on the former. Even though these two regions share a similar subordinated relation with the European core, they have undergone distinct historical trajectories entailing differentiated patterns of peripheral financialisation. Three most critical EE features set them apart: the post-socialist trajectory, the later integration into the EU, and the geographical proximity of EE countries to the European core, which shaped their process of European integration and the forms and contents of financialisation in the region. The post-socialist trajectory produced a large-scale restructuring of economic and social relations through the availability of a large pool of depreciated corporate assets and qualified cheap labour. That is, having gone through a process of industrial restructuring involving dramatic shifts from the divisions of production under 'socialist' rule, EE subsequently went through a reorientation process driven by foreign-owned multinational corporations, most notably from Germany, which outsourced parts of production to the region. Even though this inflow of foreign capital allowed a relevant industrial sector to consolidate in EE countries, this process meant also growing dependence and subordination as it was led from the outside. And while the specific nature of financialisation processes in SE countries was by and large marked by these countries' participation in the eurozone from its inception, which promoted the unprecedented rise of private indebtedness with the intermediary role of domestic banks, in mostly non-euro EE countries financialisation processes were on the whole promoted by a more critical participation of foreign banks and/or the foreign ownership of domestic banks that instilled a more moderate rise of private debt contracted on a foreign currency (Gabor, 2010, 2012). This has also entailed a subordinated position that is accentuating vulnerabilities linked with the dependence on foreign direct investment for export industrialisation, associated with strategies of labour devaluation, and, in some cases, feeding a recent expansion of household debt accompanied by the rise of public debt (Podvršič & Becker, 2019).

Though EE countries are comparatively relevant, the analytical work to be developed in this book will focus on the context-specific trajectories of SE countries, having Portugal as its paradigmatic case. Nonetheless, it is meant to offer a general framework for the analysis of (semi-)peripheral countries, given the crucial role of the process of European integration in moulding the nature of financialisation processes in the continent. We believe not only that this research contributes to a more accurate understanding of the recent trajectory of SE countries, but also that it provides paramount insights for a more systemic approach to financialisation by scrutinising both the macro and variegated nature of this process.

In previous work we have already argued that financialisation involves political and economic power relations on a world scale, and that this is a plastic process to the extent that finance expands in differentiated ways in time and space and across systems of provision (Rodrigues, Santos & Teles, 2016, 2018; Santos, Rodrigues & Teles, 2018). This book reiterates the relevance of the world scale and finance's plasticity. But the focus now is on post-crisis financialisation in SE where European institutions and the International Monetary Fund were the most relevant actors as they gained added economic and political power with the conditionality attached to the official loans granted to this semi-periphery when the GFC turned into a sovereign debt crisis in the region. It argues that the imbalances and unevenness attached to financialisation are not leading to a reversal or a slowing down of previous processes. The various chapters show instead how qualitative changes are being produced that keep those processes going in novel ways resulting in further variegation and unevenness within the EU.

The book is organised in three parts: financialisation and the euro crisis; labour relations; and social reproduction. Part 1 presents the main features of financialisation in Portugal and the ways in which it has impacted on the trajectory of the economy prior to, and after, the euro crisis. It underlines the variegated nature of financialisation in terms of the forms taken and ensuing vulnerability and financial dependency. Part 2 discusses the impacts of financialisation and the euro crisis on the labour market at theoretical and empirical levels, addressing the ways in which financialisation has altered management practices at the corporate level in general, and in relation to the workforce, in particular. It also discusses the role of the EU and national actors in promoting or resisting ongoing labour market transformations, and their impacts on employment and wage levels. Part 3 discusses the impacts of financialisation on social reproduction, thereby extending the analysis beyond the realm of capital accumulation as such (i.e. industry and industrial relations) as analysed in the previous parts. It addresses, both theoretically and empirically, changes in workers' ways and conditions of reproducing themselves, examining various indicators of inequality, including access to commodities and services that used to be collectively provided but the provisioning of which has been increasingly financialised, as illustrated with the housing and water systems of provision. The remainder of this introductory chapter further presents the structure and the constituent parts of the book. But before that, some conceptual clarification is provided on our understanding of the concept of financialisation as applied to (semi-)peripheral contexts.

## Approaching finance from a political economy perspective

Notwithstanding Epstein's (2005, p. 3) popular all-encompassing definition comprising 'the increasing role of financial motives, financial markets, financial actors and financial institutions in the operation of the domestic and international economies', the concept of financialisation is prone to diverse, although interrelated, understandings. These range from a new finance-led accumulation regime and the rise of shareholder value management to the ubiquity of finance in our daily lives (van der Zwan, 2014), and beyond (Aalbers, 2019). The adoption of such general and diverse understandings of financialisation can be taken as risking conceptual irrelevance (Christophers, 2015; Christophers & Fine, 2020). But they have also contributed to advancing research in a surprisingly unexplored subject across disciplines, from varied vantage points and increasingly addressing different geographies. This book is meant as well as a contribution to this large and expanding body of literature.

However, we would like to bring more directly into the analysis conceptual tools on finance from Marxist political economy as an important first step for the analysis of (semi-)peripheral contexts. These include the various categories of capital such as money-capital, interest-bearing capital, fictitious capital and loanable-money capital, which have different and divergent theoretical interpretations in the context of financialisation studies.[1]

Marx (1981 [1867]) long ago examined how money can be converted into capital on the basis of capitalist production, i.e. how money can be converted into money-capital used in the circuit of capital to buy labour force and the means of production. On his view, money-capital can be derived from the hoards that originated in the circuit of capital and that can be lent and invested as capital by someone else. This exposes a 'double outlay of money as capital', where interest (as a partition of surplus value) is due to the owner of this capital by the capitalist borrower and is generally below the average rate of profit in normal conditions of reproduction. This then means that money-capital can itself become a commodity, that it can be interest-bearing capital (IBC), the basis of the credit system.

Marx's initial exposition of the role of IBC in the circuit of capital, and thus in production wherein surplus value is extracted, is at the core of Fine's understanding of financialisation. According to Fine (2013, p. 49), IBC is 'distinct from money borrowed (even with interest) for other purposes'. That is,

IBC can only be located where 'production and realization of surplus value in Marxist terms' take place or when IBC acquires this character 'based on the intentions of those who are borrowing'. Fictitious capital (FC) is the 'independent circulation of IBC in paper form', in other words, it is a tradable security priced according to expected future returns (that may or may not materialise in the future, thus its 'fictitious' character). FC allows an explanation of the 'intensive' and 'extensive' growth of finance through the upstream securitisation of productive investments, which provide financial institutions the liquidity needed to finance both investment (i.e. money-capital) and non-productive loans. Hence, financialisation is understood as the accumulation of FC or 'the increasing scope and prevalence of IBC in the accumulation of capital' (Fine, 2013, p. 55). This, in turn, entails an added analytical role for the cash flows originating in production, which sustain securitisation and the trade of securities in financial markets.

Makoto Itoh and Costas Lapavitsas offer a broader conceptualisation of IBC. On their view, IBC encompasses two notions. First, IBC includes the above-mentioned role in the circuit of capital, being associated with a particular class relation, that between 'functioning [industrial] capitalists' (the borrowers) and 'monied' capitalists (the lenders), who accumulate and lend out their hoards (Itoh & Lapavitsas, 1999, p. 61). Second, IBC 'might also be created out of temporary idle parts of the money revenue of workers and other social groups', which may be used by capitalists. By the same token, 'the further advance of interest-bearing capital by the credit system need not be directed exclusively towards real accumulation, but also towards other activities not productive of surplus value' (Itoh & Lapavitsas, 1999, p. 61). That is, not only can workers' hoards fund IBC, but IBC can also fund loans to workers. This contrasts with Fine's view in which IBC exclusively derives from and is exclusively channelled to production.

Drawing on Marx's concept of loanable-money capital (LMC), Lapavitsas (2013, p. 117) asserts that this is 'the appropriate concept for analysis of the borrower-lender relationship [...] rather than interest-bearing capital'. LMC has the advantage of corresponding 'to a lower level of theoretical abstraction', which 'rests on the advanced functioning of the financial system', where 'interest takes the form of a reward for merely parting with the money lent regardless of the purposes of the loan'. Lapavitsas' approach to IBC is thus broader than Fine's even if the more expansive use of the term is generally conveyed by the notion of LMC. LMC encompasses the mobilisation of idle money by the financial sector, for whatever purpose, and the possibility open to the financial system to act on the anticipation of the accumulation of this idle money.

Even though Lapavitsas and Fine propose different understandings of IBC, both approaches have the advantage of rooting their claims in how finance interacts with capital accumulation, avoiding the somewhat naïve accounts that perceive finance as a separate realm consisting of pure parasitical 'casino speculation'. But Lapavitsas' perspective is broader, as mentioned, considering the conceptual possibility of including non-productive loans as IBC, such those granted to households that are not directly channelled to production and thus are not part of the circuit of capital. This perhaps accommodates Marx's original understanding of IBC as a form of 'antediluvian' capital that did not emerge with capitalism. Indeed, for Marx, IBC predates capitalism, then identified as usury, directed both at production and consumption in pre-capitalist times.[2]

But while IBC does not have to be directly employed as productive capital by the borrower to be considered capital, within capitalism it is subjected to the competitive pressures of capital reproduction. Thus, Itoh and Lapavitsas' conception of IBC as LMC locates the latter in a competitive environment where banks strive to attract hoards across the economy in order to support their credit creation. Moreover, even in situations where the impacts are less straightforward on the reproduction of capital, as in consumer or mortgage credit, LMC contributes to the credit system through its 'effect in the equalisation of the rate of profit' by accelerating the reproduction of capital and, thus, the production of surplus value (Itoh & Lapavitsas, 1999).

Rather than insurmountable conceptual divergences in the various categories of capital, what the above discussion entails is a different conceptual focus, either on fictitious or on loanable-money capital, resulting in nuanced different takes on financialisation. This has inevitable relevant implications for research on financialisation, and particularly for the examination of the distinctive differences between core and (semi-)peripheral contexts. In our view, the LMC concept is more apt to examine (semi-)peripheries as it allows us to analyse processes that fall outside the arena of securitisation and securities markets (i.e. FC), which are less predominant therein. In so doing, LMC more easily integrates recent phenomena, such as the increasing involvement of workers with finance, both as debtors and creditors. This while retaining the Marxist emphasis on the relation between finance and production by scrutinizing how hoards are produced and mobilized by the financial system across borders. Finally, it allows the inclusion of hierarchical power relations at the global level and how these play out in the productive and financial realms. Indeed, the focus on the channelling of idle money to credit through the banking system not only applies to different classes or sectors, but it also fits relations across countries. This is particularly relevant to the European context given the creditor and debtor relations whereby the external surplus produced in core countries, such as Germany, is turned into credit to the European periphery, either in the form of FC (e.g. public debt securities) or LMC (e.g. interbank loans). This difference provides an important indication that production and real accumulation mould financial relations and financialisation processes differently in different geographies. These links will be particularly scrutinised in the first part of the book.

## Semi-peripheral financialisation in SE

In Chapter 2, entitled 'Revisiting the concept of semi-peripheral financialisation', Rodrigues, Santos and Teles identify the main features of the Portuguese processes of financialisation taken as constituting the semi-peripheral type when analysed on a world scale. The term semi-periphery is adopted in a double sense. First, it accounts for the intermediate position of the Portuguese economy in the world economy, combining characteristics of developed and developing countries, as it has been marked by late industrialisation and backward economic development relative to the core made up of Northern and Central European countries. Second, it refers to the institutional features of its financial system, also sharing characteristics of core and peripheral countries, being mostly shaped by the predominance of loanable-money capital *vis-à-vis* that of fictitious capital given the country's relatively immature securities markets.

The notion of semi-peripheral financialisation is also meant to stress the uneven and combined nature of financialisation processes, understood in terms of the incorporation of financialised practices in non-financialised institutional environments, accounting for spatial and sectoral variegation of financialisation processes (see Fernandez & Aalbers, 2019, and references therein; Chapters 12 and 13 in this volume). In the Portuguese case, its intermediate position in the world economy under the current era of financialised capitalism has meant the subordination of a relatively backward economy to the interests of international finance and other forms of capital located in the most advanced countries, and to the national and international institutions under their influence. As in other SE countries, this subordination has been mostly exercised through the process of European integration, first through accession to the European Economic Community (EEC), and subsequently through the steps taken towards the creation of the Economic and Monetary Union (EMU).

Indeed, the creation of the single market in the domains of capital, goods and services, which dissolved trade barriers within the EU, required substantial structural transformations within a short time-span (privatisation, liberalisation and re-regulation in many sectors of the economy, including finance) and opening up to new, similar low-cost-of-labour competitors (i.e. Eastern European countries and China). The subsequent project of the single currency, set up in the Maastricht Treaty, imposed a common and tight fiscal and monetary policy for the countries willing to be part of the euro area. This was a major factor in SE financialisation. The new currency allowed almost unlimited access to loanable (money) capital at low interest rates, often unavailable to countries with similar levels of development. The combination of cheap credit, loss of competitiveness and the continued straitjacket of budgetary restrictions favoured private corporate and household indebtedness cornered around the real estate and housing sectors.

In the context of growing international competition and the lack of control over monetary and exchange rate policy at the national level, the credit-driven form of financialisation that the EMU promoted in this part of Europe led to the transfer of investment to the more protected non-tradable sectors, resulting in reduced productivity growth relative to wage and price increases, accentuating the economic weaknesses of these countries (Gambarotto, Rangone & Solari, 2019; Chapters 3, 4 and 7 in this volume; Reis et al., 2014; Rodrigues & Reis, 2012). The result was mounting current account deficits and external debt. This contrasts to the evolution of core European countries, most notably Germany, that have instead developed export-oriented models, accumulating surplus in their current trade account (Barradas et al., 2018; Johnston & Regan, 2016; Stockhammer, 2011; Stockhammer, Durand & List, 2016), thus allowing, and requiring, a continuing fuel of loanable-money capital to the SE periphery.

Increasingly integrated into a highly hierarchical and asymmetric financial system, the recent evolution of SE economies was marked by the incidence of sovereign debt crises when, in the wake of the GFC, states could no longer refinance themselves in international markets, culminating in dependence on official loans, upon request, from the Troika comprised of the European Central Bank, the European Commission and the International Monetary Fund. The most severe economic and financial crises followed, especially in Greece and Portugal, which were most forcibly compelled to implement radical structural adjustment reforms. Greece was the first country to ask for financial assistance from the international institutions, in May 2010. Portugal did so one year later, in May 2011, followed by Spain in July 2014, in the latter case with assistance subject to conditions for the banking sector only. Italy has never made such a request, but has also been severely pressured by bond markets to push through reforms and austerity measures.

After the 2009 recession, the austerity programmes imposed as a condition for institutional financial assistance produced a new round of economic crises between 2011 and 2014. While fiscal and monetary restrictive policies were already part of the EU toolkit, the memoranda of understanding that the countries signed accelerated the implementation of ever more draconian measures, most notably labour market reforms that downgraded wage income and working conditions. These measures accentuated economic and social fragilities, resulting in long recessions and unprecedented double-digit unemployment rates, especially so among the youth.

Even though, at very different paces, economic activity has recovered over the last five years, not least due to a change of monetary policy by the ECB, the distance between the EU core and periphery has grown, with significantly higher peripheral levels of unemployment and people at risk of poverty (Table 1.1). However, the situation of each is variegated even across these four relatively similar countries. Portugal presents an interesting case as it seems to have recovered better from the harsh impacts of the crisis, presenting the lowest unemployment rate and risk of poverty and social exclusion (see Chapter 10). While these measures no doubt signal an improved situation, variegated and volatile vulnerabilities within the country remain high, as this book will show.

In Chapter 3, 'Portugal as a European periphery: imbalances, dependency and trajectories', José Reis offers an historical account of the country's changing semi-peripheral condition over the last four decades in light of the process of European integration and associated trajectories of structuration of material and social life. Special attention is given to labour and industrial relations, the modes of articulation with other economic spaces within Europe, and the more recent financial dependency under the conditions of the EMU and the crisis.

*Table 1.1* Average GDP, unemployment and poverty rates, 2009–2018

|  | *2009–2013* | *2014–2018* | *2018* |
|---|---|---|---|
| **Real GDP growth rate** | | | |
| EU | -0.1 | 2.1 | 2 |
| Greece | -5.9 | 0.7 | 1.9 |
| Spain | -1.8 | 2.8 | 2.6 |
| Italy | -1.5 | 0.9 | 0.9 |
| Portugal | -1.6 | 1.9 | 2.1 |
| **Unemployment rate** | | | |
| EU | 9.9 | 8.5 | 6.8 |
| Greece | 18.4 | 23.2 | 19.3 |
| Spain | 22 | 19.7 | 15.3 |
| Italy | 9.5 | 11.6 | 10.6 |
| Portugal | 13.1 | 10.8 | 7.1 |
| **People at risk of poverty or social exclusion** | | | |
| EU | 24.1 | 23.5 | 22.4 |
| Greece | 31.3 | 35.5 | 34.8 |
| Spain | 26.4 | 28.1 | 26.6 |
| Italy | 27.3 | 29 | 28.9 |
| Portugal | 25.5 | 25.6 | 23.3 |

Source: Eurostat

Direct links are thus forged between the persistent semi-peripheral condition of the Portuguese economy at the world level and its insertion in the EU, on the one hand, and the impacts these links have had on economic and social reproduction. Reis' analysis has an important implication: appraisal of the trajectory of the economy is incomplete without a sectoral analysis of contributions to employment and social reproduction.

Reis stresses that the high rates of economic growth in the 1950s and 1960s cannot be taken as defining characteristics of an allegedly golden age in Portugal, as some historians have suggested. This is so not only because the country was then under a dictatorship, but also because those growth rates were associated with low employment rates and mass emigration. In other words, in addition to analysis of economic growth rates, attention must also be given to the sectoral composition of the economy and wider social reproduction conditions. For the same reasons, the present economic recovery, even if associated with declining unemployment and a reduction of the risk of poverty and social exclusion, can hardly be taken as an indication that the structural problems of the economy have been resolved. Even if the Portuguese economy and society have, at particular junctures, experienced some remarkable bounce-backs and achievements, significant imbalances have remained. In the last decades, these have been attached to long-lasting negative balances of trade reflecting the position of the country as a net importer, and more recently under the single currency, to current account deficits associated with unprecedented levels of private debt. The present situation is particularly difficult because the influx of foreign financial flows has not been channelled to the diversification and upgrading of economic activities, hindering the rise of productivity and wages, and social and territorial cohesion (see also Chapters 4 and 7 in this volume). Moreover, within the strict monetary and fiscal conditionality currently imposed by the EU, the country finds itself in an institutional locked-in situation that prevents it from carrying out any policy that could at least attempt to redress its semi-peripheral condition.

In Chapter 4, 'Financialisation and structural change in Portugal: a euro-resource-curse?', Ricardo Paes Mamede examines the relation between structural change and financialisation through the analysis of the growth of credit to the non-financial sector. Mamede takes as a starting point the participation of the country in the EMU that allowed an extraordinary inflow of loanable (money) capital, depicted as a financial euro-resource-curse to evoke the similarities with the recipients of capital inflows in the developing world and resultant exchange rate appreciation and financial instability, as developed in the Dutch-disease thesis. Even though the exchange rate has remained stable, similar to the countries that rapidly opened up their capital accounts, in Portugal the influx of capital fostered the development of non-tradable activities at the expense of the tradable sector. This trend was reinforced by a combination of factors, which include an economy based on a low-productivity, low-skills manufacturing sector, the increasing globalisation of trade and production, and last but not least, a strong and stable currency.

A growing divergence from the EU core has resulted, with the low-productivity sectors that already had a significant weight in the economy – construction, accommodation and food services – increasing their relative importance, in terms of both Gross Value Added and employment, while high-productivity sectors – such as information and communication technology and other business services – are growing at a slower pace. The traditional sectors – agriculture and fishing, and textiles and footwear – have declined because they have failed to keep up with the competition coming from EE countries (benefiting from an influx of foreign direct investment that targeted the manufacturing export sector as we have seen above), and China in the context of a strong euro.

## Semi-peripheral financialisation and labour relations in SE

The financialisation literature has explored the ways through which financialisation has impacted on the labour market and labour relations. This has been covered in two grand strands of literature. One of them has underlined the emergence of a finance-led accumulation regime that has undermined collective arrangements and labour protection laws (e.g. Boyer, 2000); the other has focused on the ascendency of a new form of management devoted to the maximisation of shareholder value, characterised by the restructuring of production around financial imperatives, resulting in a greater weight of finance standards, short-termism of management and increasing top management salaries (e.g. Crotty, 2005). Deregulation of the labour market together with new management practices are then deemed to have resulted in falling labour income shares and increasing inequality in the personal distribution of income, fuelling the rise of private debt to make up for wage stagnation or regression (e.g. Hein, 2015).

In Chapter 5, entitled 'Financialisation, work and labour relations', Helena Lopes examines the ascendency of new forms of governance. She argues that more analysis is needed at the firm level as the corporation is the most critical mediator between finance and workers, including listed and non-listed firms due to the contagion effects the former have on the latter. Lopes argues that financialisation has forged a finance-led management model, promoting the development of accounting practices that link financial targets to operational activities, resulting in the quantification of workers' activities through various means – quantitative work targets, quantitative performance appraisals, pecuniary incentive schemes, systemic reporting – which infuse financial criteria into workers' activity.

This mode of governance is deemed to lead to unprecedented levels of intensification, dehumanisation and devaluation of work, undermining its meaningfulness to workers as well as its collective character, furthering workers' alienation with non-negligible moral and health impacts, in addition to the loss of wage income and rights. Moreover, by normalising individualism and the lack of empathy towards others, the quantification of workers' tasks is also producing psychosocial disorders due to feelings of isolation and of culpability when performance targets are not met, emotional exhaustion, dissolution of collective solidarities, deterioration of work relations and overall depersonalisation of work interactions. What is particularly worrisome is not only that firms exploit workers' subjective engagement in such inhumane ways – this did not originate with financialisation. What is troublesome is that financialisation, by intensifying and broadening such exploitation, facilitates these practices, which are increasingly perceived by workers as reasonable and justified. As this mode of governance is increasingly generalised and accepted as legitimate, it becomes more difficult to challenge. This is so not only because individualism hampers collective forms of action, but also because it becomes more difficult to perceive these finance-led management practices as the outcome of prior political action and thus capable of being challenged and replaced by alternatives, especially those that again place production and employment at the centre of firms' activities (as opposed to short-term profitability for underpinning shareholder value and financial speculation). As this requires action at levels other than the firm, it entails conceiving the firm as an entity embedded in political struggle and part of the conditions of economic and social reproduction.

In addition to systemic transformations in corporate governance in listed firms and their contagion effects on non-listed (public and private) firms, undermining workers' rights and wages, in Europe, EU institutions have actively promoted the deregulation of labour markets, particularly of SE countries after the GFC. The conversion of the financial crisis into a public debt crisis of the weakest economies was then used to justify the implementation of particularly harsh austerity measures in those economies, which they accepted because they needed official loans as they could no longer finance themselves in the financial markets. Conditions imposed included the weakening of labour rights in national legislation, in general, and the deterioration of public employment and civil servants' rights in particular, worsening the quality of services provided in relevant areas such as health and education (e.g. Hespanha, 2019).

Since the crisis, EU institutions such as the European Council, the European Commission and the Eurogroup have pressured member states to further reduce public spending, leading to deteriorating public services. The magnitude of the crisis then created a favourable environment for instituting a 'new macroeconomic governance regime' (Kantola & Lombardo, 2017), including new sets of legislative pacts and packs – the Euro Plus Pact, the Stability and Growth Pact, the Fiscal Compact and the Six-Pack – which tied member states into a commitment to keep their annual budgetary deficit below 3 per cent and their debt below 60 per cent of GDP. This added to pressure on the economically and politically weaker member states to cut public sector employment and wages.

In Chapter 6, 'Reconfiguring labour market and collective bargaining institutions in Portugal: turning the page on internal devaluation?', Maria da Paz Campos Lima examines recent institutional changes in labour market regulation during and after the Troika intervention, to assess the amplitude and intensity of changes and the continuities and discontinuities between the two periods. She argues that during the period 2010–2014, government practices and changes to legal regulations represent a radical shift towards the erosion of collective bargaining, the weakening of trade union power and the reduction of labour rights. The new political cycle that emerged when the Socialist party came to power, in 2015, with the parliamentary support of the left parties, aroused expectations towards the reconstruction of institutions that had been damaged by the adjustment process. However, despite the reversal of some measures, such as the cuts in nominal wages and bonuses and the unfreezing of civil servants' careers, relevant mechanisms of internal devaluation, such as those weakening the role of collective agreements and of trade unions, continued in place. This then signals the long-term impacts of policies of internal devaluation and the difficulty in reverting them. While future governments may more easily alter wage policies in the public sector, it will be far more difficult to restore overall labour rights.

In Chapter 7, 'Financialisation, labour and structural change: the case of Portuguese internal devaluation', Nuno Teles, José Castro Caldas and Diogo Martins argue that the gradual loss of political power of trade unions and the implementation of regressive labour market reforms have been a deliberate outcome of EU policy. This was first initiated through soft power, as in the case of the European Employment Strategy, which explicitly and intentionally directed member states towards employment policies focused on the deregulation of the labour market conceived as a macroeconomic policy variable for the attainment of growth. The GFC provided the opportunity to harden these policies in SE. Indeed, the request for financial assistance was followed by demands for 'structural reforms', especially of the labour market, that targeted the dismantling of collective bargaining arrangements at national and sectoral levels, and the promotion of negotiations at the firm level that enfeebled trade unions. This resulted in loss of protection for workers through facilitating employee dismissals, intensifying working hours, and cuts in pay for night or extraordinary hours.

Consonant with the analyses in Chapters 3 and 4, Teles and co-authors argue that the option for internal devaluation is having lasting impacts on the economy through a structural change based on the relative rise of low-pay and low-productivity sectors, which have been the main drivers of the growth of employment and the recent economic recovery, accentuating the semi-peripheral and apparently irreversible condition of the country. Being perceived as the main instrument to tackle the crisis and thereby ensure debt repayment to foreign creditors, labour became more intricately dominated by foreign financial institutions. Having relinquished exchange rate and monetary policy, in a context of imposed fiscal austerity, financial agents prevail over ever more domains, such as the labour market and other areas of social reproduction. This is yet one more difference between peripheral and core countries, with a more relevant role of EU institutions in determining labour market regulation to the detriment of the democratic deliberation.[3]

The transformations in labour markets have impacts both on the economy and on social reproduction more broadly. The three first chapters of the first part of this volume show that the increasing economic and financial integration of SE economies in the context of a strong common currency has favoured the non-tradable sectors. The second part shows that labour market reforms have intensified the vicious circle of low wages in low-productivity sectors. The third part of the book shows that these trends have had severe impacts on social reproduction, as low-waged precarious employment compromises resources, monetised and otherwise, for sustaining norms of everyday life.

## Semi-peripheral financialisation and social reproduction in SE

The third part of the book discusses the impacts of financialisation on social reproduction, thereby extending the analysis beyond the realm of capital accumulation (i.e. industry and labour relations) analysed in the previous parts. The focus moves on to the activities that are attached to livelihoods within and beyond those delivered through the market, including the consumption of basic goods such as education, health or housing, and different forms of care needed at various stages of the life course.

There is a burgeoning literature on the social impacts of the financial crisis in Europe, which has underlined the severe consequences for SE households, mostly from austerity measures resulting in unemployment, reduced income and the rise of economic and social vulnerability (e.g. Leahy, Healy & Murphy, 2014), and of their gendered impacts (e.g. Bargawi, Cozzi & Himmelweit, 2017). An emerging literature has more recently started forging the relation between financialisation and economic and social reproduction, linking economics, politics and social outcomes (Bargawi, Cozzi & Himmelweit, 2017; Bayliss, Fine & Robertson, 2017; Bhattacharya, 2017; Elson, 2012; Fine, 2017; Kantola & Lombardo, 2017; Roberts, 2013). Within the European context, it is increasingly evident that the severe social consequences of the crisis are by and large the outcome of EU policies that have favoured the expansion of finance and rendered livelihoods more difficult for most vulnerable segments of the population.

While EU policies were already putting in place a set of 'hegemonic projects' promoting a 'finance-led regime', pushing the financialisation of social provisioning in areas such as pensions, health and elderly care (Wöhl, 2017), the crisis pushed this agenda further through austerity measures, having particularly harsh effects on SE countries and on their already weaker welfare systems. Feminist political economists have, in turn, underlined that these developments in the sphere of economic and social reproduction have significant gendered impacts (Elson, 2010, 2012; Montgomerie & Young, 2010; Roberts, 2013). This is because women tend to have fewer assets to protect themselves against social exposure and risk, and are overrepresented in insecure low-paid jobs with no benefits, while assuming greater responsibility for care.

In Chapter 8, 'The deepening of financialised social reproduction in Southern Europe', Ana Cordeiro Santos and Catarina Príncipe address the impact of financialised social reproduction in this semi-periphery and its gendered effects. They argue that the occurrence of the GFC in these countries, followed by the Troika interventions, has implied the deterioration of already poor working conditions and of their weak welfare states, meaning greater strain at the household level to ensure social reproductive activities, and putting at risk more vulnerable households, which lack resources to purchase commodified goods and services. But this does not mean that finance expansion has reached its full potential in the semi-periphery. It is instead finding new ways to expand in various systems of provisioning. Based on the Portuguese experience, it is shown how the post-crisis is bringing about new agents, such as institutional investors in real estate, further straining the livelihoods of the youth, who face not only less favourable work conditions and pay but also increasing living costs. The long-lasting impact of the EU hegemonic project in the periphery therefore means an overburden of SE households, and especially of women, as ultimate absorbers of economic and social shocks. Following feminist political economists of a Marxist tradition, they argue that the analysis of contemporary capitalism must include developments outside the strict realm of capitalist production, including critical studies on the ways in which financialised social provisioning impacts on how labour power is produced and reproduced, which analyses of aggregate levels of employment or various forms of income inequality cannot account for. They conclude that the detrimental impacts of financialised social provisioning can only be overcome through the resolution of the contradictions of capitalism at a more structural level, going beyond mere fixes of gender or other gaps within present circumstances.

The plasticity of finance to adapt to altered conditions is evidenced not only in the more recent post-crisis developments, but also in how these developments take place in distinct systems of social provision. In Chapter 9, 'Variegated financialisation: how finance pervaded (and pervades) housing and water provisioning in Portugal', Nuno Teles shows just that through comparison of two distinct systems of provision, water and housing. Given the different nature of these goods (housing as a commodity and water as commodity form), as well as their mode of provisioning (private in the case of housing and public in the case of water), the rising importance of finance in these sectors was achieved through different channels with varied outcomes.

As mentioned above, the eased access to European interbank markets in the context of a single currency favoured the shift of bank credit to housing loans and the construction of new dwellings. However, contrary to what happened in some core countries, the rise of indebtedness was scarcely linked to the rise of securitisation of mortgages. Securities markets have always been relatively small in the country. However, things changed radically after the crisis. Mired with non-performing loans, and subjected to bailout arrangements, most domestic banks were forced to follow stricter prudential rules and restrict credit. New financial actors, such as foreign investment funds searching for yield in a low-interest-rate environment, have since become more relevant. The commodification and financialisation of housing, and of real estate more generally, continued. But this time it was more concentrated in urban centres, where prices have spiked most, resulting in an ongoing housing crisis.

Following a long-lasting process of commodification through corporatisation, the water sector also benefited from the eased access to foreign capital to fund an investment surge. This also led to rising levels of indebtedness, although, in this case, funding was provided through European investment funds and the international bonds market. While remaining in the public domain, the indebtedness of the water system of provision led to added pressure to raise water bills, hence linking household bills with the payment of the financial costs of public investment. Bills have since risen well above inflation, particularly in the aftermath of the GFC when interest rates rose. The post-Troika period continued advancing the enforcement of cost-recovery billing, and the contraction of public investment has been gradually replaced by the entry of new foreign players (conglomerates and investment funds), thereby following the same trajectory as housing.

In Chapter 10, 'Financialisation and inequality in the semi-periphery: evidence from Portugal', Sérgio Lagoa and Ricardo Barradas compare the country's financialised trajectory with that of personal and functional income distribution. While several indicators point to a more intense process of financialisation between 1995 and 2008, especially in the period 2004–2008, declining since then, a generalised increase in inequality in the period in which finance grew the most is not found, as measured by the evolution of wage and profit shares, rentier income and personal income inequality.

They argue that the most severe impacts of financialisation were mostly felt after the crisis, as the rise of private debt aggravated economic and social vulnerability, and the state effort was increasingly devoted to the rescue of banks (and thereby external creditors), while public services endured underinvestment and workers' rights were increasingly undermined. Even though the country has recovered somewhat – as suggested by the recent evolution of employment, the rise of real wages and the improvement of various indicators of poverty, social exclusion and income distribution – it is too hasty and exaggerated to conclude that the country has fully recuperated. As Part 1 of the book shows, the insertion of the Portuguese economy within the EMU and the availability of credit this allowed did not contribute to the improvement of the structural composition of the economy. Part 2 subsequently explains that economic recovery has largely been achieved through the loss of workers' rights and the devaluation of labour. Finally, Part 3 shows that the financialisation of basic goods, such as housing and water, has made them less affordable and a source of greater inequality. This in turn reinforces the argument pursued throughout this book that the examination of the impacts of financialisation requires a full account of the structural composition of the economy, the labour regime and wider social reproduction.

## Semi-peripheral financialisation in post-crisis SE

Based on all the contributions in the book, which offer rich accounts of the variegated ways through which financialisation and the GFC have impacted on economic and social reproduction in Portugal, in the final chapter, entitled 'The case for semi-peripheral financialisation', we return to the semi-peripheral specificity of financialisation processes. Even though the intensity of some of these seems to have slowed down, as measured by levels of private indebtedness, the expansion of finance continues through other means and in various realms of economic and social reproduction, most notably through a growing role of foreign financial institutional investors. Moreover, the financialised trajectories of SE countries in the spheres of production, work and social reproduction reveal accentuating and growing divergences between the European core and periphery. This then reinforces the subordinated position of (semi-)peripheries in contemporary capitalism.

The book includes a final commentary section, where Ben Fine and Manuel Aalbers present their takes on the concepts of social reproduction and (semi-)periphery, and with which several chapters of this book dialogue. Taken together, the book offers a general theoretical and methodological framework for the analysis of financialisation processes in (semi-)peripheral contexts, integrating multiple scales across the international, national and subnational, for a variety of objects of study, including different domains of capital accumulation and social reproduction more broadly.

## Acknowledgements

The authors are grateful to Ben Fine and Manuel Aalbers for comments on previous versions of this chapter. All errors and omissions remain the responsibility of the authors. This work was funded by the Portuguese Foundation for Science and Technology and co-funded by the European Regional Development Fund (ERDF), within the scope of the FINHABIT project, ref. PTDC/ATP-GEO/ 2362/2014 – POCI-01-0145-FEDER-016869.

## Notes

1 This perhaps reflects Marx's own unsystematic account of finance, contained in the third volume of *Capital* (Chapters 21 to 36) where various categories of capital are presented.
2 It is true that the relation between usury and IBC is established only once in *Capital* (in Chapter 36). However, it does seem straightforward that, for Marx, IBC did not originate with capitalism. Indeed, Marx's comparison between IBC and labour force reinforces this view, when he states that while labour force 'is bought as the ability to create labour […] One might also buy it without setting it to work productively; for purely personal ends, for instance, for personal services, etc.'. On his view, 'The same applies to capital' as 'It is the borrower's affair whether he employs it as capital, hence actually sets in motion its inherent property of producing surplus-value' (1981 [1867], p. 505).
3 At the time of the writing of this introduction there is a general strike in Macron's France, while the socialist-leaning Portuguese government has just presented its first surplus budget in 45 years of democracy, which eloquently depicts the differences between the EU core and periphery. Cf. www.theguardian.com/world/2019/dec/ 18/french-unions-meet-government-as-pension-strikes-continue  and  https:// econews.pt/2019/12/17/government-forecasts-first-surplus-in-democracy-with-economy-growing-1-9 (consulted on 18 December 2019).

## References

Aalbers, M. B. (2019). Financialization. In D. Richardson, N. Castree, M.F. Goodchild, A. Kobayashi, W. Liu & R.A. Marston (eds.), *The International Encyclopedia of Geography* (pp. 1–12). Oxford: Wiley-Blackwell.

Bargawi, H., Cozzi, G., & Himmelweit, S. (eds.) (2017). *Economics and Austerity in Europe: Gendered Impacts and Sustainable Alternatives.* London and New York: Routledge.

Barradas, R., Lagoa, S., Leão, E., & Mamede, R.P. (2018). Financialization in the European periphery and the sovereign debt crisis: the Portuguese case, *Journal of Economic Issues, 52*(4), 1056–1083.

Bayliss, K., Fine, B., & Robertson, M. (2017). Introduction to special issue on the material cultures of financialisation. *New Political Economy, 22*(4), 355–370.

Bhattacharya, T. (2017). Introduction: mapping social reproduction theory. In T. Bhattacharya (ed.), *Social Reproduction Theory: Remapping Class, Recentering Oppression* (pp. 1–20). London: Pluto Press.

Boyer, R. (2000). The political in the era of globalization and finance: focus on some regulation school research. *International Journal of Urban and Regional Research, 24*(2), 274–322.

Christophers, B. (2015). The limits to financialization. *Dialogues in Human Geography*, 5(2), 183–200.

Christophers, B., & Fine, B. (2020). The value of financialisation and financialisation of value, Mimeo.

Crotty, J.R. (2005). The neoliberal paradox: the impact of destructive product market competition and impatient finance on nonfinancial corporations in the neo-liberal era. In G.A. Epstein (ed.), *Financialisation and the World Economy* (pp. 77–110). Cheltenham: Edward Elgar.

Elson, D. (2012). Social reproduction in the global crisis: rapid recovery or long-lasting depletion? In P. Utting, S. Razavi & R.V. Buchholz (eds.), *The Global Crisis and Transformative Social Change* (pp. 63–80). Basingstoke: Palgrave Macmillan.

Elson, D. (2010). Gender and the global economic crisis in developing countries: frame-work for analysis. *Gender & Development*, 18(2), 201–212.

Epstein, G.A. (2005). Introduction: financialization and the world economy. In G.A. Epstein (ed.), *Financialisation and the World Economy* (pp. 3–16). Cheltenham: Edward Elgar.

Fernandez, R., & Aalbers, M.B. (2019). Housing financialization in the Global South: in search of a comparative framework, Mimeo.

Fine, B. (2017). The material and culture of financialisation. *New Political Economy*, 22(4), 371–382.

Fine, B. (2013). Financialization from a Marxist perspective. *International Journal of Political Economy*, 42(4), 47–66.

Gabor, D. (2012). The road to financialization in Central and Eastern Europe: the early policies and politics of stabilizing transition. *Review of Political Economy*, 24(2), 227–249.

Gabor, D. (2010). (De)financialisation and crisis in Eastern Europe. *Competition & Change*, 14(34), 248–270.

Gambarotto, F., Rangone, M., & Solari, S. (2019). Financialization and deindustrializa-tion in the Southern European periphery. *Athens Journal of Mediterranean Studies*, 5(3), 151–172.

Gambarotto, F., & Solari, S. (2015). The peripheralization of Southern European capit-alism within the EMU. *Review of International Political Economy*, 22(4), 788–812.

Hein, E. (2015). Finance-dominated capitalism and re-distribution of income: a Kaleckian perspective. *Cambridge Journal of Economics*, 39(3), 907–934.

Hespanha, P. (2019). The impact of austerity on the Portuguese national health ser-vice: citizens' well-being, and health inequalities. *e-cadernos*, 31, 43–67.

Itoh, M., & Lapavitsas, C. (1999). *Political Economy of Money and Finance*. Basingstoke: Palgrave Macmillan.

Johnston, A., & Regan, A. (2016). European monetary integration and the incompati-bility of national varieties of capitalism. *Journal of Common Market Studies*, 54(2), 318–336.

Kantola, J., & Lombardo, E. (2017). Gender and the politics of the economic crisis in Europe. In J. Kantola & E. Lambordo (eds.), *Gender and the Economic Crisis in Europe* (pp. 1–25). Basingstoke: Palgrave Macmillan.

Lains, P. (2018). Convergence, divergence and policy: Portugal in the European Union. *West European Politics*, 42(5), 1094–1114.

Lapavitsas, C. (2013). *Profiting without Production: How Finance Exploits Us All*. London: Verso.

Leahy, A., Healy, S., & Murphy, M. (2014). *Crisis Monitoring Report 2014 – The European Crisis and Its Human Cost: A Call for Fair Alternatives and Solutions*. Brussels: Caritas Europa.

Marx, K. (1981[1867]). *Capital*, vol. III. London: Lawrence & Wishart.

Montgomerie, J., & Young, B. (2010). Home is where the hardship is: gender and wealth (dis)accumulation in the subprime boom (CRESC Working Paper No. 79). Manchester: Centre for Research on Sociocultural Change.

Orsi, L., & Solari, S. (2010). Financialisation in Southern European countries. *Économie Appliquée*, *63*(4), 5–34.

Oxfam (2013). A cautionary tale: the true cost of austerity and inequality in Europe (Oxfam Briefing Paper No. 174, September 2013). Oxford: Oxfam.

Podvršič, A., & Becker, J. (2019). Eurozone periphery post-crisis: financialisation and industrialisation in Slovenia and Slovakia (CEPN Working Papers 2019-10). Paris: Centre d'Economie de l'Université de Paris Nord.

Reis, J., Rodrigues, J., Santos, A.C., & Teles, N. (2014). Compreender a crise: a economia portuguesa num quadro europeu desfavorável. In J. Reis (ed.), *A economia política do retrocesso* (pp. 21–87). Coimbra: Almedina.

Roberts, A. (2013). Financing social reproduction: the gendered relations of debt and mortgage finance in twenty-first-century America. *New Political Economy*, *18*(1), 21–42.

Rodrigues, J., & Reis, J. (2012). The asymmetries of European integration and the crisis of capitalism in Portugal. *Competition & Change*, *16*(39), 188–205.

Rodrigues, J., Santos, A.C., & Teles, N. (2016). Semi-peripheral financialisation: the case of Portugal. *Review of International Political Economy*, *23*(3), 480–510.

Rodrigues, J., Santos, A.C., & Teles, N. (2018). Financialisation of pensions in semi-peripheral Portugal. *Global Social Policy: An Interdisciplinary Journal of Public Policy and Social Development*, *18*(2), 189–209.

Santos, A.C., Rodrigues, J., & Teles, N. (2018). Semi-peripheral financialisation and social reproduction: the case of Portugal. *New Political Economy*, *23*(4), 475–494.

Stockhammer, E. (2011). Peripheral Europe's debt and German wages. *International Journal for Public Policy*, *7*(1–3), 83–96.

Stockhammer, E., Durand, C., & List, L. (2016). European growth models and working class restructuring: an international post-Keynesian political economy perspective. *Environment and Planning A*, *48*(9), 1804–1828.

van der Zwan, N. (2014). Making sense of financialization. *Socioeconomic Review*, *12*(1), 99–129.

Weeks, S. (2019). Portugal in ruins: from 'Europe' to crisis and austerity. *Review of Radical Political Economics*, *51*(2), 246–264.

Wöhl, S. (2017). The gender dynamics of financialisation and austerity in the European Union – the Irish Case. In J. Kantola & E. Lambordo (eds.), *Gender and the Economic Crisis in Europe* (pp. 139–159). Basingstoke: Palgrave Macmillan.

# Part 1

# Financialisation and the Euro crisis in the Southern European periphery

# 2 Revisiting the concept of semi-peripheral financialisation

*João Rodrigues, Ana Cordeiro Santos and Nuno Teles*

## Financialisation: a context-specific process

Financialisation, broadly understood as the rise of the power of financial actors, motives and markets, has emerged as one of the most studied subjects within political economy over the past two decades (e.g. Epstein, 2005; Fine, 2010, 2013; Krippner, 2005; Lapavitsas, 2009; Van Treeck, 2009). Critical international political economy (IPE), in particular, has contributed to this literature, challenging the notion of a homogeneous erosion of state power caused by global financial markets (Helleiner, 1994; Konings, 2007). It argues instead that changes in the world economy stem from an institutional reconfiguration of international power carried out by dominant states through their capacity to devise new rules that have different national and regional impacts. The notion of structural power, i.e. 'power that is exercised indirectly and operates through shaping preferences and influencing the conditions under which other actors make decisions' (Konings, 2007, p. 37), is here decisive to account for the way in which the United States acquired a new power position in the international arena through its ability to maintain the dollar as world money after the demise of the Bretton Woods system. This was due, among other things, to the capacity of the US government to promote, and benefit from, the rise of financial markets.

Studies on financialisation have initially focused on the most mature capitalist countries of the centre, taking the USA and the UK as archetypes of financialised economies and societies. This has also been the case of IPE, with few exceptions (e.g. Abdelal, 2006). The role of European integration, in general, and of the euro, in particular, in promoting financialisation, with asymmetric contents and impacts, and its unfulfilled potential to become a hegemonic currency, have only recently received sufficient attention (Fields & Vernengo, 2013; Gambarotto & Solari, 2015; Orsi & Solari, 2010).

Increased interest in the variegated nature of the rise of finance in other geographical contexts has now emerged (e.g. Becker et al., 2010; Kaltenbrunner & Painceira, 2018; Lapavitsas & Powell, 2014). This chapter aims to contribute to this later literature by focusing on Southern European (SE) countries and, particularly, on the Portuguese case, both in its commonalities with other processes of financialisation and, most importantly, in its specificities. By drawing attention to SE semi-peripheral realities it endeavours to highlight the role of the Economic and Monetary Union (EMU) in driving their financialisation processes.

We argue that in Portugal (as well as in other SE countries) financialisation was a rapid, but effective, process of socioeconomic transformation. Within the time span of a mere decade, between the mid-1980s and the mid-1990s, the Portuguese financial system evolved from a state-controlled and 'repressed' financial regime to become a fully integrated and liberalised one, supported by solid insertion in international circuits of finance. Despite the speed of these transformations, the transition was smoothly produced without the financial instability that frequently accompanies such processes (Kaminsky & Reinhart, 1999). The Portuguese case is even more remarkable when considering the scope and depth of these transformations. The recent evolution of the (non-financial) private sector testifies to the magnitude of these changes, progressing from a very timid engagement with finance to skyrocketing levels of private indebtedness, the main culprit for turning Portugal into one of the highest externally indebted countries in the world. While some of these trends are partially shared with other semi-peripheral European countries that have common structural elements, namely Greece and Spain, the combination of high external debt and economic stagnation, starting at the beginning of the millennium, sets Portugal apart from these countries.

This chapter starts, in the next section, by setting out our theoretical starting point within political economy and advancing our understanding of semi-peripheral financialisation. It then moves on to the analysis of the recent evolution of the Portuguese financial sector and its relation with other economic agents. The third section presents the main institutional transformations of the financial sector, namely through the national transposition of progressively market-creating and market-conforming EU regulation in the financial sphere. The fourth section examines how Portuguese finance engaged with international markets, particularly money markets. The fifth section analyses the relation of finance with non-financial firms, which is pivotal to understanding the dynamics of stagnation and crisis of the Portuguese economy since 2000. The sixth section addresses the relation between finance and households, which have also become increasingly integrated with financial markets through their borrowing and saving decisions. Finally, the seventh section overviews the recent evolution of SE countries, which further accentuates the semi-peripheral nature of financialisation in the region.

## Theorising semi-peripheral financialisation

At the most general level, financialisation has been defined as a set of historical and institutional processes whereby specific financial actors, motives and markets have gained an increased weight in, and exerted a growing influence upon, the rest of the economy and society (Epstein, 2005). These processes, most visible in the Anglo-Saxon world, are deemed to encompass a wide range of socio-economic phenomena: privatisation, deregulation and market-led reregulation of financial activities, allowing the penetration of finance into ever more areas of economic and social life; the expansion and proliferation of different types of financial asset; the primacy of financial interests and imperatives in capital accumulation, increasing income inequality arising out of the weight of financial rewards; consumer-led booms based on credit, and so forth (Fine, 2010).

The term financialisation, which started to be used by Marxist political economists in the 1990s, has gained increasing currency among other heterodox economists of post-Keynesian and institutionalist, mainly regulationist, persuasions and other social scientists interested in real-world transformations of the economy. At risk of oversimplifying what has been a vibrant discussion about complex phenomena, we distinguish two main positions in the literature, focusing upon the causes and effects of the rise of finance to a hegemonic position within capitalism since the 1970s. First, a Marxist tradition takes as the main factor leading to the rise of finance the escape of capital from a stagnated or depressed productive sphere, riddled with problems of profitability, to the more rewarding financial sector (Arrighi, 1994; Foster, 2007; Sweezy, 1994). Second, from a post-Keynesian and an institutionalist tradition, the rise of finance has been interpreted as the product of dominant neoliberal economic policies and institutional transformations ranging from the privatisation of the banking sector to the opening up of capital accounts throughout the world economy and disinflationary policies, which have caused a general decline in capital accumulation in a context of growing economic inequality, wage stagnation and financial instability (Boyer, 2000; Krippner, 2005; Van Treeck, 2009). The literature has since matured, expanding the focus from the most financialised Anglo-Saxon economies to developing economies. Thus, as Fine (2011, p. 6) underlines, rather than an 'analytical tool from which outcomes can be readily and simply read off', financialisation must be first and foremost understood as a 'process that interacts with others in the context of specific economies', underlining the importance of taking into account specific, historically given conditions and particular geographical contexts.

Converging with Fine's concern, and located within the Marxist tradition, Lapavitsas (2013, p. 39) states that 'the aim of theoretical analysis cannot be to produce a generally valid abstract model of financialization but rather to specify its underlying tendencies and to ascertain the particular form and content it acquires in different contexts'. From this it follows that 'period analysis must occupy a middle ground, departing from theoretical concerns while systematically integrating historical phenomena in a theoretically informed way' (Lapavitsas, 2013, p. 169). With these concerns in mind, Lapavitsas has developed a theoretical framework that incorporates the historically specific and institution-specific nature of financialisation processes and the spatially varied interactions between finance and the rest of the economy. In this view, states, endowed with different degrees of power and capacity for intervention, are of fundamental importance in accounting for the deliberate political and institutional elements that have shaped the rise of finance in a necessarily hierarchical world economy. This does not exclude the influence of more spontaneous processes, such as those stemming from the relations among agents occupying different positions in the spheres of production and circulation, within capital accumulation. Thus, the rising political and economic power of finance results from profound changes in the social relations of financial markets, banks, non-financial firms and households, where the state is a decisive agent. This is taken as relevant since power relations in the world economy increasingly depend on a set of varied, often credit-based, social relations between finance and other economic agents.

Based on the experience of mature capitalist economies, Lapavitsas identifies several tendencies shaping the financialisation of capitalism: the rise of investment banking; the rise of finance-to-finance lending; and, most importantly, the new centrality of bank lending to households. He then highlights the importance of these tendencies to compensate for the retreat of non-financial firms from loan markets due to an increasing reliance on capital markets for investment and funding. This is deemed to signal the changing nature of banks, since 'at the root of financialisation lies loanable [i.e. hoarded funds collected either from the circuits of production and/or personal income], not fictitious [i.e. net present value of securitised assets], capital', (Lapavitsas, 2013, p. 29), while the trading of the former can be the basis for the latter.

For Lapavitsas, the concept of loanable-money capital is not circumscribed to a 'monied' capitalist class that lends interest-bearing capital (IBC) to 'functioning' capitalists who borrow it and invest in the productive sphere (see also Lapavitsas, 1997). Nor are interest payments conceived solely as the material basis of a specific group of capitalists, such as the Keynesian rentier class that profits from the mere accumulation of financial assets. Lapavitsas proposes instead a notion of loanable-money capital that also mobilises idle money from workers and other social groups and is lent for non-productive activities such as household consumption.[1] The notion of 'financial expropriation' is then advanced to account for exploitative aspects deriving from new power relations emerging between capital and labour, where profits are increasingly generated out of wage income through payments of interest to financial institutions (Lapavitsas, 2009).

This approach differs from other Marxist approaches to financialisation, most notably that developed by Fine (2010, 2013), which confines the use of IBC to the realm of production and exchange and refuses the concept of financial expropriation. In fact, Fine defines financialisation as a 'peculiar modern form of incorporating a variety of credit relations into the orbit of fictitious capital' (2013, p. 56), with the latter conceived of as 'the independent circulation of IBC in paper form' (p. 50). In this view, then, credit relations outside the realm of production also become forms of interest-bearing capital when these credit relations are converted into securitised assets and sold. The implication of this is that 'those buying the fictitious capital are advancing money capital in the expectation of a surplus even though the origins of this surplus do not lie in such an exchange' (p. 55).

While we find the notion of financial expropriation debatable, especially so in the Portuguese case (see below), and acknowledge the growing relevance of the extensive and intensive expansion of interest-bearing capital in paper form (i.e. fictitious capital), Lapavitsas's notion of loanable-money capital is more adequate to account for semi-peripheral forms of financialisation. As we shall see, in SE countries, where securities markets are less mature, national and international bank loans have been the main driving forces behind financialisation, increasingly involving non-financial firms and households in finance (particularly as debtors, but also as asset holders).

The prevalence of loanable-money capital, whose scale and forms are shaped by the political and institutional conditions of the spaces where it is rooted, is a critical source of variation in financialisation. In order to understand why 'neither the content nor the form of financialization is fixed' across countries (Lapavitsas & Powell, 2014, p. 360), it is necessary to enlarge the scope of the analysis beyond countries of the centre of the capitalist world economy. To this end, Lapavitsas (2013) and Lapavitsas & Powell (2014) put forward the concept of 'subordinated financialisation', according to which peripheral countries are compelled to join an increasingly financialised world economy, through formal and informal pressures, mainly by opening themselves up to financial flows and by accumulating reserves of quasi-world money (mostly dollars) needed to ensure their participation in international trade and financial transactions (Kaltenbrunner & Painceira, 2018).[2] While illuminating important aspects of financialisation outside the core, namely the way the periphery tends to be crucially shaped from the outside by the interests of international finance located in the major advanced capitalist countries, and by the national and international institutions under their influence, the notion of subordinated financialisation has less to say about the equally crucial relations taking place outside the core between financial institutions, non-financial firms and the new major recipients of credit, households. The domestic interactions between financial and non-financial agents are now attracting attention in other accounts of financialisation processes outside the core (Zhang, 2009; Hardie, 2011; Fine, 2013; Powell, 2013).

Lapavitsas' framework can be usefully complemented by Becker et al. (2010), which adapts the regulationist approach to grasp the heterogeneous nature of the 'regimes of accumulation' across the peripheries and semi-peripheries of the world economy. Through a tripartite typology of regimes of accumulation – productive versus financialised, intensive versus extensive, and introverted versus extraverted – they analyse the commonalities and specificities of the trajectories of four different countries, Brazil, Chile, Serbia and Slovakia.[3] Resulting from external impositions, although necessarily linked to the goals and interests of fractions of domestic capital, financialisation outside the core tends to require high interest rates in order to attract international capital flows, producing bouts of speculation and leading to overvalued exchange rates and to the erosion of productive capacities. This means that low interest rates and more substantial inflows of capital can only, and temporarily, be achieved through '(semi)dollarized or euroized models', i.e. under regimes of fixed exchange rates, with nationals having incentives to become highly indebted in foreign currency (Becker et al., 2010, p. 230).

The framework of Becker et al. is sharp and flexible enough to account for the Portuguese case (and other SE countries). With a colonial past, Portugal is a semi-peripheral country within the world economy, which combines characteristics of developed and developing countries, being marked by late industrialisation and lasting backward economic development relative to the core Northern and Central European countries (Santos, 1985). With decolonisation occurring in the 1970s, the country rapidly geared towards integration in the then European Economic Community (EEC), formalised in 1986 (Pinto & Teixeira, 2002). New foreign direct investment, benefiting from structural EU funds and lured by low wages, fuelled economic growth during the first years of integration. Despite some localised bouts of industrial modernisation and overall catching up, the Portuguese economy continued to rely on traditional labour-intensive industrial sectors such as textiles (Chapters 3 and 4 in this volume; Rodrigues & Reis, 2012).

Portugal's laggard position in the European context reinforced the role of the European Union (EU) in driving the financialisation of the Portuguese economy and society. The participation in the eurozone, in particular, brought unprecedentedly advantageous financial conditions, such as an almost unlimited access to hard currency and loanable-money capital at low interest rates, which are often unavailable to countries with similar levels of development. But this process ultimately had to face the structural contradictions of the country. The absence of an autonomous monetary policy in the face of growing international competition exacerbated the structural economic weaknesses of the Portuguese economy, manifest in a persistent and growing current account deficit, fuelling an equally growing external debt.

The notion of semi-peripheral financialisation is particularly useful to account for the convergences and divergences between the Portuguese economy and financialisation processes occurring in both core and periphery. The term semi-periphery is here adopted in a double sense. First, it accounts for the historical intermediate position of the Portuguese economy in the world economy, i.e. as an industrialised country that is increasingly unable to compete with countries with which it is most closely integrated, favouring the growth of the more protected non-tradable sector. Second, and most importantly, it refers to the institutional features of its financial system, which shares characteristics of both core and peripheral countries, being mostly shaped by the process of European integration and by the predominance of loanable-money capital.[4] As will be argued below, the notion of semi-periphery is also most helpful to underline the 'uneven and combined' character of capitalism (Ashman, 2009), accounting for the national and sectoral variegation of financialisation processes. Different financialised configurations are not only shaped by extant interests and power relations, among domestic and international agents. They are also influenced by underlying social, political, economic, geographical and historical factors, requiring us to avoid simplistic and homogenising relations of dependence between the semi-periphery and the core. Thus, the notion of semi-periphery is meant to underline both hierarchical power relations within the world system and the historical embeddedness of socioeconomic and political institutions (Chapter 11 in this volume).

The concept of semi-peripheral financialisation put forward thus points to differences in form and content relative to financialisation processes in core countries. It underlines the more predominant and critical role of banks as pivotal financial institutions in shaping recent and profound changes in semi-peripheral countries. It emphasises the role of international finance located in advanced capitalist countries. And it incorporates domestic relations between financial institutions, non-financial firms and households, which are crucial to account for variegation within semi-peripheral countries.

## The early stages of financialisation in Portugal: the international context

The Portuguese financial sector was one of the most 'repressed' financial systems in Western Europe in the early 1980s. This was due to the late democratisation of the country in 1974–1975, which led to the nationalisation of relevant private economic groups that had dominated the country's political economy during Salazar's dictatorship, including all major banks. In this highly interventionist period, interest rates were set administratively, and credit was mostly directed towards the needs of the state and of the associated public enterprises in strategic sectors; there were also strict controls on capital flows, and the exchange rate was defined using a sliding scale pegged to a basket of foreign currencies from 1978 onwards. This configuration, locked in by a socialist-leaning Constitution declaring nationalisations as 'irreversible conquests of the working class', was antithetical to the wider neoliberal international trends of the early eighties with which Portugal eventually aligned, albeit, as typical in a semi-periphery, with a time lag.

The combination of two International Monetary Fund (IMF) interventions (in 1979 and in 1983–1985), and the preparation for accession to the EEC, set a favourable context for what has been uncritically labelled as the 'modernisation' of the Portuguese financial system from the mid-eighties onwards (Nunes, 2011; Pinto, 1996). Indeed, the liberalisation of the banks began in 1984 when new private banks were allowed. The first Portuguese private bank, the Banco Comercial Português, was founded, soon followed by the entry of new foreign banks, such as the Spanish bank Santander (Mendes & Rebelo, 2003). In 1989, following a revision of the Constitution, allowing the reversing of nationalisations, the move towards privatising state banks began (Banco Totta, Banco Espírito Santo, Banco Português do Atlântico), with the exception of the Caixa Geral de Depósitos, which remains state-owned to the present day. In just seven years, between 1990 and 1996, state banks became just one fourth of the market share, falling from 74 per cent to approximately 24 per cent, while the market share of foreign banks tripled from 3 per cent in 1991 to 9 per cent in 2000 (Antão et al., 2009). However, the market share of foreign-controlled subsidiaries and branches has risen since then, reaching 23 per cent in 2016 (ECB, 2017), measured in terms of total assets. As a result of further mergers and acquisitions, activity in the sector was eventually concentrated around five major banks: Caixa Geral de Depósitos, Banco Comercial Português, Santander Totta, Novo Banco and Banco Português de Investimento. Since the 2008–2009 crisis, the Portuguese banking sector has undergone a new wave of mergers and acquisitions, further intensifying concentration in the sector, with the number of credit institutions falling 14 per cent to reach a total of 127 in 2016, 15 per cent of these belonging to foreign branches (ECB, 2017), mostly Spanish (Santander Totta and Banco Português de Investimento) and increasingly Chinese (Banco Comercial Português and Haitong Bank, previously part of the now bankrupted Espirito Santo group).

The privatisation and liberalisation of the financial sector, which put an end to credit limits and administrative interest rates, was the first set of factors contributing to the increase in bank loans in the 1990s. A second set of factors is linked to the release of (poorly remunerated) compulsory reserves deposited in the Bank of Portugal, which were subsequently transformed into public debt negotiable at market prices. The rate for compulsory reserves in the Bank of Portugal fell from 17 per cent in 1989 to 2 per cent in 1994, in line with European practice. There was, therefore, a quantity and price effect associated with the growth of credit in Portugal, i.e. greater available liquidity at lower prices, which favoured the expansion of credit.

The expansion of credit cannot therefore be separated from the monetary policy of the Portuguese state. The state's role in the necessary task of politically constructing financial markets also involved the gradual rise of securitised public debt, traded on secondary markets and open to foreign investors. Moreover, from 1990, the Bank of Portugal started to restrict its treasury loans as part of the process of breaking national links between the Treasury and the Central Bank, supposedly as a means of assuring Bank of Portugal's independence. As a result, the state became totally dependent on the financial markets for financing its deficits.

Legislation regulating the financial system under Decree-Law no. 298/92 was the last milestone in the deregulation of the financial sector, transposing the 1989 European Directive into Portuguese law. Within the framework of the European single market for goods and services, this law aimed to liberalise and harmonise the different segments and practices in the European banking sector, putting an end to the traditional distinction between investment and commercial banking, abolishing restrictions on the entry of new agents and aligning prudential requirements for the sector with the 1989 Basel Accords. European integration was therefore central to the entire process. As Pinho (1997, p. 2) states: 'without the need for alignment with single market legislation, the deregulation of the banks would have been much slower and probably less extensive'.

The removal of all national controls over the international circulation of capital, reflected in the full convertibility of the escudo, was the culmination of the process of transformation of the financial sector. It contributed to attracting foreign capital, helping to peg the exchange rate of the escudo, and generated significant revenues from privatisations. The changes in the exchange rate policy in turn meant the substitution of the goal of competitiveness by a disin-flationary target, in line with the strictures of the European Monetary System and the Exchange Rate Mechanism, to which the country adhered in the 1990s (Pinto, 1996). With the active participation of the state, this trajectory illustrates an active political commitment to a process of integration that increasingly favoured financial interests, both national and foreign.

The processes of bank privatisation and financial liberalisation, which were basically completed at the beginning of the 1990s, and the nominal conver-gence trajectory culminating in adherence to the euro, all contributing to the overvaluing of the escudo, were decisive factors in transforming the Portuguese economy into a financialised economy. Indeed, the official justifications and opti-mistic evaluations that underpinned the strategy for joining the euro explicitly underlined the aim of expanding the financial sector, perceived as being in the vanguard of 'modernisation' (Barbosa, 1998). The remarkable decrease of real interest rates was then seen as the most relevant sign of the successful insertion of national finance into international financial markets. The expectation was, on the one hand, that it would allow firms to accelerate capital accumulation, taken as a precondition for future increases in overall productivity; and, on the other hand, that it would favour accumulation of wealth on the part of households, particularly through the purchase of housing stock. From indebtedness levels below the European average in the mid-1990s, Portuguese households and firms were geared to gallop to the top in the first decade of the euro, with levels similar only to the UK and Ireland when measured in percentage of the countries' GDP or disposable household income (to be developed below).

The policy of nominal convergence, as part of the construction of the single European currency, ultimately created conditions for future troubles. Portugal, in contrast to Spain, entered the euro with an over-appreciated exchange rate and with an already unbalanced economy (Garcimartín, Rivas & Martínez, 2010; Leão & Palacio-Vera, 2011). A huge current account deficit started to mount, since the government no longer had available the traditional means to manage it, having previously relied on devaluation to boost its exports and solve its balance of payments problems even if temporarily (Ferreira do Amaral, 2006). Given already existent European economic policy constraints imposed by the Common Market on any kind of industrial policy, the strong euro aggravated this problem further. In a context marked by continuing downward pressure on prices, Portuguese firms, mostly price-takers when operating internationally, saw a decrease in their profit margins. Incentives were thus geared towards the profitable non-tradable sectors of the economy, less exposed to foreign com-petition, from construction to retail and privatised utilities, but heavily inserted internationally. The banking sector played a pivotal role in these structural transformations, channelling foreign credit, directly or indirectly (i.e. through households), to these sectors. But before moving to the analysis of the relation between the banking and the non-tradable sectors, we make a closer examination of the recent evolution of the banking sector.

## The relations between national and international finance

The rise of finance-to-finance lending is of paramount importance to understanding financialisation. In the Portuguese case, cross-border lending is particularly relevant to explain the insertion of the economy in the international financial sphere, as this has been the preferred channel of foreign financial investment over the past 20 years. Indeed, cross-border liabilities of the Portuguese banking sector with foreign financial agents grew from 9 billion to almost 50 billion euros between 1993 and 1999 (Figure 2.1).

While this growth was balanced with assets until 1999, Portuguese banks' assets and liabilities started to diverge during the 2000s, with the latter growing at a much faster pace, reflected in the concomitant widening of the current account deficit. It mirrored, on the one hand, the growing negative net investment position of the country. And it signalled, on the other hand, the unconstrained access of the Portuguese banking sector to foreign debt markets until the 2008 international crisis, which helps explain the absence of classic balance-of-payments crises typical of peripheral countries. These capital inflows were also driven by real interest rate differentials during the new millennium, favouring domestic demand for new loans. Indeed, interest rates and inflation converged during the nineties (each being part of the Maastricht Criteria), but the creation of the single currency interrupted this convergence process.

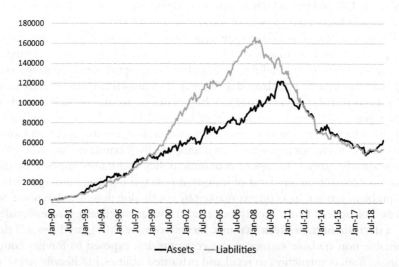

*Figure 2.1* Bank liabilities and assets with rest of the world agents, 1990–2019 (million euros)

Source: Bank of Portugal

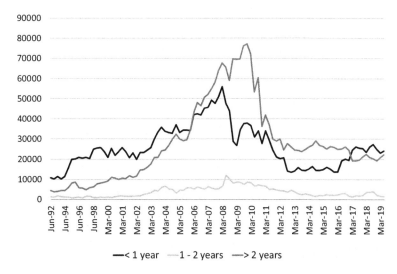

*Figure 2.2* Foreign bank credit inflows by maturity, 1992–2019 (million dollars)
Source: Bank of International Settlements

Despite having a common monetary policy, with inflation being the exclusive responsibility of the European Central Bank (ECB), inflation differentials rose between the core and the European semi-periphery.[5]

Bank credit inflows to Portugal not only changed in magnitude but also in content, noticeable in their maturities. During the 1990s, the growth of credit flows was dominated by short-term loans (Figure 2.2), mainly in the form of money-market instruments. But since 2000, after the creation of the euro, long-term funding (mainly in the form of bonds and notes) surpassed short-term flows.

This difference in maturities is common to other early experiences of financialisation, being, in a first phase, associated with the proliferation of new short-term financial instruments that promote market liquidity – T-bonds on repos, commercial paper, certificates of deposit, promissory notes, etc. – through money markets, as happened for example in the USA in the 1980s (Gindin & Panitch, 2012). These financial claims are only granted among financial institutions, and are subsumed under the evaluation criteria of payment probability. This involves a homogenisation of loanable-money capital that 'cuts across economic and geographical areas and makes it possible for idle money funds to acquire a common and general character across society' (Lapavitsas, 2003, p. 83). Credit rating criteria, internationally defined, act here as a unique set of information wherein all the relevant dimensions are integrated, submitting all the sectors, countries or individuals. Such homogenisation of underlying social relations in credit allows for money markets to prevail over context-specific realities. With a newborn private and liberalised banking sector, this has been the case too in Portugal since the 1990s.

Moreover, as pointed out by Gabor (2010), in her analysis of the evolution of Eastern European banking sectors, the pivotal role of securitised money markets was typically the outcome of a changing relation between banks and central banks. In the face of the excess of liquidity coming from abroad, central banks in this region resorted to sterilisation operations that further promoted bank securitisation operations. Central banks induced not only the regulatory stand-ardisation of financial practices that allowed these cross-border flows but also acted as active participants in the moulding of these markets. In fact, the role of central banks in financialisation should not be understood as an aberration in the newly liberalised credit markets, but instead as a consequence of their role in the credit system. Central banks need to support every financial liability in the economy, converting money market instruments into currency and reserves. Hence, there cannot be a functioning money market without a credible and robust intervention of the central bank. Without it, credibility can be damaged to the point of collapsing the credit system (Lapavitsas, 2003). However, in Eastern European countries, the role of central banks was constrained by the need to accumulate international reserves in order to sterilise capital flows. This was also the case of Portugal during the 1990s, when a rising current account deficit led to the accumulation of foreign exchange reserves.

With the euro and its own powerful central bank, the ECB, the profile of banking credit flows changed, and long-term bonds and notes became the pre-ferred form of indebtedness of the Portuguese banking sector with the rest of the world. The advantage of having access to these debt markets is apparent as it involves fewer costs, thus further enabling the leveraging and profitability of their balance sheets. At the same time, lenders' risk decreased since the single currency eliminated currency risk. Moreover, ECB independence from polit-ical power and its mandate devoted to targeting an inflation rate of no more than 2 per cent enhanced trust among financial agents in the real value of their future promises to pay.

Coinciding with the creation of the euro, mortgage securitisation also had a role in expanding credit facilities in Portugal, most importantly by serving as col-lateral in the ECB's refinancing operations. Created legally only in 1999, under Decree-Law no. 453/99, the first loan securitisation operation was carried out in December 2001. The amount of loan securities issued by Portuguese banks would reach 26 billion euros in 2011, with 39 securitisation funds operating on the market (CMVM, 2012). The scale, sophistication and variety of financial instruments available to the Portuguese banking sector show that, despite its semi-peripheral position, banks benefited from (long-term) funding only avail-able to the most financialised core countries. Hence, membership in the EMU contributed to the deepening of financialisation processes during the 2000s, going beyond the pattern of financial integration shown by peripheral countries.

The role of the EMU becomes even more salient when analysing the nationality of foreign bank credit flows into the country. Bank credit was dominated by inflows from other eurozone countries: from Spain, with which the Portuguese economy was increasingly integrated commercially, and the major financial powerhouses of the eurozone, Germany and France. Although rising, inflows from other major financial centres outside the EMU, such as the UK and the USA, were not as significant. After the Global Financial Crisis (GFC) the relation between Portugal and Spain has intensified, by and large the result of the sale of national banks and insurance companies to Spanish banks such as Santander (Figure 2.3).

This pattern shows not only the importance of the single currency, backed by the ECB, in granting the needed credibility of the Portuguese banks, but also the close relation between financial accumulation and the general dynamic of capital accumulation in Portugal. Indeed, the inflows of credit have their origins in the countries with which Portugal has more intense trade relations, and thus current account deficits, most notably Spain. Cross-border credit was thus intertwined with consumption and investment between Portuguese households and non-financial firms and their suppliers within the eurozone. The foreign and domestic national banking sectors acted as crucial mediators as they benefited from their domestic position in terms of information-gathering and power in their relation with other sectors. While the common financial architecture fostered cross-border lending, the close relation between financial flows and trade relations among European countries indicates that, from its inception, the EMU did not succeed in creating a common securities market where the national origin of capital would be irrelevant. The euro crisis of 2011 ultimately exposed the fiction of totally integrated financial markets, with the

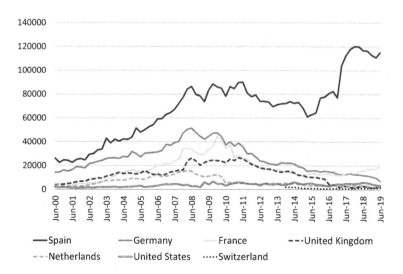

*Figure 2.3* Foreign bank assets in Portugal by nationality, 1999–2019 (non-consolidated, million dollars)

Source: Bank of International Settlements

sudden drop of capital flows from the core to the least developed EU countries, which cannot be justified by the financial health of particular agents, revealing instead the fragmentation of national financial markets.

## Finance and the non-financial sectors of the Portuguese economy

The securitisation of Portuguese public debt treasury bills and bonds has been the backbone of further financial developments, as has been the case in most developed economies (Gindin & Panitch, 2012). It has allowed the creation of exchangeable collateral essential for money market liquidity operations among financial agents and for modern monetary policy open-market operations. This strategic choice was coupled with another, also made within the EMU framework: the opening up of the public debt market to foreign investors, which further consolidated the insertion of Portuguese banks into the international circuits of finance. Portuguese banks were further helped from the late 1990s onwards in accumulating a net nega-tive financial position with the rest of the world through the supply of this internationally accepted collateral. Portuguese public debt thereby became increasingly internationalised.

In 2008, 80 per cent of public debt was held by foreigners: 50 per cent was held by foreign banks and 28 per cent by other foreign institutional investors (pension, investment and hedge funds) (Caldas, Rocha & Teles, 2012). This deteriorated the state's investment position in the first decade of the euro: from a negative position of 29 per cent of GDP in 2001, it rose to 60 per cent in 2009 (calculated from international investment position statistics; BdP, 2020), nonetheless being somewhat contained by financial engineering strategies to avoid the rise of public deficits (e.g. public-private partnerships). However, the growing dependence on and therefore vulnerability to inter-national finance partially contributed to the financial stress observed in the immediate aftermath of the international crisis. As has been pointed out (e.g. De Grauwe, 2011), while the semi-peripheral states of the eurozone appeared to have borrowed in a domestic currency at very low interest rates, it is as if they had in fact borrowed in a foreign currency over which they had no con-trol. Thus, the presumed low level of risk, and hence of defaulting, allowed an overextension of loans from core banks to the EU periphery, both in the public and private sectors.

Benefiting from the increased sophistication of the newly liberalised finan-cial system and from the privatisation of major Portuguese non-financial firms during the 1990s, major Portuguese companies began to access inter-national capital and debt markets and started to accumulate financial assets. These assets grew from around 29 billion euros in 1994, to 160.5 billion euros at current prices, in 2013, most notably in the form of shares in other companies, which grew from 5.3 billion euros to 40 billion euros in the same period (consolidated, current prices, national financial accounts statistics; BdP,

2020). However, this engagement with financial markets did not represent an accumulation of net financial assets (or of financial profit, for that matter). On the contrary, the net financial position of Portuguese firms deteriorated from -60 billion to a record negative position of -252 billion euros in the same period (consolidated, current prices, national financial accounts statistics; BdP, 2020). The negative position of non-financial firms can be partially attributed to the issuance of shares (whose importance in balance sheets depends on market fluctuations) and debt securities, such as bonds. However, (bank) loans formed the liability that most contributed to this negative position. Thus, the rising financialised profile of Portuguese non-financial firms did not imply a turning away from banking credit, but, on the contrary, a strong and growing dependence on it. And this dependence is mostly related to the domestic banking sector whose loans to domestic non-financial firms grew at a very fast pace from the beginning of the 1990s (Figure 2.4).

Far from being evenly distributed across all sectors, the boom in banking credit to non-financial firms was highly concentrated. The manufacturing sector, which at the beginning of the 1990s absorbed almost 40 per cent of all loans granted to business, saw this percentage drop by half in the 2000s (Figure 2.4). In contrast, bank credit to construction and real estate activities, which represented about 10 per cent of entire business debt in 1992, reached almost 40 per cent in 2008 (Figure 2.4). This reflects the move of domestic capital to sectors protected from international competition in the new context of a strong currency that penalised the tradable sectors such as manufacturing. The Portuguese banking business thus changed both in size and content.

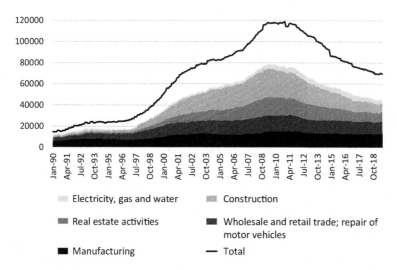

*Figure 2.4* Composition of bank loans to non-financial firms, total and by selected sectors, 1990–2019 (million euros)

Source: Bank of Portugal

These transformations were further encouraged by the adoption of inter-national banking regulations that favoured the financing of homeownership through mortgages (considered the most secure form of credit since they are based on a durable asset as collateral), and thereby the upstream activities of construction and real estate. Continued public investment in infrastructures further favoured these sectors. Even if the Maastricht fiscal criteria and the Stability Pact constrained public investment, various financial engineering arrangements, such as the creation of state-owned enterprises or public-private partnerships, allowed for averting the registration of public invest-ment in infrastructure as public expenditure (Chapter 9 in this volume). This financial engineering, primarily engendered by the banking sector, allowed for the rise of aggregate investment in the 1990s, pulled by the housing and construction boom of that period, which attained 28 per cent of GDP in 2000. But this investment would soon drop and stagnate around 23–24 per cent of GDP from then up to the crisis. This evolution reflected not so much a submission to financialised short-term investment time-horizons as a form of financial mimicry, but mainly was a slow-burn crisis in the domestic con-struction sector, starting in 2001, increasingly beleaguered by problems of housing oversupply (to be developed below).

As domestic investment stagnated, foreign direct investment by Portuguese firms abroad started to rise consistently, from around 20 billion euros at the beginning of the 2000s to more than 50 billion euros at the end of the decade (current prices, International Financial Position Statistics; BdP, 2020), indi-cating the search for new investment opportunities abroad by major Portuguese corporations. Using their holding companies, they benefited from easier access to cheap loans in a strong currency (the euro) to expand to new markets, especially outside the eurozone, such as in the Portuguese-speaking countries Angola and Brazil.

In sum, the evolution of the banking business in Portugal differs from that of US and UK banking in its relation with non-financial firms, with those firms still struggling to access capital and debt securities markets (in 2020, the Portuguese stock exchange only lists 18 companies in its PSI-20 index). However, the same cannot be said in what regards the relation between banks and households. Similar to core countries, household debt has grown unprecedentedly since the second half of the 1990s. It rose from around 45 per cent of bank lending to non-financial corporations in 1992, to 115 per cent in 1999, having grown more slowly since then (Monetary and Financial Statistics; BdP, 2020). This was promoted by various policy changes; including those relating to the creation of the EMU, inducing a significant decline in real interest rates and the expansion of foreign loanable capital; regulatory changes in the banking sector at EU level, such as those implemented by the Basel Accords, inducing a more favourable treatment of mortgage risk (Allen, 2004); and the promotion of capital markets through the introduction of the securitisation of mortgage loans (Aalbers, 2008). The centrality of household debt in financialisation is the issue to which we now turn.

## The financialisation of Portuguese households

The extraordinary growth of household debt over the past two decades, and of its weight in the overall level of indebtedness of the (non-financial) private sector, provides a remarkable synthesis of the unbalanced semi-peripheral nature of the Portuguese financialisation processes. It conveys, in particular, the financialisation of the housing sector as banks not only financed the construction of family dwellings but also home purchases, thus controlling their production and provision. Indeed, household debt is likewise the outcome of European integration, allowing unprecedented access by the Portuguese banking sector to European credit markets, as noted above, making credit available to households at low interest rates. And it is a manifestation of the structural imbalances of the Portuguese economy, favouring the non-tradable construction sector, in general, and the production of new homes, in particular, as the bulk of household debt pertains to housing loans.

In Portugal, gross debt-to-income ratio of households grew from 38 per cent in 1995 to reach its highest value of 126 per cent in 2009, declining since then and representing 95 per cent of household income in 2018 (Eurostat, 2020a). The rise in Portuguese household debt is easily identified with housing loans. It not only constitutes the main portion of household bank debt, but its weight in total household debt increased from 70 per cent in 1995 to 82 per cent in 2015, declining slightly since to 79 per cent in 2019 (Monetary and Financial Statistics; BdP, 2020). The construction of household dwellings rose in the same period, when the number of housing completions rose from 68,818 in 1995 to 125,603 in 2002, to decline sharply since then to reach 12,308 in 2018 (EMF, 2019). This growth in housing construction and mortgage debt corresponded to a rise in the proportion of property owners relative to tenants, with homeownership representing 73 per cent of accommodation in 2011, growing from 65 per cent in 1991 (INE, 2020), remaining high since (EMF, 2019).

The extraordinary growth of household debt over the last two decades, reaching levels comparable only to those of countries of the North and Centre of Europe, offers a clear illustration of the magnitude of socioeconomic transformations in Portugal. In 2009, when the crisis hit, Portuguese households were among the most indebted in Europe. In that year, the average level of household debt for the 19 eurozone countries, as measured in terms of the percentage to disposable household income, was 98 per cent, while it reached 126 per cent in Portugal (Eurostat, 2020a). Besides the financialisation of the Portuguese economy within the context of EU integration, the traditional weakness of the Portuguese system of social provisioning, together with a housing policy focused on the promotion of private ownership, helps to explain the magnitude and content of Portuguese household debt. Already prior to membership of the EEC, ownership rates were high in EU terms, as state intervention favoured private forms of provision. The financialisation of the Portuguese economy ultimately provided the conditions for the success of a policy model focused on homeownership through the use of credit which, from the second half of the

1990s onwards, became cheap and plentiful. Between 1987 and 2011, subsidies associated with loans for permanent homeownership and tax incentives granted under the Income Tax Code for the acquisition, construction or improvement of private housing reached two thirds of total public funding on housing (IHRU, 2015).

Thus, rather than being associated with the retreat of the state from this domain of social provisioning, as has been argued for other contexts, in Portugal the evolution of household debt is more directly the result of financialisation. This nonetheless points to the importance of relevant systems of provision and broader welfare provisioning, which are shaped by country-specific social, political, economic and historical factors (Bayliss, Fine & Robertson, 2017), entailing differentiated extents, natures and uses of finance. In the Portuguese case, the almost non-existent public provision of housing explains by and large the extent and magnitude of household debt. Yet the state has played a critical part, ensuring the synchronic evolution of demand to the supply of credit to households through fiscal incentives to home purchase with credit.

However, household engagement with finance is not a transversal phenomenon within Portuguese society. Unlike recent household credit expansion in the American subprime market, this expansion was not directed at all at the lower social classes at greater risk of defaulting, but to households with higher incomes and better guarantees of financial solvency. In 2017, 46 per cent of Portuguese families were in debt, approximately 32 per cent had a loan on a household home, 4 per cent had mortgages for properties other than their home, and 18 per cent had loans not secured by property. Moreover, the level of household involvement in the debt market rises in line with income level, ranging from 18 per cent for the lowest income quintile to 66 per cent for the highest income decile (BdP & INE, 2019).

That household debt consists mainly of mortgage loans and that it is concentrated in higher-income households exposes the unequal access to and the unequal impact of finance on households. For the Portuguese middle to upper classes, homeownership has emerged as the best option for meeting accommodation needs. Benefiting from low interest rates and long maturity periods on their housing loans, these households saw a reduction of their housing costs (when compared with the rental market) and accumulated wealth. This is clearly evidenced by the difference between the cost of a mortgage and of paying rent. In 2013, at the height of the crisis, only 7 per cent of families with mortgages were bearing an excessive burden of expenditure on housing (i.e. over 40 per cent of the available household income), whereas the figure was 35 per cent for households who were renting the household home; these values decreased, respectively, to 3 per cent and 26 per cent in 2018 (Eurostat, 2020b). The extraordinary expansion of household debt should thus be understood as the easiest and cheapest way for the wealthier households to gain access to housing. Departing from very low debt levels, this rise of indebtedness was not only generally sustainable in respect of a household's ability to pay, but was also a relatively safe way to accumulate wealth, due to the relatively stable and continued rise of house prices despite the drop in the immediate aftermath, between 2009 and 2013, though it has already surpassed pre-crisis levels, increasing 18 percent points in 2018 relative to 2006 (EMF, 2019). With most of these mortgages contracted at variable rates indexed to the interbank rate Euribor, monthly repayment amounts have followed the decline of ECB interest rates since 2009, allowing for a significant reduction in levels of mortgage loan repayments as reflected in the favourable evolution of the housing cost overburden rate of homeowners paying mortgages.

The participation of Portuguese households is even more unequally distributed in financial assets markets. In 2013, the top income decile concentrated all financial assets, where 33 per cent of these households held tradable assets (mutual funds, bonds and shares) and 42 per cent held voluntary private pensions or whole life assurance, while the bottom income quintile held, respectively, 1 per cent and 4 per cent of the same assets (BdP & INE, 2016).[6] This means that high-income households have substantially higher rates of participation in financial markets, both as debtors and holders of financial assets. The concentration of specific financial liabilities such as mortgage debt, and of financial assets such as mutual and pension funds, in high-income households suggests that they have a balanced and beneficial relation with finance. This is so not only because financial liabilities are contracted on more favourable terms and can be converted into real wealth, but also because these households have a more diversified and balanced set of financial assets, thus being better able to hedge their portfolios against financial volatility. In contrast, low-income households tend to contract debt with higher interest rates for the purchase of consumer goods, having fewer means to deal with liquidity or solvency problems, and being more vulnerable to personal and social contingencies that compromise their wage income. By benefiting the high-income households more and in relevant areas of provision, such as housing and retirement, financialisation is further detrimental to the most vulnerable segments of the population in promoting and reinforcing private and commodified forms of provision. This has deep implications for the way in which other parts of the system of provision adapt and adjust to the financialised parts, which will be more thoroughly developed in Part 3 of this book.

The rapid expansion of debt among Portuguese households over the past two decades has been associated with low levels of default. It was the crisis and the consequent drop in household income and overall increase in the cost of living that led to bad debt in bank portfolios. Reflecting the differentiated engagement of households with finance, the default rate on credit for consumer goods and other purposes rose fastest, from around 6 per cent in 2009 to 15 per cent in 2015, while the default rate for housing loans remained relatively contained, increasing from 2 per cent to 3 per cent in the same period. Both rates have fallen, respectively, to 7 per cent and 2 per cent in 2019 (Monetary and Financial Statistics; BdP, 2020).

It was therefore essentially the crisis itself that revealed the household vulnerability to increasing entanglement with finance, making them more vulnerable to the economic and financial instability of the country. This time, vulnerability to debt problems was not caused by the bursting of inflated mortgage markets, leading to the fall in housing prices as in the USA and to a lesser extent Spain. It was first and foremost caused by the rise in unemployment and the sudden lack of income caused by austerity conditionality imposed by the European Union and the IMF and endorsed by the government (Chapter 8 in this volume).

Thus, the claim that it has been the growth of income inequality and the rollback of the state that have forced households to engage with finance to fill the gap between income and acquired standard of living does not apply to the Portuguese case, as has been argued for the USA and the UK (see, for example, Barba & Pivetti, 2009; Cynamon & Fazzari, 2008). And while households have been a new source of revenue for the banking sector, what we observe is by and large a shift in the transfer of income stream from private landlords, positioned in a shrinking market, to banks benefiting from the rise of homeownership rates. Hence, contrary to Lapavitsas' (2009) hypothesis of financial expropriation, the financialisation of households, at least in the Portuguese case, should not be taken as a detrimental relation across all income brackets but as a phenomenon that exacerbates existing income inequality, resulting in the concentration of wealth and capital within the financial sector.

## Towards a conceptualisation of semi-peripheral financialisation for Southern Europe

Critical international political economy is now devoting more attention to the concrete institutional underpinnings of the recent rise of finance and to power relations beyond the Anglo-American world. This book tries to contribute to this burgeoning literature through scrutiny of the content of financialisation in Southern Europe, with a particular focus on the Portuguese case, bringing to the fore the role of the EU.

In contrast to EU core countries, in the SE periphery the major institutional transformations involving finance occurred at a later stage, evolved at a faster pace and were strongly determined by external factors, even if mediated by the enabling role of the state. The process of European integration since the 1980s, particularly that leading towards the creation of the EMU, has implied substantial structural transformations within a short time span (privatisation, liberalisation and re-regulation in many sectors of the economy, including finance) and required the opening up of these economies to their more direct low-cost-of-labour competitors in China and Eastern Europe. The bank credit-driven form of financialisation that the EMU promoted in this part of Europe led to an allocation of investment to the more protected labour-intensive non-tradable sectors, such as construction and real estate, resulting in reduced productivity growth relative to wage and price increases, which accentuated the decline of these countries' manufacturing sectors as expressed by the widening of their current account deficits and resulting foreign indebtedness (Gambarotto & Solari, 2015; Gambarotto, Rangone & Solari, 2019; Orsi & Solari, 2010;

Chapters 3 and 4 in this volume; Rodrigues & Reis, 2012; Weeks, 2019). This has been depicted as indicating a semi-peripheral type of financialisation, stemming from an intermediate position in the world economy and the hybrid form of financialisation where loanable-money capital still prevails vis-à-vis that of financial securities markets (Becker et al., 2010; Lapavitsas & Powell, 2014; Chapter 1 in this volume). This contrasts with the evolution of core European countries, most notably Germany, that have instead reinforced their export-oriented models, accumulating record surplus in their current trade account (Barradas et al., 2018; Johnston & Regan, 2016; Stockhammer, 2011, 2016), which funded the EU periphery deficits.

Thus, the context-specific nature of semi-peripheral financialisation in SE countries stems by and large from the hybrid nature of these economies, combining elements of relatively backward structures with a rapidly modernised financial sector, fully articulated with core financial centres and easy access to hard currency (the euro). But SE countries also differ amongst themselves in many respects. For example, while external debt rose in all countries, in Portugal and Spain it was mostly private whereas in Greece it was mostly public (Lapavitsas et al., 2012). And while household debt rose dramatically in Portugal and Spain over the last two decades, due mainly to the evolution of housing loans, only the latter displayed a housing bubble that fed high levels of investment and economic growth during the 2000s (Lopez & Rodríguez, 2011; Santos, Serra & Teles, 2015). This partially explains why the euro is associated, in Portugal, with prolonged economic stagnation before the crisis; a feature shared only with Italy within the eurozone, although the latter did not register the same high levels of external debt.

Nonetheless, increasingly integrated in a highly hierarchical and asymmetric financial system, the recent evolution of SE economies is marked by the unprecedented growth of private debt leading to a (sovereign) public debt crisis when, in the wake of the GFC, SE states could no longer refinance themselves on international markets, culminating in the request for financial bailouts to the Troika comprising the ECB, the European Commission and the IMF. These loans were partly meant to substitute German and French bank loans so that the latter would remain solvent. The most severe economic and financial crises followed, especially in Greece and Portugal, the countries which have been most forcibly compelled to implement radical structural adjustment reforms typical of the Washington Consensus of the 1980s, with the most significant rises of unemployment and decline in GDP in the period (Chapter 1 in this volume).

The structural adjustment programme imposed by the official lenders, even if with the acquiescence of national governments, induced an 'internal devaluation' process aimed at improving external competitiveness since SE countries no longer had available the instrument of currency devaluation to deal with their external account deficits (Chapter 7 in this volume). Deflationary policies based on the reduction of government expenditure and wages, particularly of civil servants, and deep labour and rental market reforms were then implemented. Especially in the Portuguese and Greek cases, the memoranda of understanding signed with the official lenders also envisaged plans of privatisation which included the most important companies that remained in public ownership, such as energy, transport, communications, postal service and insurance sectors. In the dire financial and banking conditions of these countries, this meant that these public assets would be sold to foreign private investors at sale prices. Leading SE industries were then purchased by European companies in services, public utilities and finance, especially French and German as well as Chinese (Silva, 2015; Gambarotto, Rangone & Solari, 2019).

The crisis and the fall in aggregate demand due to austerity measures deteriorated the situation of the local economies, resulting in falls in production, the shutting down of SMEs, and deflationary-induced unemployment. Moreover, the measures envisaged for the banking sector of these countries (i.e. the imposition of a more stringent capital–assets ratio) magnified the credit crunch in these economies (where production is mostly financed by credit), hindering investment and the positive feedback mechanism between producers and consumers. This in turn jeopardised the capacity of non-financial corporations to repay loans, resulting in the rise of banks' non-performing loans, aggravating the situation of banks further and its impact on local economies. This has meant an acceleration of relative deindustrialisation while services and non-traded-goods sectors deepen the processes of internal cost-cutting devaluation, leading to further 'peripheralisation' (Gambarotto, Rangone & Solari, 2019; Chapter 3 in this volume). This divergence is not expected to be reversed within the straitjacket of the EMU which preserves the real exchange rate gap between core and periphery, resulting in long-lasting external imbalances (Johnston & Regan, 2016; Lains, 2018; Weeks, 2019).

Being severely hit by the GFC, SE economic recovery has been based on labour-intensive services sectors, such as tourism and real estate. The austerity-driven, supply-side 'internal devaluation' policies have worsened the situation of these countries by downgrading their patterns of specialisation. The result has been a disappointing increase in productivity notwithstanding the implementation of regressive labour market reforms, implying greater exposure to external pressure on the sectors of their product specialisation. This led to further relative deindustrialisation (Chapter 4 in this volume), widening the gap between the core and periphery, with high-productivity activities increasingly concentrated in the centre, situated in 'the Paris-Amsterdam-Berlin-Frankfurt quadrangle', where 'former national centres (Milan, Lisbon, Athens, Madrid) are losing ground compared to continental ones, becoming less important "second order" centres' (Gambarotto, Rangone & Solari, 2019, p. 165).

A new phase of peripheral financialisation is now emerging, as the internal-demand-led process of growth, based on increasing private debt, is no longer feasible, at least not on the same scale as before. The high level of household indebtedness and the rise of newly created low-paid jobs for the younger generations constrain the expansion of the previous growth model based on the housing market. Instead, we have been observing a new influx of foreign capital restructuring both economic and social reproduction (Chapter 9 in this volume). A recent development has been the rise of foreign investment in real estate, lured by a booming tourism sector, a highly favourable fiscal system and the expectation of higher returns in the post-crisis low-interest-rate environment. This in turn has deep effects on social reproduction due to its impacts on house prices and rents in the two main metropolitan areas of the country (Chapter 8 in this volume).

This is not to say that SE countries have passively accepted the conditions of a new emerging monetary and financial hierarchy within the EMU. The construction of the EMU was based on a hierarchical alliance of sovereign states, which favoured particular fractions of capital both at the national and international levels. Under EU influence, namely through the national transposition of a progressively market-creating and market-conforming regulatory apparatus in the financial sphere, successive SE governments played a role in the insertion of their countries into the international financial circuits, thus mediating between the European and the domestic levels, which benefited not only the economic elite but large swathes of the middle-class, now property owners with low-interest-rate debt. However, such processes involved the loss of important elements of sovereignty in the economic and monetary realms as European integration moved forward. When the financial crisis then morphed into a crisis of public debt, the full extent of SE states' dependence on external funding was fully exposed. The hierarchical nature of the euro and its fragile nature as quasi-world money were yet again brought to the fore.

To conclude, the concept of semi-peripheral financialisation continues to be apt in accounting for the recent evolution of SE. Rather than retreating, finance continues expanding even if in novel ways. This expansion continues to produce a growing divergence from the core, entailing differences in form and content in financialisation processes between the EU core and periphery. It conveys a more relevant role of international finance and its intertwining with domestic agents, including financial institutions, non-financial firms and households, which are crucial to adequately account for variegation in financialisation processes in these countries. This topic is addressed in other chapters of this book, which the concluding chapter brings together.

## Acknowledgements

This is a revised and updated version of Rodrigues, Santos and Teles (2016), where the concept of semi-peripheral financialisation was first proposed. Even though a mere four have years passed since this publication, significant changes have occurred in Southern European countries. These recent changes are presented in the last section of the chapter. We thank Taylor & Francis for permission to reprint this revised version of the article in this edited book, and Ben Fine for comments. All errors and omissions remain the responsibility of the authors.

## Notes

1  For a thorough development of the concept of loanable-money capital, see Chapter 1 in this volume.
2  The term quasi-world money refers to Marx's concept of world money, and accounts for the need for a common international means of payment and hoarding (reserves) in the world market. This has been mostly assured by the dollar, which has given the USA the 'ability to exercise monetary policy domestically, to maintain foreign trade deficits and to import and export capital'. It has also 'spurred financialization in developing countries and systematically transferred value to the US' (Lapavitsas, 2013, p. 104).
3  They argue that in the peripheries and semi-peripheries, where financial securities markets are less developed, financialisation is more directly associated with the expansion of loanable-money capital provided by banks, national and international.
4  Notwithstanding the intensification of economic relations with its former colonies (namely, with Brazil and Angola), promoted too by cheap and easy access to loanable-money capital in a hard currency (the euro), these economic ties have remained of marginal importance to the Portuguese economy as a whole. For this reason, the traditional intermediation role between core/empire and periphery/colony (e.g. Wallerstein, 1974) is not taken as significant for the contemporary Portuguese case.
5  In contrast to what was observed in Portugal, in Germany wages grew at a slower pace than productivity. The difference between the unit labour costs of the two countries explains, at least partially, the continued relative loss of competitiveness in Portugal (Lapavitsas et al., 2012).
6  This data is unavailable for more recent years.

## References

Aalbers, M.B. (2008). The financialization of home and the mortgage market crisis. *Competition and Change, 12*(2), 148–166.

Abdelal, R. (2006). Writing the rules of global finance: France, Europe, and capital liberalization. *Review of International Political Economy, 13*(1), 1–27.

Allen, L. (2004). The Basel capital accords and international mortgage markets: a survey of the literature. *Financial Markets, Institutions & Instruments, 13*(2), 41–108.

Antão, P., Boucinha, M., Farinha, L., Lacerda, A., Leal, C., & Ribeiro, N. (2009). Integração financeira, estruturas financeiras e as decisões das famílias e das empresas. In Banco de Portugal (ed.), *A economia portuguesa no contexto da integração económica, financeira e monetária* (pp. 423–561). Lisbon: Banco de Portugal.

Arrighi, G. (1994). *The Long Twentieth Century: Money, Power and the Origins of Our Times.* London: Verso.

Ashman, S. (2009). Capitalism, uneven and combined development and the transhistoric. *Cambridge Review of International Affairs, 22*(1), 29–46.

Barba, A., & Pivetti, M. (2009). Rising household debt: its causes and macroeconomic implications: a long-period analysis. *Cambridge Journal of Economics, 33*, 113–137.

Barbosa, A.P. (ed.). (1998). *O impacto do euro na economia portuguesa.* Lisbon: Publicações Dom Quixote.

Barradas, R. Lagoa, S., Leão, E., & Mamede, R.P. (2018). Financialization in the European periphery and the sovereign debt crisis: the Portuguese case. *Journal of Economic Issues, 52*(4), 1056–1083.

Bayliss, K., Fine, B., & Robertson, M. (2017). Introduction to special issue on the material cultures of financialisation. *New Political Economy, 22*(4), 355–370.

BdP (Banco de Portugal) (2020). Data from BPstat Estatísticas on line. [Dataset]. Retrieved from www.bportugal.pt/EstatisticasWeb.

BdP & INE (Banco de Portugal & Instituto Nacional de Estatística) (2016). *Household Finance and Consumption Survey 2013*. Lisbon: BdP & INE. Retrieved from www.ine.pt/xportal/xmain?xpid=INE&xpgid=ine_destaques&DESTAQUESdest_boui=274564316&DESTAQUESmodo=2&xlang=en.

BdP & INE (Banco de Portugal & Instituto Nacional de Estatística) (2019). *Household Finance and Consumption Survey 2017*. Lisbon: BdP & INE. Retrieved from www.ine.pt/xportal/xmain?xpid=INE&xpgid=ine_destaques&DESTAQUESdest_boui=403895196&DESTAQUESmodo=2&xlang=en.

Becker, J., Jäger, J., Leubolt, B., & Weissenbacher, R. (2010). Peripheral financialization and vulnerability to crisis: a regulationist perspective. *Competition & Change, 14*(3–4), 225–247.

Boyer, R. (2000). The political in the era of globalization and finance: focus on some regulation school research. *International Journal of Urban and Regional Research, 24*(2), 274–322.

Caldas, J.C., Rocha, S., & Teles, N. (eds.). (2012). Conhecer a dívida para sair da armadilha: relatório preliminar do grupo técnico (Report). Lisboa: Iniciativa para uma Auditoria Cidadã à Dívida. Retrieved from http://auditoriacidada.info/facebook/docs/relatorio_iac.pdf.

CMVM (Commissão do Mercado de Valores Mobiliários) (2012). Relatório estatístico da gestão de ativos em Portugal (Report). Retrieved from www.cmvm.pt/pt/Estatisticas/EstatisticasPeriodicas/GestaoDeActivos/Documents/RGA_4%20T%202011%20VA.pdf.

Cynamon, B.Z., & Fazzari, S.M. (2008). Household debt in the consumer age: source of growth – risk of collapse. *Capitalism and Society, 3*(2), 1–30.

De Grauwe, P. (2011). The governance of a fragile eurozone (CEPS Working Paper No. 346). Brussels: Centre for European Policy Studies.

ECB (European Central Bank) (2017). Report on financial structures. Frankfurt: European Central Bank.

EMF (European Mortgage Federation) (2019). EMF-hypostat archive publication 2019 [Datatset].

Epstein, G.A. (2005). *Financialization and the World Economy*. Cheltenham: Edward Elgar.

Eurostat (2020a). Annual sector accounts database (NASA) [Dataset].

Eurostat (2020b). Income and living conditions database (ILC) [Dataset].

Ferreira do Amaral, J. (2006). O impacto económico da integração de Portugal na Europa. *Nação & Defesa, 115*, 113–128.

Fields, D., & Vernengo, M. (2013). Hegemonic currencies during the crisis: the dollar versus the euro in a cartalist perspective. *Review of International Political Economy, 20*(4), 740–759.

Fine, B. (2010). Locating financialisation. *Historical Materialism, 18*(2), 97–116.

Fine, B. (2011). Financialisation on the rebound? Retrieved from http://eprints.soas.ac.uk/12102.

Fine, B. (2013). Financialization from a Marxist perspective. *International Journal of Political Economy, 42*(4), 47–66.

Foster, J.B. (2007). The financialization of capitalism. *Monthly Review, 58*(11), n.p.

Gabor, D. (2010). (De)financialisation and crisis in Eastern Europe. *Competition & Change, 14*(34), 248–270.

Gambarotto, F., & Solari, S. (2015). The peripheralization of Southern European capitalism within EMU. *Review of International Political Economy, 22*(4), 788–812.

Gambarotto, F., Rangone, M., & Solari, S. (2019). Financialization and deindustrialization in the Southern European periphery. *Athens Journal of Mediterranean Studies*, *5*(3), 151–172.

Garcimartín, C., Rivas, L.A., & Martínez, P.G. (2010). On the role of relative prices and capital flows in balance-of-payments-constrained growth. *Journal of Post Keynesian Economics*, *33*(2), 281–305.

Gindin, S., & Panitch, L. (2012). *The Making of Global Capitalism*. New York: Verso.

Hardie, I. (2011). How much can governments borrow? Financialization and emerging markets government borrowing capacity. *Review of International Political Economy*, *18*(2), 141–167.

Helleiner, E. (1994). *States and the Reemergence of Global Finance: From Bretton Woods to the 1990s*. Ithaca, NY: Cornell University Press.

IHRU (Instituto da Habitação e Reabilitação Urbana) (2015). *1987–2011: 25 anos de esforço do orçamento do estado com a habitação*. Lisbon: Instituto da Habitação e Reabilitação Urbana. Retrieved from www.portaldahabitacao.pt/opencms/export/sites/portal/pt/portal/publicacoes/documentos/Esforco-do-Estado-em-Habitacao.pdf.

INE (Instituto Nacional de Estatística) (2020). Construction and housing statistics. [Dataset]. Retrieved from www.ine.pt.

Johnston, A., & Regan, A. (2016). European monetary integration and the incompatibility of national varieties of capitalism. *Journal of Common Market Studies*, *54*(2), 318–336.

Kaminsky, G., & Reinhart, C. (1999). The twin crises: causes of banking and balance-of-payments problems. *American Economic Review*, *89*(3), 473–500.

Kaltenbrunner, A., & Painceira, J.P. (2018). Subordinated financial integration and financialisation in emerging capitalist economies: the Brazilian experience. *New Political Economy*, *23*(3), 290–313.

Konings, M. (2007). The institutional foundations of US structural power in international finance: from the re-emergence of global finance to the monetarist turn. *Review of International Political Economy*, *15*(1), 35–61.

Krippner, G. (2005). The financialization of the American economy. *Socio-Economic Review*, *3*, 173–208.

Lains, P. (2018). Convergence, divergence and policy: Portugal in the European Union. *West European Politics*, *42*(5), 1094–1114.

Lapavitsas, C. (1997). Two approaches to the concept of interest-bearing capital. *International Journal of Political Economy*, *27*(1), 85–106.

Lapavitsas, C. (2003). *Social Foundations of Markets, Money, and Credit*. London: Routledge.

Lapavitsas, C. (2009). Financialised capitalism: crisis and financial expropriation. *Historical Materialism*, *17*(2), 114–148.

Lapavitsas, C. (2013). *Profiting without Production: How Finance Exploits Us All*. London: Verso.

Lapavitsas, C., & Powell, J. (2014). Financialisation varied: a comparative analysis of advanced economies. *Cambridge Journal of Regions, Economy and Society*, *6*(3), 359–379.

Lapavitsas, C., Kaltenbrunner, A., Lambrinidis, G., Lindo, D., Meadway, J., Michell, J., Painceira, J., Pires E., Powell, J., Stenfors, A., Teles, N., & Vatikiotis, L. (2012). *Eurozone in Crisis*. London: Verso.

Leão, P., & Palacio-Vera, A. (2011). Can Portugal escape stagnation without opting out from the eurozone? (Working Paper No. 664). Annandaleon-Hudson, NY: Levy Economics Institute.

Lopez, I., & Rodríguez, E. (2011). The Spanish model. *New Left Review*, *69*, 5–29.

Mendes,V., & Rebelo, J. (2003). Structure and performance in the Portuguese banking industry in the nineties. *Portuguese Economic Journal, 2*(1), 53–68.

Nunes, A. (2011). The International Monetary Fund's standby arrangements with Portugal: an ex-ante application of the Washington Consensus? (Working Paper No. 44). Lisbon: Instituto Superior de Economia e Gestão GHES.

Orsi, L., & Solari, S. (2010). Financialisation in Southern European countries. *Économie Appliquée, 63*(4), 5–34.

Pinho, P. (1997). The impact of the single market programme and the preparations in Portuguese banking (Working Paper Series No. 312). Lisbon: Faculdade de Economia da Universidade Nova de Lisboa. Retrieved from https://run.unl.pt/bitstream/10362/89009/1/WP312.pdf.

Pinto, A.C., & Teixeira, N.S. (2002). From Africa to Europe: Portugal and European integration. In A.C. Pinto and N.S. Teixeira (eds.), *Southern Europe and the Making of the European Union* (pp. 3–40). New York: Columbia University Press.

Pinto, A.M. (1996). Changing financial systems in small open economies: the Portuguese case (Policy Papers No. 1). Basel: Bank of International Settlements. Retrieved from http://www.bis.org/publ/plcy01.htm.

Powell, J. (2013). Subordinate financialisation: a study of Mexico and its non-financial corporations. PhD thesis, School of Oriental and African Studies, University of London.

Rodrigues, J., & Reis, J. (2012). The asymmetries of European integration and the crisis of Portuguese capitalism. *Competition & Change, 16*(3), 188–205.

Rodrigues, J., Santos, A.C., & Teles, N. (2016). Semi-peripheral financialisation: the case of Portugal. *Review of International Political Economy, 23*(3), 480–510.

Santos, B.S. (1985). Estado e sociedade na semiperiferia do sistema mundial: o caso Português. *Análise Social, 87–89*, 869–901.

Santos, A.C., Serra, N., & Teles, N. (2015). Finance and housing provision in Portugal (FESSUD Working Paper Series No. 79). Leeds: FESSUD.

Silva, J.R. (2015). Foreign direct investment in the context of the financial crisis and bailout: Portugal. In B. Galgóczi, J. Drahokoupil and M. Bernaciak (eds.), *Foreign Investment in Eastern and Southern Europe after 2008* (pp. 171–207). Brussels: European Trade Union Institute.

Stockhammer, E. (2011). Peripheral Europe's debt and German wages. *International Journal for Public Policy, 7*(1–3): 83–96.

Stockhammer, E. (2016). Neoliberal growth models, monetary union and the euro crisis. a post-Keynesian perspective. *New Political Economy, 21*(4): 365–379.

Sweezy, P. (1994). The triumph of financial capital. *Monthly Review, 46*(2), 1–11.

Van Treeck, T. (2009). The political economy debate on 'financialisation': a macroeconomic perspective. *Review of International Political Economy, 16*(5), 907–944.

Wallerstein, I. (1974). *Semi-peripheral Countries and the Contemporary World Crisis.* New York: Academic Press.

Weeks, S. (2019). Portugal in ruins: From 'Europe' to crisis and austerity. *Review of Radical Political Economics, 51*(2), 246–264.

Zhang, X. (2009). From banks to markets: Malaysian and Taiwanese finance in transition. *Review of International Political Economy, 16*(3), 382–408.

# 3   Portugal as a European periphery

## Imbalances, dependency, and trajectories

*José Reis*

## Portugal as a European periphery

The subject of this text is the trajectory of the Portuguese economy in the European framework during the last few decades. Within this context, Portugal's peripheral position is taken as a most relevant fact. Due to the heterogeneity of their internal organisation, and the relations they establish within the plurinational space of which they are a part, European peripheral economies are dependent economies. That is, they show little control over what is essential in economic and social evolution and are subjected to the development of the central countries, thus articulating the evolution of the whole of which they are a part. From this, results a position that, by the material and institutional connections that involve peripheral economies, structurally conditions the political choices and the margins of action made possible by their own specificities.

The peripheral condition of Portugal is persistent and has assumed diverse forms. Geography – the country's distance from the great centres and dynamics of the most powerful capitalisms – is not enough to determine that condition. What is essential to define it are the imbalances that result from this internal characteristic and the consequent intermediation roles that the country plays in the space where it established its fundamental economic relations. These are developed within the European framework – constituted in its dominant relational space at the end of the colonial cycle – and reproduced differently over time. The key roles have been the supply of labour force to the centre, the reception of the exports of these countries, and finally, the role of debtor in the context of a credit and debt economy.

The unbalanced internal nature and the dependency relationship do not mean, however, that we cannot distinguish moments of reconfiguration resulting from specific and relevant deliberations (even though we know that there are strong limiting tendencies). But I will admit, that the structural power and the reproduction of the asymmetric condition prevail over what the specificities might suggest. It is a game of tensions, present within the European framework itself, which, at the extreme, allows us to suggest that the peripheral condition is not inescapable. There are circumstances in which a reaction occurs in the search for other trajectories and other destinations. This is what happened with the project of advanced democracy that began to be constructed on 25 April 1974; with the European integration of the 1980s; with the recent response to the austerity shock; and – this must be admitted, at least for some – with the adoption of the euro. At these times new balances were rehearsed. But these balances have not been easily obtained. These are demanding and must start with the way in which people's lives are organised and how they are socially and economically embedded.

I assume that in any economy it is through work and employment that the essential mechanisms for inclusion are established. This means that it is in the productive system and in the internal organisation of material life that the key to social and economic problems lies – it is in the way in which wealth is created in the various sectors that the economy itself and society are qualified – and that society should be understood as a community of people where the collective well-being and the public interest must be realised. But it has happened that, in a periphery, instead of the desired balances, new imbalances succeed, perhaps deeper than the previous ones.

In 1974, at a time of radical change that reconciled the country with itself, Portugal was an anachronistic colonial 'power' and an economy that had experienced a decade of high growth and intense industrialisation without increasing employment and that, at the same time, had transformed workforce export into its main device of external relations. In fact, between 1960 and 1973, the Portuguese GDP more than doubled, and the annual investment was between 20 and 30 per cent of GDP, consisting predominantly of capital accumulation in heavy industry. Yet employment remained virtually stagnant.[1] The resident population itself decreased. By contrast, emigration, which moved to European countries in a novel way and replaced the traditional destinations of Africa and Latin America, amounted to around 900,000 emigrants in the same period, according to official numbers. But according to estimations by Maria Ioannis Baganha (1994), who also assessed clandestine emigration, total emigration volume in this timeframe was actually closer to 1.4 million. The dictatorial regime rehearsed a sort of modern industrialisation. But although this appeared as the driver of progress, it did not even modernise or give cohesion to the economy. Much less did it fulfil the immediate purpose of generating employment and 'pulling' the rest of the economy with it. Portugal arrived at the beginning of the seventies with a smaller population and with exhausted possibilities of growth. For the first time in the period under consideration, the Portuguese economy fell short of potential output. This imbalance between GDP growth and job supply is the first imbalance that we find in the formation of the contemporary Portuguese peripheral position.

The second imbalance was formed over the period of economic, social and political democratisation following the 1974 revolution and the redefinition of the country's international insertion, which led to its accession to the European Economic Community (EEC) in 1986, and to the first phase of integration. It was fundamentally an imbalance of underproduction. The result was heavy commercial dependence. At a time of major institutional change, of various external shocks, of emigration stoppage, and of the return of over half a million citizens (over 5 per cent of the resident population),[2] the 'transformation of productive structures' was one of the 'major tasks' (Lopes, 1996, p. 26), alongside addition to the country's own physical and social infrastructure. Economic policy persistently focused on the internal dimension. Between 1973 and 1985, employment registered 400,000 new jobs (10 per cent of the total volume). This was a radical change from the previous period. The generalisation of the principle of inclusion through work and the diffusion of well-being became central and brought with them two significant growth cycles with a similar duration, profile and intensity (see Figure 3.1).[3] However, this effort did not prevent, even after an initial glimpse associated with integration, the widening of the trade deficit, consolidating a negative trend that would prove to be longer and more inflexible than at other times.[4] Productive insufficiency is necessarily associated with a low-skilled workforce, scarce entrepreneurial competence, and productive specialisation in low-value-creating sectors. These were weaknesses of the economic system as a whole. The priorities were well established and the effort huge. But it was not enough. International openness through trade accelerated, exports grew, but imports increased much more, resulting in a significant imbalance that expressed the persistent structural weaknesses of the country, deterring the expectations of a population seeking access to reasonable welfare standards.

The previous imbalance was then combined with a much more profound one, which was decisive because of the institutional architecture of EMU. Portugal participated in this process with all the signs of peripherality just described. In a framework of 'happy Europeanism' this was underestimated or even ignored. A functionalist idea of convergence predominated, and it was assumed that this would blur and make irrelevant centre–periphery relations that predated the single currency (Rodrigues & Reis, 2012). But this new reality, made up of intense forms of privatisation and liberalisation that made the financial sector more powerful than it had ever been, quickly revealed that some countries' productive and commercial advantages would make them creditors to those on the other side of this asymmetrical relationship. The Portuguese economy, whose financial relations with foreign countries were balanced in the early 1990s, quickly accumulated high deficits, as shown by the International Investment Position. With no balance-of-payments mechanisms (such as transfers made by emigrant remittances or European cohesion policy at its most significant phase), placed in a situation of heavy trade dependence, devoid of economic policy instruments that would counteract this unbalanced trajectory, and caught in the trap of a financial circulation actively promoted by the institutional framework and powerful players, the Portuguese economy saw its external indebtedness rise from -13 per cent of GDP in 1996 to -119 per cent in 2014.[5] This is the third major imbalance. The subjection to credit and debt became prevalent, in a situation of impoverishment that mirrored the renewed peripheral condition of Portugal.

From these three moments of the tension game established between the Portuguese economy and its European context, there resulted, as it turned out, different internal configurations of the labour market, the productive system and the relationship with capital markets. Emigration, trade deficit and external indebtedness expressed the internally generated imbalances and dependencies. Beyond what each one means in the Portuguese economy, they have unleashed intermediation effects in relation to the central countries that have consolidated the country's peripheral condition – as a labour provider, as an open market for their exports, and as a debtor that makes the surpluses that they accumulate. These functions are essential elements of the consolidation of the asymmetrical form assumed by the European framework and, therefore, of the distinct role of central and peripheral countries.

## The difficulty of structuring a qualified productive system

Behind the previously mentioned imbalances there has always been an essential problem: the difficulty of structuring the economy around a skilled system of production and wealth creation, and consequently the building of a welfare system. The economy has often fallen short of potential and, above all, short of what a fairer country required. What the satisfaction of internal needs demanded was always greater than its ability to create wealth, resulting consequently in external dependence. This has been revealed in the employment system and the labour market, in trade relations, and in the financial balance.

This is the general and permanent difficulty of a periphery. In Portugal, the key moments in the history of this difficulty can be properly identified. In the decade prior to the 1974 democratic revolution, the salient dynamics in the economy – which existed and were occasionally acute – were limited to creating an 'insular', protected and self-centred space in which capital was accumulated and some technologies were structured without a direct result in the creation of an articulated and capable system of production and supply. Still less did this create a set of relations between the economy and society that allowed a sustainable development, in both social and economic terms. Some economic historiography saw here 'Portuguese development', and abandoned research devoted to 'explaining backwardness' (Amaral, 1998, p. 741). It was argued that we would be faced with a 'unique reality in the post-war economic scene' because 'a small and peripheral country' with a 'different socio-political structure from the typical European one', 'has grown strongly and transformed its economy into an industrial and modern economy', being considered 'one of the best examples of the growth of the "golden age" of the 50s and 60s' (Neves, 1994, pp. 1005–1006). It was even said that the fact that those 'turbulent' decades were 'governed by the same institutional structure' (i.e. by 'Salazarism') 'brought to the Portuguese economy a great unity of purpose and consistency of orientation' (Neves, 1994, p. 1006). But what happened was that Portugal was 'the last European industrial country', 'the last industrial nation of Western Europe', the one that only in 1963 saw the value of its industrial product surpass that of agriculture (Lains, 2003, p. 179).

It is clear, then, that an original process was opened up in the evolution of the Portuguese economy and that it consisted of industrialisation and unprecedented economic growth. But 'growth accounting' only records as the most important input the accumulation of capital, that is, physical capital. Therefore, the reading I propose is substantively different. The effects on the constitution of a modern economy and society were minimal. There was no political democracy, much less economic democracy. Nor was there room for positive 'production functions' and 'externalities' that would involve the whole economic sector. There is no evidence of other mechanisms that allow this industrialisation to be considered a mode of development of a society. These would be a broad and articulated productive base that would involve, through employment, an increasing number of people and set standards (technical, but above all, social) for the organisation and qualification of collective life.

The confrontation with such limits forced the regime to resort to what had been set aside: light industries producing finished goods, and agriculture, in an export turn that would rebalance the economy and the state, which in the meantime had to endure a colonial war in Africa. It was, however, an openness based on low-value goods and low remuneration, in a context in which various forms of protectionism and regulation remained, as well as a policy of low wages that protected profits and capitalist positions. This culminated in an industrialisation dictated by the 'capital factor' alone and thus absolutely mediocre in its economic and social repercussions. While the peripheral condition of the country subsisted, it had relevant political consequences. The political economy internally set the conditions for the rise of a new democratic framework.

The next phase of the Portuguese economy includes the long period of the establishment and consolidation of democracy and the first phase of European integration, until 1993. This has been the most complex period of economic, social and political evolution in the country over the last decades. The institutions that shape employment systems, social security, income sharing and access to the provision of collective services became crucial and were positively structured with remarkable achievements.[6] This is what determined a set of general drag effects. The high level of investment demonstrated that the basic elements of the structure of the economy and society were at stake. The social dimensions of democracy, as well as its political dimension, became relevant and this is the kind of deliberation that shapes the prevailing political economy. Industry kept its weight in GDP above 20 per cent. A decisive condition, which is inclusion through work, was ensured. Similar to what had already happened in most economies, the emergence of an economy of public and private services, characteristic of a tertiary economy, was, along with industrial persistence, one of the striking new features. The link between democratic deliberation and economic governance found significant expression here. A mix of economic policies prevailed where the domestic level was central, before financial transformations radically changed the rules of the game.

However, amid strong external shocks and a turbulent international economic situation, the capacity for dealing with the structural weaknesses of the productive system was scant. The Portuguese economy was too peripheral for all of the country's ambition for qualification to be fulfilled. To the 'characteristic fact' of employment growth should be added that of intense foreign trade dependence. Trade deficits widened and became particularly significant in the balance on goods. Between 1984 and 1992 they were around 10 per cent of GDP. The country's peripheral conditions were once again exposed. It became clear that this was the difficulty resulting from the way in which an economy without robust anchoring factors fitted into an international market in which very diverse economic powers operate.

In the absence of industrial reinforcement (as opposed to the deindustrialisation and banal tertiarisation that did occur), changes in productive specialisation in favour of higher-value-added activities, or a shift in the qualification of the workforce, the difficulties became worse. Admittedly, democracy and the adherence to a Europe that still had cohesion policies, especially territorial cohesion, qualified the country and disguised the problems. But it turns out that what a country means as a market is, in many circumstances, more appealing than what it represents as an economic, social and political system. Suffice it to say that even foreign direct investment has always been scarce in the Portuguese economy and its weight in the current International Investment Position is reduced, since financial transactions largely dominate without any productive counterparts. This contrasts, for example with countries on the eastern periphery of Europe (Reis, 2018, p. 203).

The most frontal and dramatic moment of encounter with its peripheral condition happened when Portugal became involved in the construction of the Economic and Monetary Union and became a member. The 'new Europe' that began to be defined and formalised with the 1992 Maastricht Treaty and the 1997 Stability and Growth Pact was establishing a set of systematic restrictions on an economy which, in 1993, had closed its third cycle of expressive growth and, then, because of the new commitments, entered into a limited and later turbulent evolution.

The scope of public policies (e.g. the exchange rate, fiscal, monetary and financial policies, as well as the organisation of production and labour market policies) was reduced and the power of market relations, especially of financial markets, prevailed over state action. The principles of real convergence that underpinned aspects of European policy were replaced by those of nominal convergence and restrictive logics of 'economic governance' that actually act in the name of markets and their powers. The preponderance of financial investment by shifting amounts of wealth from the real economy has become a new form of rentism. The centre of gravity of the economy's dynamics was shifted to sectors whose activity was facilitated not only by excessive credit availability (where real estate predominated) but also by an influx of imports, which were not subject to international payment restrictions, in view of the conditions of membership of the monetary union and of trade liberalisation worldwide.

Instead of progressing towards the improvement of the economic system, more 'extractive' than inclusive schemes were developed (Acemoglu & Robinson, 2012), resulting from the primacy of the logic of capital circulation, financial relations and credit files. Portugal was particularly fragile and ill-equipped to cope with what would emerge in this new European context. In it, in place of production and employment, which were central to the affluent phases of capitalism, canonised money management, finance and banking systems became the essential governing powers of the economy. It is in their name that all mischief is allowed, including the weakening of states, while promoting markets and their power of command.

At that time, during the 1990s, international economic relations began to give major importance to the circulation of capital in the form of credit. The balance of intra-European development, through cohesion and sustainability of each country, has been pushed to the background in favour of the accumulation of trade surpluses in the central countries, leading to a reduced convergence between EU national components. Banks frantically promoted credit and were careful not to separate speculative operations from those that could qualify the economy, thus leading to clumsy financial schemes that would create huge problems for the banking system itself. Bank refinancing has become the main external indebtedness component of the Portuguese economy, and the combination of this weakened position and the political economy of austerity, accentuating the impoverishment of the country, transfers responsibilities to the state, generating a public debt economy, which passed from reasonable values and from a minimum of 50 per cent of GDP in 2000 to a maximum of 131 per cent of GDP in 2014. Society and the economy were marked by the great restrictions already established, given the dependence generated by the indebtedness of the economy and then by public debt. The economy was hit by an absolutely unprecedented level of unemployment and an equally unprecedented stagnation. At the same time, the marks of inequality were reinforced, including again emigration and the devaluation of the country's resources. It was the strongest recessive capture of the Portuguese economy by deep ideological convictions, in favour of a reversal of social relations, especially labour relations, and of a limitation of the role of the state. The acceleration of the problems brought about by the international financial crisis occurs in an already established institutional context, favourable to financial power and inhibiting responses that could reconstitute the capacity to structure and grow productive systems.

To deindustrialisation and outsourcing through banal services would quickly be added a reduction in employment, strong precariousness, and a concentration of labour dynamics in the low-wage and higher-precariousness sectors, particularly low-cost tourism.[7] To this we may add a metropolitan concentration that weakens the country territorially. Portugal remained far from having a balanced and sensible set of economic policies, which would have combined productive investment, budgetary clearsightedness, fiscal justice and the development of society itself.[8] However, for this the European environment would have had to be different, since its presence in national deliberations became asphyxiating. This is the periphery in its most intense condition.

## Growth and forms of external dependence

Portugal had, over the period I am taking as a reference, four significant growth cycles: 1960–1974, 1975–1983, 1984–1992 and 1993–2002. The graph summarises the essentials (Figure 3.1). All have a similar duration and only the third shows slow rhythms, which I associate with the restrictions to which the economic governance of the EMU subjected the Portuguese economy. The effects of the international financial crisis then become apparent by the radical instability they give rise to, as a turbulence never felt before.

The turbulent period which we have recently entered is undergoing significant recovery effects, albeit in a new context of low and irregular increases. But there are two issues that must be addressed: one is the low starting point, which has kept the country far from the most advanced ones; the other is the dependency that each cycle generates.[9] I will now dedicate myself to this topic.

As we have already seen, there are three forms of dependency that I analyse here. The first concerns the inclusion of people in the economic system, wage ratios, income distribution and access to welfare. A developing Portugal relied on the labour markets of European economies in order for a significant part of its population to achieve these goals. Taken together, the aforementioned indicators of negative demographic evolution, non-growth in employment and

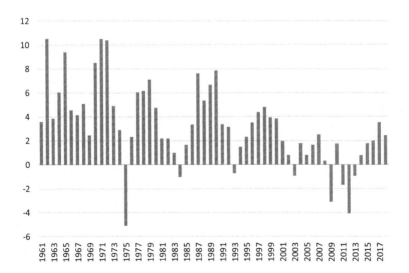

*Figure 3.1* Annual percentage rates of real GDP growth, 1960–2018
Source: Instituto Nacional de Estatística and Bank of Portugal

massive emigration in the 1960s demonstrate exactly this. When situations of fragility persist, even in different forms, this dependence may return. This is what is happening now in Portugal, with other types of emigration and other destinations.[10]

Commercial dependence is especially impactful on the industrial sector and, therefore, on the production of goods, and is mitigated by an unskilled specialisation in tourism services that make intensive use of the country's environmental conditions, from urban to seaside. The ratio of exports to imports of goods has rarely moved beyond 60 per cent and only under conditions of great economic compression, as happened under the austerity effect, has it exceeded 80 per cent. The current account deficit is obviously determined by what happens with the production of goods. There is a noticeable parallelism between both indicators. The problem increases when there is a trend towards deindustrialisation and specialisation degrades.[11] At this point, it is particularly apparent that such dependence is, in fact, a consequence of the development of the role of peripheral economies as a market for the industrial capacity of central countries.

The picture described above converged in the nineties to a new form of intense and novel dependence of the Portuguese economy, which defines the current situation. This kind of dependence had never occurred in Portugal, even in times of crisis and transition such as the ones the country experienced punctually in the late seventies and eighties. It is a new political economy, based on the financial circulation that is prevalent in the country and, ultimately, in the European context (for more details, see Rodrigues, Santos & Teles, 2016). External economic relations are the focal point of significant change.

## The intermediary functions of a peripheral economy

As I have been arguing, a peripheral society is defined by its internal condition and intermediation functions within the spaces in which it operates, at different times and at different scales. For example Portugal exerted forms of mediation within the world system when it played a colonial role. In this case, the appropriate way of conceptualising Portuguese society was as a semi-periphery (Santos, 1993; Wallerstein, 1979). Returning to its current European position, the relevance of any intermediary function in the international system has diminished sharply, highlighting the internal relations with a 'region' of that system, the European Union. It was here that Portugal's position was redefined and consolidated. And it is also here that we emphatically see that its intermediate condition also means the exercise of intermediation functions in relation to the central countries and the system itself, which thus maintain its asymmetrical nature. It is no longer political intermediation in conflict management as conceived on the scale of the world economy. It is an economic intermediation, which in the Portuguese case is expressed in labour supply, in the widening of goods and services markets, and in capital reception and debt creation, within a framework of structural asymmetry within the EMU, where the single currency has become a powerful instrument of governance between economically and politically very different countries.

The first of these functions took place when the labour markets of the developed economies showed that they were dual markets and contained within them low-skilled and lower-waged segments; these were the sectors supporting those where the dynamics driving innovative growth were based. It was the periphery that made these people available through massive waves of abundant emigration. In Portugal, the inability to structure the economy internally was combined with this function at the service of central capitalisms. And the same is happening today, in the face of an employment system that has become more fragile after the political economy of austerity, which means an inability to generate the necessary volume of employment and, in particular, to absorb the skilled population. This function of labour intermediation is thus recurrent, even when it is the result of different processes within the same structural condition of a peripheral economy.

The second intermediation function, clearly visible at the different stages of the integration process, consists of the 'supplementary' market for goods and services that a periphery offers to the central countries because it has a deficit-productive system in view of internal needs. We have already seen that what results is a trade balance deficit of more than 10 per cent of GDP for long periods of time. But of course, the structure of this market is also significant, as we are considering sectors with very different value creation capabilities. The peripheries thus legitimise the superior technological capacity of the centre and the 'organic composition' of its productive capitals. In the same vein, the shift of production chains from the centres to the peripheries can be observed as certain technological goods and processes mature and their innovative meaning and profitability decline, as was well explained by the product cycle theory. The move to Portugal by the electrical and electromechanical industries first, and later the automobile industry, illustrate this phenomenon.

The intermediation role played by the peripheries in the financialisation phase of capitalism results from indebtedness and insertion in the credit circuits and is primarily played by the recycling of surpluses accumulated in the centre and converted into financial assets. The indicators already used to illustrate external debt and public debt express this. But more immediately, we must also account for the internal devaluation that these processes push the peripheries into and the transfer of income that asymmetrical relations lead to.[12] In Portugal, the balance of primary incomes with the exterior was positive until 1996 and entered a declining path that seems difficult to change, reaching at times -4 per cent of GDP. The costs of financing public action in the periphery are high and compensate for the low costs in the centre, safeguarding the overall remuneration of capital and thus contributing to the cumulative structural surpluses already available to it.[13] In the EMU, with a common currency, the actual real exchange rates are very different between countries: the most developed act as if they had a weak currency, the peripheries as if they had a strong currency, and that establishes the terms of an asymmetric competitiveness over which the weakest cannot act because they no longer have their own exchange policy. These are the circumstances in which the periphery now has a new intermediary function vis-à-vis the centre, in the financial and monetary framework.[14]

## The persistent peripheral condition

The peripheral condition of the Portuguese economy, uniquely demonstrated at times as different as those I pointed out earlier, from the 1960s to the country's participation in the formation of the EMU, through the democratic revolution and the first phase of European integration, is, as we have seen, a persistent circumstance. The intense political economy of austerity, in the context of that last phase, in which financialisation dominates, brought the country into a new and intense confrontation with this condition. The unavoidable fact is always the same: a dramatic contradiction between internal welfare needs and the internal capacity for wealth creation, for which skilled people and advanced resources are essential. By the second decade of this millennium we have rediscovered, in a renewed way, the most primary imbalance of a periphery, which is the deficit of the employment system, whose inclusion power is much lower than the volume and quality required of the workforce. And with that returns the emigration escape valve or, more rigorously, the function of providing labour to other economies. Therefore, from 2011 on the annual volume of emigration, which was at a low level, has risen to 100,000, including permanent and temporary emigrants (INE, 2020a).

Now, it is inevitably in European terms that the peripheral condition of Portugal is defined. Moreover, it is an institutionally locked-in situation, encased in the architecture of the EMU and its economic governance processes. The profound shock of austerity, the effects of which must not be underestimated, reconfigured the economy on a material level (productive and employment systems), established powerful constraints on the state and public action, and fixed the terms of financial constraint expressed in foreign indebtedness and public debt.

It is true – and this also must not be underestimated – that Portugal has embarked on a process of recovery that has enabled the reconstruction of certain dimensions of well-being and expectations and diminished the quantitative gaps suffered by the employment system and growth indicators.[15] Having changed neither the institutional conditions nor the main restrictions, either at the European level or at the international level in general, this new phase only shows that the possibilities for political action for a country are very narrow and correspond to a trajectory on a razor's edge. The activation of an income policy that values labour and relies on a balance of growth-boosting mechanisms – which include domestic demand and the attempt to refocus the role of the state and public administration, including collective services – is confronted by strong limitations. The persistence of the constraints established by the financial powers – the restraint of the economy, the promotion of undervalued forms of international insertion, the weight of restrictions such as debt – are allied to a restrictive 'economic governance' that is the expression of these constraints.

The unavoidable feature of the peripheral condition of a country lies in its productive system and in the failure of a basic condition: employment and the existence of robust forms of inclusion through work. This is where not only the possibility of properly structuring the life of a community begins, but also the possibility of counteracting the asymmetrical relationships that weaken the peripheries.

## Acknowledgements

This work was funded by the Portuguese Foundation for Science and Technology and co-funded by the European Regional Development Fund (ERDF), within the scope of FINHABIT project, ref. PTDC/ATP-GEO/ 2362/2014 – POCI-01-0145-FEDER-016869.

## Notes

1 Chemical industry, cement, steel, heavy metalworking, and shipbuilding and repair. In 1960 and 1973 the employment volume was respectively 3,439 and 3,549 million (Amaral, 2009, p. 788).
2 This was the return to Portugal of those residing in the African colonies, especially Angola and Mozambique. This happened in a few months, coinciding with the independence.
3 This is an important point. The conventional notion that economic growth in Portugal is only the result of trade liberalisation and European integration mechanisms in the 1980s is unfounded. What I call the 'cycle of democracy' is significant and as relevant as the 'cycle of European integration' (Reis, 2018, pp. 81–90).
4 In 1985 and 1986 trade deficits amounted, respectively, to 3 per cent and 1 per cent of GDP, but soon returned to values always exceeding 6 per cent of GDP between 1988 and 2011 (Reis, 2018, p. 111).
5 Remittances reached almost 9.4 per cent of GDP in 1979, were above 5 per cent in 1991, and in recent years have reached 1.8 per cent. Between 1992 and 1999, EU transfers to Portugal were always close to 4 per cent of GDP. In 2017 and 2018 they were set at 1.8 per cent. The net balance, however, was below 3 per cent and is now below 1 per cent (Bank of Portugal, 2020).
6 It is rightly considered that the establishment of a free general health service and public education were two crucial aspects.
7 The maximum employment volume in Portugal was reached in 2001, with 5.1 million jobs, reduced to 4.4 million in 2013, and by 2017 it had only returned to close to 4.8 million, reaching 4.866 million in 2018 (INE, 2020b).
8 The form of political economy pursued in these restrictive circumstances weakens material life in different domains. The references I have made to the productive system and employment can be extended elsewhere to other forms of collective organisation. One which I consider to be among the most important is the country's spatial articulation and the generation of territorial asymmetries. Although that is not the subject of this chapter, I cannot omit to point out the profound and original effects that reduce the dynamics essentially to the Lisbon metropolis and give it a unipolar role that it never had before in Portuguese society.

9 Portuguese GDP per capita in 2017 was 77 per cent of the EU average and its most significant proximity is to peripheral economies and not, for example, to the economies of Southern Europe.

10 The United Kingdom and Spain are significant new destinations for Portuguese emigration.

11 I have described the evolution of the structure of the economy after the economic cycle of the establishment and consolidation of democracy – the cycle of the first phase of European integration – as characterised by 'two "excesses": the excess of deindustrialisation and the corresponding excess of real estate and outsourcing' (Reis, 2018, p. 154).

12 '"Internal devaluation", in fact falling workers' wages and other labour-related business costs, is seen as the only mechanism for adjusting external deficits available to a country that has no currency of its own or has decided to establish a fixed exchange rate between your currency and that of other countries' (Caldas, 2015, p. 5).

13 In 2018, ten-year sovereign bonds in Germany paid rates of 0.25 per cent. In Portugal this figure is 1.7 per cent, almost seven times higher.

14 On top of all this, it still happens that today all countries are, by the prevailing logic of liberalisation and privatisation, 'autonomous' participants in financial circulation. In 2017, residents of Portugal had EUR 340 billion (176 per cent of GDP) as foreign financial assets. A globally deficient country thus contributed to the activism of the financial markets. And it reinforced such contributions through much larger liabilities (EUR 544 billion, 282 per cent of GDP) and a debt position equivalent to 106 per cent of GDP.

15 Between 2013 and 2017 the volume of employment registered 330,000 more jobs but the difference from 2008 is still 360,000. In 2015, 2016 and 2017 the real GDP growth rate was respectively 1.8, 1.4 and 2.5 per cent.

# References

Acemoglu, D., & Robinson, J.A. (2012 [1981]). *Why Nations Fail: The Origins of Power, Prosperity and Poverty.* New York: Crown.

Amaral, L. (1998). Convergência e crescimento económico em Portugal no pós-guerra. *Análise Social, 148,* 741–776.

Amaral, L. (2009). New series of Portuguese population and employment, 1950–2007: implications for GDP per capita and labor productivity. *Análise Social, 193,* 767–791.

Baganha, M.I. (1994). As correntes emigratórias portuguesas no século XX e o seu impacto na economia nacional. *Análise Social, 128,* 959–980.

Bank of Portugal (2020). External Accounts. [Dataset]. Retrieved from https://bpstat.bportugal.pt/dominios/2.

Caldas, J.C. (2015). Desvalorização do trabalho: do Memorando à prática. Cadernos do Observatório No. 6.

INE (Instituto Nacional de Estatística) (2020a). Population. [Dataset]. Retrieved from www.ine.pt.

INE (Instituto Nacional de Estatística) (2020b). Labour Market. [Dataset]. Retrieved from www.ine.pt.

Lains, P. (2003). *Os progressos do atraso: uma nova história económica de Portugal.* Lisbon: Imprensa de Ciências Sociais.

Lopes, J.S. (1996). A economia portuguesa desde 1960. Lisbon: Gradiva.

Neves, J.C. (1994). O crescimento económico português no pós-guerra: um quadro global. *Análise Social, 128,* 1005–1034.

Reis, J. (2018). *A economia portuguesa: formas de economia política numa periferia persistente (1960–2017).* Coimbra: Edições Almedina.

Rodrigues, J., &Reis, J. (2012). The asymmetries of European integration and the crisis of capitalism in Portugal. *Competition & Change, 16*(3), 188–205.

Rodrigues, J., Santos, A.C., & Teles, N. (2016). Semi-peripheral financialisation: the case of Portugal. *Review of International Political Economy, 23*(3), 480–510.

Santos, B.S. (ed.) (1993). *Portugal: um retrato singular.* Porto: Edições Afrontamento.

Wallerstein, I. (1979). *The Capitalist World Economy.* Cambridge: Cambridge University Press.

# 4   Financialisation and structural change in Portugal

## A Euro-resource-curse?

*Ricardo Paes Mamede*

## Introduction

This chapter deals with the relation between structural change and financialisation in the Portuguese economy since the mid-1990s. In particular, it looks at the effects of the non-financial private sector's indebtedness on the country's productive structure, and how this relates to the economic crisis that hit Portugal after 2010.

As pointed out by Barradas et al. (2018) and Rodrigues, Santos and Teles (2016), bank credit was the main driving force of financialisation in Portugal after 1995. The steep rise in credit resulted from a thorough process of financial liberalisation that took place between the mid-1980s and the early 1990s and was further enhanced by the participation of Portugal in the European Monetary Union since its inception in 1999. The domestic banking sector played a decisive role in this process as an intermediary between international lenders and domestic debtors.

During the period under analysis, Portugal experienced the highest growth of bank loans to households in the euro area, and one of the largest increases of loans to non-financial corporations. According to the Bank of Portugal's data, loans by Portuguese banks to the non-financial private sector increased from 49 per cent of GDP in 1995 to 93 per cent in 2000, reaching 134 per cent in 2008. Bank credit was the main channel through which non-financial firms and households initiated involvement with finance. This has been a central feature of the Portuguese economy ever since (Barradas et al., 2018; Rodrigues, Santos & Teles, 2016).

The impact of such rise in credit on the overall economic performance of Portugal has been discussed elsewhere. Mamede et al. (2016) describe the distinctive evolution of the Portuguese economy as a long boom followed by an early bust. Like other countries in the periphery of the euro area, Portuguese GDP grew fast in the second half of the 1990s, at an average rate of 4.1 per cent per year (in constant prices). However, the growth process came to a halt much earlier than in Greece, Ireland or Spain: while these economies kept growing at an annual average rate of 3.5, 4.3 and 3.2 per cent (respectively) between 2000 and 2008, Portugal experienced one of the lowest rates of economic growth in the EU (1.1 per cent) during those years. When the international crisis hit the country in 2008/2009, Portugal had not only reached a high level of external debt (like the aforementioned countries) but had already been experiencing growing levels of unemployment since the turn of the century.

The Portuguese economy underwent a fast process of structural change during the period under analysis. For example, the weight of the non-tradable sector increased from 41.3 per cent of GDP in 1995 to 48.1 per cent in 2008, thus converging on the EU average of 49 per cent.[1] Beyond this aggregate convergence in the weight of the non-tradable sector, the patterns of structural change in the Portuguese economy differ from the EU average in many respects. In particular, this chapter analyses the relation between the growth of credit to the non-financial private sector and the structural transformation of the Portuguese economy in recent decades, by addressing the question: to what extent can the financialisation process account for the structural changes that took place in Portugal between 1995 and 2008?

We take the literature on Dutch-disease effects[2] as a starting point for answering that question. Originally, the Dutch disease refers to the impacts accruing from the discovery of natural resources, or a steep rise in their price, on the industrial composition of a country. Afterwards, similar effects on production structures were associated with events like large foreign aid and capital inflows, mostly in the context of developing economies. We will argue in this chapter that the main causal mechanisms emphasised by the Dutch-disease literature are useful to understand the links between the credit boom and the structural change experienced by the Portuguese economy since the 1990s. However, it is important to take into account some context-specific features, the most relevant of which is Portugal's participation in the euro from its inception. This leads us to put forward the concept of 'Euro-resource-curse' as a framework for our analysis.

The chapter is organised as follows. We start by discussing the literature on Dutch disease and the way it can contribute to the understanding of the links between financialisation and structural change in the Portuguese economy. The following section presents the main features of structural change in Portugal since the mid-1990s. We then discuss how those features can be related to financialisation and other processes. The chapter concludes by drawing implications from the previous discussion for understanding the crisis that hit Portugal after 2010.

## Signs of a financial Dutch disease in the euro area

The idea of Dutch-disease effects was originally inspired by the experience of the Netherlands in the 1960s, when natural gas was discovered in the North Sea (Magud & Sosa, 2010; The Economist, 1977). The discovery of natural resources, or a steep rise in their price, is associated with an increase of export revenues in the natural resource sector and of capital flows into the national economy. If the country is under a flexible exchange rate regime, both the natural resources' export boom and the capital inflows induce a nominal exchange rate appreciation. In any exchange rate regime, the growth in disposable income is expected to foster price increases in non-tradable-sector products (not in the tradable sector, since the price of tradable goods is mainly determined by international markets). As result, the country will experience a real exchange rate appreciation.

Left to itself, this can induce a change in the relative weight of different economic activities. Both the natural resource sector and the non-tradable sector will expand, experiencing a rise in prices and wages. In contrast, since price increases in the tradable sector are constrained by international competition, activities like agriculture and manufacturing will attract fewer resources (including capital and labour), and their production, employment and exports are expected to shrink, at least in relative terms.

The concept of Dutch disease was later extended to other countries (especially less developed ones) and to different economic triggers. Namely, such effects have been associated with large foreign aid transfers, capital inflows and other mechanisms that may result in real exchange rate appreciations (Williamson, 1995).

The vast literature on Dutch-disease effects is often concerned with its long-term impacts on economic growth. While the real exchange rate appreciation and the ensuing deindustrialisation can be viewed as an adjustment to a new equilibrium, a declining manufacturing sector may reduce future potential growth, to the extent that this sector is associated with higher increasing returns to scale, learning by doing, spillover effects or other positive externalities (Magud & Sosa, 2010).

Botta (2015) has considered a different type of negative, long-run impact that may result from Dutch-disease dynamics, that he called a 'financial Dutch disease'. Having in mind the impact of foreign direct investment in natural resources in less developed economies, under a flexible exchange rate regime, the author draws attention to financial developments that may have further detrimental effects on the economy of the recipient country. Specifically, a real exchange rate appreciation may reduce the perceived country's risk or increase the expectations of capital gains, thus attracting additional portfolio investment.

This, in turn, feeds back into the exchange rate dynamics and may lead to an even stronger appreciation. Imports will grow as a result of both the increase in disposable income and the decrease in the domestic supply of tradable products, while exports will decrease due to a drop in the production of tradable goods and/or the increase of their prices. As the country accumulates high levels of foreign debt, capital flows may reverse as investors perceive the exchange rate appreciation as unsustainable. Ultimately, capital reversals may lead to the collapse of the exchange rate and to macroeconomic instability, jeopardising long-run growth.

The process described by Botta (2015) is similar to the experience of many developing countries in the 1990s, even though in most cases the outbreak of capital flows was unrelated to natural resources and took place in a context of fixed exchange rates. As Calvo, Leiderman and Reinhardt (1996) show, capital flows into many Asian and Latin American countries in the early 1990s were associated with aggregate demand growth, higher inflation, real exchange rate appreciation (especially in Latin America), widening current account deficits, and macroeconomic instability. Such impacts tend to be greater in more indebted economies and in countries that initially had less access to international capital markets (since in these cases capital flows are typically associated with the fast growth of credit and steep drops in interest rates).

The idea of a 'financial Dutch disease' also fits the experience of the countries in the periphery of the euro area since the mid-1990s. Between 1995 and 2008, financial inflows grew rapidly in Portugal, Spain, Ireland and Greece, with these countries observing the highest decreases in net financial assets in percentage of GDP among the euro area's early members (see Table 4.1). These developments are associated with high increases in prices, real exchange rates and current account deficits. Ultimately, those four countries were among the economies most affected by the financial instability that hit the EU in 2010–2012.

A notable difference between the euro area periphery and the developing countries that went through severe financial instability after a period of capital inflows in the early 1990s has to do with the exchange rate regime. Although in both cases the national authorities started by fixing their currencies against a foreign one (the US dollar in the case of Asian and Latin America countries, the ECU in the European Monetary System), the exchange rate risk virtually

*Table 4.1* Evolution of euro area earlier members in selected variables

| | Change between 1995 and 2008 | | | | Net financial assets in 2008 in % of GDP | Change in nominal long-term interest rates between 2008 and 2012 (Δ p.p.) |
|---|---|---|---|---|---|---|
| | Net financial assets in % of GDP (Δ p.p.) | National consumer price index (Δ%) | Real effective exchange rates based on ULC (Δ%) | Balance of current transactions in % of GDP (Δ p.p.) | | |
| Greece | -92.9 | 66 | 22 | -12.5 | -90.0 | 17.7 |
| Portugal | -91.1 | 44 | 14 | -9.3 | -95.1 | 6.0 |
| Ireland | n.a. | 53 | 34 | -8.2 | -95.3 | 1.6 |
| Spain | -57.1 | 48 | 18 | -8.0 | -77.8 | 1.5 |
| Italy | -13.2 | 37 | 27 | -4.7 | -19.1 | 0.8 |
| Belgium | 32.6 | 31 | -3 | -3.2 | 54.4 | -1.4 |
| France | -19.3 | 24 | -2 | -2.1 | -9.3 | -1.7 |
| Austria | 3.6 | 27 | -14 | 6.8 | -10.0 | -2.0 |
| Netherlands | 78.9 | 34 | 2 | -1.0 | -10.7 | -2.3 |
| Finland | 39.0 | 24 | -9 | -1.1 | -2.6 | -2.4 |
| Germany | 13.9 | 22 | -24 | 6.8 | 13.9 | -2.5 |
| Luxemburg | n.a. | 32 | 11 | -5.0 | 82.8 | -2.8 |

Source: AMECO

disappeared for those economies that entered the euro by the turn of the century, while the credit risk was perceived to be very low (as is reflected in the strong convergence of interest rates between euro area countries until 2008).

Arguably, in the presence of higher exchange rate and credit risks, the build-up of macroeconomic imbalances would have stopped earlier, since investors would have perceived the exchange rate appreciation as unsustainable. The irrevocability of euro membership, together with the full integration of capital markets within the EU, may have encouraged capital flows even further, increasing the vulnerability of the debtor countries to financial instability events. In this sense, we may talk about a 'Euro-resource-curse' – a Dutch disease of a financial nature, with features that are distinctive of the European Monetary Union.

## Does the structural change in Portugal reflect a Euro-resource-curse?

According to the discussion in the previous section, we may expect the following changes to take place in a national economy experiencing a Euro-resource-curse:

- an increase in the value-added and employment shares of the non-tradable sector;
- within the non-tradable sector, the relative growth of financial, construction and real estate activities;
- a relative (and possibly absolute) decline of manufacturing and agriculture;
- the growth of wage rates in the non-tradable sector, but also in the tradable one;
- a decline in the profit rate of the tradable-sector industries; and
- a decline in the country's export performance.

In this section we analyse the patterns of structural change in Portugal after the mid-1990s and check their consistency with the Euro-resource-curse thesis.

Some of the changes in the productive structures were common to most EU economies, reflecting secular trends such as the growth of services and of knowledge-intensive activities. In order to take into account those common trends, the evolution of the Portuguese economy is here analysed with reference to the evolution of other EU countries.

### Patterns of structural change in Portugal

The increase in the value-added share of the non-tradable sector was a pervasive feature across the EU during the period under analysis (with the notable exception of Germany). Between 1995 and 2008, the share of the non-tradable sector in the EU as a whole increased from 46.1 to 49 per cent. Starting from much lower levels (40 to 42 per cent), the countries in the periphery of the euro area rapidly converged with the EU average, reaching a level between 47 and 49 per cent in 2008. After Spain, Portugal was the country in which the non-tradable sector's share of value-added increased the most in percentage points, from 41.3 in 1995 to 48.1.[3] A similar trend was observed in the sectoral composition of employment. However, these trends do not apply uniformly across industries.

Figure 4.1 shows how the changes in the distribution of employment across industries in Portugal compare with a benchmark group of EU countries.[4]

Most of the industries are located either in the upper-left or the lower-right sides of the graph. This means that their share of employment in Portugal has become more similar to what is observed in the benchmark. In other words, in these cases, the Portuguese productive structure converged with the average of EU countries for which data are available. For example, the share of employment in wholesale and retail trade was lower in Portugal in 1995 but increased faster than in the benchmark group between 1995 and 2008 (in this sense we can talk of a positive convergence). In the cases of agriculture and fishing, and of textiles and footwear, the opposite happened: these industries' share of

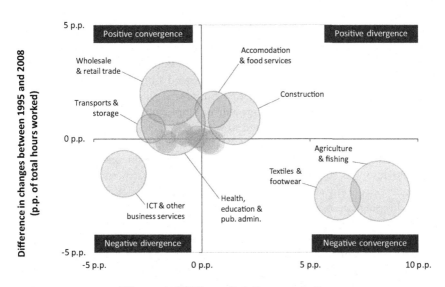

*Figure 4.1* Structural convergence/divergence in employment (hours worked) between Portugal and a benchmark group of EU countries

Note: The sizes of the circles represent each industry's share of total hours worked in Portugal in 1995. The benchmark corresponds to the weighted average of a group of EU countries for which industry-level data are available for the period under analysis, with weights given by the number of hours worked of each country. The countries included in the benchmark are Austria, Denmark, Germany, Greece, Spain, France, Italy, Netherlands, Finland, and the United Kingdom.

Source: Eurostat

employment was initially higher in Portugal but decreased more than in the benchmark group (in this case we talk of negative convergence).

Two main exceptions to the aforementioned trends of structural convergence are worth mentioning. First, construction activities and accommodation and food services, which already absorbed a higher share of employment in 1995, grew faster in Portugal afterwards (here we talk of positive divergence). Second, ICT and other business services increased in relative terms both in Portugal and in the benchmark group, but their growth was lower in the Portuguese case (therefore we talk of negative divergence).

In sum, the data on employment shares are consistent with the Euro-resource-curse hypotheses, with some exceptions. As expected, most of the non-tradable sector grew faster in Portugal than in the benchmark during the period under analysis; this is especially true in the case of construction, which already accounted for a higher share of employment in 1995. In the same vein, the most important tradable industries – namely agriculture and fishing, and textiles and footwear – lost a higher share of jobs in Portugal than in the benchmark group. All these trends seem to support the Euro-resource-curse thesis.

There are, however, three caveats to that conclusion. First, the employment performance of several manufacturing industries was better in Portugal than in the benchmark; in fact, if we exclude textiles and footwear, the share of employment of manufacturing industries decreased less in Portugal over the same period. Second, not all non-tradable industries experienced a higher growth of employment shares (namely the ICT and other business services activities). Finally, an important part of the differential growth in employment shares in Portugal as compared to the benchmark is related to what are essentially non-market services (public administration, healthcare and education activities). All these cases point to the need to consider other mechanisms, in addition to the ones put forward by the Euro-resource-curse thesis, when accounting for the structural change of the Portuguese economy after 1995. We will come back to this later.

At this stage, it is also important to note that the evolution of industries underlying these trends was non-monotonic. As said in the introduction, there is a sharp contrast in the growth of the Portuguese economy before and after the turn of the century. The growth slowdown after 2000 was asymmetric across industries, as Figure 4.2 shows. While in most of the non-tradable industries the number of employees increased during the whole period under analysis, in the case of construction it reached a peak in 2002, decreasing afterwards. As regards the tradable sector, the decline of textiles and footwear is evident since 1995, although it became steeper after 2001; other manufacturing industries followed a different path, growing in employment until 2001 and only decreasing afterwards. Overall, between 1995 and 2008, the manufacturing sector lost around 188,000 jobs, and almost 140,000 (or 74 per cent) of these were due to the decline of textiles and footwear industries alone. These asymmetric and non-monotonic developments will also be taken into account when assessing the validity of the Euro-resource-curse thesis.

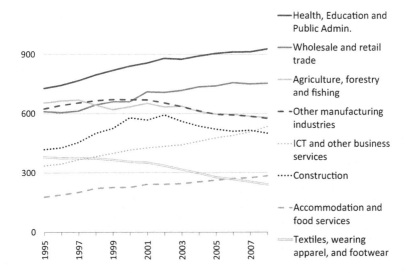

Health, Education and Public Admin.

Wholesale and retail trade

Agriculture, forestry and fishing

Other manufacturing industries

ICT and other business services

Construction

Accommodation and food services

Textiles, wearing apparel, and footwear

*Figure 4.2* Evolution of employment (thousands of employees) by industry, 2000–2008
Source: Eurostat

The analysis of the distribution of value-added across industries in Figure 4.3 adds to the evidence regarding the structural change in employment (Figure 4.1). The most relevant difference between Figures 4.1 and 4.3 is the growth of finance and insurance's share of value-added, which was not visible in the case of employment (due to the low labour-intensity of these activities). The value-added share of financial activities in Portugal was already higher than in the benchmark group in 1995, and that difference became even greater in the following years. This is consistent with the Euro-resource-curse thesis.

With respect to the remaining industries, Figure 4.3 largely confirms the conclusions drawn from Figure 4.1, the most notable exception being wholesale and retail trade activities, which grew faster in Portugal than in the benchmark in terms of employment share but grew slower in value-added share. This suggests that the profitability of those industries fell during the period under analysis, as a result of increased competition and/or higher costs. In the following section we discuss the relation between structural change and the evolution of wages and profits.

### The evolution of the wage rate and the profit rate by industry

The Euro-resource-curse thesis suggests that the Portuguese tradable sector was negatively hit by undue cost developments and losses in relative profitability, accruing from the large capital flows within the euro area. The growth of non-tradable activities leads to a rise in wages, attracting workers away from

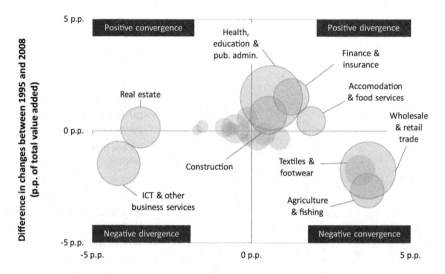

*Figure 4.3* Structural convergence/divergence in Gross Value Added
Note: The sizes of the circles represent each industry's share of total hours worked in Portugal in 1995. The benchmark corresponds to the weighted average of a group of EU countries for which industry-level data is available for the period under analysis, with weights given by the value added of each country. The countries included in the benchmark are Austria, Denmark, Germany, Greece, Spain, France, Italy, Netherlands, Finland, and the United Kingdom.

Source: Eurostat

industries that are exposed to foreign competition. In order to retain workers, the tradable sector has to raise wages in line with the non-tradable sector. Since the prices in the tradable industries are largely determined at the international level, the rise in the tradable sector's wages leads to a decrease in its profitability. Thus, both labour and capital tend to move away from the tradable sector, leading to its decline (either relative or absolute) in value-added and employment.

Figure 4.4 displays the relation between the wage rate (i.e. euros per hour worked) of each industry in 1995 and the corresponding annual growth rate between 1995 and 2008. We can see that the two industry groups that experienced the largest drops in employment during the period under analysis – agriculture and fishing, and textiles and footwear – were among the industries with the lowest wage rates in 1995, reflecting the low productivity and low skill levels of those industries. In the following period, wage growth in these industries was in line with or slightly below the national average. In contrast, the wage rates in other low-paying activities – notably construction and accommodation and food services – grew faster than the average. This is

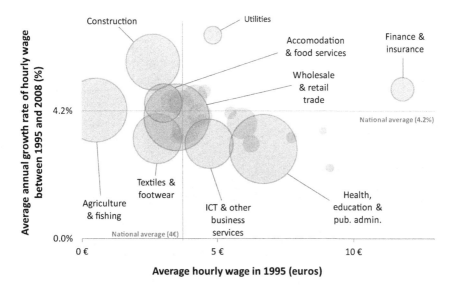

*Figure 4.4* Average initial levels and growth of wage rates by industry, 1995–2008
Note: The sizes of the circles represent each industry's share of total hours worked in Portugal in 1995.
Source: Eurostat

consistent with the idea that the expansion of non-tradable activities allowed for a faster wage growth, attracting workers away from industries that rely on similar skill levels.

In other words, the high growth in the demand for restaurants, hotels, commerce, housing and other physical infrastructures, together with the higher increase in the wage rate in some of these activities, may have led to a significant numbers of workers leaving the production of agriculture, fishing, textiles, apparel, footwear, etc., in the search for higher wages in the expanding activities. This is consistent with the Euro-resource-curse thesis.

Figure 4.5 relates each industry's profit rate (here measured as the ratio between the net operating surplus plus mixed income and the total fixed assets) and the growth of employment.[5] There is a strong positive relation between the two variables, with some notable outliers. First, in contrast with all other industries, the profit rate in financial services grew strongly, while employment slightly declined in the period. Second, within manufacturing, two industries stand out for their unusual evolution: manufacture of coke and refined petroleum products and manufacture of computer, electronic and optical products.

In sum, while it is clear that differences in profitability played an important role in shaping structural change, the discussion in this section and in the previous one suggests that the evolution of industries' profit rates during the

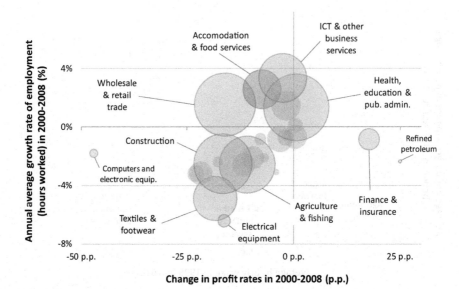

*Figure 4.5* Relative growth of profit rates and of employment by industry, 2000–2008
Note: The sizes of the circles represent each industry's share of total hours worked in
Portugal in 1995. The industries' profit rate is here measured as the ratio between the
net operating surplus plus mixed income and the total fixed assets.
Source: Eurostat

period under analysis may have been influenced by changes in factors other
than wages. In the two subsequent sections we discuss two dimensions that
are worth considering: the dynamics of international trade and the patterns of
credit allocation.

### External demand, foreign competition and structural change in Portugal

During the first decade of this century, the Portuguese export sector was hit
by a sequence of competitive shocks, including the accession of China to the
World Trade Organisation in 2001, the EU enlargement to the east in 2004,
and the strong appreciation of the euro against the US dollar between 2000 and
2008 (Mamede, Godinho & Simões, 2014).[6] These three developments, taken
together, put the Portuguese export sector under strain, given the large overlap
of its specialisation profile with those of the emerging economies of Asia and
Central Europe (IMF, 2008; OECD, 2007).

Between 2000 and 2008, the sum of shares of China and the largest Eastern
European EU economies (the so-called Visegrad countries[7]) in the euro area's
imports nearly doubled, from 6 to 11.5 per cent. Figure 4.6 relates this evolution to the changes in Portuguese manufacturing industries' profit rates.

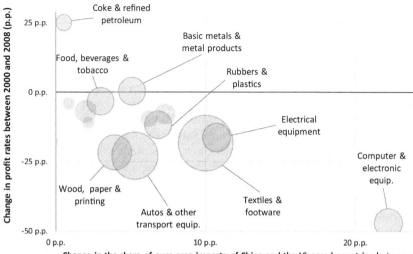

*Figure 4.6* The relation between the growth of China's and the Visegrad countries' share of the euro area's imports and the change in profit rates of Portuguese manufacturing industries, 2000–2008

Note: The sizes of the circles represent each industry's share of Portuguese exports in 1995. The industries' profit rate is here measured as the ratio between the net operating surplus plus mixed income and the total fixed assets.

Source: Eurostat

The figure shows a clear negative relation between the evolution of Portuguese industries' profit rates and the penetration of imports from China and the Visegrad countries in the euro area. In addition, by checking Figures 4.5 and 4.6 together, we see that the industries with the highest relative decline in employment are also among the ones with the largest penetration of imports from China and the Visegrad countries to the euro area (namely, manufacture of textiles, wearing apparel, leather and related products, and manufacture of electrical equipment).

The information in Figure 4.6 suggests that the mechanisms described by the Euro-resource-curse thesis are insufficient to account for the structural change in the Portuguese economy between 2000 and 2008. It may be argued that the growth of wages was an additional factor of vulnerability for industries that were highly exposed to competition from low-wage countries. However, on the basis of the information presented above, it is difficult to sustain that the growth of wages was the most decisive determinant of export performance in Portugal during the period under analysis. The sharp increase in competitive pressure from low-wage countries, together with a strong exchange rate appreciation of the euro, seem to have played a major role in the evolution of Portuguese manufacturing industries after 2000.

### Patterns of credit allocation, structural change and financial instability

In the previous sections we have seen that the structural changes in the Portuguese economy between 1995 and 2008 can be largely explained by a combination of Dutch-disease effects and a succession of competitive shocks. We will now see that the structural transformation of productive activities in Portugal may have resulted, as well, from changes in credit allocation.

Major surges of capital flows are often associated with an increase in households' share of bank credit. For example, using a sample of 36 countries over 1990–2011, Samarina and Bezemer (2016) find that the non-financial business credit share in all bank loans declined, on average, from 54 to 42 per cent and that this change is significantly associated with capital inflows.

The Portuguese economy experienced similar trends during the period under analysis. According to the Bank of Portugal, loans by Portuguese banks to the non-financial private sector increased from 49 per cent of GDP in 1995 to 134 per cent in 2008. The rise in bank loans was notable for non-financial corporations, more than doubling its value in percentage of GDP from 27 to 61 per cent, but was even steeper in the case of households (from 22 per cent of GDP in 1995 to 73 per cent in 2008). As a result, the share of non-financial corporations in the total bank loans to the non-financial private sector decreased from 55 per cent in 1995 to 45 per cent in 2008 (Chapter 2 in this volume).

The largest share of credit to households went to mortgage loans: by 2008, these represented 79 per cent of the total credit to households and 43 per cent of the total credit to the non-financial private sector. In addition, 38 per cent of the credit to non-financial corporations was granted to construction and real estate activities.

This means that at least 60 per cent of loans granted by the domestic banking system to the private sector was geared towards those two activities, by financing either the supply side (i.e. the construction and real estate firms) or the demand side (i.e. their non-corporate, private clients).[8]

Figure 4.7 illustrates the changes in the distribution of domestic banks' credit to non-financial corporations by industry between 1995 and 2008. In addition to the large increase in the share of construction and real estate activities, the figure shows that only two other industries, both in the non-tradable sector – accommodation and food service activities, and (private) health and education – increased their share of credit. In absolute terms, the increase in bank credit benefited all industries without exception. However, the comparison between the credit growth in construction and real estate activities and in manufacturing industries is telling: while bank credit grew at an average annual rate of 1.2 per cent in the latter case, it grew at 18.5 per cent in the former one.[9]

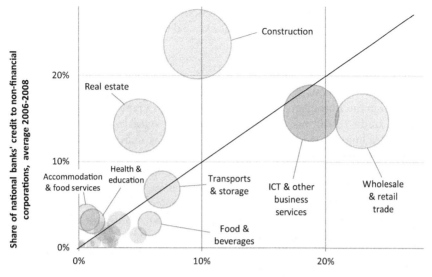

*Figure 4.7* The change of industries' share of credit granted by Portuguese banks from 1995–1997 and 2006–2008

Note: the sizes of the circles represent each industry's average share of credit granted by Portuguese banks in 2006–2008.

Source: Banco de Portugal

Major surges of capital flows are often associated with an increase in construction and real estate activities (Calvo, Leiderman & Reinhart, 1996), which is typically explained by the tradable sector industries' decline of profitability and increase in credit risk, as well as by the rise in households' share of bank credit, mostly related to mortgage loans. In a weakly regulated financial system, the rise in mortgage loans during a credit boom easily becomes a cumulative process. Banks use the houses acquired through loans as collateral. As the price of houses rises, the value of the collateral also increases, which has a positive impact on the banks' balance sheets. This allows for the continuing growth of bank credit. The availability of credit in a context of rising house prices fosters the further expansion of investment in the construction and real estate industries.

In the case of Portugal, the cumulative process of construction and real-estate-related loans was reinforced by the securitisation of mortgages. Securitisation started in Portugal in 1997 and developed rapidly after 2002, with banks using special-purpose vehicle companies to issue securities (Lagoa et al., 2014). This allowed banks to increase liquidity and to continue expanding their credit activities.

The remarkable growth of finance, insurance, construction and real estate industries in Portugal must thus be understood as a combined result of capital flows, financial liberalisation and loss of external competitiveness.

## Conclusions

In this chapter we have defined Euro-resource-curse as a process in which participation in the European Monetary Union leads to a rapid and lasting increase in bank credit to the private sector in countries with less developed capital markets, leading to a decline of the tradable sector, a sharp growth of external debt, and an increased vulnerability to international financial shocks.

Like the concept of financial Dutch disease (Botta, 2015), the idea of a Euro-resource-curse goes beyond the mechanisms that are usually considered in the more traditional Dutch-disease analysis, by considering the positive feedbacks between exchange rate appreciations and capital flows, through the increased expectations of capital gains and the decline in the perceived investment risks. However, it adds to the concept put forward by Botta (2015) by putting capital flows in a context of full capital market integration and the abolition of exchange rate risks between advanced economies. The disproportional growth of the financial sector – and not only of the non-tradable sector in general – is an expected characteristic of such a process, since domestic banks play a central role as an intermediary between international lenders and domestic debtors in the countries of the periphery of the euro area (Orsi & Solari, 2010).

We have seen that the evolution of the Portuguese economy after 1995 presents several features that point towards the presence of a Euro-resource-curse. The loans by Portuguese banks to the non-financial private sector were relatively stable between 1980 and 1995, but increased dramatically afterwards, reaching 134 per cent of GDP in 2008. During this period, the value-added share of the non-tradable sector increased rapidly, converging with the euro area average. For similar levels of skills, wages grew faster in the non-tradable sector than in industries exposed to international competition, forcing the wages of the latter to follow suit, with negative impacts on those industries' profitability. Although the slowdown in growth after 2000 was pervasive in the Portuguese economy, it was especially marked in agriculture activities and manufacturing industries, all of which lost jobs until 2008 (in contrast with most non-tradable sector industries). Finally, finance and insurance activities experienced an outstanding growth in value-added, even though their value-added share was already above the average of EU countries for which data are available.

All these trends seem to suggest that the patterns of structural change in Portugal are a result of a Euro-resource-curse. However, we need to take into account the interplay of Euro-resource-curse effects with other factors in order to explain some of the most relevant changes in the Portuguese structure of production.

In fact, there is a significant variability in the performance of manufacturing activities, including among those with similar levels of wage rate and labour-intensity. In the same vein, the outstanding growth of construction and real estate activities within the non-tradable sector also requires an explanation that goes beyond the mechanisms put forward by the Euro-resource-curse thesis. Finally, the increase in the value-added and the employment shares of non-market activities (public administration, health and education) is largely outside the realm of analysis of that hypothesis. The explanation for these distinguishing features of Portuguese structural change needs to rely on additional causal mechanisms.

While the growth of non-market activities depends mostly on fiscal policy options, we expect that the growth of market-oriented industry mostly responds to the evolution of profitability. Two main processes appear to have played a crucial role in the profitability of some Portuguese industries in the period under analysis: the dynamics of international trade and the evolution of credit allocation.

We have shown that the profitability of Portuguese manufacturing industries is strongly related to the increase of China's and the Visegrad countries' share of euro area imports. The growth of exports from those emerging economies to the EU seems to play a decisive role in explaining the employment contraction of Portuguese manufacturing industries after 2000, in addition to the wage effects related to the Euro-resource-curse.

Similarly, although the loss of external competitiveness partially explains the bias in the allocation of credit to the non-tradable sector, the specific growth of construction and real estate activities can only be fully accounted for by considering the cumulative nature of the rise in mortgage loans in the context of a deregulated financial system.

In sum, in order to understand the patterns of structural change in Portugal after 1995 we need to consider the combined effects of high capital inflows, financial deregulation and external competitive shocks in the context of Portugal's participation in the euro area. In combination, those changes resulted in the accumulation of a historically high level of external debt and in the high exposure of the domestic banking system to the real estate market, both of which made the Portuguese economy particularly vulnerable to the financial instability that followed the international crisis of 2008.

Avoiding those sources of vulnerability in a country like Portugal would require preventing unsustainable capital flows and credit allocation patterns (which could arguably be achieved by stricter financial regulation), but also reducing the risks of external competitive shocks. The latter can hardly be achieved in a country that has lost control over international trade and exchange rate policies, and in which the transition to a more advanced productive structure is hampered by the inherited industrial basis, a lack of domestic capital, and a low-educated workforce. Understanding the Portuguese crisis as a result of the interplay between financial flows, credit allocation and competitive shocks helps to highlight the complex challenges that countries like Portugal must face in the context of the euro area.

## Acknowledgements

I would like to thank Ben Fine and the editors for their useful comments and suggestions.

## Notes

1  These figures are drawn from the European Commission's AMECO database.
2  For a review see, e.g., Magud and Sosa (2010).
3  The source of these figures is the AMECO database.
4  The benchmark corresponds to the weighted average of the EU countries for which industry-level data is available for the period under analysis. These include Austria, Denmark, Germany, Greece, Spain, France, Italy, Netherlands, Finland and the United Kingdom.
5  Contrarily to the case of wages, the available data on profits only includes the period from the year 2000 onwards. As mentioned before, during this period economic growth in Portugal was already slowing down (in contrast with other countries in the periphery of the euro area); agriculture, construction activities and manufacturing industries were in clear decline; and the only industries experiencing employment growth were service activities.
6  During this period the value of the euro went from 0.83 cents to the dollar (in October 2000) to 1.59 US dollars (in April 2008).
7  These are the Czech Republic, Hungary, Poland and Slovakia.
8  To this we should add the portion of credit to non-financial corporations that is used for financing the building of production facilities and the acquisition of real estate assets.
9  The annual values of bank credit are here adjusted using the GDP deflator.

## References

Barradas, R., Lagoa, S., Leão, E., & Mamede, R.P. (2018). Financialisation in the European periphery and the sovereign debt crisis: the Portuguese case. *Journal of Economic Issues*, *52*(4), 1056–1083.

Botta, A. (2015). The macroeconomics of a financial Dutch disease (Levy Economics Institute of Bard College Working Paper No. 850). Annandale-on-Hudson, NY: Levy Economics Institute.

Calvo, G.A., Leiderman, L., & Reinhart, C.M. (1996). Inflows of capital to developing countries in the 1990s. *Journal of Economic Perspectives*, *10*(2), 123–139.

The Economist (1977). The Dutch disease. 26 November 1977, pp. 82–83.

IMF (International Monetary Fund) (2008). France, Greece, Italy, Portugal, and Spain – competitiveness in the southern euro area (IMF Country Report No. 08/145). Washington, DC: IMF.

Lagoa, S., Leão, E., Mamede, R.P., & Barradas, R. (2014). *Financialisation and the Financial and Economic Crises: The Case of Portugal* (FESSUD Studies in Financial Systems No 24). Leeds: FESSUD.

Magud, N., & Sosa, S. (2010). When and why worry about real exchange rate appreciation? The missing link between Dutch disease and growth (IMF Working Paper, WP/10/271). Washington, DC: International Monetary Fund.

Mamede, R.P., Godinho, M.M., & Simões, V.C. (2014). Assessment and challenges of industrial policies in Portugal: is there a way out of the 'stuck in the middle' trap? In A. Teixeira, E. Silva & R. Mamede (eds.), *Structural Change, Competitiveness and Industrial Policy: Painful Lessons from the European Periphery* (pp. 258–277). London: Routledge.

Mamede, R.P., Lagoa, S., Leão, L., & Barradas, R. (2016). The long boom and the early bust: the Portuguese economy in the era of financialisation. In E. Hein, D. Detzer & N. Dodig (eds.), *Financialisation and the Financial and Economic Crises: Country Studies* (pp. 255–274). Cheltenham: Edward Elgar.

OECD (Organisation for Economic Co-operation and Development) (2007). *Economic Survey of the European Union.* Paris: OECD.

Orsi, L., & Solari, S. (2010). Financialisation in Southern European economies. *Économie Appliquée, 63*(4), 5–34.

Rodrigues, J., Santos, A.C., & Teles, N. (2016). Semi-peripheral financialisation: the case of Portugal. *Review of International Political Economy, 23*(3), 480–510.

Samarina, A., & Bezemer, D. (2016). Do capital flows change domestic credit allocation? *Journal of International Money and Finance, 62*, 98–121.

Williamson, J. (1995). The management of capital inflows. *Pensamiento Iberoamericano,* January–June.

**Part 2**

# Financialisation and labour relations in the Southern European periphery

# 5 Financialisation, work and labour relations

*Helena Lopes*

## Introduction

There is now a significant body of literature that analytically scrutinises and empirically investigates the effects of financialisation on the labour market and on macro-level employment outcomes (Chapter 7 in this volume). Financialisation as a macro-level process influences macroeconomic policies and industrial relations systems, which powerfully impact on the balance of power between employers and employees, as examined in other chapters of this book, and, consequently, on work. But the relationship between financialisation and work, even though (sparsely) documented in compelling in-depth studies (Alvehus & Spicer, 2012; Cushen, 2013; Ezzamel, Willmott & Worthington, 2008), remains underspecified. Since it is firms that determine the organisation, management and assessment of paid work, the firm is the inevitable mediator between finance and work, which implies carrying out analyses, at least in part, at the firm level.

Taking Favereau's (2016) arguments as point of departure, the main aim of the present chapter is to further develop the understanding of the distinctive impact of financialisation on work. This requires examining the impact of financialisation processes on work, in addition to other macro-level trends such as globalisation or the evolution of information technology, to identify: (i) the specific channels through which financialisation processes affect and shape work management practices at the firm level, and (ii) the effects of such practices on work content and control at the individual worker level. Our first claim is that firms have gone through specific financialisation processes since the 1980s, which were stimulated by the academic and ideological influence of the agency theory of the firm.

We primarily focus on the evolution of the activity of work itself, a human activity that potentially transforms 'human nature' (Marx, 1867, p. 127), thus diverging from and complementing existing studies that concentrate on the effects of financialisation on headcount reduction, work restructuring, job insecurity or earnings polarisation (see Cushen, 2013, for references). Our second claim is that firm-level financialisation processes,[1] and related predominance of financial criteria, powerfully contribute to the diffusion of 'governance by numbers' practices (Supiot, 2015), which engender the quantification, devaluation and dehumanisation of work.

The chapter is organised as follows. The second section examines the specific channels and transmission mechanisms through which financialisation affects firm governance and work. It shows that financialisation processes at the firm level are theoretically grounded on, and normatively justified by, the agency theory of the firm. It also shows that a major transmission channel between finance and work is the reporting of the financial situation of the firm. The third section addresses two key features of work discarded in mainstream economics, namely its meaningfulness and its collective character. These features are the most affected by the individualisation and quantification of work trends brought about by financialisation. The fourth section elaborates on the indirect effects on labour relations of the dynamics previously depicted and outlines some of the institutional reforms needed to reverse current trends. The fifth section concludes.

## The effects of financialisation on firm governance and work: theoretical grounding and transmission channels

### Financialisation processes at the firm level: the key role of the agency theory of the firm

As mentioned above, since firms determine the design of the work to be performed by workers, firms are the inevitable mediators between finance and work. The agency theory of the firm provided the theoretical ground to justify and legitimate changes in the governance of the firm, which have increasingly promoted the interests of finance.

The baseline of agency theory was provided by Friedman (1970) in a seminal article where he claimed that (i) 'money profit' is the only legitimate goal of the corporate firm, and (ii) managers are 'the agents of the individuals who own the corporations', namely shareholders. Legal scholars, in both common law and coded civil law, have always noted that the idea that shareholders own the firm is wrong (Robé, 2012),[2] but most economists disregard this. The few mainstream economists who acknowledge that shareholders own only their shares of the corporation but not the firm deem this irrelevant for firm governance purposes (Fama, 1980). Thus, despite this major legal flaw, Friedman's arguments were developed and turned into an economic theory of the firm, which came to be known as agency theory, by Jensen and Meckling (1976).[3]

Jensen and Meckling view the firm as a nexus of contracts, which radically breaks with understanding it as an institution, as most social scientists, including institutional and transaction cost economists, do. In Jensen and Meckling's view, the building block of the firm is the principal–agent contract defined 'as a contract under which one person (the principal(s)) engages another person (the agent) to perform some service on their behalf which involves delegating some decision-making authority to the agent' (Jensen & Meckling, 1976, p. 308).

Jensen and Meckling focused on the relationship between shareholders as principals and managers as agents but agency theory progressively generalised the terms to all principal–agent relationships, i.e. relationships involving supervisors (principals) and subordinates (agents). The firm was hence formally reduced to a cascade of principal–agent contracts and the question of its governance was reduced to investigating which incentives would best align the interests of each worker with those of the owners of the firm.

On this view, shareholders bear the greatest investment risk since their revenues depend on what is left after the contracts with other input providers are honoured; that is, they are the 'residual claimants'. To protect their investments, they are given control over governance, i.e. over the board of directors (management). The maximisation of share value, as determined by allegedly efficient financial markets (Fama, 1980), then became the final criterion of the good governance of firms. Agency theory's nexus-of-contracts metaphor soon evolved into the most influential theory of the firm in mainstream economics and management (Goshal, 2005).

As underlined by Davis (2016), there is something odd about a finance-based approach becoming the dominant theory of the firm since only a tiny proportion of firms are listed on stock markets. In both mainstream economic theory and within real-world large firms, the view of the firm, and consequently its governance, progressively changed from that of a centre of production and employment to that of a centre for the management of an asset portfolio.[4] Despite the misrepresentation of real-world firms, agency theory pervaded business schools, being taught to millions of students and executives around the world. It then became a normative model (Goshal, 2005), one that has provided a powerful normative justification, from both moral and efficiency standpoints, for management practices suiting broader financialisation processes (Favereau, 2016). It is in this way that the theory of the firm has promoted the interests of finance.

Corporate law scholars, within the influential law and economics field, readily adopted agency theory, especially Jensen and Meckling's (1976) approach, which became the dominant paradigm in the 1990s in corporate scholarship (Armour, 2005; Bodie, 2012). The primary purpose of corporate governance became that of assuring that managers/directors act in the interest of shareholders: 'both boardrooms and courts have taken the normative call for shareholder value maximisation increasingly at heart' (Bodie 2012, p. 1033).[5] Accordingly, the 'shareholder primacy' model, grounded on the principal/shareholders–agent/directors relationship, eschews employees (Bodie, 2012) and, indeed, the productive organisation itself. The fact that agency theory 'provided a quasi-scientific rationale for de-institutionalizing the corporation' (Davis, 2016, p. 509) – being theoretically grounded on voluntary contracting and private ownership – helps explain its extensive influence in the neo-liberal era. Notwithstanding, the shareholder governance model is now being increasingly criticised for focusing on financial transactions and leaving corporate law disconnected from the strategic and operational management of the firm (Bodie, 2017; Greenfield, 1998). In particular, it is being denounced for hindering innovation and the long-term sustainability of many listed and non-listed firms (Cushen & Thompson, 2016; Marsden, 2016).

### From the shareholder governance model to the quantification of work: transmission channels

It follows from the above that the shareholder governance model is characterised by managers being impelled by their incentive structures to create 'value' for the shareholders. In the financialisation era, the previous Fordist implicit alliance between managers and employees is replaced by an explicit alliance between managers and shareholders (Boyer, 2005), often to the detriment of employees since the latter's interests disappeared from firm governance object-ives. Institutional investors now constrain management decisions by imposing the financial returns that are to be obtained. It is important to note, in this con-text, that accounting standards, rather than corporate law, define what 'profit' or 'value creation' are. Maximising 'shareholder value' does not simplistically mean maximising dividends and keeping stock prices high; it also involves accounting systems and their rules to calculate financial profits and distribute them across shareholders.

Naturally, accounting systems have evolved historically in accordance with the broad stages of capitalism and, specifically, with the needs of the dom-inant social forces at given points in time (Richard, 2015). Unsurprisingly, the accounting model associated with financialisation emerged, like agency theory and efficient financial markets theory, from the 'Chicago School' and was largely financed by big firms. The key and distinctive feature of this accounting model is based on the notion of 'fair value' (for an asset), defined as 'the price that would be received to sell an asset in an orderly transaction between market participants at the measurement date' (Richard, 2015, p. 23). Its consequence is 'the retention of funds and the distribution of dividends, normally tied to the concept of financial profit, based on the anticipation of future sales and results' (Richard, 2015, p. 24). Because the major intention and outcome of fair-value accounting is to focus on short-term gains by distributing dividends even before they are realised, Richard named this approach *futuristic accounting*. With fair-value accounting, 'residual claimants' shareholders then became 'ex ante claimants'.

Fair-value accounting was introduced in the USA in the 1990s and became dominant elsewhere in the early 2000s; in 2005, the European Union made its appliance compulsory for consolidated accounts, through the adoption of the International Financial Reporting Standards (IFRS) and the International Accounting Standards (IAS). A number of case studies reveal how accounting practices are used to meet financialised metrics (Alvehus & Spicer, 2012; Cushen, 2013; Ezzamel, Willmott & Worthington, 2008).[6] They highlight how these practices are put at the service of organisational control, an issue long emphasised by critical accounting scholars (Cooper & Hopper, 2007). The domination of financial criteria typical of the financialised era fosters 'govern-ance by numbers' practices (Supiot, 2015), i.e. practices that translate centrally defined profit targets into numbers to be delivered at the point of production. Localised versions of profit targets cascade downwards and are disseminated throughout the organisation to prescribe and measure progress and perform-ance (see Figure 5.1). Accounting practices are in this way used to link finan-cial targets to operational activities, down to the individual level, and make such links visible – a phenomenon named 'performance exposure' (Cushen & Thompson, 2016). The quantified localised versions of financial targets thereby permeate every service and office through information systems, electronic monitoring and middle management, as depicted in this first-hand account: 'I joined the organization close to four years ago and when I came there were three goals: make the numbers, make the numbers, make the numbers. That's how people referred to them' (extract of an interview quoted in Ezzamel, Willmott & Worthington, 2008, p. 120). In this case, middle managers were to inform employees of their goals by 'face-to-face, eyeball-to-eyeball' contact to ensure employees understood that they would be accountable in case they failed to deliver the numbers. The individual responsibility for attaining quanti-tative targets is thus the way financial goals are pushed down to the workplace to impose workers' behaviour. Finance and operational activities in the firm are thereby closely connected, which represents a major break with pre-finance times, when the two spheres were maintained relatively separated (Robé, 2019).

Figure 5.1 (adapted from Favereau, 2016, p. 47) represents the transmis-sion process from finance or, more specifically, from financial objectives and expectations, prioritised above other objectives, to the quantification of work. This process involves two phases; while the first phase, described above, involves translating financial targets into (localised and quantified) objectives (Translation 1), the second involves reporting what has been done and translating it in finan-cial values (Translation 2). Accounting metrics underpin the whole process.

Since quantification of work allows for the 'financialisation' of the whole firm by infusing financial criteria into every activity, the governance of work by numbers proved to be a set of practices – namely, the quantification of work targets, quantified performance appraisals, pecuniary incentive schemes, systematic reporting – particularly suited to the pursuit of shareholder value maximisation. However, the governance of work by numbers does not per-vade only publicly listed and financialised firms but all types of organisations, including public services (e.g. academia and health). The growing influence of agency theory in turn favoured the dissemination of management practices that conform to a finance-based conception of the firm throughout the whole pro-ductive system. Even though there is, to our knowledge, no sound theoretical or empirical account of this contagion phenomenon, some tentative explanations can be advanced. The proliferation of governance-by-numbers practices may be explained by the powerful organisational control it makes possible. Because of the compelling influence it exerts on workers' behaviour, it helps control labour costs, allegedly raising productivity and enhancing economic efficiency. But

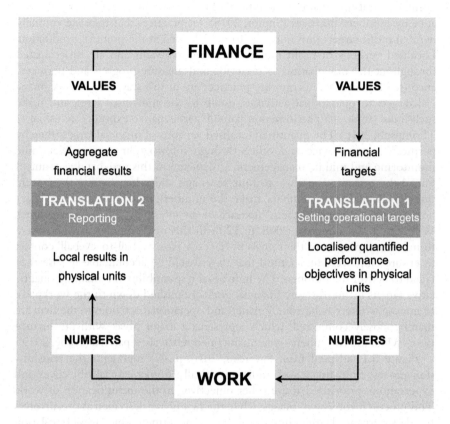

*Figure 5.1* From finance to the quantification of work: transmission channels

it may also be explained by the huge influence of agency theory, propagated by business schools all around the world, which turned it into a normative model, contributing to the expansion of its assumptions and recommendations and incorporation in managers' world-views (Goshal, 2005). Most importantly, agency theory succeeded because it has served financial actors' interests through the adoption of the shareholder governance model, leading to the financialisation of firms in all areas, from the definition of the purpose of the firm – maximising shareholder value – to the way it is governed at the board and the operational levels. To summarise, the governance of work by numbers comprises a set of management practices suited to a finance-based conception of the firm, practices that came to be used as benchmarks for advocating transformation in all economic sectors and that now permeate all kinds of organisations.[7]

Ultimately, financialisation processes at the firm level contributed to expanding the use of numerical evaluation in ever more spheres of life in our societies. All types of work, from knowledge production and creative activities to domestic work, are presently subject to more intense commodification and quantification processes, which betrays the human character of work.

## The devaluation of work in the financialisation era

### *The meaningful and collective character of work*

Neoclassical economics portrays work as a source of disutility for workers, an activity engaged in for the sole purpose of having access to income or consumption. It is this conception of work that underpins agency theory and its core concept, agency costs: since workers are assumed to be rational utility-maximisers, they try to minimise the disutility generated by the effort exercised at work and are thus likely to behave opportunistically whenever possible, which compels firms to engage in agency costs such as incentive schemes and monitoring.

In the last decades, experimental labour economists have shown that the propensity to provide effort is largely dependent on the nature of social interactions at work, and specifically on whether principal–agent relationships are perceived to be trusting and fair (Charness & Kuhn, 2011). Interactions with co-workers also significantly influence productivity. New behavioural assumptions, generically named 'social preferences', are being introduced in extended agency models by adding new arguments into utility functions. These arguments are considered 'non-standard' preferences and are weighed against the standard ones in the usual utility maximisation calculations, which leaves the calculative and individualistic ground of rational choice theory untouched. Furthermore, regarding management practices, appropriately designed pay structures are supposed to efficiently perform the multiple duties of taking workers' intrinsic motivations and social preferences into account, mitigating their opportunism and mobilising their trustworthiness (Rebitzer & Taylor, 2011).

Even though workers are here endowed with social preferences, they continue to be modelled as *abstract and calculative* agents rather than *particular people interacting* with one another, privileging formal, mathematical representation, and specifically the use of *numbers*, the elementary particles of mathematical formalism. Standard as well as behavioural agency models of work are thus theoretically consistent with the quantification of work observed in the last decades, discarding real-world work contexts and leaving out (i) the meaningfulness of work, and (ii) its collective character, features that need to be brought back into economic analysis.

Psychological and organisational research has not only gathered evidence supporting the claim that employees find meaning in work, but also that there are various sources of meaningfulness, stemming from the self and others, from the work context and content, as well as spiritual life. Based on this research, Rosso, Dekas and Wrzesniewski (2010) build an overarching model based on the two most fundamental dimensions to the creation or maintenance of meaningful work. One dimension consists in a continuum that ranges from a desire for agency to a desire for communion, which captures the extent to which the source of meaning lies either within the individual or in the group; the other dimension consists in a continuum ranging from self-directed to other-directed action (Lopes, 2018). The validity of the model is supported by empirical research that highlights 'the importance of reciprocal dynamics between individuals and groups [... whereby] the individual works to benefit the self and the collective, and the fruits of this work enhance both self and collective' (Steger, Dik & Duffy, 2012, p. 324). From this it follows that work, to be meaningful, must simultaneously benefit society and possess an intrinsic value for the worker herself. Overall, empirical evidence suggests that work is both a matter of judgement (on the usefulness for others and oneself) and calculation (of whether wage compensates for its disutility).

Coase (1937, p. 393) captured long ago the collective dimension of work: 'A firm consists of the system of relationships which comes into existence when the direction of resources is dependent on an entrepreneur'. It lies in a 'system of relationships', which, in the case of firms, involves direction. A wide list of reasons is presented that argue for the superior efficiency of collective and directed work over isolated work. For example directed work lessens transactions costs (Coase, 1937; Williamson, 1980, 1975); team production generates the unique productivity gains that distinguish firms from markets (Alchian & Demsetz, 1972); collective work allows the building of complementarities through specialisation and employees' (complementary) firm-specific investments (Rajan & Zingales, 1998; Williamson, 1975). Notwithstanding these cogent arguments, agency theory sticks to seeing firms as a nexus of contracts established between separate individuals rather than as directed 'systems of relationships'.

In real-world firms, working involves entering into a large set of relationships within various groups, involving both peers and supervisors. Moreover, the employment contract is not a market transaction; rather, it is a relationship established between a person, who will perform the work *in* and *as a person*, and a firm, which is a collective entity. The exchange of work between the worker and the firm is a *social institution*; more specifically, it is not a market but a 'social exchange' (Fehr & Gintis, 2007), one that involves a series of interactions that generate over time informal obligations, trust and mutual commitments.

A work collective is a set of persons *plus* the rules, technical and behavioural, that they build together to perform their work. Empirical research shows that interpersonal interactions at work influence the meaning of work and, in particular, that membership in work groups provides individuals with meaningfulness by making them experience a sense of belonging (Kluver, Frazier & Haidt, 2014; Rosso, Dekas & Wrzesniewski, 2010). Work is thus characterised by several kinds of *interpersonal* interactions, i.e., interactions between people who interact as *particular* individuals and *cooperate* with one another. Indeed, no organisation would function or survive without cooperation (technical and social, Barnard, 1938) among its members, which makes it necessary to give a sound account of cooperation (something attempted by neoclassical economists but unsatisfactorily achieved). Adopting Sugden's (2005) perspective inspired by Adam Smith's concept of sympathy in *The Theory of Moral Sentiments*, my claim is that the interpersonal relations in which workers engage when working together generate affective states that help sustain *norms of cooperation*. Adam Smith's basic psychological assumption is that individuals have a capacity to feel imaginatively the experience of others and so to share their pleasures and pains; this leads to a 'correspondence of sentiments' – or 'emotional contagion'.[8] This correspondence of affective states is in turn the basis for judgements of approval or disapproval of others' and one's own actions. The whole process thus involves cognitive (judgemental), as well as affective elements and, importantly, it is fundamentally unconscious and involuntary, which renders it useless to any kind of calculation. Therefore, through recurrent interactions, as in the case of workers facing common problems in pursuit of common goals, the members of the work collective share the sentiments of others and as a result tend to converge on common normative behaviours. Of course, processes of affective dissonance and related judgements of disapproval may also occur and lead to severe disruptive events and breaks of cooperation.

Smith's insights are now recognised by organisational scholars, who have acknowledged that cognitive processes do not give a complete picture of shared social processes. For example emotional contagion greatly affects individual-level attitudes *as well as* group processes, leading to greater cooperativeness (Barsade, 2002). To conclude, Smith's concept of sympathy in the end provides a powerful explanation of (i) why the meaningfulness of work is so closely related to its usefulness for others and its relational and collective character, and (ii) why collectives of work tend to cooperate.

### The key features of work management in financialisation: the devaluation of work and its consequences

Governance by numbers, as described above, makes it clear that it is the outcomes of work rather than the workers as persons that are presently the primary focus of management. Being based on numbers, this kind of governance is supposed to be axiologically neutral but it actually contributes to overlooking the subjective and collective experience of work – a highly axiological phenomenon. As the subjective and collective dimensions of work are neglected, empathic concern progressively disappears from workplaces and managers disregard and are not held accountable for the socio-psychological well-being of their subordinates.[9] The process of work quantification is intimately linked to that of the individualisation of work (Dejours, 2009), both marked by practices such as the setting of individualised and quantified performance targets, quantified appraisal systems and rankings, rising wage differentials, 'unobstructive' monitoring like standardisation of practices, extensive reporting procedures, etc. The human activity of work is being translated into numbers of products, clients, articles, reports, etc., in a prodigious endeavour to transcribe work into an abstraction intelligible and suitable for financial analysis (Supiot, 2015).

That management rhetoric solicits the cognitive and affective investment of workers in the pursuit of, and identification with, organisational goals makes the quantification of work especially paradoxical. Indeed, good managers are well aware that workers' loyalty and cooperative spirit are more efficiently fostered by granting them greater decision-making scope than submitting them to technical prescriptions and quantified control. A solution has been found to solve this paradox: workers are sometimes involved in the setting of the objectives they are required to achieve and for which they are made accountable, and they are very often free to decide on the means to reach these objectives. The latter are quantified but no longer look like prescriptions imposed by someone else; rather the workers feel like they are acting 'freely', driven by their own will and self-control, which makes them give their best.

However, there is a problem with this solution: it affects workers' mental health. These management practices have resulted in a significant intensification of work, emotional exhaustion, dissolution of collective solidarities, depersonalisation, deterioration of work relations, feelings of isolation, and of culpability when performance targets are not met (Le Gall, 2011). As a result, in the last decades, workers' vulnerability and psychosocial disorders have intensified considerably (Netterstrom et al., 2008; Dejours, 2009; Theorell et al., 2015).

Various explanations may be given for this increase in psychosocial disorders. First, having to agree with their work objectives puts workers in a psychologically perverse situation; they are free to decide on the means and methods but their choice and opportunities for self-direction are actually limited. Indeed, the autonomy workers are supposed to enjoy is an illusion; it involves the means used to reach the targets but the latter are actually decided elsewhere. In truth, this autonomy aims at getting them objectively accountable and subjectively involved. But, second, the workers' subjective (cognitive and affective) involvement at work is unrespected and unrecognised. Governance dominated by numbers exclusively focuses on outcomes, which perversely eclipses the fact that the latter result from workers' subjective involvement – workers as persons are being made invisible. Third, workers face a tension between the need for meaningful work, which includes the feeling of usefully contributing to and being part of a collective, and the pressure to enter into a competitive game which often compels them to behave selfishly (if not opportunistically, Alvehus & Spicer, 2012) to meet their quantified targets. This pressure often generates a generalised competition between workers and the deterioration of trust and solidarity, which are replaced by isolation, suspicion and anomie (which are, unsurprisingly, the ontological basis of neoclassical economics).

What the quantification of work is actually fostering in many workplaces is what Brons (2017) denounces as 'cultural psychopathy', namely the acceptance or even approval that the individual lack of empathy (sympathy in Smith's terms) is *normal* rather than deviant; leading to the normalisation of individual psychopathy.[10] An interviewee of an accounting firm goes as far as claiming that firms are 'the headquarters of egoistic behaviour' (cited in Alvehus & Spicer, 2012, p. 503); in another study, a middle manager reported that 'no sympathy was shown for failure to meet the targets' even though it was recognised that 'people are getting pretty thinly stretched in terms of being able to accomplish them' (Ezzamel, Willmott & Worthington, 2008, p. 128). For Brons (2017), if mainstream economics succeeds in empirically promoting *Homo economicus*, whom he associates with the picture of a psychopath, then it promotes psychopathy. The substitution of governing numbers for managing workers as persons in firms may well be the most emblematic instance of such promotion. Contemporary work may well be transforming 'human nature' (Marx, 1867).

## Outlining the institutional reforms needed to counteract the effects of financialisation on labour relations

### *A tentative explanation of workers' weakening disposition for collective action*

Chapter 6 of the present book examines the factors through which macro-level financialisation processes affect labour relations and continuously strengthen the power of capital over labour. The goal of this chapter is instead analysing the effects of financialisation on the weakening of labour relations because of its reinforcing of market attitudes in workers' behaviours.

The quantification of work processes has not only impacted on the content of work, but it has also affected the way work is experienced, with wide influence on workers' values and behaviours. Various studies show that trust and employee engagement levels are declining while organisational cynicism and disaffection are rising (see Cushen & Thompson, 2016, for references), which may seriously threaten organisational efficiency in the long run; or that governance by numbers prompts calculative behaviours by transforming workers' experiences. For example Alvehus and Spicer (2012) report that 'billable hours'[11] practices lead workers to understand their work as a kind of investment that should be manipulated so as to reap maximal benefits, sometimes at the expense of colleagues lower in the hierarchy. Instead of experiencing the quantification of their work as an oppressive form of control, workers come to see their work life as an investment which may pay dividends in the future. This seriously deteriorates collective solidarity, which in turn undermines the conditions and dispositions for collective action.

Workers' resistance takes individual forms – organisational disaffection, cynicism, work withdrawal – with most ending up contributing to rather than resisting governance by numbers. This lack of resistance and, most importantly, workers' relative disengagement from collective action worryingly signal that management practices are succeeding in spreading the individualistic values that ground financialisation, which contributes to legitimise and 'naturalise' them, in a vicious circle. For what is new in present times is not that firms exploit workers' subjective engagement at work – this did not appear with financialisation – but that quantification and individualisation practices are increasingly seen and accepted by workers and citizens as reasonable and justified. Workers increasingly come to accept processes and practices that engender inequality, injustice and mental suffering (Dejours, 2009). This generalised acceptance of quantified and individualised practices obfuscates the fact that this state of affairs is the outcome of political choices. The representation of the firm, its governance and the organisation of work are highly *political* issues.

Bringing back the political into the firm requires that the latter must be understood again as a centre of production and employment rather than conceived of as a bundle of assets or a nexus of contracts. Workers must, then, be managed as members of a production collective instead of being regarded as separate (human) assets whose contribution to financial performance is to be quantified. This implies recognising that workers' subjective involvement and cooperative dispositions together ground firms' proper functioning, and that firms are composed of a complex set of groups, each of which pursues often divergent goals (shareholders, chief executives, departments with different functions, etc.) even while contributing to a *common goal*: the productive goal of the firm. Insofar as workers perceive themselves as contributing to a common goal, they will perceive each other as being members of the same collective. This is why the quantification and individualisation of work ultimately threaten the firm by leading workers to perceive themselves as separated individuals rather than members of a collective, which is also a condition for the mobilisation of collective resistance against detrimental management practices.

Inasmuch as firms are composed of groups pursuing divergent goals, conflicts of different sorts will inescapably arise because the aims of all groups cannot be simultaneously realised. However, these divergent aims and interests can be negotiated, which once again brings to the fore the political nature of firms that must be explicitly and formally recognised. One solution to counteract the governance of work by numbers and associated weakening of collective action is having workers participate in the governance of firms. Indeed, in view of the power gained by financial actors at the macro-level, resisting financialisation at the firm level – the level where decisions about work organisation are taken – may be more viable through the setting up of appropriate institutional reforms, a point developed below.

### The needed institutional reform: democratising firm governance

In the last decades, the study of the evolution of work has been virtually abandoned by economists, handing over to managerial sciences the examination of how work should be organised. This has contributed to legitimising the long-standing liberal contention that work governance is an exclusively private matter (Lopes, 2016). Yet, as stated above, the monopolisation of firm governance by shareholders on the grounds that the latter are the firm's owners is a legal non sequitur and is largely responsible for the downgrading of workers' power.

In the present context, notwithstanding the shortcomings of top-down solutions in the work domain, the institutional reforms needed to revert the situation must be part of an agenda openly assumed as political, since it touches upon crucial political, economic and social issues. As Favereau (2016, p. 65) puts it, what is needed is a dynamic inversion, namely 'corporate governance should be reconstructed around labour to allow policy to gradually regain control of the financial sphere'. This would have the merit of inverting the anti-democratic bias of firms through having workers deciding themselves about work organisation and management practices.

McMahon (2017) advances three interrelated ways through which corporate law can introduce more democratic practices within the firm: (i) by having employees participate in boardrooms on an equal footing with shareholders, (ii) by creating the conditions for making management accountable to employees, and (iii) by having employees elect the directors and/or managers. Most of these suggestions are not new, having long been advocated by progressive legal scholars (Bodie, 2017; Greenfield, 1998). Presently, they are being discussed in some countries engaged with the revision of the corporate statute of firms (e.g. France, the UK, Italy). The idea is to consider managers as agents serving not a principal (shareholders) but rather the whole collective of workers (bearing in mind that the latter is composed of very heterogeneous groups), which indeed implies a radical reshaping of corporate law.

The German codetermination (*Mitbestimmung*) system and its Scandinavian counterparts provide a real-life model that, if legally instituted at the European level[12] – to avoid institutional competition between countries and 'law shopping' by firms – could help implement the 'dynamic inversion' described above. It would also contribute to rebalancing the unequal balance of power between the financial system and the productive system since, contrary to CEOs, the workers would not ally with shareholders.[13] It must be emphasised that this model is only complete and effective when the participation of employees in board-level bodies – where the German and Scandinavian experiences show that they must hold at least one third of the seats – is complemented by plant-level workers' councils. Moreover, historical evidence shows that such effectiveness is largely dependent on the strength of trade unions (Gumbrell-McCormick & Hyman, 2006) but it must be noted that the reverse might well also be true. Codetermination does not make the conflicts of interests disappear and the extent to which it may change power relations in firms is a justly contested issue. But it has the advantage of not eliding conflict in the firm governance system, being based on a conflictual rather than consensual conception of democracy. Codetermination may presently be the only pragmatic solution able to reverse the quantification of work processes; it may also be the most effective way to help recognise and value the creative character of human work by influencing the firm's management decisions. However, the representatives of workers on governance boards are supposed, like any other member, to pursue the interest of the firm as a whole, not only the interest of some particular group; the principle is to ensure that the interests of all members are taken into account by having them participating in decisions. Codetermination does not eliminate managerial authority; rather, authority directives are now also influenced by workers' interests.

As for economic efficiency, the benefits and shortcomings of codetermination are difficult to capture. The empirical evidence collected on the German experience concludes that the effect on productivity and other economic variables is non-significant or positive, but small; overall, it may be safely assumed that codetermination does not impair economic efficiency (Fitzroy & Kraft, 2005; Mueller, 2015) nor innovation (Kraft, Stank & Dewenter, 2011).

Two final points are worth making. First, instituting codetermination as a European firm governance model would introduce a cooperation principle that contrasts with the competition principle prevailing in EU policies and would strengthen the European Social Model (Favereau, 2016). Second, the changes in corporate law required to provide an appropriate and deep-rooted grounding for codetermination should be accompanied by reforms in accounting standards.

## Concluding remarks

The aim of the present chapter was to enhance the understanding of the distinctive impact of financialisation on the human activity of work. Four main arguments were developed.

First, we argued that financialisation is not solely a macro-level phenomenon; it is also a micro-level process whereby firms have been subject to deep transformations in their governance and management practices since the 1980s. This process is theoretically grounded on, and legitimated by, the agency theory of the firm which progressively became a dominant theoretical and normative paradigm in economics, corporate law and management sciences. Second, we argued that this firm-level financialisation process heavily uses accounting metrics to translate financialised targets into operational strategies and measures, resulting in 'governance by numbers' (Supiot, 2015), a powerful mode of organisational control. In the case of work, governance by numbers – a type of work governance that has disseminated throughout all countries, as can be inferred from the fact that the 2008 financial and economic crisis had very contrasting impacts on all spheres of life across countries but work (Santos, Lopes & Costa, 2016) – has brought about the quantification and individualisation of work, which means its intensification and dehumanisation.

That the objectives, remuneration and evaluation of workers are pervasively quantified suggests that firms are becoming blind to what distinguishes the work of humans from that of machines, since everything is reduced to numbers. Of course, work, in the form of wage labour, has always somehow been reduced to numbers. However, the quantification and individualisation of work that mark present times comprise a qualitatively different phase of this phenomenon because they pervade the whole spectrum of management and because they make workers obsessed with their productivity and 'the numbers'. Our third argument is that these quantified managerial practices are threatening to transform firms into psychopathic institutional environments (Brons, 2017). The deteriorating social climate in firms, denounced by scholars of all social sciences (Alvehus & Spicer, 2012; Dejours, 2009; Le Gall, 2011), combined with the total lack of recognition and valuation by firms of workers' dispositions for sympathy, ultimately negatively impacts the latter.

In Barnard's (1938, p. 110) terms, a firm is a 'system of cooperative services of persons' rather than just the 'sum of services of individuals' driven by incentive contracts. Yet, this is exactly how agency theory depicts firms – as a nexus of contracts. The crux of the issue is that collective actions (political as well as productive), collective entities and, consequently, common goals are not only a blind spot of mainstream economics but what it explicitly denies. Due to its individualistic ontological framework, interpersonal interactions and the affective and normative bonds of obligations associated with the abilities of 'sympathetic' humans are ultimately discarded. This disregard is crucially impacting the world of work and, more broadly, the progressive trends in advanced capitalist societies, on the purely ideological grounds that this is required by technology and economic efficiency.

To conclude, in corporate firms, financialisation ultimately ensures the returns to capital even before economic results are achieved, thus transferring economic risks to labour. In our view, and this is our fourth argument, the most pragmatic way to reverse such an imbalance of power and such a disdain for the common good is to give more decision power to workers at the firm governance level. But this requires substantive institutional transformations at national and EU levels, and thus political struggle to enforce it.

## Notes

1 The focus of the chapter is transformations at the firm level, specifically what the literature dubs 'financialisation as shareholder value' (e.g. van der Zwan, 2014). Note, however, that firm-level financialisation processes are obviously intimately linked with other, macro- or meso-level, processes dealt with in other chapters of this book.

2 Shareholders only own their shares of the corporation, not the firm; while they suffer or benefit from their share (de)valuations, they are not accountable for the firm's economic performance. It is crucial to distinguish the firm, which is an economic entity, from the corporation, which is a legal entity; nobody can own the firm. See Roger and Favereau (2012) for the deep, far-reaching, consequences of this distinction in terms of firms' purposes and responsibilities.

3 Indeed, in 2006, Jensen and Meckling (1976) was the third most cited paper published in economics after 1970 (Kim, Morse & Zingales, 2006).

4 Lazonick (2014) calculated that, between 2003 and 2012, 449 of the 500 firms listed in *Standard & Poors* stock market index devoted 54 per cent of their net revenue to buying back their own shares and an additional 37 per cent to distributing dividends, which means that, on average, only 9 per cent of these firms' revenues were applied to increase production capacity or employment.

5 Although it recognises that firms have responsibilities to other stakeholders, the *OECD Principles of Corporate Governance*, revised in 2015, still states that maximising shareholder value should be the primary objective of firms.

6  Labour cost reduction (through redundancies or work intensification) is signalled to financial markets by the use of specific accounting techniques such as OPEX (operational expenditure) or ABC (activity-based costing) (Cushen & Thompson, 2016).

7  Kaillo et al. (2016) show how such practices were progressively introduced in higher education systems, transforming the position and function of universities all around the world. In Finland, for example, detailed objectives are set out by the government to universities, whose accounting systems were restructured, and funding is allocated in exchange for measurable output.

8  Adam Smith's psychological assumptions have been supported by contemporary neuroscience and psychology research, which use the term 'empathy' rather than 'sympathy' (Hein & Singer, 2008; Zaki & Ochsner, 2012).

9  Of course, this is an ongoing trend. Many managers and employers still concern themselves with their employees (particularly in Nordic countries, even if this concern is also declining there).

10  For Brons (2017, p. 51) mainstream economics is partly responsible for this circumstance because it never 'returns from abstraction to the real world' and believes that efficiency requires unbridled competition, thus 'abstracting away cooperation, mutual support and everything else that makes us human'.

11  Billable hours refers to time that can be included in costumers' invoices; it used to be common practice in professional service firms such as attorneys, accountants and consultants, but it is now pervading internal practices.

12  www.etuc.org/en/pressrelease/european-appeal-companies-and-employees-blazing-new-european-trail.

13  As the reader may have inferred, we advocate the participation of workers in management rather than the mere possession of firms' shares.

# References

Alchian, A., & Demsetz, H. (1972). Production, information costs and economic organization. *American Economic Review, 62*(2), 777–795.

Alvehus, J., & Spicer, A. (2012). Financialization as a strategy of workplace control in professional service firms. *Critical Perspectives on Accounting, 23*, 497–510.

Armour, J. (2005). The proprietary foundations of corporate law. ESCR Working Paper No. 299. Centre for Business Research, University of Cambridge.

Barnard, C. (1938). *The Functions of the Executive.* Cambridge, MA: Harvard University Press.

Barsade, S. (2002). The ripple effect: emotional contagion and its influence on group behavior. *Administrative Science Quarterly, 44*, 644–675.

Bodie, M. (2012). The post-revolutionary period in corporate law. *Seattle University Law Review, 35*, 1033–1059.

Bodie, M. (2017). Employment as fiduciary relationship. *Georgetown Law Journal, 105*(4), 819–870.

Boyer, R. (2005). From shareholder value to CEO power: the paradox of the 1990s. Competition and Change, *9*(1), 7–47.

Brons, L. (2017). *The Hegemony of Psychopathy.* Santa Barbara: Brainstorm Books.

Charness, G., & Kuhn, P. (2011). Lab labor: what can labor economists learn from the lab? In O. Ashenfelter & D. Card (eds.), *Handbook of Labor Economics* (pp. 229–330). Amsterdam: Elsevier.

Coase, R. (1937). The nature of the firm. *Economica, 16*(4), 386–405.

Cooper, D.J., & Hopper, T. (2007). Critical theorising in management accounting research. In C. Chapman, A. Hopwood and M.D. Shields (eds.), *Handbook of Management Accounting Research* (207–245). Oxford: Elsevier.

Cushen, J. (2013). Financialization in the workplace: hegemonic narratives, performative interventions and the angry knowledge worker. *Accounting, Organizations and Society*, *38*, 314–331.

Cushen, J., & Thompson, P. (2016). Financialization and value: why labour and the labour process still matter. *Work, Employment and Society*, *30*(2), 352–365.

Davis, G. (2016). What might replace the modern corporation? Uberization and the web page enterprise. *Seattle University Law Review*, *39*, 501–515.

Dejours, C. (2009). *Travail vivant – travail et émancipation* [Lively work – Work and emancipation]. Paris: Payot.

Ezzamel, M., Willmott, H., & Worthington, F. (2008). Manufacturing shareholder value: the role of accounting in organizational transformation. *Accounting, Organizations and Society*, *33*, 107–140.

Fama, E. (1980). Agency problems and the theory of the firm. *Journal of Political Economy*, *88*(2), 288–307.

Favereau, O. (2016). *The Impact of Financialisation of the Economy on Enterprises and Labour Relations*. Geneva: International Labour Organization.

Fehr, E., & Gintis, H. (2007). Human motivation and social cooperation. *Annual Review of Sociology*, *33*, 43–64.

Fitzroy, F., & Kraft, K. (2005). Codetermination, efficiency and productivity. *British Journal of Industrial Relations*, *43*(2), 233–247.

Friedman, M. (1970). The social responsibility of business is to increase its profit. *New York Times Magazine*, 13 September.

Goshal, S. (2005). Bad management theories are destroying good management practices. *Academy of Management Learning and Education*, *4*(1), 75–91.

Greenfield, K. (1998). The place of workers in corporate law. *Boston College Law Review*, *39*(2), 283–327.

Gumbrell-McCormick, R., & Hyman, R. (2006). Embedded collectivism? Workplace representation in France and Germany. *Industrial Relations Journal*, *37*(5), 473–491.

Hein, G., & Singer, T. (2008). I feel how you feel but not always. *Current Opinion in Neurobiology*, *18*, 153–158.

Jensen, M., & Meckling H. (1976). Theory of the firm: managerial behavior, agency costs and ownership structure. *Journal of Financial Economics*, *3*(4), 305–360.

Kaillo, K-M., Kaillo, T., Tienari, J., & Hyvonen, T. (2016). Ethos at stake: performance management and academic work in universities. *Human Relations*, *69*(3), 685–709.

Kim, H., Morse, A., & Zingales, L. (2006). What has mattered to economics since 1970. *Journal of Economic Perspectives*, *20*(4), 189–202.

Kluver, J., Frazier, R., & Haidt, J. (2014). Behavioral ethics for Homo economicus, Homo heuristicus and Homo duplex. *Organizational Behavior and Human Decision Processes*, *123*, 150–158.

Kraft, K., Stank, J., & Dewenter, R. (2011). Co-determination and innovation. *Cambridge Journal of Economics*, *35*(1), 145–172.

Lazonick, W. (2014). Profits without prosperity. *Harvard Business Review*, September. Retrieved from https://hbr.org/2014/09/profits-without-prosperity.

Le Gall, J.-M. (2011). *L'entreprise irréprochable*. Paris: Desclée de Brower.

Lopes, H. (2016). The political and public dimensions of work. *Journal of Australian Political Economy*, *76*, 5–28.

Lopes, H. (2018). The moral dimensions of the employment relationship – institutional implications. *Journal of Institutional Economics*, *14*(1), 103–125.

Marsden, D. (2016). Norms of exchange and the socio-economics of labor markets. In B. Kaufman (ed.), *Labor Market Models* (pp. 2–40). Palo Alto: Stanford University Press.

Marx, K. (1867). *Capital, Vol. I*. Retrieved from www.marxists.org/archive/marx/works/1867-c1/ch07.htm.

McMahon, C. (2017). *Authority and Democracy*. 2nd edn. Princeton, NJ: Princeton University Press. (1st edn 1994.)

Mueller, S. (2015). Works councils and labor productivity: looking beyond the mean. *British Journal of Industrial Relations*, *53*(2), 308–325.

Netterstrom, B., Conrad, N., Bech, P., Fink, P., Olsen, O., Rugulies, R., & Stansfeld, S. (2008). The relation between work-related psychosocial factors and depression. *Epidemiological Review*, *30*, 118–132.

Rajan, R.G., & Zingales, L. (1998). Power in a theory of the firm. *Quarterly Journal of Economics*, *113*(2), 387–432.

Rebitzer, J., & Taylor, T. (2011). Extrinsic rewards and intrinsic motives: standard and behavioural approaches to agency and labor markets. In O. Ashenfelter & D. Card (eds.), *Handbook of Labor Economics* (pp. 701–772). Amsterdam: Elsevier.

Richard, J. (2015). The dangerous dynamics of modern capitalism (from static to IFRS futuristic accounting). *Critical Perspectives on Accounting*, *30*, 9–34.

Robé, J.P. (2012). Being done with Milton Friedman. *Accounting, Economics and Law*, *2*(2), Art. 5.

Robé, J.P. (2019). The shareholder value mess (and how to clean it up). *Accounting, Economics, and Law*, *9*(3), 1–27.

Roger, B., & Favereau, O. (eds.) (2012). *L'entreprise, formes de propriété et responsabilités sociales*. Paris: Éditions Lethilieux.

Rosso, B.D., Dekas, K.H., & Wrzesniewski, A. (2010). On the meaning of work: a theoretical integration and review. *Research in Organizational Behavior*, *30*, 91–127.

Santos, A.C., Lopes, C., & Costa, V. (2016). FESSUD finance and well-being survey: report. FESSUD Working Paper No. 130. Leeds: FESSUD.

Steger, M., Dik, B., & Duffy, R. (2012). Measuring meaningful work. *Journal of Career Assessment*, *20*(3), 322–337.

Sugden, R. (2005). Fellow-feeling. In B. Gui & R. Sugden (eds.), *Economics and Social Interactions* (pp. 52–75). Cambridge: Cambridge University Press.

Supiot, A. (2015). *La gouvernance par les nombres*. Nantes: Fayard.

Theorell, T., Hammarström, A., Aronsson, G., Bendz, L.T., Grape, T., Hogstedt, C., Marteinsdottir, I., Skoog, I., & Hall, C. (2015). A systematic review including meta-analysis of work environment and depressive symptoms. *BMC Public Health*, *15*, 738–752.

van der Zwan, N. (2014). State of the art – making sense of financialization. *Socio-Economic Review*, *12*, 99–129.

Williamson, O. (1980). The organization of work. *Journal of Economic Behavior and Organization*, *1*, 5–38.

Williamson, O. (1983[1975]). *Markets and Hierarchies*. New York: Free Press.

Zaki, J., & Ochsner, K. (2012). The neuroscience of empathy. *Nature Neuroscience*, *15*(5), 675–680.

# 6 Reconfiguring labour market and collective bargaining institutions in Portugal

## Turning the page on internal devaluation?

*Maria da Paz Campos Lima*

## Introduction

Labour market and industrial relations institutions in EU countries were profoundly challenged by the 2008 international crisis and by the austerity and neoliberal policies the European Union introduced in 2010, under the New European Economic Governance (NEEG). This was most evident in the countries under the surveillance of the European Commission (EC), European Central Bank (ECB) and/or International Monetary Fund (IMF) within the framework of the Memorandums of Understanding (MoUs) with the governments of 'bailed out' countries – imposed for around four years in Ireland, Portugal and Cyprus, for around eight years in Greece, and also in Hungary, Latvia and Romania. Neoliberal austerity policies combined wage depreciation measures with measures for the deregulation of labour and social institutions in order to achieve internal devaluation, making labour and social policy the main factors of adjustment to the financial and economic crisis, while austerity budget cuts escalated (Pochet & Degryse, 2013).

Broadly speaking, institutional changes in advanced capitalist societies towards neoliberalism have been seen as a 'gradual transformation' since the 1980s, through a process of incremental change, representing a discontinuity with the past (Streeck & Thelen, 2005). Abrupt processes of institutional change leading to discontinuity as a result of 'breakdown and replacement' were considered quite exceptional, a view shared by Baccaro and Howell (2011, 2017). In Europe, the exception would be the neoliberal breakdown of industrial relations institutions under Thatcher in the UK, in the early 1980s.

Nonetheless, following the 2008 international crisis, research on the variegated impact of the neoliberal agenda on the reconfiguration of labour market and industrial relations institutions in European Union (EU) countries regained critical importance. Notwithstanding different approaches and answers to the convergence/divergence debate, the emphasis on the intensification of liberalisation and its consequences has been a common denominator of recent comparative analysis looking at challenges to national patterns and trajectories. Baccaro and Howell (2011, 2017) argued that industrial relations in

EU countries have, since the middle 1970s, taken a 'common direction' converging towards neoliberalism, although this does not mean the homogenisation of national institutions towards the neoliberal archetype, nor alignment with the formal institutions of the so-called 'liberal market economies' (LMEs) variety of capitalism. The recognition of such intensification is acknowledged in the shift from the 'varieties of capitalism' approach (Amable, 2003; Hall & Soskice, 2001) to the 'varieties of liberalisation' approach (Thelen, 2012, 2014). Recent research on the reconfiguration of employment regimes (Gallie, 2013; Heyes, 2013) has also highlighted the erosion of welfare protection for the unemployed in the 'inclusive regimes' of Nordic countries; the further liberalisation of 'liberal regimes', weakening social protection and intensifying workfare-style policies, in Ireland and the UK; and the further dualisation of 'dualist regimes', like in Germany, reducing employment and social protection and expanding low-paid, irregular and weakly protected forms of employment, initiated with the Hartz reforms in 2002 (Heyes, 2013). On the other hand, with specific regard to industrial relations, comparative studies highlighted the neoliberal shift and the challenges of disorganised industrial relations and erosion of trade union power (Gumbrell-McCormick & Hyman, 2013; Hyman, 2018; Lehndorff, Dribbusch & Schulten, 2017). In sum, the 'strange non-death of neoliberalism' (Crouch, 2011) became the 'strange' intensification of the neoliberal agenda in Europe.

There is no doubt that the impact of the international crisis and of EU neoliberal austerity policies, in particular in the countries under 'bailout' agreements, such as in Southern Europe, unleashed abrupt processes challenging welfare, labour market and collective bargaining institutions in various ways: in some cases, leading to a breakdown of labour-protective institutions; in some other cases, intensifying ongoing incremental processes of liberalisation (Cruces et al., 2015; Koukiadaki, Távora & Martínez Lucio, 2016). The 'Troika' of official lenders (EC, ECB and IMF) and stand-alone IMF interventions in various countries (eurozone and non-eurozone) combined a mix of such policy aims. Imposed abruptly, they corresponded to a kind of 'institutional change by invasion' (Streeck & Thelen, 2005), regardless of or against well-established institutions, actors' views and strategies; although, in some cases, aligned with old claims of national actors who saw the opportunity to intensify the implementation of the neoliberal agenda. The variation of processes between incremental liberalisation and abrupt breakdown was clearly illustrated by the expression used by Marginson (2014) to account for the developments in collective bargaining coordination in European countries 'from incremental corrosion to frontal assault'. That is also the picture that emerges from the findings of recent European comparative studies with a focus on wage-setting and collective bargaining (Müller, Vandaele & Waddington, 2019; Van Gyes & Schulten, 2015; Visser, Hayter & Gammarano, 2015).

This chapter critically examines the significance of the transformations in employment regulations in Portugal with particular focus on industrial relations and collective bargaining. It critically reviews the significance of changes in institutions and practices following the 2008 international crisis, in particular those resulting from neoliberal austerity policies, under the shadow of the Troika (EC, ECB and IMF), implemented by a centre-right coalition government (PSD/CDS). The exercise is twofold. In the one hand, it examines the amplitude and intensity of changes and the continuities and discontinuities compared with past trajectories since the turn of the century, when the country became integrated into the eurozone and subjected to fiscal discipline, increasing competition and asymmetrical shocks. On the other hand, it examines whether the changes in institutions and practices – which were imposed abruptly in exceptional times of economic hardship and contributed to the escalation of the crisis – survived or were abandoned entirely or partially in the post-Troika period (2015–2019). The question is highly relevant, insofar as the post-Troika period has been a period of economic recovery, a recovery which, since November 2015, benefited markedly from the policies launched in the new political cycle, when the Socialist Party came to power, with the parliamentary support of left parties, the Left Bloc (BE) and the Communist Party (PCP), as well as the Greens (PEV), an unprecedented alliance aiming to turn the page on austerity policies. Furthermore, such an unprecedented alliance and the concrete commitments it entailed aroused expectations, not only of the reconstruction of institutions and new practices breaking with austerity and the neoliberal shift of the so-called 'adjustment' period, but also of a more ambitious agenda in terms of labour, welfare and public policies.

## The cycle of economic crisis and Troika intervention (2008–2014)

European policies determined to a great extent the successive policy 'packages' implemented by governments at various stages of the crisis in Portugal (Caldas, 2012). In the immediate aftermath of the Lehman Brothers collapse, the Portuguese government adopted the 'Initiative to Strengthen Financial Stability' (Iniciativa de Reforço da Estabilidade Financeira – IREF) with the aim of consolidating financial institutions. In January 2009, the government responded to calls from European institutions with the 'Initiative for Investment and Employment' (Iniciativa para o Investimento e o Emprego). The fiscal austerity stage was set in Portugal in March 2010 with the 'Stability and Growth Programme' (Programa de Estabilidade e Crescimento), the so-called PEC I, which was followed by the PEC II (May 2010), and by the PEC III (setting the national budget for 2011). Following the rejection by the national parliament, on 23 March 2011, of the proposal of a fourth austerity package (PEC IV) presented by the Socialist government, the prime minister Sócrates resigned. A turbulent period of extreme international pressure resulted in the financial bailout under the terms of the Memorandum of Understanding on Specific Economic Policy Conditionality (MoU) with the Troika institutions (EC, ECB and IMF), signed on 17 May 2011 by the interim government of the Socialist Party (PS), with the agreement of the centre-right parties, the Social-Democratic Party (PSD) and the Democratic and Social Centre (CDS). However, it was the government which was formed from the following legislative elections, the centre-right PSD-CDS coalition (coming into power on 21 June 2011), that was to implement the policy requirements of the MoU. Therefore, the new cycle of externally imposed austerity coincided with a new political cycle.

### Between regulation and deregulation and the emergence of neoliberal austerity (2008–2010)

When the global financial crisis emerged, important labour market reforms launched by the PS majority government (2005–2009) were already ongoing, which entered into force in 2009: the new Labour Code (LC), set by Law 7/2009, ruling employment relations in the private sector; and the reforms redefining employment relations in the public sector, with a view to aligning these with those governing the private sector.

The LC 2009 represented an incremental change in comparison with the LC 2003. The LC 2009 defined a number of areas where collective agreements (CAs) could not establish less favourable rules for employees than those defined by law, while the LC 2003 allowed for less favourable rules in all matters.[1] The LC 2009 extended the rules facilitating the expiry of agreements by unilateral decision to those agreements with a 'survival clause' (Naumann, 2014) and opened, for the first time, the possibility that non-union workers' representatives could conclude agreements at company level – in the case of companies with at least 500 employees – if they had a trade union mandate. Having a trade union mandate is a condition imposed by the Portuguese constitution that establishes that trade unions have exclusive prerogative of collective bargaining (Campos Lima, 2017, 2019).

In the area of labour market flexibility, the LC 2009 introduced restrictions to temporary work, reducing the duration of fixed-term contracts from six to three years; and facilitated dismissal procedures, limiting the time for court dismissal claims and reducing the cases of mandatory reinstatement. In the area of working-time flexibility, the LC 2009 introduced schemes of individual and group adaptability, working-time accounts and concentrated timetables. The rules on working-time accounts – allowing an increase of four hours of paid work per day or up to 60 hours a week (up to a maximum of 200 hours a year) – were to be defined by means of CAs. The CGTP trade union confederation opposed this trade-off, considering that some of the positive measures limiting the use and duration of fixed-term contracts did not compensate for the increased flexibility of dismissals and working time or for the added pressure on collective bargaining resulting from the rules allowing partial withdraw from statutory regulations and reinforcing the possibility of unilateral expiry (CES, 2008; Campos Lima & Naumann, 2011).

The reforms established two types of employment relationship in the public sector – by appointment (limited to the core functions) and by employment contract. The system governing employment contracts followed LC 2009 provisions, albeit adjusted. In turn, the right to conclude CAs in public administration was established for the first time, which had the same standing as private sector agreements, although with a much more limited scope: basic-ally circumscribed to the definition of working-time limits and working-time adaptability and minimum services during strikes (Stoleroff, 2013).

Eventually, within the framework of Employment Initiatives of 2009 and 2010, the government launched temporary measures to tackle rising unemploy-ment and social crisis, among which were alterations to the unemployment protection system, extending the period during which claimants were entitled to receive unemployment insurance (UI) and unemployment assistance (UA) and increasing the coverage of UI by reducing the number of days a claimant must have worked to be eligible. These temporary protective measures were reversed at the end of 2010, when austerity escalated.

### The emergence of austerity and the turn to internal devaluation prior to Troika intervention

The fiscal 'package' initiated in Portugal in March 2010 with the 'Stability and Growth Programme' corresponded to the escalation of austerity and internal devaluation measures, preceding the Troika intervention. Among the measures was the reconfiguration of the unemployment benefit system (Decree-Law 72/ 2010) reinforcing the logic of *workfare* (Albo & Fast, 2003). The basis for calcu-lating UI changed, limiting it to no more than 75 per cent of the net amount earned during the claimant's previous job (instead of the previous maximum of 65 per cent of gross earnings) and to no more than three times the value of the social support index (IAS), which in 2010 was set at 419.22 euros per month; and beneficiaries were obliged to accept a job offer even if the wage was only 10 per cent higher than their UI (when previously the wage had to be 25 per cent higher).

The EU and national turn to austerity policies heavily targeted the public sector, with the aim of reducing public expenses. The PEC III austerity package, integrated into the national budget for 2011, included nominal cuts (between 3.5 and 10 per cent) in public sector wages above 1,500 euros for the first time. On 23 March 2011, the PS government presented a new austerity package, the PEC IV, which was rejected by parliament. In fact, the PEC III and the PEC IV already reflected extreme EU pressure and integrated policies designed to be adjusted to European circumstances, in the hope of preventing Troika interven-tion. Wage freezes and wage cuts had already been implemented in the public sector in Greece and in Ireland (Glassner & Watt, 2010). In the context of emer-gent austerity, the minimum wage increase for 2011 did not reach the envisaged 500 euros, increasing only to 485 euros (by 2 per cent) in that year.

### The centre-right political cycle and the implementation of MoU: the escalation of internal devaluation and the great regression

During the three years of Troika intervention (May 2011 to May 2014) and until the end of its mandate in October 2015, the centre-right government implemented MoU measures as well as some not foreseen by the MoU but endorsed by the Troika, which represented a significant break with institutions and practices. The internal devaluation strategy that was implemented covered four main areas: changing wage-setting practices and reconfiguring the collective bargaining legal framework to enable downwards wage flexibility and increase employers' discretion; reengineering flexible working-time forms and decreasing overtime pay to reduce labour costs; reducing employment protection, facilitating the deregulation both of temporary work and of dismissals; and last but not least, reducing the duration and amount of unemployment benefit. Together they represented a process of liberalisation of industrial relations through 'institutional deregulation' including almost all the neoliberal features conceptualised by Baccaro and Howell (2017, p. 18): shifts from higher levels of collective bargaining to lower ones; greater recourse to individual bargaining between employer and employee or unilateral employee decision-making; a shrinking in collective organisation capacity of class actors; and a restructuring of labour market institutions to reduce the level and duration of unemployment benefits, making benefit payment contingent on active job search and willingness to accept available jobs, and lower employment protection. Trade unions responded to the escalation of neoliberal austerity in this period with extraordinary social mobilisations and five general strikes (Campos Lima & Martin Artíles, 2014).

### Direct government intervention in wage-setting

One group of government measures consisted of a direct intervention in wage-setting, first of all as an employer in the public sector, where measures required by the MoU and beyond aligned with the MoU austerity goals of reducing public expenses. The centre-right coalition froze wages and careers in the public sector as required by Troika, while keeping in force during 2012, 2013, 2014 and 2015 the cuts in public sector nominal wages implemented by the previous government in 2011.[2] In 2011, Christmas bonuses were cut by 50 per cent; and in 2012 the payment of Christmas and holiday bonuses (adding the equivalent of two months' salary to the annual income of workers) was cancelled.[3] In 2013, the government increased the weekly working hours for the public sector from 35 to 40 hours with no equivalent wage increase, therefore reducing in practice the sector hourly wage (Law 68/ 2013). Nominal wage cuts, cuts in bonuses and working-time increases were not part of the MoU, but were 'justified' as a form of complying with the MoU public deficit targets. All these measures resulted from unilateral state action and none of them followed negotiations or social dialogue with the unions (Stoleroff, 2013).

On the other hand, government's direct intervention consisted of other measures impacting both the public and the private sector. Two were required by the Troika: unilaterally freezing the minimum wage (at 485 euros), during the whole period of the bailout programme (2011–2014); and reducing significantly the amount of overtime payment. Two were not required by the Troika: the cut in holidays by three days and the abolition of four public holidays, without pay (Table 6.1). Moreover, the government imposed labour law reform over more favourable provisions of CAs and individual contracts in relation to overtime payment and severance pay (see Table 6.2). With the exception of the minimum wage, these measures were part of the amendment to the LC 2009 introduced by Law 23/2012.

It was only in September 2014 that the government agreed to increase the national minimum wage, setting a minimum wage of 505 euros per month to be applicable from 1 October 2014 until 31 December 2015. In connection with this measure, employers' contributions to social security per employee were reduced by 0.75 per cent between November 2014 and January 2016.

The most all-encompassing and significant changes to the LC 2009 were set by Law 23/2012, in line with MoU requirements but going beyond them. Most of the measures weakening collective bargaining, employment protection and unemployment protection were contained in this amendment (see Tables 6.1, 6.2 and 6.3). This amendment was 'legitimised' to a certain extent by the tripartite agreement of 2012 (CES, 2012), proposed by the government and signed by social partners, with the opposition of the CGTP. The UGT trade union confederation signed the agreement, under the government's threat to increase the daily working time by half an hour in the private sector; and in consideration of the government's promise (broken afterwards) that future labour changes would not be made without consultation with social partners. While some accounts presented this agreement as a sign of the resilience of tripartite

*Table 6.1* Direct government intervention and wage-setting, 2011–2014

| Measures | Context of political decision |
| --- | --- |
| Nominal cuts (between 3.5 and 10 per cent) in public sector wages above 1,500 euros (2011–2015) | Not included in MoU – government unilateral decision |
| Suspension of holiday and Christmas bonuses equivalent to two months' wages in the public sector (2012) | Not included in MoU – government unilateral decision |
| Increasing the weekly working time from 35 to 40 hours without pay, in the public sector (2013, 2014, 2015) | Not included in MoU – government unilateral decision (Law 68/2013 and Law 35/2014). |
| Freezing wages and career progression in the public sector | MoU and government unilateral decision |
| Freezing the minimum wage (private and public sector – 2012/2013/2014) | MoU and government unilateral decision |
| Reducing overtime payment (private and public sector) | MoU and tripartite agreement 2012 – Law 23/2012) |
| Cut in holidays by three days and abolition of four public holidays, without pay | Not included in MoU – but in tripartite agreement 2012 – Law 23/2012 |

consultation (Ramalho, 2014), it stood out as a clear case of 'institutional conversion' (Streeck & Thelen, 2005; Baccaro & Howell, 2011, 2017), insofar as tripartite consultation – under the shadow of the Troika – was 'redeployed' in a new direction, towards a significant transferral of power resources and income from labour to capital (Leite et al., 2014), representing a zero-sum game heavily penalising labour.

## *Deregulating employment protection and the unemployment benefit system*

The promotion of 'external flexibility' was clearly one of the tools foreseen to accomplish internal devaluation, in addition to wage-setting and collective bargaining policies. The tool kit comprised the reduction of employment protection by facilitating dismissals – an old aim of Portuguese employer confederations – and facilitating temporary forms of work, alongside the reduction of the duration and amount of the unemployment benefit (Table 6.2). The most radical changes referred to the reduction of severance pay by successive amendments to the LC of 2009. The principle of 30 days of payment per year of tenure was successively reduced to 18 and 12 days. They established a cap for the overall amount of severance pay which cannot exceed 12 times the monthly

*Table 6.2* Deregulating employment protection and the unemployment benefit system, 2011–2014

| Measures | Context of political decision |
| --- | --- |
| Substantially reducing severance pay | MoU – tripartite agreement 2012 – Law 53/2011; Law 23/2012; and Law 69/2013 |
| Extending the conditions for individual dismissals based on unsuitability and suppression of job positions | MoU – tripartite agreement 2012 – Law 23/2012) |
| Amendments in criteria for selection of workers in the case of suppression of job positions | Unilateral decision – Law 27/2014 |
| Extraordinary renewal and maximum duration of fixed-term employment contracts – to 2 additional renovations and an additional maximum duration of 18 months | Not in MoU – government unilateral decision – Law 3/2012 and Law 76/2013 |
| Regime of dismissals in public sector | Not in MoU – government unilateral decision (Law 35/2014) |
| Reducing the maximum amount of unemployment benefit and reducing its amount by 10 per cent after six months of benefit; and reducing the duration of unemployment benefit | MoU – tripartite agreement 2012 – Decree-Law 64/2012 and Decree-Law 65/2012 |
| Extending the coverage – reducing period of contributions and including self-employed | |

base salary and seniority of the worker; or a limit of 240 times the amount of the mandatory minimum wage; or in the case of monthly wages (and seniority) 20 times the amount of the mandatory minium wage. Furthermore, they eliminated the payment of three months irrespective of tenure. The grounds for dismissal were also extended, increasing the employer's discretion: individual dismissals linked to unsuitability of the worker became possible even without the introduction of new technologies or other changes in the workplace. Last but not least, temporary forms of work were facilitated by unilateral decision (Table 6.3). As observed by the most recent ILO (2018, p. 4) report on Portugal:

> At the onset of the latest global economic recession, the legal framework favoured the use of temporary contracts, a situation that was reinforced by the reforms introduced between 2011 and 2013. Further ease in the use of temporary contracts was accompanied by a reduction in employment protection for permanent workers without leading to a change in the share of temporary workers among employees. Thus, adjustment reforms reduced protections without benefit to employment or the labour market.

As envisaged in MoU and in the 2012 tripartite agreement, unemployment protection was reduced. The maximum amount of the unemployment benefit decreased from 1,258 euros to 1,048 euros (corresponding to two and a half times the value of the Social Support Index, IAS) and reduced by 10 per cent after a period of six months in daily benefit. The duration of unemployment benefit was also reduced in line with the MoU, which required a maximum duration of 18 months. The new law required workers to have a period of two years of contributions to be entitled to such duration. Previously the allocation period varied between a minimum of nine months and a maximum of 38 months (depending on the worker's age and period of contributions), while with the new law the duration varies from 5 months up to 26 months. The maximum envisaged – 26 months – applies only to workers aged over 50 years with a minimum of 20 years of contributions.

Although the law included a positive measure to extend the coverage of unemployment benefit by reducing the necessary contributory period to access unemployment benefits from 450 days to 360 days, the reduction of its duration combined with the increase in unemployment, especially long-term unemployment, led in practice to the exclusion of a large number of unemployed people from unemployment benefits.

### Reconfiguration of collective bargaining rules and practices

As explained, for the public sector wage freezes and wage nominal cuts were not negotiated. In addition, in 2014 and 2015, the government blocked around 500 CAs signed in local government for the return of the weekly working time of 35 hours. In all matters regarding wages or other pecuniary benefits, collective bargaining was also paralysed in state-owned companies. Eventually these practices in the public sector sent clear signs to the private sector to contain wage demands, which combined with escalating unemployment, created an extremely unfavourable context for unions' claims and demands.

The so-called structural reforms of collective bargaining envisaged by the Troika had a clear focus on the private sector. Mostly the legislation that implemented these reforms was part of the amendment set by Law 23/2012. Nevertheless, one of the most critical measures with impact on bargaining coverage was the government's unilateral blockade of extension ordinances and the imposition of new criteria for the extension of CAs requiring signatory employers' organisations to comprise more than 50 per cent of all employees in the industry concerned (see Table 6.3). These criteria faced strong opposition not only from trade union confederations but also from employers' confederations.[4] The quasi-automatic extension of CAs played a very important

*Table 6.3* Measures with a direct impact on collective bargaining, 2011–2014

| Measures | Context of political decision |
| --- | --- |
| Collective bargaining (private sector and public-owned companies): | MoU and tripartite agreement 2012 – Law 23/2012 |
| Derogation from higher-level agreements. Lowering of the firm-size threshold above which it is possible to conclude firm-level agreements negotiated by non-union workers' representative structures | |
| Introduction of stricter criteria for the extension of CAs: | MoU requirement of representativeness of signatory organisations |
| 2012 – Employers' associations must represent 50 per cent of employment in the sector | Government unilateral decision – Resolution 90/2012 |
| 2014 – Amendment – as an alternative, employers' associations must include 30 per cent of medium and small companies | Tripartite consultation – Resolution 43/2014 |
| Shortening the survival of CAs that are expired but not renewed – reducing the period of expiry of CAs from 5 to 3 years, and their period of validity after expiring from 18 to 12 months. | MoU and tripartite agreement – Law 55/2014 |
| Individual working-time accounts – negotiated between individual employees and employer, circumventing collective bargaining. | MoU and tripartite agreement 2012 – Law 23/2012 |
| Measures imposing labour law over CAs and individual contracts: nullity of the provisions of CAs providing for amounts higher than the Labour Code in relation to severance pay; suspension for two years of the provisions of CAs on overtime payment higher than those established in the Labour Code | Not in MoU – tripartite agreement 2012 – Law 23/2012 |
| Possibility of suspending CAs in force in companies in crisis by mutual agreement. | Tripartite consultation – Law 55/2014 |

role in securing the influence of Portuguese trade unions in deciding wage and working conditions, despite their low membership rate (Távora & González, 2014; Schulten, Eldring & Naumann, 2015). The combination of neoliberal reforms reconfiguring the legal framework of collective bargaining, freezing the minimum wage, and legislative measures downgrading labour standards plunged the country into the most dramatic crisis of collective bargaining in four decades of democracy (Campos Lima, 2019).

After Troika intervention came to an end, on 26 May 2014, the PSD/CDS government, under pressure from trade unions and employers' confederations, made an amendment to this law which added new alternative criteria for the extension of CAs, a mitigated solution, considering the proportion of small and medium companies that employers' associations represented. Eventually, in the second half of 2014, the government fulfilled the promise made to the Troika to shorten further the time limits of CAs and to introduce mutually agreed temporary suspension of CAs clauses for enterprises facing economic difficulties.

## The left-leaning political cycle (2015–2019): turning the page on internal devaluation?

In contrast with the economic downturn of the period 2011–2014, which was marked by a dramatic decline of GDP and unprecedented unemployment levels, the period between 2014 and 2019 was marked by significant economic recovery (ILO, 2018; OECD, 2019). This recovery, notwithstanding the positive external economic outlook, benefited from the new political cycle that started in November 2015, when the Socialist Party (PS) came to power with the support of left parties, namely the Left Bloc (BE), the Communist Party (PCP) and the Greens (PEV). The four-year mandate has since been renewed by the victory of the Socialist Party in the recent elections, in October 2019. All in all, the economic and political context became more favourable for improvements in employment relations and collective bargaining.

In the last five years, economic indicators have improved markedly: GDP per capita increased between 2014 and 2018 by 11.4 per cent; the unemployment rate decreased by 7.1 percentage points; and the employment rate increased by 1.9 percentage points. On the other hand, the country's fiscal position was strengthened considerably. After attaining its peak at 11.2 per cent of GDP in 2010, the fiscal deficit gradually declined to 0.5 per cent of GDP in 2018, the lowest budget deficit in 45 years of democracy – lower than the initially budgeted 1.1 per cent of GDP (OECD, 2019). The PS government's goal during its mandate (2015–2019) was to implement social and labour market policies to 'turn the page on austerity' and at the same time to reduce public deficit and debt in line with EU budgetary constraints. This strategy has been understood as a

> shift to a more accommodative fiscal policy stance in recent years, in the effort to maintain a balance between, on the one hand, a credible

commitment to gradual public debt reduction and, on the other hand, the need to support incomes, domestic demand.

(ILO, 2018, p. 11)

The measures negotiated between the PS government and the left parties gave priority to reversing the 'extraordinary' austerity cuts imposed by the previous PSD-CDS centre-right government, improving the trajectory of the minimum wage and combating precarious work.

During this period two tripartite agreements covering a broad range of issues were concluded, which did not have the support of the CGTP: the Tripartite Commitment for a Mid-Term Consultation Agreement (CES, 2017), signed on January 2017; and the tripartite agreement on combating precarious work and labour market segmentation and promoting greater dynamism in collective bargaining (CES, 2018), signed on June 2018. The most significant and wide-ranging changes to the LC2009 introduced by Law 93/2019 were a result, firstly, of the government commitments with the left parties, and secondly, of government commitments with social partners made in the 2018 tripartite agreement. However, Law 93/2019 did not receive a favourable vote from the left parties, as some provisions of the law, reflecting the tripartite agreement, were understood as undermining to a certain extent the original party deals. As will be examined below, this process and other legislative initiatives showed the limits and the potential of the attempts to combine tripartite consultation and left-oriented politics.

### Direct government intervention, income recovery and wage-setting

In the first year of its mandate, the government with the support of the left parties reversed the austerity cuts in retirement pensions, in social integration income (*rendimento social de inserção*, RSI) and in family allowances; and re-established four civil and religious holidays (Law 8/2016). Also in 2016, the nominal wage cuts in the public sector were eliminated (Law 159-A/2015). The 35-hour week was re-established in the public sector, through the second amendment (Law 18/2016) to the General Labour Law in Public Functions.

On the other hand, the left deal assigned priority to the recovery of the trajectory of the minimum wage, raised in October 2014 to 505 euros. In this period (2015–2019), the minimum wage increased regularly, reaching 600 euros in 2019. The government strategy for implementing minimum wage increases linked its commitments with the left parties and social dialogue with trade unions and employers' confederations. It should be noted that despite initial concerns raised about potential negative effects – notably expressed in 'European Semester' country recommendations (European Commission, 2015, 2016) – the increase in the minimum wage by around 19 per cent in four years was accompanied by a significant increase in employment, with the creation of around 400,000 jobs between the end of 2014 and the end of 2018. Furthermore, in all those years, nominal minimum wage updates were significantly higher than average salary growth. Updating the minimum wage was crucial to explaining the higher wage growth of sectors with the highest share of workers earning the minimum wage (Martins, 2019).

### Labour rights and employment protection: blockages and incremental improvements

In the new political cycle, the Troika legacy of structural reforms – reducing employment protection in relation to the grounds for dismissals and the level of severance pay – remained intact, despite the legislative proposals and attempts of the supporting left parties to reverse these measures. As to the envisaged plan to combat temporary forms of employment, the new legislation (Law 93/2019) regulating the grounds, conditions of use and duration of fixed-term and temporary forms of labour contracts only entered into force at the end of the government mandate, in October 2019. The delay in re-regulating these matters shows the difficulties in combating labour precariousness.

During the government mandate, a number of legislative measures re-regulating employment relations and labour rights, some of which were an initiative of the supporting left parties, came into force:

- Combating modern forms of forced labour, considering not only the criminal responsibility of subcontractors and temporary staffing agencies, but also the responsibility of company users (Law 28/2016).
- Improving the regulations governing the recognition of an employment contract, established by Law 63/2013, and extending the procedural mechanisms to combat 'bogus self-employment' to all forms of undeclared work, including false internships and false volunteer work (Law 55/2017).
- Reinforcing the fight against harassment at work in the private and public sectors (Law 73/2017).
- Protecting workers' contractual and acquired rights in the case of transfer of business or establishment – namely, remuneration, seniority, professional category and functional content and social benefits acquired (Law 14/2018).
- Introducing measures to promote equal pay between women and men who perform equal work or work of equal value (Law 60/2018).

Moreover, the deal with the left-leaning parties was crucial to launching the Extraordinary Programme of Regularisation of Precarious Employment Relationships in Public Administration (PREVPAP) to tackle the escalation of precarious work in the public sector originated by budgetary restrictions on recruiting public sector employees on permanent/open-ended contracts. The PREVPAP (Law 42/2016 and Law 112/2017) targeted workers performing functions corresponding to permanent needs, and subjected to hierarchical authority, discipline or direction, without a 'proper legal employment relationship'. The programme comprised various phases, from mapping the incidence of temporary contracts in the public sector and defining evaluation criteria and procedures, to examination of workers' requests and decisions by Bipartite Evaluation Committees (including sector trade unions), and eventually the integration of workers into respective services. Despite positive achievements,[5] at the end of the programme significant challenges remained, such as in the case of integrating university researchers performing permanent functions in adequate employment relationships (Campos Lima, 2018).

*Recent developments and challenges concerning atypical labour contracts*

Law 93/2019 amending the 2009 LC, which came into force in October 2019, introduced significant changes in relation to atypical labour contracts, some of which may improve employment protection, although others risk generating new forms of precariousness. The new law restricts the possibilities of using fixed-term contracts (FTCs), beyond temporary needs. In particular, it forbids hiring on FTCs of *first-time jobseekers* and *long-term unemployed* to perform jobs corresponding to permanent company needs, a practice that was previously allowed in the context of employment policies. The duration of FTCs will be reduced from three to two years (for certain term); and six to four years (for uncertain term). Among the measures that generated controversy was extending the trial period from 90 to 180 days when hiring first-time jobseekers and the long-term unemployed; and increasing the duration of *very short-term contracts* from 15 days to 35 days and allowing their use beyond seasonal activities in the agriculture and tourism sectors. These two measures are at the moment under the examination of the Constitutional Court, after a request by the left parties BE, PCP and PEV to review these provisions on the grounds that they violate the constitutional principles of fairness and security at work.

## Reconstructing unemployment social protection: mixed directions

In the new political cycle, the cuts introduced in the Troika period on the duration of unemployment benefit and its maximum amount remained in place, with a ceiling of 1,089.40 euros (corresponding to two and a half times the value of the Social Support Index, IAS). However, the 10 per cent reduction in the amount of unemployment benefit after 180 days was gradually eliminated (Decree-Law 53-A/2017, and Law 114/2017). Moreover, in 2016 an extraordinary social benefit for long-term unemployed was created, to be allocated to the unemployed enrolled in the general social security scheme, for whom the period for granting the social benefit has expired.[6]

Eventually, the social protection of self-employed workers improved with the publication of two laws: Decree-Law 2/2018 lowered their contributions for social security and increased contributions of entities hiring self-employed workers, redefining the conditions of economically dependent work – those who perform 50 per cent of their yearly activity for the same entity (before it was 80 per cent). In addition, Decree-Law 53/2018 improved the access conditions of self-employed workers to sickness benefits (getting closer to the regulations on contractual work); and extended to them maternity and paternity cash benefits. As to the unemployment benefit regulations for the 'economically dependent' self-employed, the record of contributions for access to unemployment benefit became equal to that of contractual workers – 360 days in the previous 24 months.

### Collective bargaining: persistent blockages and incremental adjustments in the public sector

#### Continuous blockage in the public sector

In the public sector, the recovery of collective bargaining was extremely limited. Trade union claims concerning wage updates faced irreducible opposition from the PS government still concerned with containing public expenses and bringing down the deficit below even the EU target. Trade union pressure escalated from the last quarter of 2018 with a wave of strikes involving various categories of public sector workers, including the education and the health sector, and with the public sector general strikes called by trade unions affiliated with CGTP and UGT, first on 25 October 2018, and again on 14 and 15 February 2019. The government response consisted in upgrading the minimum wage for the public sector from 600 to 635 euros (Decree-Law 29/2019). Furthermore, only in 2017 did the PS government decide to unfreeze civil servants' career progression/promotion and related wage updates, to start in 2018 and with a transition period of seven years. The process of unfreezing careers for public sector workers with 'general careers', no longer dependent on seniority, was not problematic. However, the negotiations with trade unions representing workers with 'special careers' still dependent on seniority (combined with performance evaluation), such as teachers, has been particularly difficult, generating a wave of strikes in 2018 and 2019. The first proposed wage increase for all public sector workers was made by the new PS government, in December 2019, at the beginning of its second term, as part of the 2020 budget proposal: a 0.3 per cent increase based on past inflation rather than on the expected (and higher) inflation for that year – after ten years of frozen wages.

#### Collective bargaining in the private sector: uneven slow progress and incremental change

Since 2015, bargaining dynamics started to improve, although not reaching pre-crisis levels. While the trajectory in terms of the number of agreements signed annually and extension ordinances published shows a clear increase and is getting closer to pre-crisis times (Figure 6.1), and agreed wage increases seem to have undergone a real recovery in 2018–2019 (Figure 6.2), there are still reasons for concern in relation to the trends in wage agreements – which show that in 2018 the agreements signed had not been updated, on average, for the past two years (Figure 6.3); and above all, the most worrying trend is the slow trajectory' of potential wage bargaining coverage (Figure 6.4). Despite

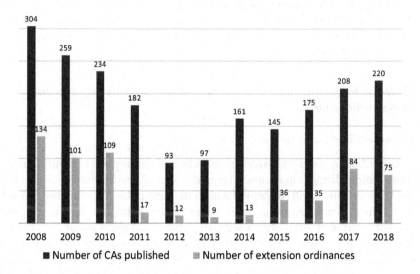

*Figure 6.1* Number of collective agreements published and number of extension ordinances, 2008–2018

Source: DGERT/MTSS

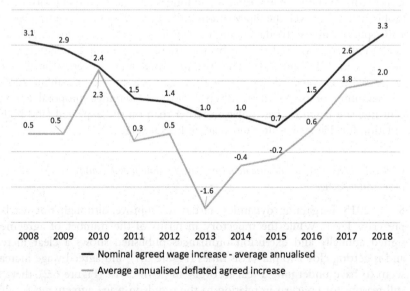

*Figure 6.2* Nominal and real agreed wage increases, 2008–2018

Source: DGERT/MTSS

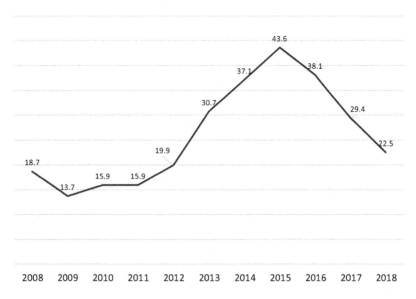

*Figure 6.3* Average duration (months) of previous CAs wage scales, 2008–2018
Source: DGERT/MTSS

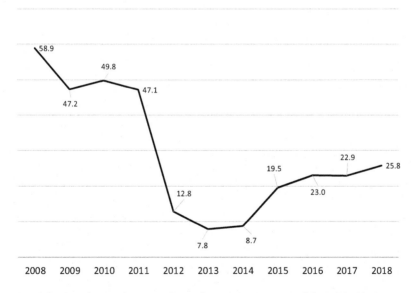

*Figure 6.4* Potential coverage rate of wage bargaining increases (%), 2008–2018
Note: Number of wage earners in *Quadros de Pessoal* does not include public administration.

Source: Author's own calculations based on DGERT/MTSS

the positive developments, there is a long way to go to reach pre-crisis levels. One has to keep in mind that in 2018, the agreed wage increases (nominal and real) set by collective agreements in that year only covered 26 per cent of the workers in the private sector.

In addition to economic recovery and falling unemployment – increasing workers' bargaining power – three important initiatives stimulated the dynamics and coverage of collective bargaining. First and foremost was the increase in the minimum wage, which acted as a catalyst to get bargaining actors back to the negotiating table, in particular in sectors with a large share of workers earning the minimum wage. Secondly, the two initiatives following the 2017 tripartite agreement (CES, 2017): a bipartite agreement between trade union and employer confederations committing their members to suspend temporary unilateral requests for the expiry of agreements; and the government decree (Resolution 82/2017) replacing the criteria for extending agreements based on employers' associations representativeness with new, more inclusive criteria, based on the constitutional principle of 'equal pay for equal work' with the explicit aim of promoting social equality and gender equality.[7] The first initiative suspended employers' potential threat of unilateral expiry of agreements, for 18 months, allowing trade unions a breathing space. The second initiative facilitated the signing of collective agreements, in particular at sector level, once bargaining actors had ensured that the negotiated provisions could be extended to the whole sector. However, the PS opposed the legislative initiatives of the other left parties to reintroduce the joint decision of agreements' signatories as a prerequisite for the expiry of agreements; and opposed their initiatives to fully reinstate the principle of *favor laboratoris*.

Law 93/2019, which entered into force in October 2019, kept intact the possibility of unilateral expiry of CAs and the rule set by the MoU reducing their survival period after expiring. It introduced some positive incremental measures: a measure reinforcing arbitration and mediation mechanisms through the creation of an arbitration court under the framework of the Economic and Social Council (CES), as a last instance before the expiry of collective agreements; and a measure mitigating the impact of the expiry agreements by enlarging the scope of rights that workers keep when collective agreements expire, adding parental rights and rights to health and safety at work. Secondly, it introduced a controversial measure that extended the grounds for the expiry of agreements to the extinction of one of the signatory organisations, enhancing employers' opportunities to exit from collective bargaining regulations. This last measure generated a strong reaction from the CGTP and the left parties BE, PCP and PEV that required the Constitutional Court to review its legality. Last but not least, the measure to replace the regulations on 'individual working-time accounts' determines that 'working-time accounts'[8] can be decided *either* by collective bargaining *or* by 'group agreements' resulting from the consultation of workers in company referendums organised by the employers. The amendment foresees that workers' committees (non-union structures) and trade union delegates at company level or labour inspection in their absence (the case of the majority of Portuguese companies) will have a role in overseeing such referenda. The potential for bypassing collective bargaining seems to be one of the new risks.

## Conclusion

In this chapter we provided a comparison of policies with an impact on the reconfiguration of labour market and collective bargaining institutions in Portugal, in two contrasting periods which followed the emergence of the EU austerity and 'internal devaluation' strategy: the period 2010–2014, including Troika intervention in the country imposing such a strategy; and the period 2015–2019, which coincided with a new political cycle with a focus on 'turning the page on austerity'. The exercise of scrutinising the directions of institutional change, from the therapy of austerity and neoliberal shocks to the attempts to nail the neoliberal mantra 'there is no alternative to austerity', also took into account the significant political and economic differences between these two periods: from the right to the left spectrum of politics; from economic crisis to recovery; from escalating unemployment to creating employment.

While the recent political and economic shifts have inspired optimism and hope in the sombre EU landscape, we examined how far the legacy of austerity and internal devaluation reconfigured institutions in a neoliberal direction and the extent to which this legacy has been challenged in recent years. The case of Portugal documents the critical role of the strategy of internal devaluation for the unprecedented intensification of institutional change in a neoliberal direction. Unprecedented, first of all, because all the main systems underpinning employment law – supporting employment protection, unemployment protection and collective bargaining – were seriously and simultaneously weakened to serve the purpose of downward wage flexibility. The interaction between such changes, in a context of escalating unemployment combined with austerity in the public sector, succeeded in achieving the internal devaluation foreseen, as is documented in various chapters in this book (e.g. Chapter 7).

On the other hand, the long-lasting impact of internal devaluation became apparent during the recovery period, not only in terms of collective bargaining and slow wage recovery, but also because of its impact on the reconfiguration of employment structure, favouring the growth of low-wage sectors and poor-quality employment (Caldas & Almeida, 2018; Chapters 3, 4 and 7 in this volume). Notwithstanding the cumulative negative effects on the country's economy as a whole, it is important to stress that the most significant institutional changes observed in the period 2010–2014 that constitute significant internal devaluation mechanisms in a neoliberal direction continued in place in the period 2015–2019. That is the case with the rules reducing severance pay and extending the grounds for dismissals; the limits to the maximum duration and amount of the unemployment benefit; and the rules reducing overtime payments. As for collective bargaining, while the new extension rules launched in 2017 were a positive step in favour of coverage and recovery of sector bargaining, other critical negative institutional changes persist (despite some incremental changes to mitigate their effects), as is the case with the persistence of *favor laboratoris* being limited in scope; and the persistence of the expiry mechanism of CAs by unilateral decision of any of the signatory parties, a radical change introduced in 2003, aggravated in 2009 and worsened once again in 2014, as required by the Troika. Furthermore, the new amendment to the LC2009 that entered into force in October 2019 raises new concerns: namely the possibility of expiry of collective agreements in case of extinction of any signatory party, which risks generating exit behaviour; and the possibility of company referenda organised by employers to decide on working-time accounts, instead of collective bargaining, which risks bypassing collective bargaining and undermining union influence. In contrast, the new measures limiting fixed-term contracts and temporary work negotiated between the PS government and the left parties, and the new labour and social rights for vulnerable workers, including the self-employed, and the measures combating 'bogus' self-employment represent an important shift in the new cycle, in the attempt to tackle the persistence of temporary work in Portugal. Finally, and perhaps most significantly, the rise in the minimum wage began to combat internal devaluation. This had a considerable impact on the growth of average wages (Martins, 2019) and also on the dynamics of collective bargaining.

Alongside improving the trajectory of the minimum wage, the move to 'turn the page on austerity' promoted by the PS government in the 2015–2019 cycle consisted mostly of reversing the 'extraordinary' unilateral measures imposed on the public sector: reversing nominal cuts in wages and bonuses, re-establishing the 35-hour week, and unfreezing wages and careers. However, the developments in the last two years have shown that integral 'normalisation' in the public sector has not been a government option so far, at least as regards unblocking certain specific careers with full rights or increasing public sector wages (frozen for a decade). While formally in place, the right to collective bargaining in the public sector seems like an empty shell – unions might put forward their claims and strike for them, but with no influence on the outcomes, which are the result of unilateral decisions – this has been the trajectory of the neoliberal transformation in employment relations in the public sector, which is still under the shadow of New European Governance.

## Acknowledgements

This work was financed by Portuguese funds through FCT – Foundation for Science and Technology in the framework of project no. 028811, 'REVAL – From internal devaluation to the revaluation of work: the case of Portugal' Reference: PTDC/SOC-SOC/28811/2017.

# Notes

1  CAs cannot provide less favourable rules than statutory regulations on the following issues: personal rights, equality and non-discrimination; protection of parenthood; minimum age to work; workers with reduced working capacities, disabilities or chronic illnesses; working students; rights to information; limits to the duration of the normal daily and weekly working time; minimum duration of rest periods, including the minimum duration of the annual holiday period; maximum hours for night work; form and guarantees of payment; prevention and repair for work accidents and occupational diseases; transfer of undertaking or business; rights of the elected representatives of the workers.
2  In 2014, the government extended these cuts to public sector wages above 675 euros, a measure which the Constitutional Court overturned (Judgment 413/2014).
3  A measure also planned for 2013 but overturned by the Constitutional Court (Judgment 353/2012).
4  Besides its strictness, the requirement of representativeness of employers' organisations posed a problem: the lack of updated information regarding the employment covered by the non-affiliated companies, which undermined its implementation.
5  According to Portuguese newspaper Público (30 January 2019), the Ministry of Labour estimated that, in January 2019, around 24,000 precarious workers were to be integrated in regular labour contracts, of whom 14,530 were in the Central Administration (out of a total of 33,478 applications received), and around 9,364 in Local Administration. Retrieved from www.publico.pt/2019/01/30/economia/noticia/14500-precarios-estado-luz-verde-comissoes-1859990.
6  This extraordinary social benefit (means tested) is allocated over a period of 180 days and takes the form of a monthly amount equal to 80 per cent of the amount of the last paid social unemployment benefit (Article 80, Law 7- A/2016).
7  Resolution 82/2017 considers the following more inclusive criteria: the impact on the wage scale and on the reduction of inequality; the percentage of workers to be covered; and the share of women who will benefit.
8  The regulations allow normal working time to increase by two hours a day, up to a maximum of 50 hours a week, with a maximum of 150 hours a year.

# References

Albo, G., & Fast, T. (2003). Varieties of neoliberalism: trajectories of workfare in the advanced capitalist countries. Paper presented at the Annual Meetings of the Canadian Political Science Association Congress of the Humanities and Social Sciences, Dalhousie University, Halifax, Nova Scotia, 30 May 2003.

Amable, B. (2003). *The Diversity of Modern Capitalism*. Oxford: Oxford University Press.

Baccaro, L., & Howell, C. (2011). A common neoliberal trajectory: the transformation of industrial relations in advanced capitalism. *Politics and Society*, *39*(4), 521–563.

Baccaro, L., & Howell, C. (2017). *Trajectories of Neoliberal Transformation – European Industrial Relations since the 1970s*. New York: Cambridge University Press.

Caldas, J.C. (2012). The impact of 'anti-crisis' measures and the social and employment situation (European Economic and Social Committee – Workers Group.)

Caldas, J.C., & Almeida, J.R. (2018). Emprego e salários: pontos de interrogação (*Barómetro das crises*, No.19). Lisbon: Observatório sobre Crises e Alternativas.

Campos Lima, M.P. (2017). A grande regressão da negociação coletiva: os desafios e as alternativas'. In M.C. Silva, P. Hespanha and J.C. Caldas (eds.), *Trabalho e políticas de emprego: um retrocesso evitável* (pp. 219–270). Coimbra: Almedina.

Campos Lima, M.P. (2018). Portugal: Innovative social dialogue to combat precarious work in the public sector. Eurofound. Retrieved from www.eurofound.europa. eu/et/publications/article/2018/portugal-innovative-social-dialogue-to-combat-precarious-work-in-the-public-sector.

Campos Lima, M.P. (2019). Portugal: reforms and the turn to neoliberal austerity. In Müller, Vandaele & Waddington, 2019 (pp. 483–505).

Campos Lima, M.P., & Martin Artíles, A. (2014). Descontentamento na Europa em tempos de austeridade: da ação coletiva à participação individual no protesto social. *Revista Crítica de Ciências Sociais, 103,* 137–172.

Campos Lima, M.P., & Naumann, R. (2011). Portugal: from broad strategic pacts to policy-specific agreements. In S. Avdagic, M. Rhodes & J.Visser (eds.), *Social Pacts in Europe: Emergence, Evolution, and Institutionalization* (pp. 147–174). Oxford: Oxford University Press.

CES (2008). *Acordo tripartido para um novo sistema de regulação das relações laborais, das políticas de emprego e da proteção social em Portugal.* Lisbon: Conselho Económico e Social, Comissão Permanente de Concertação Social. Retrieved from www.ces.pt/storage/app/uploads/public/58b/f17/f79/58bf17f79da4e681625862.pdf.

CES (2012). *Compromisso para o crescimento, competitividade e emprego.* Lisbon: Conselho Económico e Social, Comissão Permanente de Concertação Social. Retrieved from www.ces.pt/storage/app/uploads/public/58b/f17/f57/58bf17f573aeb017446575.pdf.

CES (2017). *Compromisso tripartido para um acordo de concertação de médio prazo.* Lisbon: Conselho Económico e Social, Comissão Permanente de Concertação Social. Retrieved from www.ces.pt/storage/app/uploads/public/58b/f17/f44/58bf17f449b 88132493082.pdf.

CES (2018). *Combater a Precariedade e Reduzir a Segmentação Laboral e promover um maior Dinamismo da Negociação Coletiva.* Lisbon: Conselho Económico e Social, Comissão Permanente de Concertação Social. Retrieved from www.ces.pt/storage/app/uploads/public/5b2/7e5/2f6/5b27e52f6b180834433182.pdf.

Crouch, C. (2011). *The Strange Non-death of Neoliberalism.* Cambridge: Polity Press.

Cruces, J., Álvarez, I., Trillo, F., & Leonardi, S. (2015). Impact of the euro crisis on wages and collective bargaining in Southern Europe: a comparison of Italy, Portugal and Spain. In Van Gyes & Schulten, 2015 (pp. 93–138).

European Commission (2015). Council recommendation of 14 July 2015 on the 2015 National Reform Programme of Portugal and delivering a Council opinion on the 2015 Stability Programme of Portugal (2015/C 272/25). Official Journal of the European Union. Retrieved from https://eur-lex.europa.eu/legal-content/EN/TXT/PDF/?uri=CELEX:32015H0818(26)&from=EN.

European Commission (2016). Council recommendation of 12 July 2016 on the 2016 National Reform Programme of Portugal and delivering a Council opinion on the 2016 Stability Programme of Portugal (2016/C 299/26). Official Journal of the European Union. Retrieved from https://eur-lex.europa.eu/legal-content/EN/TXT/PDF/?uri=CELEX:32016H0818(26)&from=EN.

Gallie, D. (2013). Economic crisis, the quality of work, and social integration: issues and context. In D. Gallie (ed.), *Economic Crisis, Quality of Work, and Social Integration: The European experience* (pp. 1–29). Oxford: Oxford University Press.

Glassner, V., & Watt, A. (2010). Cutting wages and employment in the public sector: smarter fiscal consolidation strategies needed. *Intereconomics, 45*(4), 212–219.

Gumbrell-McCormick, R., & Hyman, R. (2013). *Trade Unions in Western Europe: Hard Times, Hard Choices.* Oxford: Oxford University Press.

Hall, P.A., & Soskice, D. (eds.) (2001). *Varieties of Capitalism: The Institutional Foundations of Comparative Advantage.* Oxford: Oxford University Press.

Heyes, J. (2013). Flexicurity in crisis: European labour market policies in a time of austerity. *European Journal of Industrial Relations, 19*(1), 71–86.

Hyman, R. (2018). What future for industrial relations in Europe? *Employee Relations, 40*(4), 569–579.

ILO (2018). *Decent Work in Portugal 2008–2018: From Crisis to Recovery.* Geneva: International Labour Office.

Koukiadaki, A., Távora, I., & Martínez Lucio, M. (2016). Joint regulation and labour market policy in Europe during the crisis: a seven-country comparison. In A. Koukiadaki, I. Távora and M. Martínez Lucio (eds.) *Joint Regulation and Labour Market Policy in Europe during the Crisis* (pp. 7–134). Brussels: ETUI.

Lehndorff, S., Dribbusch, H., & Schulten, T. (2017). European trade unions in a time of crisis – an overview. In S. Lehndorff, H. Dribbusch and T. Schulten (eds.), *Rough waters – European Trade Unions in a Time of Crisis* (pp. 7–37). Brussels: ETUI.

Leite, J., Costa, H., Silva, M.C., & Almeida, J.R. (2014). Austeridade, reformas laborais e desvalorização do trabalho. In J. Reis (ed.), *A economia política do retrocesso* (pp. 127–188). Coimbra: Almedina.

Marginson, P. (2014). Coordinated bargaining in Europe: from incremental corrosion to frontal assault? *European Journal of Industrial Relations, 21*(2), 97–114.

Martins, D. (2019). *Quando a decisão pública molda o mercado: a relevância do salário mínimo em tempos de estagnação salarial* (*Cadernos do Observatório*, No. 14). Lisbon: Observatório sobre Crises e Alternativas.

Müller, T., Vandaele, K., & Waddington, J. (eds.) (2019). *Collective Bargaining in Europe: Towards an Endgame*, vol. III, (pp. 483–505). Brussels: ETUI.

Naumann, R. (2014). Collective bargaining in Portugal: Study on the survival of contracts that are expired but not renewed (sobrevigência). ICF, GHK, European Commission, DG Employment, Social Affairs and Inclusion.

OECD (2019). *OECD Economic Surveys: Portugal 2019.* Paris: OECD Publishing.

Pochet, P., & Degryse, C. (2013). Monetary union and the stakes for democracy and social policy. *Transfer: European Review of Labour and Research, 19*(1), 103–116.

Ramalho, M.R. (2014). Portuguese labour law and relations during crisis. In K. Papadakis & Y. Ghellab (eds.), *The Governance of Policy Reforms in Southern Europe and Ireland* (pp. 147–163). Geneva: International Labour Organization.

Schulten, T., Eldring, L., & Naumann, R. (2015). The role of extension for the strength and stability of collective bargaining in Europe. In Van Gyes & Schulten, 2015 (pp. 361–401).

Stoleroff, A. (2013). Employment relations and unions in public administration in Portugal and Spain: from reform to austerity, *European Journal of Industrial Relations, 19*(4), 309–323.

Streeck, W., & Thelen, K. (2005). *Beyond Continuity: Institutional Change in Advanced Political Economies.* Oxford: Oxford University Press.

Távora, I., & González, P. (2014). The reform of joint regulation and labour market policy during the current crisis: national report on Portugal. In A. Koukiadaki, I. Távora & M. Martínez Lucio (eds.), *Joint Regulation and Labour Market Policy in Europe during the Crisis* (pp. 321–393). Brussels: ETUI.

Thelen, K. (2012).Varieties of capitalism: trajectories of liberalisation and the new politics of social solidarity. *Annual Review of Political Science, 15*(1), 137–159.

Thelen, K. (2014). *Varieties of Liberalisation and the New Politics of Social Solidarity.* Cambridge: Cambridge University Press.

Van Gyes, G., & Schulten, T. (eds.) (2015). *Wage Bargaining under the New European Economic Governance: Alternative Strategies for Inclusive Growth.* Brussels: ETUI.

Visser, J., Hayter, S., & Gammarano, R. (2015). Trends in collective bargaining coverage: stability, erosion or decline? (Labour Relations and Collective Bargaining Policy Brief, No. 1). Geneva: International Labour Office.

# 7 Financialisation, labour and structural change

## The case of Portuguese internal devaluation

*Nuno Teles, José Castro Caldas and Diogo Martins*

## Introduction

In the wake of the Global Financial Crisis (GFC) of 2008–2009, the euro-zone experienced its own crisis. Initially triggered by the inability of Southern European (SE) peripheral countries to refinance their sovereign debt, the crisis was aggravated when the European Union (EU) turned its attentions to fiscal austerity and internal devaluation in 2010. As debatable as austerity measures were (Lapavitsas et al., 2012), their imposition was justified by policymakers as a necessity given the ballooning of public deficits and sovereign indebtedness in 2009–2010. Internal devaluation, however, was far from being considered a straightforward priority in the face of the devastating effects of the GFC in the eurozone. The crisis was largely blamed on financial sector wrongdoings and subsequent public sector profligacy. Nevertheless, internal devaluation was placed at the top of the list of priorities by European institutions, particularly in the SE peripheral countries subjected to the political conditionality of 'bailout' agreements, namely Greece, Portugal and Spain. These countries subsequently embarked on deep-seated labour market reforms with the intention of restructuring their economies, achieving competitiveness and redressing their external balances. More recently, Portugal has been heralded as a successful showcase for such reforms. In fact, after a deep recession with the unemployment rate peaking at 17 per cent in 2013, economic growth has since recovered, the external deficit vanished and unemployment is now under 7 per cent.

This chapter argues that the financialisation process of the SE periphery, fostered by the Economic and Monetary Union (EMU), is crucial in explaining the EU focus on internal devaluation as a preferred policy instrument for economic adjustment. This conjecture is presented against a theoretical background in which the link between labour restructuring in these countries and financialisation is either ignored or downplayed. The financialisation literature on labour relations is often focused on the short-term behaviour of listed corporations towards their workforce in a new context of myopic shareholder value, narrowing its research to listed companies and to countries with sizeable stock exchange markets.

We take a different approach. Drawing on previous work on the specific form of financialisation within the SE periphery (see Chapter 2 in this volume), we broaden the scope of the analysis and argue that a new macroeconomic policy regime aimed at preserving financial agents and their interests, a regime which coincides with the rise of neoliberalism, has deprived peripheral states of economic policy instruments traditionally available to them. The tight control of inflation and public deficits alongside the banning of trade and capital controls which limit the reach of monetary, fiscal or industrial policies benefiting the preservation of financial value, has left labour as the main adjustment variable to exogenous shocks. This new macroeconomic regime, although present in most countries that followed the financialised path, is particularly salient in the eurozone, where countries were led to relinquish their sovereign monetary, fiscal and trade policies. As the GFC transmuted into the eurozone crisis, labour rigidity was targeted as one of the structural causes of European financial fragility, and labour market reform came to the fore as the appropriate instrument for achieving an 'internal devaluation' that would boost price competitiveness and redress external imbalances. While the financial sector was becoming the focal point for state rescue operations at the national and European level, SE peripheral countries were led to impose harsh fiscal austerity measures and, in the absence of any other economic policy instruments (most notably the use of exchange rates), steered into depressing wages as a way of replicating the effect of currency devaluation and raising their respective positions in terms of external competitiveness. Weakening collective bargaining agreements, the freezing or cutting of minimum wages, and the enhancing of ease of dismissal were some of the instruments implemented for such purposes (see Chapter 6 in this volume).

In Portugal, the effects of austerity and labour reform were particularly harsh, with the loss of several hundred thousand jobs, mass emigration and a rise in levels of poverty and inequality (Chapter 10 in this volume). Nonetheless, following the adjustment, the Portuguese economy not only experienced an abrupt fall in the external deficit but has, since 2015, been benefiting from the combination of an alleviation of austerity under a new left-leaning government and a new activist monetary stance carried out by the European Central Bank (ECB) supporting (low) sovereign interest rates through massive 'quantitative easing', leading to a decrease in overall interest rates and the nourishing of an international drive for yield by financial agents. Such a favourable economic context and the resulting economic recovery have thus served as a vindication for the policies imposed by the EU. We argue, instead, that the recent success of the Portuguese economy in terms of current balance, fiscal consolidation, employment and, to a lesser extent, growth, is obfuscating the fact that internal devaluation has triggered a process of structural sectoral change which accounts for the persistence of stagnant wages and precarious labour relations, now seen as part and parcel of a new economic growth model. This recent growth pattern is still financialised, though less dependent on debt and more reliant on the 'hot' money coming from abroad and the consequent asset alienation, particularly through real estate. The prospect of stagnant growth, wages and productivity along with the risk of further financial instability is still looming.

This chapter is organised as follows. The second section overviews the literature on financialisation and labour, pointing out some of its shortcomings and presenting an alternative approach which stresses macroeconomic policy regime changes and the new role of labour as a macroeconomic adjustment variable. The third section addresses the rise of the labour market as a policy area in the EU and of 'flexibility' as the mantra for structural reform. The fourth section scrutinises the rise of internal devaluation as a policy priority in the context of the euro crisis. The fifth section deals empirically with the consequences of internal devaluation in Portugal during the adjustment and recovery periods, pointing to the structural changes taking place within the Portuguese economy. The conclusion summarises the main findings.

## Financialisation and labour: a complementary approach

Financialisation and the restructuring of labour relations has proved to be a difficult topic. One of the reasons behind this difficulty is related to the concept of financialisation itself (Christophers, 2015; Chapters 1 and 2 in this volume). Part of the literature on the financialisation of labour relations emphasises the deleterious effects of a financialised accumulation regime on workers, expressed in the declining wage share to total income during the last decades (Stockhammer, 2008). The causality channel of financialisation on the declining power of labour and on the labour share is ascribed to the evolution of capitalism in the direction of dominance through the financial sector, the rise of dividends, interest payments and 'shareholder value' management practices (Hein, 2015; Lazonick & O'Sullivan, 2000; Chapters 5 and 10 in this volume). Trade union weakness and labour market deregulation are also taken into account as contributing to the decline of wage share, even if understood as being the result of the described finance-dominated accumulation regime. The financial(ised) motives behind the political drive for governments to embrace labour market reform are ignored.

In her comprehensive review of financialisation, Natasha van der Zwan (2014, p. 107) confirms the focus of the 'ascendancy of the shareholder value orientation' as the main research topic on the relationship between financialisation and labour, dividing it into two streams:

> First, it considers how financial markets exert pressures on nonfinancial corporations, and the managers running them, to adopt business practices promoting shareholder value. Second, it interrogates how these corporations themselves establish shareholder value by diverting financial market pressure onto other constituents of the firm, in particular the employees.

Cushen and Thompson (2016) and Thompson (2013) further elaborate on the impact of financialisation on labour relations by considering two main interrelated channels: (1) the decomposition of capital assets, enabling a stronger monitoring of performance of different capital assets categories, now increasingly dismembered across multiple firms, and thus an enhancement of tightening controls on the labour force involved in each of the different categories (see also Martin, Rafferty & Bryan, 2018); (2) the new corporate governance, aligning the incentives of shareholders and executives, setting objectives from above, which serve to constrain 'appropriate rewards and opportunities to employees, even when they have delivered high performance' (Thompson, 2013, p. 478; see also Chapter 5 in this volume).

Despite its many findings, this literature still operates under a narrow conception of financialisation, understood as a process only present in countries with vibrant stock markets or, more broadly, in countries where debt and equity securities markets are dominant. As discussed in Chapter 1, if the dominance of market-based finance were the main criterion of financialisation, few countries would have undergone such transformations. Specifically, it would necessitate excluding the SE periphery from these systemic changes since stock markets play only a marginal role in their economies due to the relatively small number of listed companies. Even in countries with developed stock markets, such a narrow focus would leave out non-listed corporations, limiting analyses insofar as both listed and non-listed companies face significant pressures (Chapter 5 in this volume).

Further analysis of these shortcomings falls beyond the scope of this chapter. However, presenting a perspective which avoids the potential pitfalls of a narrow conception of financialisation, and which may contribute to furthering greater appreciation of the loss of power by labour relative to capital due to financialisation, is deemed necessary. We seek to build on the concept of financialisation presented in previous chapters of this book, which departs from the approach excessively centred on the 'rise of securities markets', favouring instead the importance of continued, though transformed, roles that banks and bank credit play in the rise of finance. We understand financialisation as being variegated depending on the position and history that each country and its financial sector (bank or market-based) brings with respect to the international economy, but argue that the rise of finance and financial interests and the associated accumulation regime have imposed a new macroeconomic policy paradigm which increasingly takes labour as the major economic policy adjustment variable in order to preserve and foster financial streams of revenues. Driven by financial motives and interests, this regime reduces public policy to regressive labour market reforms while allowing for different timelines and institutional designs in each country. Depending on their size and insertion within the international economy, the role of nation states, and international organisations including the International Monetary Fund (IMF), the European Union and the World Bank, may also vary in terms of institutional vehicles for furthering financialised interests. Policy, particularly labour market reforms, aimed at promoting a model of corporate management favourable to financial interests at the expense of labour is thus the main channel through which finance and labour relations interact.

This type of link between finance and labour is most salient in the SE periphery. Given their structural weaknesses and associated undeveloped capital markets, the construction of the EMU was most significantly about fostering financialisation in the peripheral countries and setting a precedence in the policy agenda of labour market reforms. Early in the process those reforms were perceived as an instrument for counterbalancing the financial strictures of the euro. In this context, the Portuguese experience, along with that of Greece, is of major interest, as these two countries have undergone deep labour market reforms deliberately and explicitly imposed on them (with the consent of their respective governments) by the official European lenders when the eurozone crisis struck in 2010–2011. The Portuguese case is of special relevance since it is now presented as a success story.

## Labour as an adjustment variable in the eurozone

Since the end of the seventies, the major economies have withdrawn from pursuing full employment policies, favouring instead 'sound' macroeconomic policies which would avoid inflation as well as facilitate economic and employment growth (Mitchell & Muysken, 2008). This neoliberal turn of public policy has several causes (economic, political, intellectual, etc.), but the rise of finance and its specific demands must not be ignored as a driving force. Monetary policy, determined by 'independent' central banks, has been oriented towards the preservation of financial value through (low) inflation targeting and light-touch regulation. Fiscal policy, in turn, has privileged low or non-existent public deficits and controlled public debt stocks relative to GDP, assuring financial markets of the solvency of the respective states and implying new forms of control through the almost exclusive role of finance in funding public deficits. Within the setting of the international arena, trade and capital account liberalisation, deeper financial integration and currency internationalisation have subjected economic policy to external monitoring and the respective economies to continuous threats of harsh penalties from financial markets. Any deviation from financial market demands would be paid for dearly in the form of either capital flight, exchange rate instability or inability to roll over public debt.[1]

More saliently than anywhere else in the world, the EU effected the neoliberal turn in its treaties and policies. After having established the single market in 1992, under rules that interdict any form of trade or industrial policy (e.g. through procurement rules or state ownership) and that significantly enhanced the integration of financial services at the European level, the single currency project piled on the pressure for member states to relinquish any control over their economic policy.

The architecture that underpinned the monetary union, established through the Maastricht treaty of 1992, focused on the downward convergence of inflation rates across the EU, understood as a condition for the creation of an independent European Central Bank. The ECB was itself constituted on a mandate that prioritised inflation targeting (below but close to 2 per cent) above any other economic objective. Furthermore, the monetary stability ensured by dis-inflation and nominal interest rates convergence was to be assured through continued fiscal tightening, namely a public deficit under 3 per cent of GDP and public debt level under 60 per cent of GDP. The reasoning behind these targets was that controlled fiscal deficits and public debt would forestall any incentive to monetise deficits or 'overheat' the economy above the 'non-inflationary unemployment rate', thereby appeasing financial markets.

Nonetheless, labour market regulation was until the end of the nineties out-side the scope of EU integration policies, remaining an exclusive prerogative of the individual member states. In the Common Market, European interference in labour issues remained marginal. That changed on the eve of the implemen-tation of the euro in the latter part of the nineties. Facing high unemploy-ment rates that afflicted various European countries at the time, a European Employment Strategy (EES) was introduced in 1997 at the Luxembourg summit (Mosher & Trubek, 2003). The EES presented a number of annual guidelines for each country and introduced financial support for labour market reform in the member states (Goetschly, 1999). This strategy and subsequent regular European employment summits in combination with the introduc-tion of another 'soft power' tool – the open coordination method[2] – directed members towards employment policies focused on 'supply-side' proposals and the associated jargon of 'employability', 'entrepreneurship', 'adaptability' and 'equality' in defining new employment opportunities (Goetschly, 2003). In a context of combined homogeneity and rigidity of macroeconomic public policy, despite uneven economic structures between countries that shared the same currency, labour 'flexibility' emerged as an economic mantra for the attainment of growth and convergence across the whole eurozone. Labour flexibility was understood as a necessity for better adjusting to asymmetric exogenous shocks (Turrini et al., 2014).

The results of the EES were asymmetric, with labour reforms moving along very different timelines within the eurozone. In Germany the Hartz reforms of the mid-nineties produced a complete overhaul of the German labour market, cutting social protection for unemployed workers, introducing a new form of precarious labour contract (the infamous *mini-jobs*) and promoting temporary work and labour outsourcing (Streeck & Trampusch, 2006), while attempts to deregulate labour contracts in France, such as the introduction of the Contrat Premier Embauche (CPE) aimed at workers under the age of 26, was met with fierce resistance by both the student and trade union movements. In the SE per-iphery, liberalising labour market reforms were also introduced, though proving not as profound as in Germany. In Portugal, a major reform expanding the use of fixed-term contracts and eroding collective bargaining schemes was pursued in 2003 (Chapter 6 in this volume; Teles, 2017). Despite varying degrees of successful implementation across member states, the EES did obtain important achievements: namely, it de-linked monetary and fiscal policies from employ-ment targets and subsumed employment policies into macroeconomic policies focused on inflation control.

Economic policy has since focused on ensuring 'flexibility' within labour markets in order to make them better able to adjust to asymmetric economic shocks, such as that caused by the GFC. While originally a domain outside the scope of European institutions, the creation of the EMU and the constraints it created turned the labour market into a highly significant political arena. Even if this was to some degree disguised as EU 'soft policy', EU policy prescriptions were increasingly hardened, culminating in the labour reforms imposed on the SE peripheral countries during 2010–2011 in exchange for EU loans.

## The eurozone crisis and the enforcement of labour market reform

While prior to the GFC the EU lacked the means to enforce labour market reforms upon its member countries, this changed when the eurozone crisis struck in 2010. Ignoring the origins of the GFC and the flaws in the architecture of the monetary union, European institutions chose instead to blame national governments and peoples, specifically those of the SE periphery, for the crisis. Two main criticisms were levelled against them: the first, was the fiscal profligacy of their governments, and the second, their wage levels compared to those registered in the North of Europe. The rise of nominal unit labour costs and consequent reduction in competitiveness were taken as the main causes of the macroeconomic imbalances and the over-indebtedness problems in the peripheral zone. Such reasoning was presented by Mario Draghi, the ECB president, in 2013, when he stated that the divergence between productivity and wages in the SE periphery was caused by overly protective labour market arrangements. Indebtedness and financial fragility of the European peripheral countries was thus attributed to the structural rigidity of labour relations. Yet, this kind of analysis compares productivity, a variable discounting inflation, with wages in nominal terms. While in Portugal real wages had been aligned with productivity growth since the creation of the euro (Reis et al., 2014), Germany went through wage growth below that of productivity growth (Lapavitsas et al., 2012), but the divergent unit labour costs can be mostly attributed to different inflation rates within the eurozone, a variable supposedly controlled by the ECB.

In the final analysis, with blame being attributed to labour costs and government fiscal irresponsibility, the behaviour of financial agents and the serving of financial interests were both acquitted as key drivers of the crisis. The role of Northern European banks in fuelling SE periphery indebtedness and the aftershock effects of a public 'bailout' of the financial sector on public deficits were ignored. European policy was to be conducted to protect debt-exposed European banks, imposing austerity across the eurozone as a necessary cost to help meet debt repayments in full in an improvised new official financial architecture which now included the *European Stability Fund Facility* and later the *European Stability Mechanism*, aimed at avoiding any debt defaults. At the same time, while providing a battery of policy tools to support European banks –from the *Securities Market Program* to *Long Term Refinancing Operations* – the ECB avoided any monetary relief to eurozone member states until the integrity of the eurozone itself was put at risk in 2012.

SE peripheral countries, such as Portugal and Greece, were forced to request official 'bailout' loans from the EU institutions and the International Monetary Fund. The loans were subject to strong political conditionality, with the countries putting in requests being forced to sign a 'Memorandum of Understanding' with the so-called Troika (European Commission, ECB and IMF) in charge of monitoring the process. Greece's and Portugal's Memoranda were comprehensive policy documents, with a wide range of sectoral policies to be enforced, but with labour market reform at the top of the agenda. Other peripheral countries subject to rising interest rates on their sovereign bonds and with broken banking systems as, for instance, Italy and Spain, suffered EU pressure through more 'informal' channels, such as letters from the ECB to their national leaders (Berlusconi and Zapatero, respectively), explicitly demanding labour market reforms. Either through harsher and more direct means or through softer and more informal means, the SE peripheral countries endured increasing demands for labour market reform involving the dismantling of collective bargaining arrangements at national and sectoral levels, and the fostering of firm-level negotiations that enfeebled trade union power and enhanced greater wage 'flexibility' (Chapter 6 in this volume).

For the EU, only the (downward) flexibility of wages could readjust national economies on a path towards stability within the monetary union. This preference is clearly confirmed by Yannis Varoufakis (2017, p. 200), former Greek finance minister, in his memoir *Adults in the Room* in which he reports a brief exchange between the Italian finance minister and Wolfgang Schäuble:

> Pier Carlo said that he had asked Schäuble to tell him the one thing he could do to win his confidence. That turned out to be 'labour market reform' – code for weakening workers' rights, allowing companies to fire them more easily with little or no compensation and to hire people on lower pay with fewer protections. Once Pier Carlo had passed appropriate legislation through Italy's parliament, at significant political cost to the Renzi government, the German finance minister went easy on him.

The internal devaluation which has now taken place in the euro area as a stated policy aim is, in fact, the resurrection of an old idea (Petroulakis, 2017). The origins go back to the intentional deflation of nominal wages meant to correct current account negative imbalances implemented specifically in peripheral countries under the gold standard (O'Rourke & Taylor, 2013). More recent episodes, though still prior to the introduction of the euro, include the 'competitive disinflation policy' adopted in France in the 1980s (Uxó, Paúl & Febrero, 2014). The same authors (O'Rourke & Taylor, 2013; Uxó, Paúl & Febrero, 2014) have isolated the main theoretical foundation for the resurrection of internal devaluation in Optimum Currency Area Theory. According to this theory, in a currency area where states have surrendered their ability to use monetary and exchange policies, in which a central fiscal authority is absent as well as a common budget that may alleviate the consequences of adverse shocks through transfers, wage and price flexibility, together with labour mobility, are supposed to operate the external balance adjustment.

Despite its distant origins, the term 'internal devaluation' was coined as recently as the 1990s in connection with the debates in Sweden and Finland on euro accession. Since then, the idea has gained ground to the point of becoming one of the main components of the Troika toolkit in the SE periphery adjustment programmes.

In Portugal, the idea of an internal-devaluation-based adjustment process was presented even before the GFC in an influential paper by Olivier Blanchard published in 2007. In this paper, Blanchard, who would come to co-preside as IMF chief economist during the Troika intervention in Portugal, advocated 'competitive disinflation' as a means of addressing a considerable current account deficit coupled with a similarly large budget deficit and low GDP and productivity growth which, in his view, were the result of a previous 'investment boom' triggered in the second half of the nineties 'by the commitment by Portugal to join the euro' and the resulting 'drop in interest rates and expectations of faster growth' (Blanchard, 2007, p. 2).

Blanchard explored the policy options available in this context for Portugal alongside other euro area countries in similar situations. In his view, the Portuguese problem, whose symptom was the large current account deficit, was one of competitiveness, with only two remedial options available. The first (and most attractive) was to achieve a sustained increase in productivity growth. The second (considered less attractive) was 'lower nominal wage growth', or rather, given the context of low wage inflation in Portugal and the EU, 'a large decrease in the nominal wage' (Blanchard, 2007, p. 2). Since the more attractive alternative for Blanchard was simply not available because productivity growth was unlikely to increase overnight, the faster, and less painful, track left open was to 'achieve a decrease in nominal wages – without relying on unemployment to do the job over time' (Blanchard, 2007, p. 8).

Blanchard then concentrated his efforts on the means by which to decrease nominal wages with the least possible cost in terms of unemployment. Noting that currency devaluation was blocked by Portugal's membership in the euro, he stated that 'the same result can be achieved …, at least on paper, through a decrease in the nominal wage and the price of non-tradables, while the price of tradables remains the same'. This would require 'coordinated decreases in nominal wages' (Blanchard, 2007, p. 15). The workers should understand that 'the adjustment of wages has to come sooner or later if competitiveness is to be improved', that 'coordinated wage adjustments … can decrease the unemployment cost of the adjustment', and that, given that tradable prices remain unchanged and that non-tradable prices are set by a mark-up on wage costs, 'any decrease in nominal wages implies a smaller decrease in real consumption wages' (Blanchard, 2007, p. 16). Blanchard was not very specific on which policy tools should be mobilised to achieve nominal wage devaluation. Implicit, however, was a thorough reform of the institutions regulating employment protection. The 'Portuguese labor market', Blanchard wrote, 'is dysfunctional', and 'the main cause appears to be the high degree of employment protection' (Blanchard, 2007, p. 14).

Blanchard's paper suggests that the rationale for the 'adjustment within the euro', which was to be enacted from 2010 on in the EU peripheral countries, was well developed within the IMF even before the crisis (Caldas, 2015). However, internal devaluation was only fully implemented in Portugal in 2010 to 2011 in the context of a series of Programs of Stability and Growth (PECs) adopted by the Portuguese government in response to EU pressures. The Troika bailout extended and accelerated the process. In 2011, the Staff Report included in the IMF Country Report *Portugal: Request for a Three-Year Arrangement under the Extended Fund Facility* echoed, to some extent, though in a more ruthless tone, Blanchard's analysis:

> Restoring competitiveness in a currency union will undoubtedly be challenging. With no recourse to changing the exchange rate, the key question is whether the Government will succeed in reducing the external deficit through productivity boosting reforms that make the economy more competitive at current wage levels. If it fails, membership of the Euro Zone means that the economy will instead be forced to rebalance through a deep recession, including through a painful adjustment in nominal wages as unemployment surges.
>
> (IMF, 2011a, p. 25)

Measures aimed at internal devaluation in the Memorandum included (a) reducing severance payments for all new contracts; (b) reducing the maximum duration for unemployment insurance benefits and unemployment benefits; (c) freezing any increase in the minimum wage; (d) reducing compensation and pay for overtime hours; (e) limiting the extension of collective agreements; and (f) promoting negotiation at the firm level. Other measures on fiscal consolidation also converged to produce an internal devaluation, namely: (a) a 5 per cent average cut in public sector wages, followed by a freeze on pensions alongside a special contribution levied on pensions above 1,500 euros; and (b) new means-testing procedures for social security non-contributory benefits (IMF, 2011b). These measures, as highlighted by Campos Lima (Chapter 6 in this volume), were not only faithfully implemented but backed up by other measures aimed at speeding up internal devaluation.

Presently, eight years down the line, the consequences of internal devaluation in the SE euro area countries – Portugal included – have materialised and are open to assessment. Two lines of criticism have come to the fore, both converging on the claim that the pass-through of the lower labour costs to export prices was imperfect. The first, exemplified by a recent ECB study

(Petroulakis, 2017), states that this is due mostly to 'trade costs', implying a lower relative reduction of export prices to domestic prices. In all the countries considered in this study – Greece, Italy, Portugal, Spain and Ireland – internal devaluation achieved the goal of reducing the current account deficit. However, in the case of Greece, unlike in the other countries, this result was obtained through a steep fall in imports, rather than enhancement of exports, arguably due to the special relevance of trade costs in this country. The second line of assessment criticising internal devaluation (Uxó, Paúl & Febrero, 2014) attributes the imperfection of the pass-through of the lower labour costs to an increase in profit margins.

However, our assessment of internal devaluation in Portugal in the next section takes on board, not the issue of pass-through mechanisms, but rather the distributive effects of devaluation and its long-term effects on the development path. Drawing on ongoing research on this topic, we adopt a sectoral approach that highlights the effects of devaluation on the structure of the Portuguese economy and its consequences.

## Internal devaluation and its persistent effects

The adjustment programme in Portugal delivered its main stated goal. The external deficit, which had reached almost 10 per cent of GDP in 2008, was eliminated by 2013 (see Figure 7.1). This was achieved between 2010 and 2013 through a combined boost in exports and reduction in imports. In the subsequent years, exports and imports grew simultaneously, preserving the external

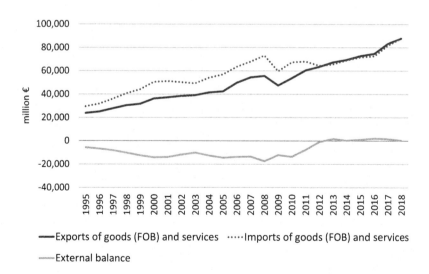

*Figure 7.1* Imports, exports and external balance (current prices), 1995–2018
Source: INE

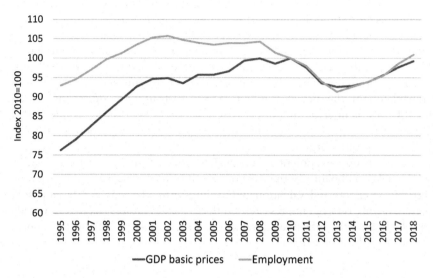

*Figure 7.2* Real GDP and employment, 1995–2018
Source: INE

balance, while more recently (2016–2018) imports have grown marginally faster than exports.

Over the same time period, GDP and employment suffered major contractions until 2013, at which point a sustained recovery can be seen to have taken place (see Figure 7.2). Real average wages had begun to drop markedly by 2010 while a paradoxical increase in productivity, combined with real wage deflation, resulted in a steep decline of the labour share lasting beyond 2013. Despite the recovery initiated that same year, real average wages decreased further until 2015 and have remained virtually stagnant since then. Productivity has decreased, while the labour share has improved marginally, mostly due to the decrease of average productivity. This suggests a persistence of the effects of internal devaluation beyond the adjustment period, despite the recovery of employment and the reduction of unemployment; a persistence which has seen average wages and labour share stagnate, combined with a decline in productivity (see Figure 7.3).[3] Such persistent effects call for an explanation.

A sectoral approach based on a shift-share analysis of all major sectors (excluding agriculture[4]) is appropriate in analysing internal devaluation and its persistent effects with respect to wages, productivity and the labour share. This allows for the decomposition of variations of the variable of interest in a given time period into (a) effects taking place within sectors – namely, shift effects; and (b) effects resulting from structural change – share or static structural effects. A third component – covariance or dynamic structural effect – which is usually small, is discarded in the analysis (for details, see Annex 1).

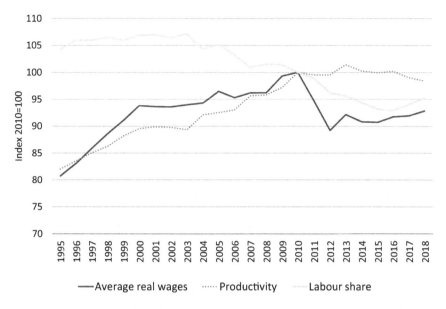

*Figure 7.3* Wage, labour share and productivity, 1995–2018
Source: INE

The shift-share analysis relies on data from the National Accounts. Since at the time of writing this chapter the available sectoral data only extended to 2016, the overall period considered has been restricted to 2010–2016 and decomposed into two sub-periods: 2010–2013 (employment and GDP contraction) and 2013–2016 (employment and GDP recovery).

### Wages, productivity, and labour share: a shift-share decomposition

Between 2010 and 2013, real average wages[5] (excluding the agricultural sector) decreased 7.7 per cent. Intra-sectoral (shift) effects alone would have registered a larger decrease of 8.6 per cent. However, the intra-sectoral effect was countered by a smaller inter-sectoral effect of 1.2 per cent. The co-variance term is negative but residual (see Figure 7.4).

During this period – the peak of the 'adjustment' – wage deflation cut across all sectors (except for 'B – mining'). The sectoral decomposition of effects in Figures 7.5 and 7.6 highlights the sectors making a larger contribution to the overall real wage deflation. The sectors that contributed the most to shift (within-sector) effects were 'Q – public administration', 'P – education' and 'Q – human health and social work' – all three carrying considerable weight within the employment structure as well as being related to social reproductive activities (Chapter 8 in this volume).[6] With respect to share (inter-sector)

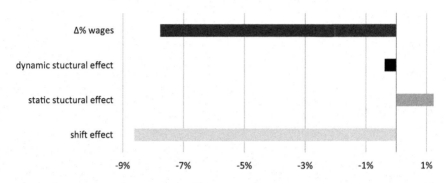

*Figure 7.4* Shift-share decomposition for real wages, 2010–2013

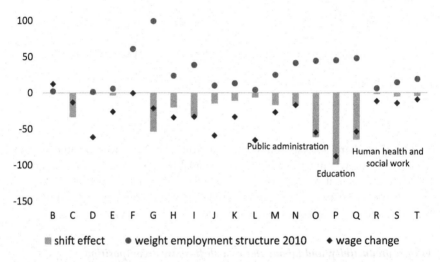

*Figure 7.5* Sectoral shift effects for wages, 2010–2013

effects, 'F – construction' provided a large positive contribution to the evolution of the average wage. This is because this sector, with wages below the mean and having carried considerable weight within the employment structure, has, due to the crisis and the adjustment, reduced its weight within the structure.

In the same period, productivity increased in annual terms by 2.4 per cent. It is important to note that the overall increase in productivity is due not to a rise in Gross Value Added (GVA) greater than that in employment growth but rather to a decrease in employment greater than the decrease in GVA (except in 'G – the wholesale and retail trade', where GVA slightly increased and employment decreased, and 'S – other service activities', where GVA increased more than employment; see Figure 7.7). 'F – construction' stands out in terms of

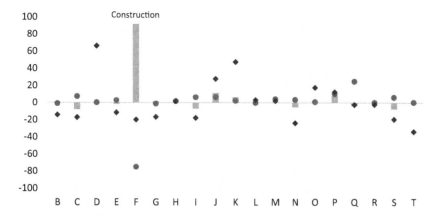

share effect ● change of weight in employment structure ◆ distance from mean wage

*Figure 7.6* Sectoral share effects for wages, 2010–2013

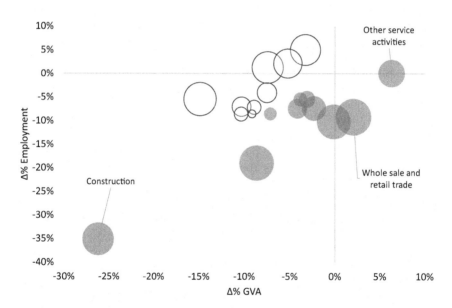

*Figure 7.7* Percentage variation in Gross Value Added, employment, productivity (as shown by diameters of shaded (positive) and unshaded (negative) balloons) and sectoral share effects for wages, 2010–2013

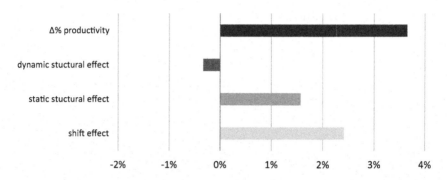

*Figure 7.8* Shift–share decomposition for productivity, 2010–2013

sector contribution to this type of (paradoxical) productivity enhancement during this period.

With respect to productivity during the 2010–2013 period, shift and share effects were both positive and of similar values (see Figure 7.8), mainly due to the contribution of two sectors – 'G – wholesale and retail trade' and 'F – construction'. 'G –Wholesale and retail trade', a sector carrying considerable weight within the employment structure, stagnated with respect to GVA and lost a significant number of jobs, giving rise to an important positive shift contribution to the overall productivity. Part of this positive shift effect was countered by 'K – financial and insurance services', in which a fall in productivity was pronounced. 'F – construction', with productivity below the mean, lost weight within the employment structure, giving rise to a positive share contribution (see Figures 7.9 and 7.10).

Because of the combined changes in wages and productivity, the overall labour share lost 2.9 percentage points between 2010 and 2013. As pictured in Figure 7.11, the variation of the labour share reflects the predominance of negative variations within sectors. The overall variation was, for the most part, negatively affected by the increase in 'productivity' of 'L– real estate' and, in positive terms, by the decline of productivity (greater than nominal wage increase) in 'K – financial and insurance activities'.

During the 2013–2016 period, real wages fell by a lesser amount of 0.39 per cent. However, this negative variation was propelled, not by processes taking place within sectors, but by a structural change. The shift (within-sector) effect was positive (0.27 per cent), while the share effect was negative (-0.75 per cent); see Figure 7.12. As shown in Figure 7.13, which depicts shift effects, positive contributions to the variation of wages in sectors carrying a significant weight in the employment structure, as with 'C – manufacturing' and 'G – the wholesale and retail trade', were compensated by shift effects in the opposite direction in 'K – financial and insurance activities' and 'O – public administration'.

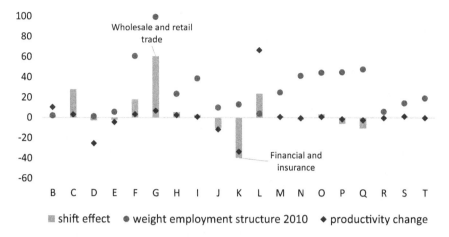

*Figure 7.9* Sectoral shift effects for productivity, 2010–2013

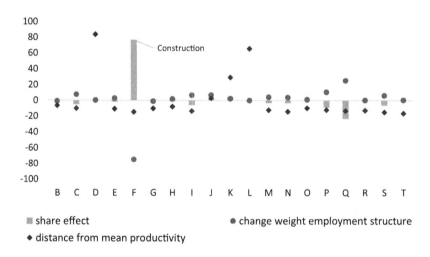

*Figure 7.10* Sectoral share effects for productivity, 2010–2013

The negative share effect, significant during this period, was in turn propelled, on the one hand, by the reinforcement in the employment structure of sectors with wages below the mean, namely, 'I – accommodation and food services' and 'N – administrative and support services', and, on the other, by the demise of one of the sectors with wages above the mean, namely, 'K – financial and insurance activities' (see Figure 7.14).

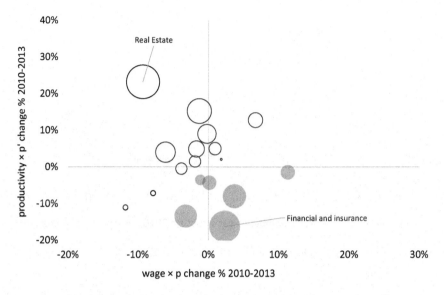

*Figure 7.11* Variation of wages and productivity adjusted by relative prices and variation of sectoral labour share, 2010–2013 (as shown by diameters of shaded (positive) and unshaded (negative) balloons)

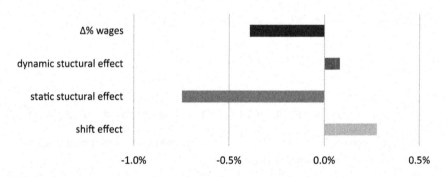

*Figure 7.12* Shift-share decomposition for real wages, 2013–2016

With respect to aggregated productivity, a significant decline of 3.7 per cent took place during this period with shift effects accounting overwhelmingly of this negative variation (see Figure 7.15). The share effect is negative but minimal.

However, the predominance of shift (within-sector) effects over structural effects with respect to productivity may be misleading. Regarding shift effects, it is important to note that the overall negative sign results from the marked

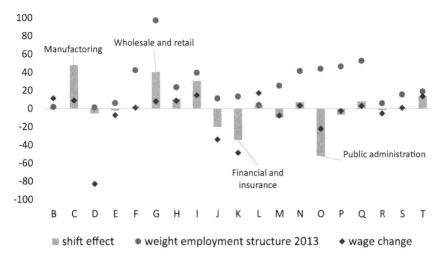

*Figure 7.13* Sectoral shift effects for wages, 2013–2016

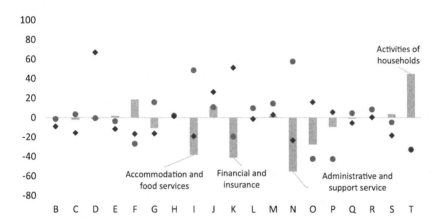

*Figure 7.14* Sectoral share effects for wages, 2013–2016

negative contributions of two sectors, namely, 'K – financial and insurance activities' and 'L – real estate' in a setting of (within-sector) stagnant productivity. While the negative productivity change in the financial sector was determined by the decline in GVA, the same effect in real estate was mostly the result of an expansion of employment in the sector (see Figure 7.16).

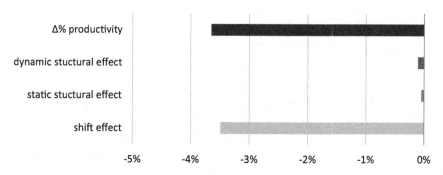

*Figure 7.15* Shift-share decomposition of productivity, 2010–2016

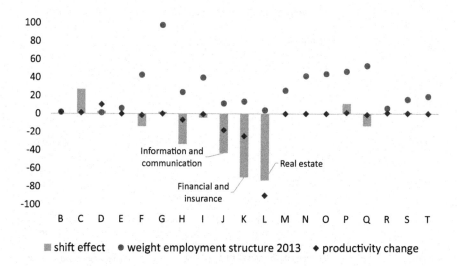

*Figure 7.16* Sectoral shift effects for productivity, 2013–2016

Conversely, the irrelevance of the overall share effect is the result of the large positive share effect of real estate – a sector with a very low weight within the employment structure but registering a large contribution to GVA. The reinforcement of the weight in the employment structure for this sector, with 'productivity' largely above the mean, compensated for negative variation stemming from the large-scale reinforcement of weight of sectors emerging as large-scale employers in this period, namely, 'I – Accommodation and food services' and 'N – Administrative and support services'. If real estate is excluded from the shift-share analysis, the negative shift effect would be lower and the structural negative effect much higher (see Figure 7.17).

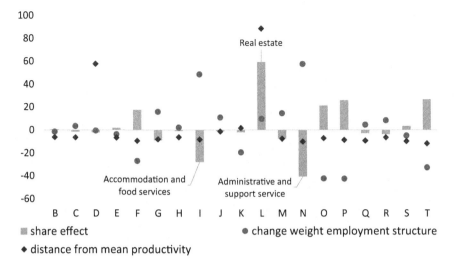

*Figure 7.17* Sectoral share effects for productivity, 2013–2016

Over this period the aggregated labour share fell 0.65 percentage points. However, the small scale of this negative variation is once again mostly determined by the positive contribution of real estate, whose 'productivity' decline made a considerable positive contribution to the aggregate labour share. On the other hand, 'G – electricity, gas, steam and air conditioning supply' made a strong negative contribution due to the combined large-scale increase in productivity and decrease in average wages (see Figure 7.18).

To sum up, during the 2010–2013 period, changes in aggregated real wages, productivity and labour share were dominated by processes taking place within sectors. Negative shift effects with respect to wages were mainly propelled by cutbacks on compensation for civil servants and counteracted by the retrenchment of one large-scale low-pay employer – 'F – construction'. The increase in productivity in this period is merely apparent, since it originated mostly from employment retrenchment, not from growth in GVA.

Conversely, in the subsequent 2013–2016 period, processes of structural change converged with within-sector processes to preclude the revalorisation of real average wages and productivity enhancement, leading to the persistence of a depressed labour share. The main drivers of structural change during this period were four sectors: (a) two low-pay/low-productivity sectors associated with tourism – 'I – accommodation and food services' and 'N – administrative and support services' – which, by increasing weight in the employment structure, drove average wages and productivity down; (b) two high-pay/high-productivity sectors, namely, 'K – financial and insurance activities' and 'L – real estate', the first losing weight in the employment structure and driving average

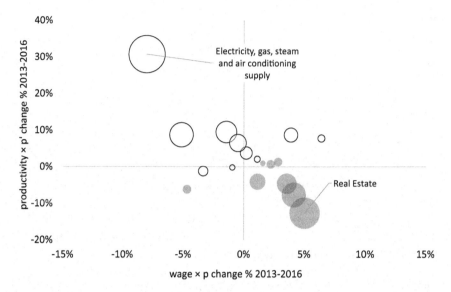

*Figure 7.18* Variation of wages and productivity adjusted by relative prices and variation
of sectoral labour share, 2013–2016 (as shown by diameters of shaded (positive) balloons, unshaded (negative) balloons)

wages down, the second, reinforcing weight in the employment structure and
obfuscating the general trend to productivity decline.

A structural change concomitant with internal devaluation occurred in
the Portuguese economy, which biased the employment structure and GVA
towards low-pay (and low-productivity) sectors, accounting for the persistent
stagnation of real wages, productivity and labour share despite the recovery of
employment and GDP (see Figures 7.19 and 7.20 below).

More recent developments, beyond 2016, seem to confirm the persistence
of the effects of internal devaluation. Sectoral data available for 2017 confirms
that the bulk of job creation throughout the year (71 per cent) took place in
low-wage/low-productivity sectors (see Figure 7.21).

### Other neglected aspects of internal devaluation

Concomitant with its impact on the employment structure and GVA accounting
for the persistence of wage deflation, stagnant productivity and depressed labour
share beyond the 'adjustment' period, internal devaluation has put in motion
other processes weighing down on prospects for future recuperation which
deserve consideration.

The first of these processes is demographic. In the case of Portugal, the combination of mass unemployment with wage deflation led to a 3.5 per cent fall in
active population numbers between 2011 and 2016 (see Figure 7.22). This decline,

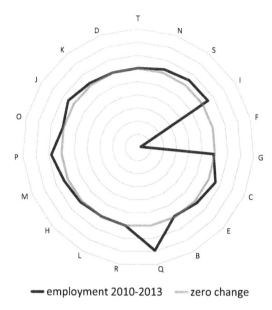

*Figure 7.19a* Sectors arranged from N (low-wage) to T (high-wage), change of weight in the employment structure, 2010–2013

Source: INE

*Figure 7.19b* Sectors arranged from N (low-wage) to T (high-wage), change of weight in the employment structure, 2013–2016

Source: INE

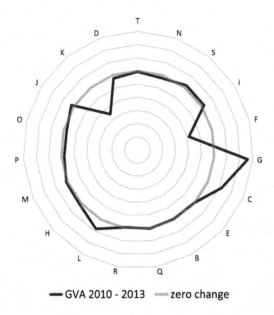

*Figure 7.20a* Sectors arranged from N (low-wage) to T (high-wage), change of weight
in the Gross Value Added structure, 2010–2013

Source: INE

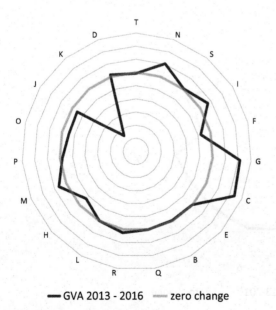

*Figure 7.20b* Sectors arranged from N (low-wage) to T (high-wage), change of weight
in the Gross Value Added structure, 2013–2016

Source: INE

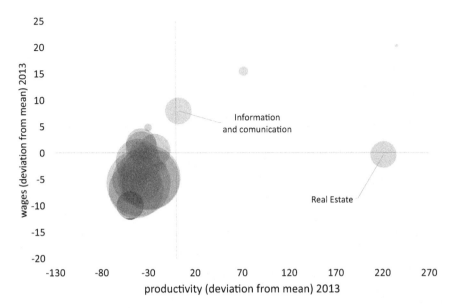

*Figure 7.21* Distribution of job creation across sectors, 2017 (the area of the balloons represents employment creation)

Source: INE

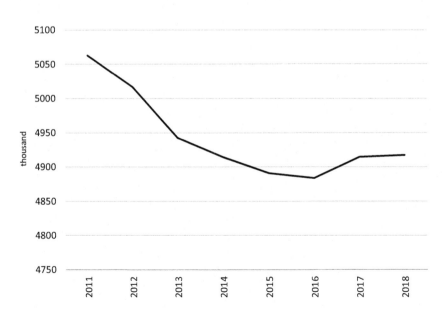

*Figure 7.22* Active population (20- to 64-year-olds), 2011–2018

Source: INE

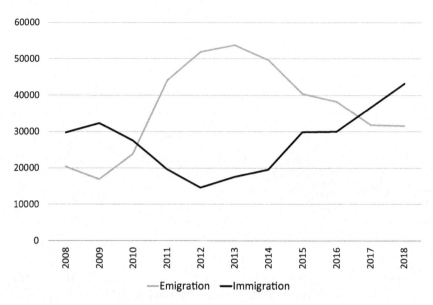

*Figure 7.23* Permanent immigration and emigration, 2008–2018
Source: INE

due to an inversion of previously positive migration flows, was followed by a slight recovery in response to a new reversal of the sign of migration flows initiated in 2016. Nonetheless, despite the recovery of employment, emigration in 2017 and 2018 remained above the threshold prior to the adjustment (see Figure 7.23). This may be partially due to the widening of wage differentials within the EU during and after the adjustment. Given an absence of increased productivity, this decline in the active population, difficult to reverse in the context of protracted wage deflation, weighs down on the prospect of future GDP growth.

The second point to consider is that conditions for productivity growth have also been depleted by the adjustment. Between 2010 and 2016, investment (Gross Fixed Capital Formation) decreased 23 per cent in nominal terms. Moreover, its sectoral distribution changed markedly, biasing the structure in favour of expanding low-wage, low-productivity sectors. Between 2013 and 2016, with the anomalous exception of 'L – real estate', those sectors increasing weight in the investment structure were low-wage ones, specifically 'N – administrative and support service activities', 'I – accommodation and food service activities', 'G – wholesale and retail trade' and 'C – manufacturing' (see Figure 7.24). Since these sectors, with the exception of 'C – manufacturing', are also low-productivity and low-productivity-growth sectors, the prospects for a productivity-led push forward are bleak.

A third aspect worthy of investigation is the changes in channels of financing within the Portuguese economy. During the GFC, the eurozone crisis

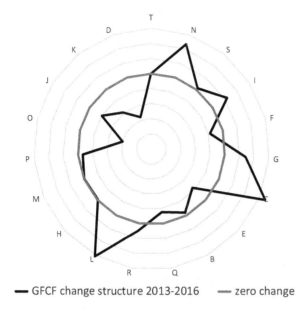

*Figure 7.24* Sectors arranged from N (low-wage) to T (high-wage), change of weight in the investment structure, 2013–2016

Source: INE

and the subsequent adjustment, bank-mediated capital flows (under the form of credit) seem to have been partially replaced first by official lending, and subsequently by the outright alienation of assets to non-residents. This is most salient in the case of privatisations and bank bailouts that took place during the adjustment and, more recently, in the real estate boom presently underway, which is fed mainly by capital flows from non-resident real estate funds and individuals. To the extent that the acquisition of assets by non-residents will increase outward flows of capital as a future counterpart, such a shift in the regime of financing the economy may also converge cumulatively in Portugal to preclude a full recovery from the crisis.

### *The cumulative (and potentially circular) mechanisms of internal devaluation*

Internal devaluation in Portugal, albeit effective in terms of rebalancing the current account, served financial interests while triggering a regressive process of structural change leading to the stagnation of real wages, productivity and labour share. The stylised features of this process are as follows:

(1) Internal devaluation in the context of massive unemployment has impacted across all sectors.

(2) While low-pay/low-productivity labour-intensive sectors producing for the internal markets have failed to benefit from devaluation due to its detrimental effects on internal demand, sectors exposed to external demand (mainly those linked with tourism, in the case of Portugal) have been able to absorb an impressive proportion of the labour market 'slack' at low-wage levels.

(3) Exports have grown more than imports (due to the reduced imported content of these exports and the compression of internal demand).

(4) Driven by external demand targeted at labour-intensive sectors, overall GDP and employment have responded positively. Employment is being created mostly in the expanding low-pay/low-productivity sector and a decline in unemployment has served to feed a mitigated expansion of internal demand.

(5) Due to the combined effect of emigration and less unemployment, nominal wages tend to increase, affecting costs and returns in the emergent low-wage, labour-intensive, tradable sectors.

(6) Wage revaluation and absence of productivity enhancement will either deplete capital margins in the emergent labour-intensive export-oriented sectors or drive supply prices up, thereby eroding the price competitiveness of these sectors. The balance of current accounts tilts towards a new deficit.

(7) A closing of the circular loop is brought about through mounting pressure for internal devaluation stemming from the labour-intensive export sector and external creditors.

## Conclusions

This chapter has argued that financialisation in the Southern European periphery is crucial to explaining how internal devaluation became a preferred policy instrument of economic adjustment in the context of the GFC and the eurozone crisis. Departing from the financialisation literature on labour, which focuses on the short-term behaviour of listed corporations towards their workforce in the context of financial dominance and myopic shareholder value, we argue instead that financialisation among the peripheral countries impinged first and foremost on them in the form of a new macroeconomic policy regime aimed at preserving financial value and interests by making labour the main adjustment variable to 'asymmetric shocks'.

The effects of this new macroeconomic regime on labour have taken on a dual character. On the one hand, worker vulnerability has risen due to the externally imposed 'internal devaluation' guided by labour reform. On the other hand, the structural change that this process has brought about in the Portuguese economy in recent years has led to the prevalence of sectors characterised by low-productivity and low-pay employment, thus further raising the social vulnerability of the workforce. This structural change reflects, not only the post-Troika adjustment policies, but also a new outlook on how the Portuguese economy is now integrated in international financial markets. Rather than through inter-bank credit flows from other European countries, it has now become a recipient of investment funds in real estate, searching for yield in a low-interest-rate environment, by taking advantage of (and fostering) the booming touristic sector and the relative low prices of Portuguese assets brought on by the crisis.

Internal devaluation came to the fore in the context of the GFC as the structural policy needed to restore competitiveness and redress the external imbalances in the SE periphery. The EU, which previously lacked the coercive powers to enforce recessive labour market reforms, seized an opportunity to advance its long-standing flexibilisation agenda through the conditionality of the Troika. In Portugal, internal devaluation and fiscal austerity delivered their stated main goals – the rebalancing of the government's budget alongside the external accounts. When austerity relaxed, there was a degree of recovery in employment and GDP. However, this recovery still lags behind the pre-adjustment levels of real wages, productivity and labour share. In exhibiting a path typical of hysteresis processes, these variables remain stagnated below previous thresholds.

This suggests that the (regressive) adjustment process in the 2010–2013 period has triggered a cumulative (and potentially circular) regressive process, deepening the peripheral condition of Portugal within the EU. Researching the regressive adjustment process from a sectoral perspective, we found that reductions in real wages, productivity and labour share, which were determined between 2010 and 2013 by processes taking place within sectors, gave rise, during the subsequent 2013–2016 period, to processes of structural change which converged with within-sector processes to preclude revalorisation of real average wages and productivity enhancement, leading to the persistence of a depressed labour share.

We may therefore conclude that a structural change process, concomitant with internal devaluation, occurred in the Portuguese economy, one which biased the employment structure and GVA towards low-pay (and low-productivity) sectors, thus accounting for the persistent stagnation of real wages, productivity and the labour share. Addressing the mechanisms prone to producing this structural reconfiguration leads to the conjecture that the reversal of the regressive processes put in motion by internal devaluation may be hard to achieve (being cumulative and potentially circular). In a political economy tilted towards the 'export' of low-cost (low-pay) services and real estate assets, the vested interests entrenched in the low-cost export sector will not be isolated in trying their utmost to block progressive labour market reforms (and urban planning), but they will seek out legitimacy in claiming that a new imbalance of external accounts, a profit margins squeeze and an upsurge in unemployment will arise should a wage recovery be permitted to take place.

Difficult as it may be to reverse, the cumulative process of wage, productivity and labour share decline put in motion by the regressive internal devaluation adjustment is jeopardising prospects for the Portuguese economy and society. Demographic decline, dilapidation of the productive potential of fixed capital, and reliance on investment funds feeding a real estate bubble are all symptoms of a disease difficult to cure, at least within the present financialised policy strictures of the euro. In light of this, claiming success for the Portuguese adjustment that has taken place must, at the very least, be viewed as an exaggeration.

## Acknowledgements

This research was partially financed by Portuguese funds through FCT – *Fundação para a Ciência e a Tecnologia* – in the framework of project no. 028811, 'REVAL – From internal devaluation to the revaluation of work: the case of Portugal'. Reference: PTDC/SOC-SOC/28811/2017.

## Annex 1: labour income and shift-share decomposition

### (a) Estimating labour income

Labour income may be estimated from data in National Accounts by adjusting the aggregated or sectoral compensation of employees (AcE) as follows:

$$AcE = \frac{compensation\ of\ employees}{employees} \times employment$$

This includes the income of both dependent and independent workers in labour income by assuming that the average income from the labour of independent workers is the same as the average compensation of employees in each sector, or in the economy as a whole. In Portugal, given pluri-activity in the rural areas, this assumption leads to large distortions of labour income in the case of agriculture, and of the overall labour share. The analysis included here therefore excludes agriculture.

### (b) Computing labour share, average wages and productivity

Once labour income is estimated for all sectors, the sectoral labour shares – $LS_i$ – are computed as:

$$LS_i = \frac{AcE_i}{GVA_i}$$

and the aggregated labour share – $LS_T$ – as:

$$LS_T = \frac{\sum_{i=1}^{n} AcE_i}{\sum_{i=1}^{n} GVA_i}$$

Note that the labour-share, expressed in nominal terms as $LS = \dfrac{AcE}{GVA}$, may also be written as $LS = \dfrac{w \times l}{GVA}$, where $w$ is the average nominal remuneration of labour and $l$, employment. Dividing by $l$ dividend and divider, we get $LS = \dfrac{w}{\frac{GVA}{l}}$, or $\dfrac{real\ average\ wage \times p}{labor\ productivity \times p'}$, with $p$ denoting the consumer price index and $p'$ the deflator of GVA.

This means that (leaving aside relative price fluctuations) the analysis of the dynamics of the labour share may be decomposed into an analysis of the dynamics of real wages and of the dynamics of labour productivity. When real wages grow faster (or decrease less) than productivity, the labour share will increase. Conversely, when real wages grow less or decrease more than productivity, the labour share will decline.

$$\text{Real wages are computed as } w_i = \frac{AcE_i}{l_i} \times \frac{1}{p} \text{ and productivity as } \pi_i = \frac{GVA_i}{l_i}.$$

### (c) Shift-share equations and analysis

Real wages and productivity may vary as a result either of changes taking place within sectors or of a change in the employment structure. By decomposing the dynamics of real wages and productivity with a shift-share analysis, we separate intra-sector effects (shift effects) on those variables from inter-sector effects (share effects), allowing for the assessment of both types of effects on the overall evolution of wages, productivity and thus labour share. The shift-share decomposition of real wages and productivity relies on the following arithmetic expressions.

### (i) For real wages

$$\Delta w = \underbrace{\sum_{i}^{n} \Delta w_i \times l_{i0}}_{\text{shift effect}} + \underbrace{\sum_{i}^{n} (w_{i0} - w_{T0}) \times \Delta l_i}_{\substack{\text{share effect} \\ \text{(static structural effect)}}} + \underbrace{\sum_{i}^{n} \Delta w_i \times \Delta l_i}_{\substack{\text{covariance effect} \\ \text{(dynamic strutural effect)}}}$$

where $\Delta w$ is the variation of the aggregated average wage in the period of analysis (between time 0 and time t), $\Delta w_i$ is the variation between 0 and t of the average wage within each sector, $l_{i0}$ is the weight in the employment structure for each sector at time 0, $\left(w_{i0} - w_{T0}\right)$ is the deviation of the wage for each sector from the mean of all sectors at time 0, and $\Delta l_i$ is the variation between 0 and t of the weight in the employment structure of the same sector.

*(ii)  For productivity*

$$\Delta \pi = \underbrace{\sum_i^n \Delta \pi_i \times l_{i0}}_{\text{shift effect}} + \underbrace{\sum_i^n \left(\pi_{i0} - \pi_{T0}\right) \times \Delta l_i}_{\substack{\text{share effect} \\ (\text{static structural effect})}} + \underbrace{\sum_i^n \Delta \pi_i \times \Delta l_i}_{\substack{\text{covariance effect} \\ (\text{dynamic strutural effect})}}$$

where $\Delta \pi$ is the variation of the aggregated average productivity for the period of analysis, $\Delta \pi_i$ is the variation of the average productivity for each sector, $l_{i0}$ is the weight in the employment structure for each sector at time 0, $\left(\pi_{i0} - \pi_{T0}\right)$ is the deviation of the productivity for each sector from the mean of all sectors at time 0, and $\Delta l_i$ is the variation of the weight in the employment structure for each sector.

The overall shift effect quantifies the contribution of within-sector effects to the variation of the aggregated wage (or productivity). For each sector the contribution to the overall shift effect is positive if the variation of the average wage (or productivity) is positive, and vice versa in the case of a negative.

The overall share effect quantifies the effects on the aggregated average wage (or productivity) for changes in the employment structure. A sector with wages (or productivity) below the mean at time 0 contributes negatively to the share effect when its weight in the employment structure increases and contributes positively to this effect when its weight decreases. Conversely, a sector with wages above the mean contributes negatively to the share effect when its weight decreases and contributes positively when its weight increases.

The dynamic structural effect (or covariance effect), usually residual, is positive when both positive or both negative correlated variations of wages (or productivity) and weight in structure predominate over uncorrelated variations. Otherwise it is negative.

On a final note, the shift-share equation (for the average wage in this case) is usually given as:

(i)

$$\Delta w = \underbrace{\sum_i^n \Delta w_i \times l_{i0}}_{\text{shift effect}} + \underbrace{\sum_i^n w_{i0} \times \Delta l_i}_{\substack{\text{share effect} \\ (\text{static structural effect})}} + \underbrace{\sum_i^n \Delta w_i \times \Delta l_i}_{\substack{\text{covariance effect} \\ (\text{dynamic strutural effect})}}$$

Instead, we used:

$$\Delta w = \underbrace{\sum_{i}^{n} \Delta w_i \times l_{i0}}_{\text{shift effect}} + \underbrace{\sum_{i}^{n} (w_{i0} - w_{i0}) \Delta l_i}_{\substack{\text{share effect} \\ \left(\text{static structural effect}\right)}} + \underbrace{\sum_{i}^{n} \Delta w_i \times \Delta l_i}_{\substack{\text{covariance effect} \\ \left(\text{dynamic strutural effect}\right)}}$$

(ii)

However, given that,

$$\sum_{i}^{n} \left(w_{i0} - w_{T0}\right) \times \Delta l_i = \sum_{i}^{n} \left(w_{i0} \times \Delta l_i - w_{T0} \times \Delta l_i\right)$$

$$= \sum_{i=1}^{n} \left(w_{i0} \times \Delta l_i\right) - \sum_{i=1}^{n} \left(w_{T0} \times \Delta l_i\right)$$

and,

$$\sum_{i=1}^{n} \left(w_{T0} \times \Delta l_i\right) = w_{T0} \times \sum_{i=1}^{n} \Delta l_i = 0, \text{ Since } \sum_{i=1}^{n} \Delta l_i = 0$$

equations (*i*) and (*ii*) are equivalent with respect to aggregate (shift, share and covariance) effects, but (*ii*) provides more appropriate values for the share effect of each sector.

With equation (*ii*), we are able to obtain:

(1) Shift effects (sectoral and total): changes in average wage for each sector weighted by its initial share of total employment and overall changes in average wage due to changes within sectors.
(2) Share effects (structural static effects): changes in average wage due to changes in the allocation of employment; for each sector the term is positive if the employment share for a sector (or sectors) having an average wage above the mean in the initial period has increased.
(3) Covariance effects (structural dynamic effects): changes in sectoral average wage interacted with changes in the allocation of labour across sectors; a positive value for the sector means that variations in average wage and share of total employment were either positive or negative. A positive value for the aggregate means that positive sectoral changes predominate across sectors.

## Annex 2: industry

*Table 7.A1* National Accounts classification of industry

| Industry |
| --- |
| B   Mining and quarrying |
| C   Manufacture |
| D   Electricity, gas, steam and air-conditioning supply |
| E   Water, sewerage, waste management and remediation activities |
| F   Construction |
| G   Wholesale and retail trade, repair of motor vehicles and motorcycles |
| H   Transportation and storage |
| I   Accommodation and food service activities |
| J   Publishing, audiovisual and broadcasting activities; telecommunications; computer programming, consultancy and related activities; information service activities |
| K   Financial and insurance activities |
| L   Real estate activities |
| M   Legal and accounting activities; activities of head offices; management consultancy activities; architecture and engineering activities; technical testing and analysis; scientific research and development; advertising and market research; other professional, scientific and technical activities; veterinary activities |
| N   Administrative and support service activities |
| O   Public administration and defence; compulsory social security |
| P   Education |
| Q   Human health services; social work activities |
| R   Arts, entertainment and recreation |
| S   Other services activities |
| T   Activities of households as employers of domestic personnel and undifferentiated goods and services production of households for own use |

## Notes

1 The neoliberal transformation of macroeconomic policy aimed at relinquishing full employment objectives in favour of targeting inflation was already theoretically encapsulated in the (now outmoded) concept of the NAIRU (Non-Accelerating Inflation Rate of Unemployment). Originally introduced by Milton Friedman as the natural level of employment, and later elaborated by Layard, Nickell and Jackman (2005), the NAIRU would set the threshold above which a rise in inflation would hurt financial interests.

2 The method of open-coordination does not enforce any policy on any member state, resorting instead to non-binding recommendations, establishing 'best-practices' and evaluation metrics for successful reforms. Inspired by OECD methodologies (Dostal, 2004), this method has been adopted in other social policy domains such as pension reform (Rodrigues et al., 2016).

3 For the concepts and methods for computation of average wages, labour share and productivity, see Annex 1.

4 On reasons for excluding agriculture, see Annex 1.
5 For simplicity we use the expression 'real average wages' to denote what would be more properly called 'real average labour income' (see Annex 1).
6 The full list of sectors can be consulted in Table 7.A1 of the annex.

## References

Blanchard, O. (2007). Adjustment within the euro: the difficult case of Portugal. *Portuguese Economic Journal, 6*(1), 1–21.

Caldas, J.C. (2015). Desvalorização do trabalho: do memorando à prática (*Cadernos do Observatório*, No. 6). Coimbra: Observatório sobre Crises e Alternativas. Available at www.ces.uc.pt/observatorios/crisalt/documentos/cadernos/CadernoObserv_VI_jun2015_final.pdf.

Christophers, B. (2015). The limits to financialization. *Dialogues in Human Geography, 5*(2), 183–200.

Cushen, J., & Thompson, P. (2016). Financialization and value: why labour and the labour process still matter. *Work, Employment and Society, 30*(2), 352–365.

Dostal, J.M. (2004). Campaigning on expertise: how the OECD framed EU welfare and labour market policies — and why success could trigger failure. *Journal of European Public Policy, 11*(3), 440–460.

Goetschy, J. (1999). The European Employment Strategy: genesis and development. *European Journal of Industrial Relations, 5*(2), 117–137.

Goetschy, J. (2003). The European Employment Strategy, multi-level governance, and policy coordination: past, present and future. In Jonathan Zeitlin and David M. Trubek (eds.), *Governing Work and Welfare in a New Economy: European and American Experiments* (pp. 59–87). Oxford: Oxford University Press.

Hein, E. (2015). Finance-dominated capitalism and re-distribution of income: a Kaleckian perspective. *Cambridge Journal of Economics, 39*, 907–934.

IMF (International Monetary Fund) (2011a). Request for a three-year arrangement under the Extended Fund Facility. IMF Country Report, No. 11/127. Available at https://www.imf.org/external/pubs/ft/scr/2011/cr11127.pdf.

IMF (International Monetary Fund) (2011b). Letter of Intent, Memorandum of Economic and Financial Policies and Technical Memorandum of Understanding. Available at www.imf.org/external/np/loi/2011/prt/051711.pdf.

Lapavitsas, C, Kaltenbrunner, A., Lambrinidis, G., Lindo, D., Meadway, J.S, Michell, J., Painceira, J.P., Pires, E., Powell, J., Stenfors, A., Teles, N., & Vatikiotis, L. (2012). *Crisis in the Eurozone*. London: Verso.

Layard, R., Nickell, S., & Jackman, R. (2005). *Unemployment: Macroeconomic Performance and the Labour Market*. 2nd edn. Oxford: Oxford University Press (1st edn 1991).

Lazonick, W., & O'Sullivan, M. (2000). Maximising shareholder value: a new ideology for corporate governance. *Economy & Society, 29*, 13–35.

Martin, R., Rafferty, M., & Bryan, D. (2018). Financialization, risk and labour. *Competition & Change, 12*, 120–132.

Mitchell, W., & Muysken, J. (2008). *Full Employment Abandoned: Shifting Sands and Policy Failures*. Cheltenham: Edward Elgar.

Mosher, J.S., & Trubek, D.M. (2003). Alternative approaches to governance in the EU: EU social policy and the European Employment Strategy. *Journal of Common Market Studies, 41*(1), 63–88.

O' Rourke, K., & Taylor, A.M. (2013). Cross of Euros. *Journal of Economic Perspectives*, 27(3), 167–192.

Petroulakis, F. (2017). Internal devaluation in currency unions: the role of trade costs and taxes. European Central Bank Working Paper No. 2049. Available at www.ecb. europa.eu/pub/pdf/scpwps/ecb.wp2049.en.pdf.

Reis, J., Rodrigues, J., Santos, A.C., & Teles, N. (2014). Compreender a crise: a economia portuguesa num quadro europeu desfavorável. In J. Reis (ed.), *Economia política do retrocesso: crise, causas e objectivos* (pp. 21–87). Lisbon: Almedina.

Rodrigues, J., Santos, A.C., & Teles, N. (2016). A financeirização do capitalismo em Portugal. Lisbon: Conjuntura Actual Editora.

Stockhammer, E. (2008). Some stylized facts on the finance-dominated accumulation regime. *Competition & Change*, 12(2), 184–202.

Streeck, W., & Trampusch, C. (2006). Economic reform and the political economy of the German welfare state. In K. Dyson and S. Padgett (eds.), *The Politics of Economic Reform in Germany* (pp. 60–81). Oxford: Routledge.

Teles, N. (2017). O trabalho como variável de ajustamento: da teoria à prática. In M. Carvalho da Silva, P. Hespanha & J. Caldas (eds.), *Trabalho e políticas de emprego: um retrocesso evitável* (pp. 35–79). Lisbon: Almedina.

Thompson, P. (2013). Financialization and the workplace: extending and applying the disconnected capitalism thesis. *Work, Employment and Society*, 27(3), 472–88

Turrini, A., Koltay, G., Pierini, F., Goffard, C., & Kiss, A. (2014). A decade of labour market reforms in the EU: insights from the LABREF database, European Economy Economic Papers No. 522. Brussels: European Commission.

Uxó, J., Paúl, J., & Febrero, E. (2014). Internal devaluation in the European periphery: the story of a failure. Working paper 2014/2, University of Castilla-La Mancha. Available at:   www.researchgate.net/publication/270896333_Internal_devaluation_in_the_ European_periphery_the_story_of_a_failure.

van der Zwan, N. (2014). Making Sense of Financialization. *Socioeconomic Review*, 12(1), 99–129.

Varoufakis, Y. (2017). *Adults in the Room*. Bodley Head: London.

# Part 3

# Financialisation and social reproduction in the Southern European periphery

# 8   The deepening of financialised social reproduction in Southern Europe

*Ana Cordeiro Santos and Catarina Príncipe*

## Introduction

This chapter brings together the strands of literature on financialisation and feminist political economy in the analysis of financialised social reproduction in Southern Europe (SE). Specifically, it draws on the Systems of Provision (SoP) approach that has examined the diverse ways in which finance has penetrated economic and social reproduction, including connections with material culture (Bayliss, Fine & Robertson, 2013, 2017; Fine, 2017a). And it draws on the feminist political economy take on social reproduction, with a more circumscribed focus on the activities required for the reproduction of labour power carried out of the wage labour relation and mostly by women (Bakker & Gill, 2003; Bhattacharya, 2017; Luxton, 2006). Admittedly, these two strands of literature are not completely attuned, conceptually or in their concerns or focuses. But together they will allow us, or so we will argue, to deepen the analysis of the vulnerabilities generated by financialised social reproduction. The SoP approach does so by offering a broader conception of social reproduction, allowing extension of the analysis of financialisation to various systems of provisioning, bringing to the fore the variegated nature of financialisation processes and associated volatilities and vulnerabilities. Feminist political economy does so by focusing on the impacts of financialisation outside of the sphere of capitalist production, bringing to the fore less visible inequalities based on class, gender, race, ethnicity and nationality.

The chapter is organised as follows. The next section reviews the SoP approach to financialised social reproduction. The subsequent third section illustrates this approach by presenting the Portuguese financialised housing system. The fourth section then reviews the feminist political economy contribution. The fifth section analyses financialised social reproduction in SE, in general, and in Portugal, in particular. The final section reasserts the differentiated nature of financialised social reproduction in time and place and what can be termed, following Fine (Chapter 12 in this volume), the resulting variegated, volatile vulnerabilities ($V^3$), even within a fairly homogeneous region such as Southern Europe. It then concludes that analyses of the impact of financialisation are incomplete without explicit consideration of social reproduction in its broader and narrower terms. That is, financialised social reproduction goes beyond reducing it to the financialisation of everyday life, as expressed in the rise of household indebtedness and privatised pensions. It also includes the linkages with capital accumulation and what occurs outside commodity production, and its vulnerability-producing effects.

## Social reproduction, the Systems of Provision approach and the Material Culture of Financialisation

Fine proposes a broad conception of social reproduction that includes the domain of capital accumulation, involving the production of commodities and the circulation of value; what occurs outside that sphere of commodity production, complementing what is capitalistically produced as means of consumption; and broader social relations as well as social norms underlying the provision of commodity and non-commodity goods. In short, besides the production of commodities, social reproduction also concerns 'the political and ideological superstructure … filled out by the state and civil society, both of which are engaged in, but not reducible to, value relations'. The implication of this is that 'the shifting boundaries of economic reproduction structurally create, or vacate, the space where the broader social reproduction is situated' (Chapter 12 in this volume). This then means that capitalist social relations play a crucial role in social reproductive activities carried out by the household in the domestic sphere because the majority of people must sell their labour force to ensure their own subsistence and capitalist accumulation needs this work force in turn. Thus, on this view, the reproduction of labour power within the household is only a part of social reproductive activities, which include collective and privatised forms of provision (as in health, care, education), other classes than labour, and other social relations beyond those between labour and capital.

The Systems of Provision (SoP) approach, originally developed for the analysis of private consumption and applied to food and clothing industries among others (Fine & Leopold, 1993; Fine 2002), has been extended to examine social provisioning and underlying social norms (Bayliss, Fine & Robertson, 2013). It conceives the economy as constituted by overlapping, commodity-specific systems of provision, each of which is defined in terms of structures, processes, relations and agencies that characterise the entire chain of production of that commodity, and is shaped by multiple social, political, economic, geographic and historical factors. Taking the system of provision for a good as the integral unit of analysis, the SoP approach then builds on a vertical analytical framework that focuses on the whole chain of activity, bringing together production, distribution, access and the context in which these occur, underlining in this way the specific nature of each system of provision. In so doing it offers a sectoral framework for the analysis of the (re)production of labour power, allowing for shifts in commodification and de- or re-commodification with impact on capitalist production and social reproduction.

The SoP approach has also addressed the cultural aspects of financialisation through the lens of the Material Culture of Financialisation framework (Bayliss, Fine & Robertson, 2017; Fine, 2017a). The application of the approach to the investigation of the role of finance in particular systems of provision has brought to the fore the ways in which, and with what impacts, particular systems have been restructured by the expanded presence of finance and the distinct commodity-specific cultures of consumption, that is, the practices, ideas and meanings attached to associated patterns of consumption. Thus, it challenges the hegemony of a uniform financialised culture. For one thing, agents' capacities for reflection and resistance oppose such trends, and the influences of finance on subjectivities are multiple because they derive from factors other than those directly associated with acts of financing, purchasing and consuming. Moreover, examining what financialisation means to its subjects and how those meanings are generated depends on other individual and social characteristics as, for example, a single mum who needs to get credit to pay for medicine for a sick kid as opposed to a CEO who has diversified financial assets.

While the examination of the impact of financialisation on social reproduction comprises the expansion of economic reproduction through privatisation of state provision, it also invites analysis of the complex relation between economic and social reproduction, which cannot be simply put in terms of a shift of responsibility from the state to the market, or from non-commodified to commodified forms of provision, as the state is always deeply involved in both. These different gradients of commodification have been distinguished as commodification (C), commodity form (CF) and commodity calculation (CC), ranging from commodity production, various forms of market mimicry as charges for public services, to monetary valuations without monetary transactions, all contributing to expanding the role of finance in social provisioning. Particular attention has thus far been given to the provisioning of housing, pensions, health and water, giving due account of ongoing processes and forms of commodification (Bayliss, Fine & Robertson, 2017; Fine, 2017a; Rodrigues, Santos & Teles, 2018; Santos, Rodrigues & Teles, 2018; Chapters 9 and 12 in this volume).

Housing has been one of the most studied systems of provisioning due to the historically unprecedented explosion of mortgage markets in most advanced economies, being fed by and feeding the industry of securitisation of such debt and its trade on financial markets. This has been a general trend across the globe, even if variegated by different timings and paces (Aalbers, 2008, 2016; Jordá, Schularick & Taylor, 2015), the result of deep transformations in financial markets producing a 'shift from regulated mortgage and capital markets, limited cross-border capital flows and a low private-debt-to-GDP-ratio towards higher private debt levels and an increasingly "liberalized" financial environment' (Fernandez & Aalbers, 2016, p. 72). The growth of mortgage markets has also been associated with the redefinition of policymaking marked by the deliberate reduction in the stock of public housing, even if this remains relevant in some cases (Robertson, 2017a, 2017b), and by an inversion of policy instruments from the development of new homes to housing allowances (NHF, 2017). Nonetheless, the particular ways in which the housing system has been financialised are variegated in form and content, producing different mixes of owner-occupation and other forms of tenure across and within countries, and with very differentiated impacts.[1]

Indeed, while both the UK's and Portugal's housing systems are marked by relevant private and commodified forms of provision, the growth of mortgage markets in these two geographies has undergone different paths producing distinct effects. Britain's planning system together with the speculative nature of housebuilding resulted in credit being channelled more into demand than into supply, producing a formidable escalation of house prices. In Portugal, mortgage-led demand for new homes grew in tandem with housing supply. This was favoured by lax land use regulation and state investment in infrastructure, allowing for a construction boom which helped curb house prices inflation, but ultimately led to a dysfunctional use of land and oversupply of dwellings. Moreover, in Portugal, the rise of homeownership occurred in a context of debilitated state provision, with almost non-existent public housing, and a deficient private rental market. In the UK, social housing has instead been (and still is) significant even if subject to intense waves of privatisation through the discounted sale of council housing to sitting tenants (Santos & Robertson, 2016).

But the financialisation of housing has not been merely a matter of replacing one form of tenancy with another. The rise of owner-occupation through participation in (prime) mortgage markets has had impacts on other parts of the system, namely in social and private rental markets. In the UK, it has reduced the supply of social housing, pushing those unable to access either homeownership or social provisioning to the private rental market. In Portugal, it has instead curbed the development of non-commodified forms of provision as well as the rental market, with homeownership being the dominant policy model for decades (Santos, 2019; Santos, Serra & Teles, 2015). The political privilege of homeownership has thus deepened inequalities. It has favoured the better-off, those better able to participate in mortgage markets and on better terms, improving housing conditions, ensuring housing security, and contributing to wealth accumulation as the growth of mortgage markets and homeownership rates has induced rising house prices. Those unable to participate in these markets have instead faced reduced supply of affordable homes in social and private rental. This growing dominance of owner-occupation has in turn shaped housing cultures in ways that further favour owner-occupation and undermine other forms of provisioning, changing people's experiences as homeowners or private or social tenants (Robertson, 2017a).

Even if these tendencies have slowed down in the aftermath of the financial crisis, financialisation trends in the sector continue in new guises. In recent years we have been observing the emergence of a new housing crisis triggered by the rise of prices and rents as real estate has become, on a larger scale, an important class of assets for capital, especially for the wealthy and new financial actors, such as real estate funds and societies (Fernandez, Hofman & Aalbers, 2016; Wijburg, Aalbers & Heeg, 2018). Again, this cannot be perceived merely in terms of a retreat of the state creating room for new financial agents. This has been the deliberate result of public policy; and public expenditure continues expanding as the states have to continue to provide for those excluded from the housing markets (NHF, 2017).

Moreover, the financialisation of housing has impacts on other systems of provision and well-being more generally. The rise of homeownership is increasingly taken by policymakers as a (partial) substitute for collective forms of welfare provision, as housing is becoming the most relevant asset on which households increasingly rely to insure themselves against other social and individual risks (Doling & Ronald, 2010). The dominance of homeownership coupled with the expectation of ongoing rising house prices, together with the implementation of neoliberal policies in other areas of social provisioning, continues to promote the private accumulation of residential assets over the life cycle. Indeed, the diminishing significance of collective forms of provisioning funded by taxes, and the rising importance of financialised forms of provision based on the channelling of individual savings into privately funded schemes, as in pensions and health insurance, promote the accumulation of residential assets. This means that income after retirement or access to health services become an individual matter, dependent on individual investments. This entails particularly severe impacts on disadvantaged groups and particularly on women since they tend to accumulate fewer assets due to their more intermittent work careers, childbearing and other social reproductive activities, and due to overall labour market inequalities (Oran, 2017).

## From the SoP approach to semi-peripheral financialised systems of provision

The concept of semi-peripheral financialisation was deliberately put forward to underline the role of hierarchical power relations at the world and regional level (see Chapter 2 in this volume). Within the EU, this has meant the deepening of a subordinated-dominating relationship between peripheral and core EU countries stemming from a debtor-creditor relation. Thus, in SE countries the financialisation of the various systems of provision is not only marked by the increasing dominance of finance, as in core countries, but it is also crucially marked by asymmetric power relations in the access to these markets – meaning an increasing outflow of financial resources from domestic to foreign agents.

These dominating-subordinated relationships were fully exposed when, in the wake of the Global Financial Crisis, SE states were unable to refinance themselves on international markets, having to request loans with strict conditionality from the Troika comprising the European Central Bank (ECB), the European Commission (EC) and the International Monetary Fund (IMF). Such financial support was by and large meant to ensure payment to external creditors (mostly German and French) so their banks would remain solvent, and was used to restructure the banking system at the EU level, aiming at higher concentration (Chapter 2 in this volume). And it was also used to impose radical structural adjustment reforms typical of the Washington Consensus of the 1980s.

The structural adjustment programmes imposed by the official lenders, with the acquiescence of national governments, and serving particular interests of domestic capital, consisted by and large of 'internal devaluation' policies since these countries no longer had available the instrument of currency devaluation to deal with their external account deficits (Chapters 6 and 7 in this volume). Deflationary policies based on the reduction of government expenditure and wages, particularly of civil servants, were then implemented, including the privatisations of the few sectors that remained in the public domain. These austerity-driven, supply-side policies have worsened the situation of these countries. The most severe outcomes of economic and financial crises were felt harshly in SE countries when compared to the EU as a whole, resulting in negative GDP growth rates, double-digit unemployment rates and significantly higher levels of risk of poverty or social exclusion (Chapter 1 in this volume).

This has resulted in further 'peripheralisation' as SE economies have become increasingly deprived of the benefits of participating in the global division of labour (Chapters 3 and 4 in this volume). And it has meant a growing divergence that is not expected to be reversed within the straitjacket of the Economic and Monetary Union (EMU) which preserves the real exchange rate gap between core and periphery, resulting in long-lasting external imbalances (Gambarotto & Solari, 2015; Gambarotto, Rangone & Solari, 2019). This is leading to a new phase of peripheral financialisation as the internal-demand-led process of growth, based on increasing private debt, is weakening. The high level of household indebtedness and the disproportionate rise of newly created low-paid jobs constrain the expansion of the previous model based on internal demand (Chapter 7 in this volume). Instead, we have been observing a new influx of foreign capital restructuring both economic and social reproduction. A recent development has been the rise of foreign investment in real estate, lured by a highly favourable fiscal regime and the expectation of higher returns in the post-crisis low-interest-rate environment.

As discussed at length in Chapter 2 of this book, the expansion of finance in Portugal was the result of reforms in the financial sector leading to the expansion of bank loans that favoured non-tradable sectors, namely construction and real estate, and fuelled growing household debt, specifically mortgage loans, resulting in the extraordinarily unprecedented rise of private debt in the country. The expansion of bank loans has had a tremendous impact on the Portuguese system of housing provision as it absorbed a great part of loans granted to business and households, as lending has gone into the construction of dwellings as well as into their purchase. Within the SE region, this was particularly so in the Portuguese case since loans for the purchase of the household main residence consisted of more than 80 per cent of total household debt, reaching 33 per cent of Portuguese households, in 2013 (cf. Table 8.A1 in the Annex to this chapter), and has remained at these levels since (BdP & INE, 2019).

Rather than being the result of the retreat of public provisioning in this domain of social policy, as in the UK, these developments expose instead the traditional weakness of the Portuguese welfare state, historically favouring a policy model based on the promotion of private ownership, conceding only a marginal role to social housing (representing 2 per cent of the total housing stock of permanent homes). Already prior to membership of the European Economic Community, ownership rates of primary residence were high in European terms (56.6 per cent in 1981). But the financialisation of the Portuguese economy ultimately provided the conditions for the success of a policy model based on homeownership through mortgage loans. Ownership rates of main residence reached the highest value of 75.7 per cent in 2001, declining to 73.2 per cent in 2011, while second and seasonal homes rose from 5.4 per cent in 1981 to 18.4 per cent in 2001 and 19.3 per cent in 2011, with the rise of ownership of main residences and second homes being associated with an extraordinary growth of new dwellings in the peripheries of the main cities and touristic areas (Ribeiro & Santos, 2019).

The role of the central government in this process is evident when it is considered that subsidies associated with loans for permanent homeownership constituted almost three-quarters of total expenditure on housing between 1987 and 2011 (IHRU, 2015). State support was thus relevant to ensure that mortgage-led demand for new homes grew in tandem with the rise in housing supply. Thus, in the Portuguese case, the system of housing provision has accounted for a large portion of households' financial activities through mortgage markets, which the unprecedented access by the Portuguese banking sector to European credit markets allowed.[2] The financial crisis put this model on hold. With public debt reaching record highs, a shaky banking sector requiring continual assistance from public authorities, and an impoverished middle class slowing down reliance upon private indebtedness, household debt to GDP began a downward trend from 92 per cent in 2009 to 69 per cent in 2017 (Eurostat, 2020).

The large-scale programme of quantitative easing carried out by the ECB to ensure that interest rates remained at very low levels, reducing yields on government bonds, bank deposits and pension annuities, raised the relative attractiveness of investment in real estate. Many capital cities have since received a substantial amount of foreign investment from wealthy individuals and institutional investors (Fernandez, Hofman & Aalbers, 2016). Moreover, the conditionality attached to the Portuguese bailout included the liberalisation of the Portuguese rental market, facilitating the termination of rental contracts and thereby the supply of real estate for more profitable uses in the prime market (European Commission, 2011). The major cities of SE have become a desirable destination for investment, contributing to the escalation of housing prices in these areas. This is visible in the two major urban centres of the country, Lisbon and Porto, and also in the country's traditional tourist region of the Algarve. Lisbon indeed ranked in first position in the 2019 list of investment and development prospects for real estate markets (PwC & ULI, 2018).[3]

In a stagnated domestic market, both central and local governments have actively promoted foreign investment in real estate, for example by facilitating residency permits in exchange for the purchase of expensive properties (i.e. 'Golden Visas'), by conceding reductions in or temporary exemptions to the payment of personal income tax to particularly attractive groups of foreigners, or foregoing municipal taxes for rehabilitation such as the IMI (Property Tax) and the IMT (Property Transfer Tax).[4] With domestic banks having trouble accessing European debt markets, the direct involvement of international finance in the form of real estate investment became an alternative for the over-indebted and capital-depleted Portuguese economy, turning real estate financialisation into a state strategy.

This means that finance continues to expand in the housing and real estate domains through the use of fiscal and other incentives, and the creation of novel agents and markets, such as the recently created Sociedades de Investimento e Gestão Imobiliária (SIGI), the Portuguese equivalent to REITS (Real Estate Investment Trusts) or the Spanish SOCIMIS (Sociedades Anónimas Cotizadas de Inversión Inmobiliaria). Building on the recent interest of international investors, the goal is clearly to keep investment flowing into real estate while promoting the expansion of capital markets (Santos, 2019). With the end of the Troika intervention and more optimistic prospects for economic growth, international agents started investing in Portugal. Investment in real state began to recover in 2014, with new investment surpassing 2,100 million euros in 2015 and 2017 and reaching a record volume of 3,500 million euros in 2018. This is deemed to reflect Portugal's late entry into the post-GFC investment cycle, with the growing participation of new foreign investors, representing 91 per cent of total incoming investment in 2018. Big American hedge funds, such as Lone Star and Apollo, have been central players, purchasing real estate portfolios from distressed banks and insurance companies for almost immediate resale. More patient capital, such as pension funds, has also been purchasing properties for redevelopment and sale for the high-end market segment, stimulated by the attractive incentives mentioned above, but also including commercial real estate (CBRE, 2019). This means that global institutional investors, such as pension funds, perceive Portuguese real estate as a relatively profitable and safe long-term investment as well. This suggests a new phase of financialisation in the SE periphery characterised by a shift from aggressive strategies to invest short- to mid-term with the aim of buying low and selling high, i.e. 'pure speculation', to long-term investment where land and real estate are increasingly part of capital accumulation (Wijburg, Aalbers & Heeg, 2018).

The anticipation of the end of the 'property cycle', due to the foreseeable termination of the ECB's policy of quantitative easing, is pushing investors to look for alternative investments in real estate. The rental market is now targeted to 'the millennial generation and a growing number of foreigners working in Portugal, for whom rental is an option that better suits their lifestyle' (CBRE, 2019, p. 43). In contrast to the previous phase marked by the rise of loans, this is expected to launch a new phase of financialisation in housing based on the rise of investment in real estate assets in anticipation of predictable flows of income coming from residential and commercial rents. This type of investment is particularly attractive for pension funds searching for more moderate risk-return, bringing capital and real estate markets closer together in novel ways, and thereby the housing and pension systems of provision.

The qualitative transformation generated by the gradual substitution of domestic by foreign investment in real estate also suggests the emergence of a new phase of peripheral financialisation in SE. This means not only that financialisation is accentuating divergence between core and periphery within the EU, but also that this divergence has severer socio-spatial impacts for the underprivileged. In urban areas, highly vulnerable to global and systemic pressures, there has been an accentuation of socio-spatial segmentation in the uses of space through the restructuring of location, with a concentration of high-value activities and high-income groups in particularly attractive areas – whereas low-value activities disappear and low-income groups are expelled to the outskirts of urban areas. As urban space becomes an attractive asset for investment funds and the transnational wealthy – resulting in the dispossession and displacement of the local poor – extant class, race and gender inequalities accentuate spatial segregation and discrimination, impairing equal access to jobs, schools, public services, transportation, recreation and so forth (Ribeiro & Santos, 2019). This has deep impacts on social reproductive activities. As the lower segments of the labour force are pushed out from the city centres, their working lives and livelihoods are severely undermined due to their more difficult access to collective, commodified or community services.

The straitjacket of the EMU maintains the pressures on SE governments, ever more dependent on foreign investment under ever more dysfunctional and, for some, unfavourable conditions. It is thus unlikely that the situation of these countries will improve as the EU continues to support financialisation by prescribing the reduction of public expenditure in deference to financialised social provision. This in turn entails added political power to (foreign) wealthy proprietors and their representatives, who exercise more influence on the control of local land and mobilise against perceived threats to property devaluation, further reinforcing socio-spatial segmentation.[5]

## Feminist political economy on social reproduction

Marxist feminists adopt a more circumscribed notion of the term 'social reproduction' to refer to the activities that ensure that 'labour power', the 'special commodity' that the capitalist needs to keep the system going, is itself produced and made available to the capitalist. This term and meaning have been retained since the 1970s and 1980s when this line of research first emerged (Vogel, 2013 [1983]; for a review, see Ferguson & McNally, 2013; Luxton, 2006). This is a narrower conception than that entailed by Fine (Chapter 12 in this volume), focusing mainly on the material conditions for the reproduction of the labour force carried out outside of capitalist production and mostly by women.

Indeed, the most popular definition of social reproduction within feminist scholarship defines it in terms of the activities 'directly involved in the maintenance of life on a daily basis, and intergenerationally', which include 'how food, clothing, and shelter are made available for immediate consumption, the ways in which the care and socialisation of children are provided, the care of the infirm and elderly, and the social organization of sexuality'. Or, in short, all the 'care necessary to maintain existing life and to reproduce the next generation' (Laslett & Brenner, 1989, pp. 382–383).

Lise Vogel (2013 [1983]) offers one of the seminal works on the reproduction of human beings and labour power. Two key ideas that the concept of social reproduction underlines are, first, that labour power is produced and reproduced outside of capitalist production; and second, the production and reproduction of labour power is mainly carried out by women. The Marxist lineage of the concept is, in turn, deemed to accomplish two interrelated things: first, it aims at articulating the sphere of production of commodities within that of the production of labour power, seeking to develop an approach that would enclose both production and reproduction within a unitary framework, even if setting them analytically apart; and, second, it puts gender (as well as its intersections with other forms of oppression) at the centre of analysis of both production and reproduction. Thus, feminist scholarship also sees the domains of economic and social reproduction as deeply interconnected, even if its focus is the analysis of the reproduction of the labour force in the domestic realm.

Vogel develops her analytical proposal through the understanding of domestic labour – which she deems a part of the overall necessary labour (i.e. the labour necessary to reproduce one's own and others' labour power) – as a key contradictory component of capitalism. The domestic part of the necessary labour is produced outside of the capitalist forms of production. But if production has to occur, reproduction *must* occur, and if reproduction *must* occur, then domestic labour *has to* be performed. However, capitalism's drive for maximum profit and accumulation tends to demand the full availability of labour power. The underlying contradiction is, then, that 'From the point of view of capital, domestic labour is simultaneously indispensable and an obstacle to accumulation' (Vogel, 2013 [1983], p. 163). This contradiction creates a tension between the capitalist class (trying to keep the costs of reproduction at a minimum) and the labourers themselves, sometimes in fragmented ways, sometimes in unified ways, trying to gain the best possible conditions for their own reproduction. This tension is what allows for different resolutions at different times and moments, not only in the level and type of domestic labour performed, but also in who performs it and how. From this follows a very dynamic understanding of how social reproduction in general is organised: whether in privatised, familial models;

through a strong welfare state; in a privatised fashion, having recourse to formal or informal labour markets; making use of waves of migration; accentuating already underlying inequalities or smoothing them; with or without female participation in the labour market; or all of the above, at different moments and to various degrees.

Thus, even if the focus is on domestic non-waged work, a key point of Marxist feminists is to explain women's oppression under capitalism in terms of a unitary, materialist framework, providing an integrated account of both women's oppression and the capitalist mode of production. Hence, the analytical distinction forged between economic production and social reproduction is meant to bring closer to the surface the links between the two so as to underline that women's oppression is grounded on the central relations of the capitalist mode of production such that 'in order to secure the production and reproduction of current and future supplies of labour-power, capitalism requires institutional mechanisms through which it can exercise control over biological reproduction, family-forms, child-rearing, and maintenance of a gender-order' (Ferguson & McNally, 2013, p. xxvi). Indeed, capitalist societies are deemed to have repeatedly reproduced male-dominated family forms as the changes occurring in time and place 'have not inherently undermined the gendering of fundamental responsibilities for the birthing, nurturing, and raising of young children' (Ferguson & McNally, 2013, p. xxxiii).

An important aspect of bringing together economic production and social reproduction in a unitary system, with underlying interrelations of the various parts of the system, is that it facilitates identifying the various sources of oppression within capitalism that magnify the burdens and constitute the main obstacles to overcoming them. To put it another way, the feminist approach to social reproduction allows a systemic analysis of capitalism which 'is incomplete if we treat it as simply an economic system involving workers and owners, and fail to examine the ways in which wider social reproduction of the system ... sustains the drive for accumulation' (Ferguson quoted in Bhattacharya, 2017, p. 2). This is deemed to bring to the fore the forms of oppression that have been marginalised, such that 'oppression is theorized as structurally relational to, and hence shaped by, capitalist production rather than on the margins of analysis or add-ons to a deeper and more vital economic process' (Bhattacharya, 2017, p. 3).

The analytical role of the concept of social reproduction is taken to be particularly timely in contemporary neoliberal times as the burdens of social reproduction have intensified, implying increased

> subsistence and domestic labour to offset the cutbacks to social reproduction in both the labour market (with reduced prices for subsistence products, pay cuts, jobs losses and the expansion of contingent work) and the state (with cuts to welfare payments, education and health care, and new or increased user fees).
>
> (Luxton, 2006, p. 39)

Indeed, since the new millennium the interest in social reproduction seems to have re-emerged to account for the gendered detrimental impacts of neo-liberal policies.[6] Under neoliberalism, the reconstitution of labour markets, with the reduction of pay and rights, and the focus on restrictive fiscal policies, implying cuts in budgetary expenditures, have implied a new redistribution of social reproductive work within the household, and among women based on their class, ethnic origin and citizenship. These changes imply a shift of activities previously guaranteed by the state or corporations to the household, which must now be performed within the household, be shifted to paid domestic workers within the household or substituted through bought services in the market. This means not only that with neoliberalism the material conditions of households are being eroded and that more burdens are being pushed onto them, but also that these affect particularly women given the persistence of gendered norms. As social risks are being increasingly privatised, commodified and individualised, old and new inequalities arise. This is so because, depending on class and ethnicity, at least some women will be able to buy the domestic services of other women even if they both face the conflict between their paid work and their social reproduction needs (Bakker, 2003, 2007).

This in turn brings into the analysis the variegated nature of these trans-formations, even if the term is not used by these scholars. Their systemic nature, resulting from the increasing role of global actors, means uneven and combined impacts at the national level, especially considering that social reproductive activities are increasingly done 'across borders'. This entails the 'the painful irony for a majority of women migrants' that 'they end up, despite their qualifications for other employment, working as domestics and nannies for women in the host country in order to make money to support their own dependents in their home country' (Luxton, 2006, p. 39).

This is a mark of 'the neoliberal moment in the global political economy' inducing the 're-privatisation of the governance of social reproduction' and it is associated with 'a general increase in the range, depth and scope of socio-economic exploitation in global capitalism amid wider conditions of primitive accumulation'. This is carried out through transnational trade organisations and mechanisms, such as the World Trade Organisation and the General Agreement on Trade in Services, that impose restrictive fiscal policies and fiscal austerity measures that adversely affect social provisioning in many developing countries (Bakker, 2007, pp. 541–545). The problem is not only that increased demands for autonomisation and responsibilisation place added burdens on women, by hindering the supply and quality of the public services on which they depend both as workers and as beneficiaries, but also that this shift of responsibility renders women's work invisible once again, as well as their class and racial intersections (Bakker, 2007, p. 547).

The same arguments have been developed for the European context, addressing the impact of austerity policies to tackle the crisis: producing more economic and social vulnerability (e.g. Leahy, Healy & Murphy, 2014), accentuating their gendered impacts (e.g. Bargawi, Cozzi & Himmelweit, 2016; Kantola & Lombardo, 2017), and pushing the financialisation of economic and social reproduction (e.g. Wöhl, 2017). They, too, stress the role of EU policies putting in place a set of 'hegemonic projects' that have been promoting a 'finance-led regime', which has meant 'the advancement of financial products into private households ... such as private pension schemes, privatised health and elderly care provision' (Wöhl, 2017, pp. 141–142), and the instrumental role of the crisis in pushing this agenda further through austerity measures (Chapter 7 in this volume; Rodrigues, Santos & Teles, 2018; Santos, 2017; Santos, Rodrigues & Teles, 2018).

This is in line with the SoP approach to financialisation, understood as the contemporary neoliberal stage of capitalism in which economic and social reproduction has become increasingly governed by finance (Fine & Saad Filho, 2016; Chapter 12 in this volume). Indeed, an emerging stream of research is now beginning to address the growing role of finance in social reproductive activities and their gendered impacts. Focusing on housing, Roberts (2013) has argued that the individualisation and re-privatisation of relations of social reproduction, by assuming formal equality of individuals, is erasing gender (as well as class and ethnicity) inequalities in paid labour markets, in asset ownership and in the division of unpaid labour. This is not only because access to housing through mortgage debt reproduces extant inequalities due to differentiated access to these markets, but also because these inequalities have been magnified by regressive fiscal policies (e.g. tax deductions) that promote private homeownership for the better-off while reducing the availability of collective forms of housing for the worse-off. Roberts (2013, p. 23) then concludes that mortgage markets ultimately have served 'to redistribute wealth upward, from the poor to the rich, from single women to men and from certain racial minorities to white men and their families'.

By looking into social provisioning in a systemic way, the SoP approach stresses that the growing predominance of mortgage markets in accessing housing has additional detrimental impacts on other subsystems of housing provisioning through the privileging of selectivity over a policy of universal scope. This is so because policymakers, in the context of crisis and recession, find themselves torn between 'the pressures both to reduce individual and overall benefits and to protect the most vulnerable' (Fine, 2017b, p. 35). These in turn impose added pressures on single women with children as those more likely to be the targets of selective and intrusive measures (Montgomerie & Tepe-Belfrage, 2016).

The systemic proposal of the different strands of social reproduction theory can also be aligned with the basic stance of the SoP approach to the determination of the value of labour power in the various stages of capitalism, which means that differentiated forms of social reproduction affect the determination of the value of labour power. That is, as different systems of provision are de-commodified, re-commodified or re-privatised into the familial sphere, different elements redefine the value of labour power. These pertain to those factors determining the levels of absolute and relative surplus value and how they evolve, and the increased presence of finance, both directly and indirectly, in economic and social reproduction. In the present stage, 'neoliberalism seeks avenues for renewing accumulation that draws upon expanding the role in social reproduction of private capital and of finance in particular' (Chapter 12, p. 269). Returning to the contradictory role of the domestic portion of necessary labour, we can then state that:

> so-called domestic labour can be seen to be not only a vital component of social reproduction alongside health, care, education and so on, but also mutually to constitute the social norms associated with the value of labour power in which the content of each and the balance between them can shift as well as be transformed.
>
> (Chapter 12, p. 261)

The links between financialised social reproduction and the determination of the value of labour power, and how it varies across the labour force, have been recently forged by Horton (2019) through the analysis of the financialisation of care homes in the UK. Her case study shows, not only that increasing ownership of domains of social provisioning by private equity firms is partly driven by the realisation of value from the purchase of associated property assets (such as care homes, which can be resold or leased back to the service provider), but also how the interests of finance are advanced through the downgrading of the work conditions of care givers, who are mostly low-status female workers. This in turn suggests that privatisation and the presence of finance are facilitated in fragmented and low-status sectors due to the composition of a powerless workforce dominated by women, migrants, black and minority ethnic groups, who face barriers in other parts of the labour market. By producing worsening work and social conditions, financialised social reproduction accentuates exploitation in the sphere of production and further strains the social reproduction of the labour force, implying new forms of extracting both absolute and relative surplus. But Horton also shows that these sectors create resistance and pose limits to further financialisation as the already extraordinarily high levels of exploitation in this sector curb further exploitation and the continuing downgrading of relevant care service by conflicting with care ethics. Thus, the rise of financialised social reproduction in an increasing number of domains does

> signal not just a flow of surplus to capital via interest payments [and others resulting from the purchase of financial products such as health insurances and pension funds], but also the increased likelihood of each household offering more workers to the market and each worker's commitment to deliver productivity growth and longer working weeks

as the condition of meeting her own costs of subsistence [i.e. absolute and relative surplus].

(Bryan, Martin & Rafferty, 2009, p. 470)

Feminist political economists offer relevant clues for further research on these distributive impacts of financialisation. A critical point of social reproduction literature is that the privatisation of social provisioning accentuates extant inequalities, as access to these services becomes more dependent on market provisioning (for those who can afford it) and is shifted onto the domestic sector (for those who cannot). This then implies the deterioration of the situation of women from the lower classes given that the labour force continues to be segregated by gender and gender-based pay gaps persist, and domestic work still relies mostly on women (INE & Eurostat, 2017).

To conclude, the key contradiction of capitalism that Marxist feminists identified four decades ago is still, if not more, relevant today as the burdens of social reproduction are pushed to the domestic sphere, even if in contradictory ways due to the active roles of the state and the market. What is at stake is not only a gender issue. It is a profound crisis of social provisioning compromising the livelihoods of increasing segments of the population through the production of ever more 'variegated, volatile vulnerabilities' (Chapter 12, p. 268).

## The reproduction of labour power in Portugal

SE households have been facing increasing hardship due to the Troika austerity measures, especially in Greece and Portugal, which faced stricter programmes that reinforced an agenda driven by disengagement from public involvement in social reproduction and its re-privatisation. The negative impacts of these policies have been magnified by the deficient capacity of the welfare states of these countries to protect their citizens. Notwithstanding their similarities, the trajectories of the SE countries have been differentiated. Apparently, Portugal is the country that has recovered the most, presenting in 2018 a positive growth rate, the lowest unemployment rate and the lowest risk of poverty and social exclusion within the SE region (Chapters 1 and 10 in this volume).

Nonetheless, the effects of the adjustment programmes implemented in Portugal through 2011 to 2014 have accentuated inequality across groups and between men and women, as well as among groups of women. These tendencies are not exclusive to Portugal, but a closer look is essential if we are to grasp the adversities caused by austerity and how they deepened gender and other disparities.

With the rise in unemployment and precarious working conditions, and the deterioration of already weak systems of provision, Portuguese households developed, in those years, 'coping strategies' in order to deal with lower incomes. According to Frade and Coelho (2015), Portuguese households mobilised, first and foremost, coping strategies of 'self-mobilisation'. These are strategies that imply 'either downsizing consumption habits and lifestyles, seeking out new sources of income, or both'. They also note that this overall reduction in spending was unequally distributed, since 'the tendency is to maintain spending on children as long as possible' (Frade & Coelho, 2015, pp. 640–641). Other forms of coping strategies – such as 'solidarity-based mobilisation' – are premised on a weak welfare state that prompts the necessity of mobilising the so-called 'welfare society', here understood as 'the networks of relationships of inter-knowledge, mutual recognition and mutual help based on kinship and community ties, through which small social groups exchange goods and services on a nonmarket basis and with a logic of reciprocity' (Santos in Frade & Coelho, 2015, p. 643). So-called 'institutional mobilisation' was only used as a sort of last resource. The authors note that an underlying problem with 'self-mobilisation' and 'solidarity-based mobil-isation' is that they perpetuate norms and forms of familial organisation that tend to be conservative and thereby detrimental to women's individual and autonomous life prospects. Moreover, a closer look at strategies of 'self-mobilisation' indicates that they are not equally shared within the house-hold. According to Coelho (2016), intra-familial arrangements of Portuguese households to cope with the crisis have meant that it was the women who mostly cut on their personal spending. Thus, if living conditions deteriorated during the crisis, women made most sacrifices through either cutting on their personal consumption or through work overload, waged (through the rising in working hours for those who found employment) and unwaged (due to the reduction of outsourced, normally informal) labour to perform domestic work (Coelho, 2016; Ferreira & Monteiro, 2015). Although unemployment contributed to a higher degree of participation of men in domestic work, it did so only in certain tasks and to a limited extent (Coelho, 2016; INE & Eurostat, 2017).

This happened despite the fact that women in Portugal have tradition-ally held higher rates of participation in the labour market, even by EU standards (see Table 8.A2 in the Annex). But the crisis has lowered female participation in the (formal) labour market by 2.4 per cent from 2010 to 2017 (Observatório das Desigualdades, 2017). The decrease in public employ-ment, a highly feminised sector, has played an important role in this evolution (between 2011 and 2014, 40,814 women lost their jobs, while 30,551 men did so in the same period) (Ferreira & Monteiro, 2015). Moreover, women are over-represented in more precarious forms of employment, such as part-time work, or in the informal labour market (Observatório das Desigualdades, 2018). During the Troika years, they were targeted by 'pro-birth' policies that promoted female part-time work by paying 60 per cent of a wage to 'mothers, who like to spend more time with their children' (Ferreira & Monteiro, 2015), while at the same time, the country witnessed an outflow of population of active and fertile age unregistered since the 1960s. Between 2008 and 2018, more than 400,000 people emigrated, and 51 per cent of these emigrants were aged between 20 and 34 (INE, 2020).

Like their European counterparts, Portuguese female workers also face a high rate of gendered occupational segregation. Coelho and Ferreira (2018) depict a clear and common tendency: while professions associated with economic and political decision-making are highly masculinised, the professions related to care and social reproduction are highly feminised. Interestingly, they note that traditionally male-dominated, non-qualified professions in construction, manufacturing and transport show a high speed of feminisation. This is interpreted as resulting from the recent evolution of the labour market wherein men find better opportunities (e.g. IT being highly paid, viable as a career, and also highly masculinised), and from a sort of 'race to the bottom' phenomenon, where women begin to take on male professions that require less education and training, associated with worse wages and reduced career possibilities. The highly feminised sectors, such as those comprising social reproductive activities, are still perceived as 'inherently feminine' and therefore undervalued. The specific tasks that women perform in the manufacturing, construction and transport sectors (e.g. assembly of small components, sewing, ironing or activities that require patience and attention to detail) follow the same trend.

In sum, as feminist scholars have underlined in relation to other geographies, in Portugal women are over-represented in devalued sectors and assume most of the burden of domestic labour. However, these inequalities and burdens are not felt in the same way and to the same extent within this very heterogeneous group, affecting most the underprivileged, migrant and racialised women. Although this is a rather understudied subject in Portugal, some studies suggest that women with a migration background, including second and third generations possessing Portuguese nationality, continue to assume a big part of outsourced and/or informal domestic labour (Góis et al., 2018; Roldão, 2015; Vasconcelos, 2012), pointing to the low social mobility of the descendants of female domestic workers and the class and racialised intersections that cut through them.

Despite the economy and employment recovering to their pre-crisis levels, incomes remain among the lowest in the EU. In 2018, GDP per capita (in PPS) constituted 76 per cent of the average for the EU.[7] While the percentage of population at risk of poverty is declining, in 2018 it still remained high (affecting 17.2 per cent of the total population; 16.6 per cent of men and 17.8 per cent of women), and it is rising for particular segments of the population, namely for single-adult households with at least one child (affecting 33.9 per cent of this group) and the unemployed (affecting 47.5 per cent of this group), the typical vulnerable groups. But more surprisingly, between 2017 and 2018, this risk has also risen for the employed (comprising 10.8 per cent of workers; 11 per cent of male workers and 10.6 per cent of female workers), meaning that having a job is becoming less of a warranty against such risk (INE, 2019).

While employment is rising and income inequality is generally declining, social provisioning remains under-budgeted and under-resourced. The health sector is a case in point. The now chronic under-budgeting of the national health system, resulting in a slow decay of the quality of health provisioning in the country, is associated with the expansion of large health corporations and the rise of the share of expenditure supported by households (Rosa, 2019). This means that despite economic recovery, households continue to make unusual adjustments to their expenditure and living standards, at least in health and housing provisioning. This, combined with low wages and precarious employ-ment, especially for the younger generation (Observatório sobre Crises e Alternativas, 2018), results in the compression of social reproduction activities.

Given the utter importance of housing for individual autonomy, younger generations are facing increasing difficulties in establishing themselves as inde-pendent adults, being forced to postpone important life decisions, such as forming a separate household and family. The rising rates of female participa-tion in the labour market, together with longer working careers required for qualifying for retirement, in turn mean that it is increasingly difficult to shift social reproduction responsibility to the domestic domain. The deterioration of work conditions in turn constrains the possibility for purchasing these services in the formal or informal market. One focus for adjustment is liable to be social reproduction, implying reduced fertility rates and less care provided within the household for family members. This is already evident in some indicators of social reproduction in SE. Relative to their counterparts, on average, Southern Europeans leave parental homes later, have fewer children and increasingly later. The strain on Portuguese women is particularly evident in that they have par-ticularly high employment rates relative to their SE counterparts, as mentioned, spending significantly less time caring for their children (see Table 8.A2 in the Annex to this chapter).

## Conclusion

Financialisation is variegated within the realms of economic and social reproduc-tion in SE as elsewhere. In the aftermath of the GFC, and as a result of the bailout programmes, financialisation in the SE periphery has meant growing economic and social divergence from the EU core (Chapters 2, 3, 4 and 7 in this volume). The SE periphery is a particularly interesting case in which to examine the various scales and layers of the uneven impacts of financialisation on economic production and social reproduction. Given its position in the world economy in general and in the EU in particular, the financialisation of the SE periphery deepened its structural weaknesses. The sovereign debt crisis in these countries, even if with varying degrees of intensity, led to official loan arrangements con-ducive to austerity measures, which have aggravated the situation of these coun-tries further. Such measures aggravated and prolonged recession through their effects on income, as a result of the cuts to salaries, the rise of unemployment and underemployment, and the contraction of public services, leaving increasing segments of the population in greater vulnerability. This has meant a greater strain at the household level to ensure social reproductive activities.

The recent economic recovery in Portugal does not seem to have alleviated much these burdens given the low levels of wages and the rising costs of relevant services such as health, housing and water. The Portuguese panorama does not differ much from what has been described as the crisis of care or the crisis of social reproduction elsewhere. During the last decades, the 'male bread-winner' model was substituted by the 'double-wage' model that, together with the building of the welfare state, allowed for the relocation of domestic and reproductive labour outside of the private sphere through processes of de-commodification. This lowered the 'double burden' for some women. However, the impacts of financialisation and of the economic crisis have shaken the capacity for social reproduction to be performed, which means a more unequal access to increasingly financialised social provisioning, resulting in a higher degree of inequality between men and women, through the devaluation of women's labour power. The contributions coming from both feminist scholarship and the SoP approach suggest that the detrimental impacts of financialised social provisioning can only be overcome through the resolution of the contradictions of capitalism at a more structural level, going beyond mere fixes of gender or other gaps within present circumstances. It implies more favourable labour relations for the working classes and a return to policies of universal scope in public provisioning, exactly the opposite of trends and shocks around the GFC which have witnessed austerity and commercialisation under the imperatives of financialised neoliberalism.

## Acknowledgements

The authors are grateful to Ben Fine, Manuel Aalbers and Nuno Teles for comments on previous versions of this chapter. All errors and omissions remain the responsibility of the authors. This work was funded by the Portuguese Foundation for Science and Technology and co-funded by the European Regional Development Fund (ERDF), within the scope of FINHABIT project, ref. PTDC/ATP-GEO/2362/2014 – POCI-01-0145-FEDER-016869.

## Annex

*Table 8.A1* Household main residence mortgages

|  | Netherlands | Portugal | Spain | Germany | Greece | Italy | Euro area |
|---|---|---|---|---|---|---|---|
| EUR thousands (median) | 132.8 | 63.7 | 68.6 | 73.9 | 35.2 | 65 | 75.5 |
| % of total houshold debt | 73 | 82 | 65 | 63 | 68 | 77 | 66 |
| % of households | 41 | 33 | 28 | 17 | 11 | 10 | 20 |

Source: Household Finance and Consumption Survey – Wave 2

Table 8.A2 Social reproduction: selected indicators, 2016

| | EU | | Greece | | Spain | | Italy | | Portugal | |
|---|---|---|---|---|---|---|---|---|---|---|
| | Males | Females | Males | Females | Males | Females | Males | Females | Males | Females |
| Leaving the parental household (age) | 27.1 | 25.1 | 30.4 | 27.8 | 30.4 | 28.3 | 31.3 | 29 | 29.9 | 28.2 |
| Tertiary education (%) | 28.9 | 32.5 | 28.5 | 31.9 | 33 | 38.4 | 15.3 | 20.1 | 19.4 | 27.9 |
| Employment rates (%) | 71.8 | 61.4 | 61 | 43.3 | 64.8 | 54.3 | 66.5 | 48.1 | 68.3 | 62.4 |
| Caring/educating children (hours) | 20.4 | 37.1 | 16.9 | 34.7 | 23.2 | 38.4 | 18.4 | 39.9 | 19.3 | 29.4 |
| Caring for disabled/sick relatives/ friends aged over 75 (hours) | 10.6 | 12.1 | 9.8 | 18.9 | 13.6 | 18 | 13 | 12.3 | 16 | 8.4 |
| Fertility rate (no. of children) | | 1.60 | | 1.38 | | 1.34 | | 1.34 | | 1.36 |
| Age of women at birth of first child | | 29.0 | | 30.3 | | 30.8 | | 31.0 | | 29.6 |

Source: Eurostat and Eurofound

# Notes

1 The general agreement on the variegated impacts of financialisation on housing coexists with different understandings of underlying definitions of financialisation. Ben Fine (2014; Chapter 12 in this volume) draws on the Marxist notion of 'interest-bearing capital' as the distinctive feature of financialisation, meaning by this 'capital that is lent for the purposes of reaping rewards out of profitmaking capital' (Chapter 12, p. 263). Building on Epstein's popular definition, Manuel Aalbers (2019, p. 3) adopts a broader notion encompassing 'the increasing dominance of financial actors, markets, practices, measurements, and narratives, at various scales, resulting in a structural transformation of economies, firms (including financial institutions), states, and households'. As discussed in the Introduction to this book, we adopt a broader notion considered more apt to account for financialisation processes in (semi-)peripheral contexts.
2 Another aspect of financialised housing is the securitisation of mortgages even if to a lesser extent than in other EU countries (Barradas et al., 2018; Santos, Serra & Teles, 2015).
3 This ranking includes 4 SE cities in a list of 22 cities offering good prospects for investment in 2019. In addition to Lisbon, ranked in 1st position, Madrid ranks 4th, Athens 14th and Milan 20th.
4 From October 2012 to December 2019, 8,207 Golden Visa residence permits were awarded; 94 per cent of these were granted through the acquisition of a real estate property, mainly to Chinese nationals (54 per cent), followed by Brazilians (11 per cent) and Turkish (5 per cent), corresponding to 4509 million euros of investment (www.sef. pt/pt/Documents/2012_2019%20MAPA%20ARI.pdf, consulted 10 January 2020). In January 2019 there were 27,367 citizens benefiting from the 'Non-habitual Tax Residents Regime' that promises a very favourable tax regime applicable to individuals transferring their tax residence to Portugal; the most represented nationalities are French (24 per cent), British and Italians (11 per cent each) and Brazilian and Swedish (9 per cent each) (http://app.parlamento.pt/webutils/docs/doc.pdf?path=614852306 3446f764c324679595842774f6a63334e7a637664326c75636d56785833426c636d643 1626e52686379395953556c4a4c3342794f4455324c58687061576b744e4331684c6e4 26b5a673d3d&fich=pr856-xiii-4-a.pdf&Inline=true, consulted 10 January 2020).
5 Indeed, the cancellation of incentives for foreign investment, such as the 'Temporary Residence Permit for Investment' and the 'Non-habitual Tax Residents Regime', are obvious measures for curbing current house price and rent inflation. However, this is not forthcoming given the economic and political power of the real estate sector, which has been very vocal arguing against policies that alter the incentive structure for investors demanding so-called 'fiscal stability'.
6 See, for example, the December 2019 special issue of *Capital & Class*.
7 These values were 68, 91 and 95 for Greece, Spain and Italy, respectively, all below the average for the 28 EU countries (https://ec.europa.eu/eurostat/databrowser/view/ tec00114/default/table?lang=en, consulted 10 January 2020).

# References

Aalbers, M.B. (2008). The financialization of home and the mortgage market crisis. *Competition & Change, 12*(2), 148–166.

Aalbers, M.B. (2016). *The Financialization of Housing: A Political Economy Approach.* New York: Routledge.

Aalbers, M.B. (2019). Financialization. In D. Richardson, N. Castree, M.F. Goodchild, A. Kobayashi, W. Liu & R.A. Marston (eds.), *The International Encyclopaedia of Geography* (pp. 1–12). Oxford: Wiley-Blackwell.

Bakker, I. (2003). Neo-liberal governance and the reprivatization of social reproduction: social provisioning and shifting gender orders. In I. Bakker & S. Gill (eds.), *Power, Production and Social Reproduction* (pp. 66–82). Basingstoke: Palgrave Macmillan.

Bakker, I. (2007). Social reproduction and the constitution of a gendered political economy. *New Political Economy, 12*(4), 541–556.

Bakker, I., & Gill, S. (2003). Global political economy and social reproduction. In I. Bakker & S. Gill (eds.), *Power, Production and Social Reproduction* (pp. 3–16). Basingstoke: Palgrave Macmillan.

Bargawi, H., Cozzi, G., & Himmelweit, S. (eds.) (2016). *Economics and Austerity in Europe: Gendered Impacts and Sustainable Alternatives.* London and New York: Routledge.

Barradas, R., Lagoa, S., Leão, E., & Mamede, R.P. (2018). Financialization in the European periphery and the sovereign debt crisis: the Portuguese case. *Journal of Economic Issues, 52*(4), 1056–1083.

Bayliss, K., Fine, B., & Robertson, M. (2013). From financialisation to consumption: the Systems of Provision approach applied to housing and water (FESSUD Working Paper Series, No. 2). Leeds: FESSUD.

Bayliss, K., Fine, B., & Robertson, M. (2017). Introduction to special issue on the material cultures of financialisation. *New Political Economy, 22*(4), 355–370.

BdP & INE (Banco de Portugal and Instituto Nacional de Estatística) (2019). Survey to the financial situation of households 2017. Lisbon: BdP and INE. Retrieved from www.ine.pt/xportal/xmain?xpid=INE&xpgid=ine_destaques&DESTAQUESdest_boui=403895196&DESTAQUESmodo=2.

Bhattacharya, T. (2017). Introduction: mapping social reproduction theory. In T. Bhattacharya (ed.), *Social Reproduction Theory: Remapping Class, Recentering Oppression* (pp. 1–20). London: Pluto Press.

Bryan, D., Martin, R., & Rafferty, M. (2009). Financialization and Marx: giving labor and capital a financial makeover. *Review of Radical Political Economics, 41*(4), 458–472.

CBRE (2019). CBRE research Portugal: Real Estate Market Outlook. Retrieved from http://cbre.vo.llnwd.net/grgservices/secure/CBRE%20Portugal%20Market%20 Outlook%202020_ENG.pdf?e=1590272314&h=b1c6e80f825cd35aab2ef463e0d1 696c.

Coelho, L. (2016). Finanças conjugais, desigualdades de género e bem-estar: facetas de um Portugal em crise. *Revista Crítica de Ciências Sociais, 111*, 59–80.

Coelho, L., & Ferreira, V. (2018). Segregação sexual do emprego em Portugal no último quarto de século – agravamento ou abrandamento? *e-cadernos CES, 29*, 77–98.

Doling, J., & Ronald, R. (2010). Home ownership and asset-based welfare. *Journal of Housing and the Built Environment, 25*(2), 165–173.

European Commission (2011). Memorandum of understanding on specific economic policy conditionality, 17 May 2011. Retrieved from https://ec.europa.eu/economy_finance/eu_borrower/mou/2011-05-18-mou-portugal_en.pdf.

Eurostat (2020). Eurostat National Accounts Database. [Dataset]. Retrieved from https://ec.europa.eu/eurostat.

Ferguson, S., & McNally, D. (2013). Capital, labour-power, and gender-relations. Introduction to Vogel 2013 [1983] (pp. xvii–xl).

Fernandez, R., & Aalbers, M. (2016). Financialization and housing: between globalization and varieties of capitalism. *Competition & Change, 20*(2), 71–88.

Fernandez, R., Hofman, A., & Aalbers, M.B. (2016). London and New York as a safe deposit box for the transnational wealth elite. *Environment and Planning A, 48*(12), 2443–2461.

Ferreira, V., & Monteiro, R. (2015). Austeridade, emprego e regime de bem-estar social em Portugal: em processo de refamilização? *Revista ex æquo, 32*, 49–67.

Fine, B. (2002). *The World of Consumption: The Cultural and Material Revisited.* London: Routledge.

Fine, B. (2014). Financialisation from a Marxist perspective. *International Journal of Political Economy,* 42(4), 47–66.

Fine, B. (2017a). The material and culture of financialisation. *New Political Economy, 22*(4), 371–382.

Fine, B. (2017b). The continuing enigmas of social policy. In L.Yi (ed.), *Towards Universal Health Care in Emerging Economies: Social Policy in a Development Context* (pp. 29–59). London: Palgrave Macmillan.

Fine, B., & Leopold, E. (1993). *The World of Consumption.* London: Routledge.

Fine, B., & Saad-Filho, A. (2016). Thirteen things you need to know about neoliberalism. *Critical Sociology, 43*(4–5), 685–706.

Frade, C., & Coelho, L. (2015). Surviving the crisis and austerity: the coping strategies of Portuguese households. *Indiana Journal of Global Legal Studies, 22*(2), 631–664.

Gambarotto, F., Rangone, M., & Solari, S. (2019). Financialization and deindustrialization in the Southern European periphery. *Athens Journal of Mediterranean Studies, 5*(3), 151–172.

Gambarotto, F., & Solari, S. (2015). The peripheralization of Southern European capitalism within the EMU. *Review of International Political Economy, 22*(4), 788–812.

Góis, P., Marques, J.C, Valadas, C., Leite, A., & Nolasco, C. (2018). *Discriminação no recrutamento e acesso ao mercado de trabalho de imigrantes e portugueses de origem estrangeira.* Lisboa: Alto Comissariado para a Migrações.

Horton, A. (2019). Financialization and non-disposable women: real estate, debt and labour in UK care homes. *Environment and Planning A: Economy and Space,* advance online publication. DOI: https://doi.org/10.1177/0308518X19862580.

IHRU (Instituto da Habitação e Reabilitação Urbana) (2015). 1987–2011: 25 Anos de esforço do orçamento do estado com a habitação. Lisbon: Instituto da Habitação e Reabilitação Urbana.

INE (Instituto Nacional de Estatística) (2019). Income and living conditions. Retrieved from www.ine.pt/xportal/xmain?xpid=INE&xpgid=ine_destaques&DESTAQUESdest_boui=354099803&DESTAQUESmodo=2.

INE (Instituto Nacional de Estatística (2020). Statistical database. https://www.ine.pt.

INE (Instituto Nacional de Estatística) & Eurostat (2017). The life of women and men in Europe: a statistical portrait. Retrieved from https://www.ine.pt/scripts/wm_v_final/index.html?lang=en.

Jordá, O., Schularick, M., & Taylor, A.M. (2015). Betting the house. *Journal of International Economics, 96*(S1), 2–18.

Kantola, J., & Lombardo, E. (2017). Gender and the politics of the economic crisis in Europe. In J. Kantola & E. Lambordo (eds.), *Gender and the Economic Crisis in Europe* (pp. 1–25). Cham: Palgrave Macmillan.

Laslett, B., & Brenner, J. (1989). Gender and social reproduction: historical perspectives. *Annual Review of Sociology, 15*, 381–404.

Leahy, A., Healy, S., & Murphy, M. (2014). Crisis Monitoring Report 2014 – the European Crisis and Its Human Cost. Brussels: Caritas Europa.

Luxton, M. (2006). Feminist political economy in Canada and the politics of social reproduction. In M. Luxton & K. Bezanson (eds.), *Social Reproduction: Feminist Political Economy Challenges Neo-liberalism* (pp. 11–44). Montreal: McGill-Queen's UniversityPress.

Montgomerie, J., & Tepe-Belfrage, D. (2016). A feminist moral political economy of uneven reform in austerity Britain: fostering financial and parental literacy. *Globalizations, 13*(6), 890–905.

NHF (National Housing Federation) (2017). Public expenditure on housing: the shift from capital spend to housing allowances. A European trend? Retrieved from http://s3-eu-west-1.amazonaws.com/pub.housing.org.uk/public_spending_housing_europe_uk_briefing.pdf.

Observatório das Desigualdades (2017). Participação feminina no mercado de trabalho diminuiu nos últimos seis anos em Portugal. Retrieved from www.observatorio-das-desigualdades.com/2017/04/26/participacao-feminina-no-mercado-de-trabalho-diminuiu-nos-ultimos-seis-anos-em-portugal/?print=print.

Observatório das Desigualdades (2018). Subutilização da força de trabalho: o perfil social. Retrieved from www.observatorio-das-desigualdades.com/2017/10/13/subutilizacao-da-forca-de-trabalho-o-perfil-social/?print=print.

Observatório sobre Crises e Alternativas (2018). Retoma económica: o lastro chamado precariedade (Barómetro das Crises, no. 18). Lisbon: Centre for Social Studies, University of Coimbra.

Oran, S.S. (2017). Pensions and social reproduction. In T. Bhattacharya (ed.), *Social Reproduction Theory: Remapping Class, Recentering Oppression* (pp. 148–170). London: Pluto Press.

PwC & ULI (2018). *Emerging Trends in Real Estate: Europe 2019.* London: PricewaterhouseCoopers and the Urban Land Institute.

Ribeiro, R., & Santos, A.C. (2019). Financeirização da habitação e desigualdades socioterritoriais: um estudo comparado das áreas metropolitanas de Lisboa e do Porto. *Análise Social, 54*(233(4)) , 726–758.

Roberts, A. (2013). Financing social reproduction: the gendered relations of debt and mortgage finance in twenty-first-century America. *New Political Economy, 18*(1), 21–42.

Robertson, M. (2017a). (De)constructing the financialised culture of owner-occupation in the UK, with the aid of the 10Cs. *New Political Economy, 22*(4), 398–409.

Robertson, M. (2017b), The great British housing crisis. *Capital & Class, 41*(2), 195–215.

Rodrigues, J., Santos, A.C., & Teles, N. (2018). Financialisation of pensions in semi-peripheral Portugal. *Global Social Policy, 18*(2), 189–209.

Roldão, C. (2015). Fatores e perfis de sucesso escolar inesperado': trajetos de contratendência de jovens das classes populares e de origem africana. Phd thesis, ISCTE-IUL.

Rosa, E. (2019). A parcela da riqueza criada no país que é aplicada na saúde diminuiu, a despesa das família aumentou. *Crítica Economia e Sociedade, 20*, 25–40.

Santos, A.C. (2017). Cultivating the self-reliant and responsible individual: the material culture of financial literacy. *New Political Economy, 22*(4) 410–422.

Santos, A.C. (2019). Habitação em tempos financeiros em Portugal. In A.C. Santos (ed.), *A nova questão da habitação em Portugal: uma abordagem de economia política* (pp. 15–52). Coimbra: Conjuntura Atual Editora.

Santos, A. C., & Robertson, M. (2016). Definancialising well-being: the case of housing (FESSUD Working Paper Series, No. 178). Leeds: FESSUD.

Santos, A.C., Rodrigues, J., & Teles, N. (2018). Semi-peripheral financialisation and social reproduction: the Case of Portugal. *New Political Economy*, *23*(4), 475–494.

Santos, A.C., Serra, N., & Teles, N. (2015). Finance and housing provision in Portugal (FESSUD Working Paper Series, No. 79). Leeds: FESSUD.

Vasconcelos, J. (2012). Africanos e afrodescendentes no Portugal contemporâneo: redefinindo práticas, projectos e identidades. *Cadernos de Estudos Africanos*, *24*, 15–23.

Vogel, L. (2013 [1983]). *Marxism and the Oppression of Women: Toward a Unitary Framework.* 2nd edn. Chicago, IL: Haymarket.

Wijburg, G., Aalbers, M.B., & Heeg, S. (2018). The financialisation of rental housing 2.0: releasing housing into the privatised mainstream of capital accumulation. *Antipode*, *50*, 1098–1119.

Wöhl, S. (2017). The gender dynamics of financialisation and austerity in the European Union – the Irish case. In J. Kantola & E. Lambordo (eds.), *Gender and the Economic Crisis in Europe* (pp. 139–159). Cham: Palgrave Macmillan.

# 9 Variegated financialisation

## How finance pervaded (and pervades) housing and water provisioning in Portugal

*Nuno Teles*

## Introduction

Research on financialisation has recently addressed how its configurations vary across geographies according to the position countries occupy in the financial international sphere (Becker et al., 2010; Bonizzi, 2013; Kaltenbrunner & Painceira, 2015). In this book, Southern European (SE) semi-peripheral specificities have been highlighted to better grasp theoretically the nature and content of financialisation, while avoiding the risk of treating this process as a homogeneous one across national economies. This chapter aims at showing that finance also has differentiated impacts across the various economic sectors of the same country.

This chapter compares the financialisation processes (and their changing forms) of two different systems of provision in Portugal: housing and water provision. Housing has been of paramount importance for the Southern European semi-periphery political economy for a variety of reasons, not least, its impact on overall economic growth and employment (see Chapters 2 and 8 in this volume). Being a basic good for social reproduction, whose provision has been broadly left to the market (due to residual interventions by the state), feeding the expansion of the financial sector through credit to construction and mortgages, housing is a pivotal case study for sectoral research on financialisation. The water provision case study may seem less obvious. Considered a success case given its trajectory of expanding access over the past decades, water provision is seldom under public scrutiny in Portugal, with its provision largely remaining in public hands (Teles, 2015). However, it is precisely the predominantly public nature of water provision that makes this case study suitable for a comparative exercise with the mostly privately provided housing sector.

This chapter argues that a comparative sectoral analysis is critical for a broader understanding of financialisation for three sets of reasons. First, each commodity, commodity form or commodity calculation has behind it specific processes of production, distribution and cultural meanings that convoke different agents, motives and markets (Bayliss, Fine & Robertson, 2017).[1] It would then be analytically poor to enclose financialisation as a homogeneous process of rising importance of finance, financial agents and financial markets across sectors of the economy, only variegated according to national borders. Financialisation would then be a catch-all concept, where finance blurs diverse historical paths, forms of production, labour processes, etc. (Christophers, 2015). Secondly, sector variegation in Portugal, each with its specificities, nonetheless brings to the fore common features identified as characterising semi-peripheral financialisation (Chapters 2 and 7 in this volume). Comparative sectoral analyses illustrate how financialisation as a national process has evolved and been transformed in the semi-periphery, particularly after the euro crisis of 2010. Thirdly, this exercise helps us to better understand the relation of financialisation and social reproduction in two sectors that provide goods and services understood as fundamental for the reproduction of labour power. Indeed, as elaborated by Santos and Principe (Chapter 8 in this volume), the recent revival of social reproduction theory in feminist studies has not only underpinned the importance of female domestic work and the increasing burden put on women in social reproduction, but also highlights how financialised access to basic goods and services, such as housing and water, increasingly strains labour force reproduction. This is stressed by the current international post-crisis context, featuring stagnant wages, but also stagnant inflation, thus shedding light on the importance of scrutinising the hardships in household access to particular goods and services, which may be blurred in macro/national analysis.

Building on previous work (Santos, Rodrigues & Teles, 2018), this chapter adopts the Systems of Provision (SoP) approach. The SoP approach argues for an interdisciplinary exercise that goes beyond 'horizontal' and disciplinary frameworks, such as the utility maximisation principle of neoclassical economics, the emphasis on social emulation and distinction of sociological perspectives, or the deconstruction exercises of postmodern studies (Bayliss, Fine & Robertson, 2013). Instead, the SoP approach studies each good and service separately, adopting a 'vertical' approach that focuses on the agents, institutions and relations involved in each SoP (state, private firms, labour unions, consumers, finance, etc.). It aims to capture the specificity of each good and service through the analysis of the diverse interests and power relations involved in its provision, going beyond the homogenising character attributed to consumption by neoclassical economics (Fine, 2013). Special attention is paid to the way in which agents relate to each other, grounded on 'the premise that outcomes emerge from settlements between agents who are themselves embedded in historically evolved social and economic structures and processes' (Bayliss, Fine & Robertson, 2013, p. 2). In this context, finance and ongoing financialisation play a major role, since 'The presence or intervention of finance shapes processes of provision and the behaviour of other agents' and 'financial agencies are often proactive in trying to shape SoPs in favourable directions' (Bayliss, Fine & Robertson, 2013, p. 11).

The chapter is organised as follows. The second section will deal with the financialisation of housing in Portugal and its historical evolution, whilst recent developments are addressed, stressing its renewed importance for the overall

Portuguese economy. Being a topic present across this book, some overlapping is unavoidable, but kept to the bare minimum. The third section presents the case for water financialisation as an ongoing process in Portugal, where finance has decisively contributed (and still contributes) to its commodification albeit its control being still predominantly public. The fourth section concludes, summing up the convergences and divergences between the two sectors and stressing the need for analytical variegation at the sectorial level if one wants to draw consequent political implications.

## Housing: boom, bust … and boom again

Housing is now one of the most researched themes in the financialisation literature (see, for instance, Aalbers, 2016; Ryan-Collins, Lloyd & Macfarlane, 2017; Santos, 2019). It is easy to understand why. Housing was at the centre of the Global Financial Crisis (GFC) and has been the main conduit for household entanglement with finance, either through indebtedness or through its role as an investment asset. Portugal does not escape this pattern, albeit with common and divergent points.

The contemporary housing SoP in Portugal was unequivocally marked by social demands born from the 1974–1975 revolution. Still, contrary to other sectors of social provisioning (e.g. health and education), it was left largely unmet by public provision. In parallel with the persistent presence of slums in the major urban centres, private provision gradually met a growing demand caused by the urbanisation of the 1980s and 1990s.

This 'success' story can only be understood in the context of European Economic Community (EEC) membership and the ways in which European integration paved the way for growing financial influence. During the 1980s, ensuing financial liberalisation and the Basel Agreements, imposing norm-conformity, provided the newly privatised Portuguese banks with the liquidity and regulatory mortgage-lending orientation needed to reallocate credit towards households and the construction sector (Santos, Serra & Teles, 2015). Moreover, the prospect of euro membership gave Portuguese banks access to European loanable-money capital on an unprecedented scale to fund both household mortgages and the construction sector (Chapter 2 in this volume). In fact, one of the most distinguishing features of housing financialisation in Portugal, a country with relatively small securities markets, is the scant importance of mortgage securitisation in the growth of household indebtedness (Santos, 2019). Although securitisation rose during the 2000s, it was not, contrary to what seems to have happened in core countries, the main source of added liquidity. This was mostly found in European interbank markets.

Financialisation of housing in Portugal – signalled by the rising percentage of residential loans to GDP (Figure 9.1) – cannot be understood as a mere matching of growing supply and demand for mortgages. The enhanced commodified configuration of the Portuguese housing SoP was decisively structured by public policy. The state actively promoted household mortgage indebtedness

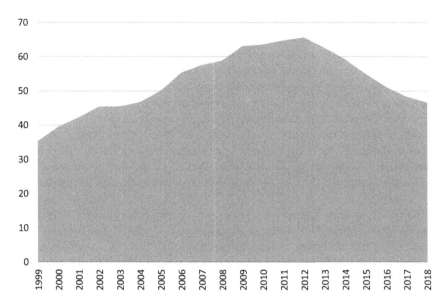

*Figure 9.1* Outstanding residential loans as percentage of GDP
Source: Hypostat

through subsidies associated with loans for permanent homeownership, total-ling 71 per cent of all the public budget for housing between 1987 and 2011 (Santos, Serra & Teles, 2015). Local governments also played a central role. Lax land regulation – fostering municipal capacity to levy real estate taxes and stimulate local economies – allowed around 55,000 hectares of rural land to be converted into urban land between 1985 and 2000, resulting in the con-struction of 1.3 million homes during that period (Caetano, Carrão & Painho, 2005). Access to European Union (EU) structural funds also enabled infrastruc-ture investment across the country (not least in water supply, see next section), opening vast areas for housing construction.

A construction boom ensued during the nineties, supporting economic growth in a period when the Portuguese economy faced new foreign competi-tive pressures (Chapter 4 in this volume). The construction sector was clearly one of the winners of the processes of European integration and financialisation of housing provision. The dynamism of the sector is reflected in the growth of its weight in national Gross Value Added during the period of strong economic growth in the second half of the 1990s, and in the growth of its relative weight in employment, which covered 12 per cent of the entire working population in 2002 (Santos, Serra & Teles, 2015). Nonetheless, the housebuilding industry was highly fragmented and heterogeneous with thousands of small companies co-existing alongside new multinationals of Portuguese origin. A symbiotic relationship based on outsourcing strategies by major national construction companies developed, whereby certain phases of the work were passed to (small) subcontractors. This allowed big firms to manage the intermittent volume of work, benefiting at the same time from the typically precarious labour relations within the sector (Baganha, Marques & Góis, 2002).

Finally, the housing needs of households living in slums and without access to mortgage markets showed the social contradictions entailed by the new configuration of the housing SoP. These social needs were met by the EU-funded Programa Especial de Realojamento (PER, Special Rehousing Programme), mainly during the nineties (Santos, Serra & Teles, 2015). Although this was marginal in the public housing budget (4 per cent of housing public expenditure between 1987 and 2011), the state, with the aid of EU-sponsored rehousing programmes, patched the gaps produced by ongoing commodification processes (Fine, 2014).

Contrary to what happened in other semi-peripheral countries, most notably in Spain (López Hernández & Rodríguez López, 2010), the housing (and economic growth) boom, fuelled by international flows of loanable-money capital and household indebtedness, came to a halt with the 2001 international recession. Construction started on a declining path and the numbers of new houses built slowed down, dragging down economic and employment growth. The sharp reduction of public investment due to the strictures of the Stability Pact –which Portugal was one of the first countries to breach – led to stagnation in prices and housing supply. However, there was no significant bust as the causes for this slowdown were mainly domestic. The credit-fuelled financialisation of the 1990s continued in the new millennium. Portuguese banks easily refunded their new liabilities abroad at low rates, continuing their model of household lending, albeit at a slower pace, for the purchase of second homes by the middle-upper classes (Santos, Serra & Teles, 2015). Nonetheless, stagnation was the main feature of the housing SoP, and the overall economy, in Portugal during the early 2000s.

The slow-burn crisis accelerated with the 2008–2009 Global Financial Crisis and subsequent euro crisis of 2011–12, when European loanable-money capital inflows froze. While the most salient indicator of this foreign capital 'sudden stop' was to be found in the sovereign debt markets, the highly leveraged domestic banks also suffered from the shutting down of European interbank money markets. However, contrary to the Portuguese state, banks could rely on European Central Bank (ECB) emergency funding, extended in 2012 to long-term financing (Long Term Refinancing Operations). This credit lifeline was eventually used by the ECB to force the Portuguese state to request official lending from the Troika (comprising the European Central Bank, the European Commission and the International Monetary Fund), thereby inaugurating the period of externally imposed austerity and adjustment for the banking sector (Rodrigues, Santos & Teles, 2016).

The following recession had a deep and lasting impact on Portuguese banks. Banks were forced to accept official funding to meet their raised their capital requirements and to reduce their leverage, thereby reducing mortgage

*Figure 9.2* Housing price index (2006 = 100)
Source: ECB

credit to households. Now dealing with record high non-performing loans rates, particularly to non-financial firms, such as construction companies, losses were inevitable. Large private banks went bankrupt, as was the case of Banco Espírito Santo in 2014, with remaining assets being sold to the American Lone Star hedge fund, and Banco Internacional do Funchal in 2015, bought by the Spanish bank Santander.

With Portuguese banks in shambles and a radical fiscal adjustment programme in place that sacrificed public investment and depressed household income, the financialised mechanisms of the Portuguese housing SoP broke. For the first time, house prices dropped (Figure 9.2). The weight of the construction sector in the economy reached a record low. Between 2000 and 2014, Gross Value Added fell from 8 to 4 percent, employment from 12 to 6 percent, and investment (gross capital formation) from 6 to 2 percent (Figure 9.3).

Since 2014, the housing SoP has gone through a profound revival, with finance again at its helm. Expansionary monetary policy of the ECB drove European interest rates to negative terrain, starting a search for yield by investment funds that found real estate as one of its favourite recipients. In this context, the Portuguese housing market looked particularly undervalued, having suffered from years of price stagnation and depression. Additionally, the restructuring of the domestic banking sector provided vast real estate portfolios available to be sold (Santos, 2019). Foreign real estate funds have since bought up masses of real estate in the city centres. In 2017, 80 percent of all commercial

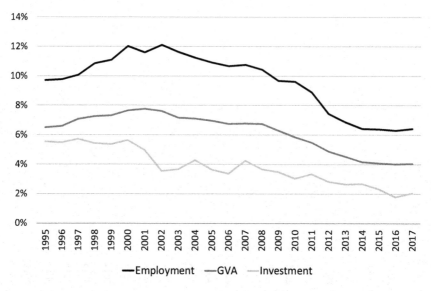

*Figure 9.3* Construction: percentage to total Gross Value Added, employment and investment

Source: INE

real estate sales had non-residents as buyers (Bank of Portugal, 2018). While these massive purchases are concentrated in the tourist destinations of Porto, Lisbon and the southern Algarve region, average Portuguese house prices rose 27 per cent in real terms between the second quarter of 2013 and the end of 2017 (Figure 9.2).

The changing external financial conditions had profound domestic impacts. The ensuing economic recovery in the rest of Europe from 2013 on, coupled with the rise of low-cost carriers in Portugal and the turmoil in touristic markets in direct competition with the Portuguese (particularly in the Middle East and North Africa), gave domestic tourism a boost (annual growth rates of 10 per cent), turning Portuguese real estate into a more attractive investment (Teles, 2019). This dynamism in tourism provided the opportunity for Portuguese homeowners to explore the emerging short-term rental market that had been developing with the proliferation of touristic websites, such as Airbnb, thus contributing to further commodification of the housing SoP (Figure 9.4).

Public policy once more had a paramount role in this new configuration. One of the impositions of the official lender agreement was the liberalisation of the housing rental market, considered a necessary means to increase the supply of housing stock for rentals so as to give households another option besides homeownership. It instead reduced the rental market by facilitating evictions and, thus, the transformation of long-term tenancy contracts into short-term

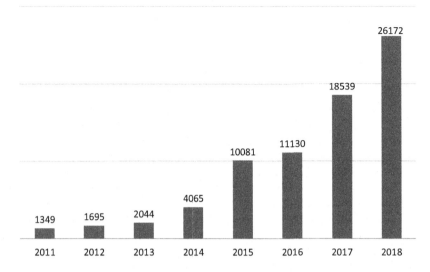

*Figure 9.4* Short-term rental licences
Source: RNAL

rentals. Another important measure was the creation of a new regime of residence permits ('Golden Visas') for foreigners who bought real estate property
above half a million euros, intended to attract foreign funds in an economy shut
out from international financial markets (Santos, 2019).

While the combination of these different factors enabled the recovery of
the housing market, particularly in urban centres, the chaotic and contradictory outcomes of such policies have given rise to new social tensions to
be addressed by public policy. In 2017, the new left-leaning Portuguese government announced a 'new generation' of housing policies. As shown by
Santos (2019), the new policies have adapted to the new financialised configuration, shifting public subsidies from household mortgages to rentals.
Public investment funds have been created to refurbish housing to be allocated
at controlled prices for rental. However, the rents have been benchmarked
not by affordability criteria but by their market prices since the landlords
have to offer a discount of 20 percent, which kept rents unaffordable to the
working classes of the main cities where rents have risen well above those
levels. Mimicking private investment funds, these public investment funds are
subjected to target investment returns which limit their capacity to contribute
to the supply of affordable rents. Moreover, the public investment originates
from state-guaranteed loans from the European Investment Bank (EIB) and
the Social Security Stability Fund, reflecting the permanent limits imposed
by the European institutions on public investment and the recurring need for
debt as the funding source.

The state-sponsored promotion of foreign private financial inflows continues in other forms. Recently, new regulation has been approved to enable the creation of the domestic version of Real Estate Investment Trusts (REITs). Although real estate investment funds have been a feature of housing financialisation since 1985, these funds have been created by the domestic banking sector which has been under close scrutiny by EU authorities since the euro crisis. The new REITs are instead financial entities whose shares can be publicly traded in the stock exchange market, being considered a most suitable vehicle for foreign investment in the Portuguese real estate sector. Committed to making these trusts work, the state ensures their returns through handsome tax benefits on capital gains and exemptions on real estate municipal tax and on value-added tax (Santos, 2019).

The financialised outlook of the Portuguese housing SoP has shifted from a bank-based mortgage lending model to the increasing relevance of foreign (financial and non-financial) direct investment in real estate. Public policy has realigned itself with the changing external financial conditions, relying on this model to revive housing and the real estate sector, and thereby overall growth and employment (Chapter 7 in this volume). New contradictions have arisen. Contrary to the previous model of funding, investment is concentrated in particular territories where tourism is booming and space has become scarce, thereby enhancing new territorial inequalities (Reis, 2019). More dramatically, the combination of frozen mortgage markets and rising house and rental prices has rendered housing less and less affordable to new cohorts of the population (Silva, 2019). To the territorial inequalities and the social reproduction strains, to which current public policy does not seem able to find an answer, one must add the enhanced external financial vulnerability of this new financialised configuration. Housing financialisation is increasingly driven by direct foreign investment from financial agents rather than by the mediation of domestic banks. In the case of a reversal of domestic and/or external financial conditions, capital flight is a likely outcome. And it is likely the absence of mechanisms to prevent or compensate for such flight, as happened in the euro crisis, will lead to the sole alternative: ECB emergency bank lending.

## Water provision: financialisation by other means

Water provision worldwide underwent major changes throughout the past decades, including new management practices (corporatisation), privatisation and an increasing role of private finance. Pioneered in high-income countries, particularly in England and Wales (Bayliss, 2014), these transformations have been replicated around the globe, often with the sponsorship of international organisations, such as the EU, the World Bank or the Organisation for Economic Co-operation and Development (OECD). Notwithstanding context-specific differences, the international movement towards the commodification and privatisation of water has been contested. Successful opposition has resulted in significant setbacks for this policy agenda, such as the re-municipalisation of many systems, as was the case in Buenos Aires, Paris and Berlin (Ahlers, 2010).

While major multinationals have retreated from many markets and been replaced by public entities, private finance has continued to expand and become increasingly influential at the global level (Hall, Lobina & Terhorst, 2013). Indeed, as financialisation processes progressed, the debate over public or private ownership of the water utilities has lost relevance as a measure of the continued expansion of private interests in the sector. Financialisation of water provision can then take diverse configurations in different countries, ranging from more conventional privatisation processes (e.g. in the UK) to the rise of varied forms of public-private partnerships (PPPs), where public property may be preserved (Bayliss, 2014). This new environment reinforces the importance of considering context-specific interactions between finance and water provision systems in order to better pinpoint the contents of financialisation in its geographically variegated forms.

Recent evolution of water provision in Portugal is again shaped by the context of European-driven financialisation already described for housing. The Portuguese water SoP was also marked by social demands in the years after the 1974–1975 revolution, forcing considerable investment effort by public entities in the then highly deficient water and waste systems. However, management of these systems remained in the hands of the newly constitutionally empowered local municipalities.

In 1993, the sector was reorganised, introducing three major institutional transformations in order to commodify water: the corporatisation of the public sector; the introduction of private enterprise practices in water management, which aimed to bring cost recovery practices to water bills; and private capital investment. These changes were justified by the need to enhance investment, taking advantage of available, although conditional, European funding.

Corporatisation involved the de-verticalisation of water provision systems, separating the (capital-intensive) bulk sector (capture, treatment and storage of water) and the retail sector (storage and final distribution). The retail sector remained in the hands of local municipalities, which held the power to fix and charge tariffs to domestic users, but the bulk sector was regionally integrated into 19 newly created multi-municipal companies where municipalities only kept a 49 percent capital share. Control was transferred to the newly created public holding AdP (Águas de Portugal – Waters of Portugal). Corporatisation, through the creation of these new public companies, was understood as a way to enhance efficiency while converging with European rules in order to meet the conditions for accessing investment subsidies and loans from the then European Economic Community and European Investment Bank (Pato, 2011). Given the municipal control of water provision, the transfer of power to AdP had to be agreed voluntarily by municipalities. Allured by the promise of new investment in the capital-intensive bulk sector, without incurring further costs, most municipalities accepted this new architecture. Corporatisation was also introduced at the retail level. Various municipal companies were created with the single purpose of managing retail provision of water and waste water treatment. While most of these companies retained public ownership by being owned by the local municipality, several municipal companies were created in partnership with private capital. Domestic construction companies were the main new private partners, which, in many cases, benefited directly and indirectly from contracts with these municipal companies (Teles, 2015). But the biggest change at the retail level, introduced from 1993 onwards, was the entry of private capital through PPPs in municipal concessions. Coinciding with the expansion of water multinationals across the world, a small number of municipalities covering large populations conceded their retail systems to multinational companies, such as Veolia or Suez, for extended periods.

The introduction of private management practices in the provision of water was enforced through the creation of a regulatory agency for the sector (also encompassing solid waste management). First established in 1995, it was restructured to become, in 2014, ERSAR (Entidade Reguladora dos Serviços de Águas e Resíduos – Water and Waste Services Regulation Authority), an independent body with growing autonomy and strengthened regulation powers. The ERSAR mandate rests on the principle that a natural monopoly ought to be regulated to ensure the adequate protection of consumers. Still, the concern with market efficiency is pervasive. While ERSAR clearly endorses as its mission 'to ensure adequate protection of consumers … by promoting the quality of the service provided by the operators and guaranteeing socially acceptable pricing', it emphatically stresses the need to safeguard 'the financial viability and best interests of the operators, irrespective of their status' (ERSAR, 2012, p. 17). This concern is explicitly conveyed in its endorsement of the total cost recovery principle in the calculation of the prices of water and waste water services, and the recommended targets for the return on capital on these investments of about 5–10 per cent, which have been legally established since the mid-1990s and are based on the ten-year government bond market rate to which is added a 'risk premium' of 3 per cent (Silva, 2010).

Since the early 1990s, European grants and abundant foreign credit (from the European Investment Bank, domestic banks and foreign bonds) funded an impressive evolution of investment in the water and waste water systems. Coverage of water supply and waste water improved, particularly in treated water waste, with coverage rising from 28 percent in 1995 to 85 percent in 2017 (Figure 9.5). The expansion of coverage was followed by an improvement in the quality of water supply. The percentage of 'safe water' to total supply – calculated by ERSAR on the basis of required frequency of water analysis and compliance with defined parameters of water quality – has evolved from 84 percent to 98 percent in the same period (Figure 9.5). Besides household services, there was also significant progress in the treatment of river basins and coastal waters.

Annual investment in the sector grew extensively in the 2000s, from 364.5 million euros in 1999 to almost 1,400 million euros in 2010 (nominal terms) but has decreased to a record low of 464 million in 2016, recovering

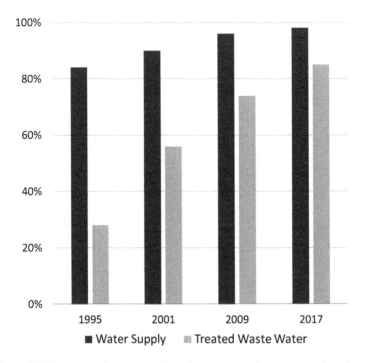

*Figure 9.5* Coverage of water supply and waste water (percentage of total population)
Source: INE

slightly in 2017 (Figure 9.6). Without any funding from the state budget, due to EU Stability Pact deficit limits, the scale of the investments was achieved with foreign capital loans, to which the Portuguese economy had privileged access from the beginning of the 1990s. As in the housing sector, participation in the Economic Monetary Union (EMU) allowed Portuguese firms to benefit from a new and unconstrained access to capital at historically low interest rates in international (European) markets. In the bulk sector, debt for the different AdP subsidiaries increased from 438 million euros in 2003 to 2,470 million in 2012 (representing about 39 percent of the sector's assets). In the retail sector debt rose from 119 million euros in 2003 to 552 million euros in 2012 (representing about 55 percent of the sector assets) (ERSAR, 2014).[2]

AdP, with its corporate structure, was of pivotal importance, channelling most of its external funding to the regional bulk companies that it controls. The scale of AdP enabled it to acquire financial know-how in domestic and foreign financial markets, having had access to three different funding sources: European subsidies, long-term debt (mainly coming from the European Investment Bank (EIB) and bond issuance) and short-term loans from the domestic banking sector. Debt grew from 744 million euros in 2003 to a record of 3,000 million

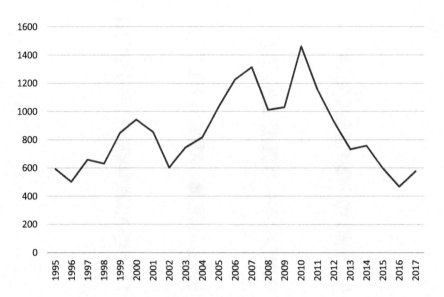

*Figure 9.6* Total annual investment (million euros, current prices, public and private) in water supply and waste water sectors

Source: INE

in 2013. However, reflecting the financial stress of the euro crisis, AdP stopped their investments and pursued a deleveraging strategy, leading to a reduced debt of 1,924 million euros in 2019 (Figure 9.7).

About 70 percent of AdP debt now consists of EIB loans with long maturities and low interest rates, whose relative importance as a funding source rose from the beginning of the 2000s. Private banking debt, still accounting for about 20 percent of total debt in 2013, has disappeared from AdP's balance sheet (AdP, 2019). The rest of the debt refers to external bond markets. AdP issued bonds of around 600 million euros to a very small number of foreign investors during the 2000s. Reflecting the 'capital sudden-stop' of the euro crisis, there were no such bond issuances during the crisis years. But benefiting from the recent change in external financial conditions described above, AdP returned to the international bond market in 2016 (AdP, 2019). Finally, the financial sophistication of AdP and its financialised profile were clearly attested by the value of the interest rate and exchange rate SWAP derivatives taken before the crisis. Contracted mainly with foreign banks, the use of these sophisticated financial products was in the public spotlight during the crisis due the losses incurred by many public corporations. However, AdP was one of the least affected, having nonetheless suffered notional losses of 25 million euros in 2011 and of 14 million euros in 2012.

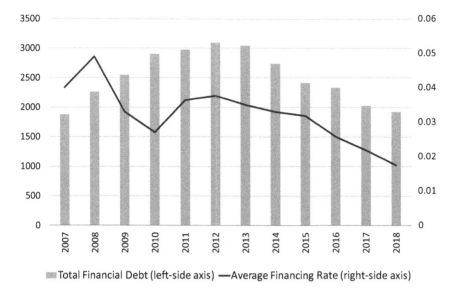

Total Financial Debt (left-side axis) —Average Financing Rate (right-side axis)

*Figure 9.7* Águas de Portugal debt (million euros) and average interest rate
Source: AdP

Reflecting increased debt, investment and output, overall annual costs significantly increased in bulk sector concessionaires, from 258 million euros in 2002 to 572 million euros in 2012. Financial costs played a non-negligible part in this evolution, having gone from 15 million euros in 2003 to 106 million euros in 2012. This spectacular rise of financial costs resulted from the combined effect of rising debt levels and the rise in interest rates due to the eurozone crisis, growing from 3.3 percent in 2002 to 4.2 percent in 2012. Costs also rose in the retail sector (including the waste water system). Again, this evolution was due to rising levels of debt contracted with significantly higher interest rates than the bulk sector. On average, interest rates paid by the retail sector were 5.7 per cent in 2012, reflecting the small scale of most of these providers (mainly municipal public companies) (ERSAR, 2014).

Reflecting both higher bulk tariffs and the costs of investment in retail, retail tariffs increased at a consistently higher rate than inflation (Figure 9.8). Although financial information on the sector has since stopped being published by ERSAR, it is expected that financial costs were reduced from 2014 onwards as interest rates fell in financial markets for Portuguese agents, which may explain the slower growth of tariffs since 2012. Nonetheless, the link between rising tariffs and rising financial costs of debt was undeniable, giving rise to concerns on water affordability for poorer households. Such problems were dealt with through the introduction of subsidised social tariffs so as to ensure conformity with the market-conforming principle of total cost recovery (Teles, 2015).

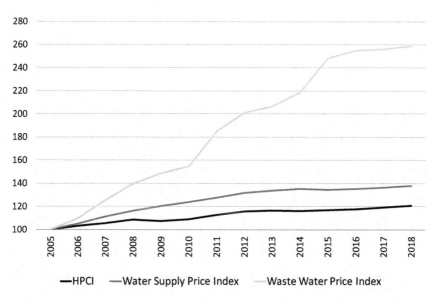

*Figure 9.8* Water provision prices, inflation and disposable income evolution (2005 = 100)

Source: INE

The international financial crisis contributed to further expanding financialisation processes in water provision in Portugal. Building on the transformations of the previous two decades, the new financial and economic constraints created yet more favourable conditions to deepen the financialised character of the Portuguese water sector. The financial conditionality imposed by official foreign lenders created a favourable climate for deepening transformations of water provision in Portugal. The reinforcement of the power of the regulator was key. In 2014, and again in 2019, new powers were granted to ERSAR, which now has legal powers to impose tariffs on municipalities to adopt the full cost recovery principle. Municipalities have been contesting these news laws, having taken up a legal battle against the government on the grounds that it constitutes a loss of constitutionally protected municipal power (Teles, 2015). AdP, even if still formally publicly owned, has been partially privatised, and it has gradually integrated corporate interests and financial criteria in its management practices. For instance, in the waste management segment, a subholding company of AdP, Empresa Geral do Fomento (EGF), was privatised in 2015, being bought by the Portuguese construction company Mota-Engil. In stark contrast to the water segment, all regional corporations belonging to EGF were financially viable. Plans to privatise EGF faced strong resistance from some municipalities, who issued court orders against it, but ultimately failed in their intent.

Although not on the agenda of the current left-leaning government, pre-vious proposals for the privatisation of the public holding company AdP are set to be resumed in the near future. Straightforward privatisation of AdP is not the only option. Given the ongoing verticalisation of provision and reinforced control over the whole water delivery process, from source to water waste management, water commodification can take other forms. It may be partially privatised with private capital buying a part of the com-pany or, most likely, remain in public hands while expanding private retail concessions, particularly in major urban centres where water provision is already a profitable business, such as in the Lisbon area, where investment is older and not reliant on debt.

The impact of the crisis and of the changing financialised character of the Portuguese economy on the domestic private sector is also relevant. With Portuguese firms still heavily indebted, new opportunities arise for foreign players. This means that the Portuguese private water sector is now more open and attractive to foreign investors, offering the guarantee of a stable stream of future cash flows stemming from the provision of an essential, but ever more expensive, good. Private companies in the sector consist of companies that hold municipal retail concessions, covering around 13 per cent of the popula-tion (Teles, 2015). The biggest private player, Aquapor, initially part of the AdP group, was privatised in 2008 and is now owned by a Portuguese construction company DST. Indaqua, which was controlled by three different Portuguese construction companies, now has two major shareholders, Miya Waters, which belongs to the British private equity group Bridgepoint, and the German financial group Talanx. AGS, formerly controlled by a consortium of Spanish and Portuguese construction companies, is now part of the Japanese conglom-erate Marubeni.

The growing participation of foreign capital in the Portuguese water SoP reflects the new phase of semi-peripheral financialisation in Portugal, where for-eign financial flows take the form of direct purchase of assets. Recent investments are understood as foothold in the Portuguese market, placing new private contenders in a more favourable position for future privatisations, in the form of new concessions, as was explicitly stated by the Marubeni conglomerate.[3]

The importance of household payments through tariffs and the need for total cost recovery are again apparent, since they secure essential cash flows for financial innovation. For instance, Veolia Portugal was sold in 2014 to the Chinese group Beijing Water Systems, thus confirming their international disinvestment strategy of the past years. The latter case has been pointed to as following the financialised model already seen in England and Wales. This Chinese company uses a sophisticated financial scheme, where an off-shore company based in Bermuda bought the retail concessions run by Veolia through a shareholder loan which was to be paid by the cash flows provided by rising water tariffs (Bayliss, 2014). It should also be noted that, stressing the historical legacy of the semi-peripheral Portuguese economy, all these major private players have internationalised their operations, particularly to

Portuguese-speaking countries (Aquapor in Angola, Mozambique and Cap Vert; Indaqua in Angola; and AGS in Brazil).

These institutional changes (corporatisation and transfer of responsibilities from municipalities, private capital involvement, new regulatory framework) did not face much popular resistance during the 1990s and early 2000s. Such transformations coincided with extraordinary progress in the provision of water and waste water services and relatively contained growth of the tariffs set by municipalities.[4] Being a sector where public involvement is still prevalent, resistance to further commodification and privatisation of the sector has come from the trade union movement, which is still strong within the public sector. The Agua é de Todos (Water for All) movement, founded in 2011 by several trade unions, has fought to 'enshrine the 2010 United Nations (UN) resolution of "water and sanitation are a human right" in national legislation and legally prevent any kind of privatisation' (Bieler and Jordan, 2018, p. 949).

Nonetheless, the increasing role of finance in water provision – through debt that funded most of the new investment – set the scene for a new stage where the relation between finance and domestic water consumers is increasingly tighter. Hence, the new corporate structures, lead to the streaming of income from households to finance through tariffs, which have risen considerably and above inflation in the past decade. Growing financialisation of water provision, slowly but surely, constructed a market for the sector. The burden of debt, the entry of new foreign financial agents and a regulatory model that enforces market discipline on the different agents involved in this SoP have opened the path for further privatisation, this time with the more likely direct involvement of foreign financial agents.

## Why variegation matters

The analysis of the housing and water SoPs shows that there is no straight-forward mechanism for the financialisation of any given sector. Different historical paths, agents and configurations of provisioning of a given good produce different outcomes (Bayliss, Fine & Robertson, 2013). Researching financialisation for each SoP shows that common assertions that directly link financialisation with privatisation or with a shrinking role of the state should, at least, be taken with caution. The plasticity shown by finance in its perme-ation in different sectors is a paradigmatic example of how financialisation has been progressing throughout different sectors in a variegated manner. However, one should highlight not only the specificities of each commodity or com-modity form, but also the specificity of the wider context that affects them. Of particular relevance is the specific trajectory of each country in integrating the international financial hierarchy that constrains and moulds financialisation processes (Rodrigues, Santos & Teles, 2016).

The financialisation of housing was and still is the cornerstone of financialisation in Portugal, having a strong influence on economic growth in the country. Built around a newly liberalised financial system, open to foreign finance, the main financial conduit to households and to the private real estate and construction sectors was domestic bank credit, the latter obtained in the European credit market. Contrary to what happened in other 'core' countries, housing financialisation was not so much the result of the expansion of financial securities markets or even of the emergence of new financial agents, but the outcome of a larger process of financial and monetary integration that enabled access to loanable capital money from the eurozone. Thus the financialisation of housing is not the outcome of the state retreating from collective forms of provisioning. The state had a most active role in the whole process. It led the integration process and the reforms of the financial sector leading to the economic and monetary union, and it purposefully fostered the financialisation of housing through varied means, such as the creation of tax incentives, re-regulation of land and rental markets, and public investment.

Being a basic good where competition between providers at endpoint is difficult to implement and the institution of property rights is challenging, the state has remained the hegemonic provider of water. However, this did not prevent the whole reorganisation of the sector along neoliberal lines (corporatisation, market conformity re-regulation, private capital entry) that enabled the growing influence of finance in the production and distribution of water, furthering its commodity form. Similar to the housing sector, this influence was mostly exercised through a European-sponsored debt model. The difference was that this credit consisted of public investment. In return, the sector was subjected to a new management model, with water tariffs increasingly based on the cost recovery principle, entailing a growing share for the repayment of debts. Given the amounts involved, finance expansion was mainly carried out by financial official institutions, such as the EIB, that channelled loans to the Portuguese corporate public providers with the mediation of the state. It also involved, even if to a lesser extent, the participation of international securities markets. Domestic banks played only a marginal role. European cross-border banking loans are thus relevant in both sectors, with other forms of finance, such as the bond markets, playing a minor role. Meanwhile, water bills, though set by municipalities, are increasingly mimicking market prices, allowing guaranteed cash flows for the financial sector. In fact, having households as primary sources of income in both water and housing provisioning allows reasonably guaranteed cash flows to the financial sector, in the form of either mortgage payments or bills, making household social reproduction vulnerable to conjectural financial conditions.

More recently, both SoPs have been going through common transformations. The continuing expansionary ECB monetary policy and consequent drop of interest rates has enabled both sectors to recover from the euro crisis, although at different paces. In housing, a new boom has taken place, although very concentrated in urban centres and leading to a housing crisis. Driven by new foreign financial inflows in search of yield, domestic banks are no longer the central agents of financialisation. Foreign investment funds are taking up their role. In water provision, financial debt and costs have fallen and investment recovered slightly, but new foreign financial agents have entered the market, replacing Portuguese construction companies and water multinationals, now disinvesting from direct provision. Both sectors are thus more vulnerable to uncertain external conditions and to the risk of capital flight since the weight of domestic agents and interests in the Portuguese political economy has diminished. Future financial instability may be costlier than ever for the Portuguese economy. The semi-peripheral character of the Portuguese economy seems to have been reinforced in the post-crisis recovery that the country has since been experiencing.

The divergent and convergent points between both SoPs also have diverse political dynamics underpinning them. As we have seen, the ongoing com-modification of both goods is different, at least in pace. The municipality con-trol of retail water access is a significant brake in the cost recovery principle for bills. Moreover, being a sector still in the public domain allows (local) workers to be organised in a strong union that has been at the forefront of the fight against privatisation. The same is not true for the construction and real estate sectors, where the private and atomised structure of firms and recurrent precar-ious labour relations hinder any kind of relevant intervention of construction unions in the current debate on the housing crisis.

This variegation has strong policy implications for how to de-financialise social provisioning. Political action and policy proposals must adapt to the specificities of each sector and the agents involved, refusing a catch-all approach. For example, the current housing crisis in Portugal must imply a comprehensive diagnosis and critical analysis of the changing nature of the financialisation process in the country and the ineffective and perverse char-acter of tax incentives and publicly subsidised investment funds in reinforcing the financialised outlook. The role of public property and provision must be set as a comprehensive alternative able to answer social demands. Nonetheless, regulation of financial agents (e.g. reversing the creation of REITs) must be part and parcel of a comprehensive housing policy. In the case of water, the focus should not only be resistance to (foreign) private capital provision, but the reversal of public policies that enhanced the continuing transformation of water as a commodity, namely corporatisation and the regulatory framework, and insistence on the role of municipalities as locus of democratic decision-making and as the adequate governance scale. Again, finance should not be outside the policy focus. Public investment in infrastructure should not be exclusively dependent on corporate (privately sourced) debt, not least because this is more expensive than public debt.

Finally, such a case-by-case approach should not forfeit a more systemic approach where finance, and the Portuguese subordination as a semi-periphery, take a central role, stressing the dependence on foreign financial flows and how European strictures on monetary and fiscal policy hinder other policy approaches. Capital controls, adequate fiscal policy and financial sector regula-tion are some of the economic arenas where any policy effort to de-financialise housing and water SoPs has to intervene. These imply economic, financial and monetary sovereignty that is part and parcel of any attempt to break with the reinforced semi-peripheral position of the Portuguese economy.

## Acknowledgements

This work has received the financial support of the Portuguese Foundation for Science and Technology (FCT/MEC), through national funds, and of the ERDF through the Competitiveness and Innovation Operational Program COMPETE 2020 (Project FINHABIT-PTDC/ATP-GEO/2362/2014-POCI-01-0145-FEDER-016869).

## Notes

1 The distinction between commodity, commodity form and commodity calculation rests on how the production of different goods and services is brought about. Commodities are produced to be sold for the market driven by the profit motive. Commodity forms involve regular payments for goods and services not driven by the profit motive, such as tariffs for publicly provided water utilities. Finally, commodity calculation refers to the production of goods and services where there is an absence of payment, i.e. where production is not driven by actual monetary transactions, but monetary valuation nonetheless occurs, for example through measurement of the cost of provision (Fine, Bayliss & Robertson, 2015).
2 Since 2014, ERSAR has stopped publishing detailed financial information on providers.
3 www.marubeni.com/en/news/2014/release/ags_eng.pdf.
4 Despite recent steady increases, tariffs are still below costs in most municipalities. Only a few retail private concessions reflect costs and adopt tariffs well above the national average (Teles, 2015).

## References

Aalbers, M.B. (2016). *The Financialization of Housing: A Political Economy Approach.* London: Routledge.
AdP (Águas de Portugal) (2019). Annual report and accounts, 2018. Lisbon: AdP. Available at www.adp.pt/en/adp-group/financial-information/annual-reports/downloads/file258_gb.pdf.
Ahlers, R. (2010) Fixing and nixing: the politics of water privatization. *Review of Radical Political Economics, 42*(2), 213–230.
Baganha, M.I., Marques, J.C., & Góis, P. (2002). O sector da construção civil e obras públicas em Portugal: 1990–2000 (Oficina do CES, No. 73). Coimbra: Centro de Estudos Sociais.
Bank of Portugal (2018). *Relatório de estabilidade financeira, Junho de 2018.* Lisbon: Bank of Portugal.
Bayliss, K. (2014). The financialization of water. *Review of Radical Political Economics, 46*(3), 277–291.

Bayliss, K., Fine, B., & Robertson, M. (2017). Introduction to special issue on the material cultures of financialisation. *New Political Economy, 22*(4), 355–370.

Bayliss, K., Fine, B. & Robertson, M. (2013). From financialisation to consumption: the systems of provision approach applied to housing and water (FESSUD Working Paper Series, N° 2). Leeds: FESSUD.

Becker, J., Jäger, J., Leubolt, B., & Weissenbacher, R. (2010). Peripheral financialization and vulnerability to crisis: a regulationist perspective. *Competition & Change, 14*(3–4), 225–247.

Bieler, A., & Jordan, J. (2018). Commodification and 'the commons': the politics of privatising public water in Greece and Portugal during the eurozone crisis. *European Journal of International Relations, 24*(4), 934–957.

Bonizzi, B. (2013). Financialization in developing and emerging countries. *International Journal of Political Economy, 42*, 83–107.

Caetano, M., Carrão, H., & Painho, M. (2005). *Alterações da ocupação do solo em Portugal continental*. Lisbon: Instituto do Ambiente.

Christophers, B. (2015). The limits to financialization. *Dialogues in Human Geography, 5*(2), 183–200.

ERSAR (Entidade Reguladora dos Serviços de Águas e Resíduos) (2012, 2014), Relatórios anuais do sector de águas e resíduos em Portugal. Available at www.ersar. pt.

Fine, B. (2014). The continuing enigmas of social policy (UNRISD Working Paper 2014-10). Available at www.unrisd.org/unrisd/website/document.nsf/(httpPublications)/30B153EE73F52ABFC1257D0200420A61?OpenDocument.

Fine, B. (2013). Consumption matters. *Ephemera: Theory and Politics in Organisation, 13*(2), 217–248.

Fine, B., Bayliss, K., & Robertson, M. (2015). Housing and water in light of financialisation and 'financialisation' (FESSUD Working Paper Series, No. 156). Leeds: FESSUD.

Hall, D., Lobina, E., & Terhorst, P. (2013). Re-municipalisation in the early twenty-first century: water in France and energy in Germany. *International Review of Applied Economics, 27*(2), 193–214.

Kaltenbrunner, A., & Painceira, J.P. (2015). Developing countries' changing nature of financial integration and new forms of external vulnerability: the Brazilian experience. *Cambridge Journal of Economics, 39*, 1281–1306.

López Hernández, I., & Rodríguez López, E. (2010). *Fin de ciclo: financiarización, territorio y sociedad de propietarios en la onda larga del capitalismo hispano (1959–2010)*. Madrid: Traficantes de Sueños.

Pato, J. (2011). *História das políticas públicas de abastecimento e saneamento de águas em Portugal*. Lisbon: ERSAR/ICS.

Reis, J. (2019). O território ainda existe? Sistemas de provisão de habitação e o desperdício do país. In A.C. Santos (ed.), *A nova questão da habitação em Portugal* (pp. 53–87). Lisbon: Almedina.

Rodrigues, J., Santos, A.C., & Teles, N. (2016). Semi-peripheral financialisation: the case of Portugal. *Review of International Political Economy, 23*(3), 480–510.

Ryan-Collins, J., Lloyd, T., & Macfarlane, L. (2017). *Rethinking the Economics of Land and Housing*. London: Zed Books.

Santos, A.C. (2019). Habitação em tempos financeiros em Portugal. In A.C. Santos (ed.), *A nova questão da habitação em Portugal* (pp. 15–52). Lisbon: Almedina.

Santos, A.C., Rodrigues, J., & Teles, N. (2018). Semi-peripheral financialisation and social reproduction: the case of Portugal. *New Political Economy, 23*(4), 475–494.

Santos, A.C., Serra, N., & Teles, N. (2015). Finance and housing provision in Portugal (FESSUD Working Paper Series, No. 79). Leeds: FESSUD.

Silva, J. (2010). Modelo de cálculo de ganhos de produtividade no sector de águas e resíduos em Portugal. Master's thesis. Instituto de Ciências do Trabalho e da Empresa.

Silva, R. (2019). Crise e desigualdade habitacional: como (não) se vive em Lisboa. In A.C. Santos (ed.), *A nova questão da habitação em Portugal* (pp. 233–258). Lisbon: Almedina.

Teles, N. (2019). Financeirização e habitação: A terra e renda fundiária como elos em falta. In A.C. Santos (ed.), *A nova questão da habitação em Portugal* (pp. 87–110). Lisbon: Almedina.

Teles, N. (2015). Financialisation and neoliberalism: the case of water provision in Portugal (FESSUD Working paper, No. 102). Leeds: FESSUD.

# 10 Financialisation and inequality in the semi-periphery

## Evidence from Portugal

*Sérgio Lagoa and Ricardo Barradas*

## Introduction

Despite being a disputed concept in the literature (van der Zwan, 2014), financialisation broadly refers to the growing weight of finance in modern economies. This salient trend has been visible in various countries since the 1980s, fostered by the deregulation of the financial system and the liberalisation of the cross-border movement of capital (Stockhammer, 2012).

In Barradas et al. (2018), we have dealt with the various features of financialisation (or financed-dominated capitalism) in Portugal. A key element, also stressed by Rodrigues, Santos and Teles (2016, and Chapter 2 in this volume), is the strong growth in household and non-financial corporation (NFC) indebtedness from 1995 to 2009, leading to one of the highest indebtedness rates among euro area countries in 2009. From the mid-1990s, the growth of bank credit fed one of the fastest growths in the financial sector in the EU and, by 2009, Portugal had one of the highest shares of finance and insurance activities as a percentage of GDP amongst euro area countries. The weight of financial assets relative to GDP increased from nearly 450 per cent in 1995 to over 700 per cent in 2011, indicating indirectly the accumulation of financial rents (Cingolani, 2013), which are, according to Kalecki, (cited by Power, Epstein & Abrena, 2003) the income earned by owners of financial institutions and of financial assets. The growth in financial services meant that a growing fraction of the economy's profits was coming from financial corporations: between 1997 and 2008, the gross operational surplus (GOS) of financial corporations rose from nearly 12 per cent to more than 23 per cent of the total GOS of Portuguese firms (including both financial and non-financial corporations).

Santos and Teles (2016) show that households increased their involvement with the financial system not only as debtors (especially through mortgage credit) but also as financial asset holders (especially in the form of deposits and pensions and life insurance funds). Financialisation also drives changes in NFC behaviour, notably the rise of financial receipts, due to higher engagement in financial activities, and the rise of financial payments in order to satisfy impatient capital (Hein, 2012). In Portugal, dividends paid and received by NFCs as a percentage of GOS had a positive trend between 1995 and 2008, notably over the period 2004 to 2008.

Due to the Global Financial Crisis and the change in growth strategy, several indicators of financialisation declined between 2008 and 2017, notably the indebtedness of corporations (bank credit, other loans and securities), which went from 146.5 per cent of GDP to 135.5 per cent, and above all household debt, which fell from 92 per cent to 72.4 per cent.

Therefore, the financialisation process was particularly visible between 1995 and 2008 – alternatively, the final year can be considered 2009, depending on the indicator used. Given the decline in GDP in 2009, we choose to define the period of stronger financialisation as between 1995 and 2008 to assess whether there was an increase in the inequality of income distribution in this period.

The growing weight of finance may increase inequality and poverty in Portugal for several reasons. Firstly, indebted households and corporations are more exposed to changes in interest rates and to business cycles. Indeed, after 2008, non-performing loans rose considerably in the segments of credit to consumption and to some industries, showing the difficulties that economic agents experienced during the economic crisis. Notably, households with excess debt have more difficulty in adjusting to falling wages, to a rise in unemployment, and to a fall in gains from trading financial products and selling their houses and are, therefore, more likely to have financial difficulties or even fall into poverty. Although debt and financial assets are more concentrated in high- and middle-income households, under severe conditions the latter may also fall below the poverty line.

Secondly, the poorest households may not benefit from the growth in credit or, when they do, the financial conditions are worse. Unequal access to both house mortgages and fiscal benefits for house purchase has meant that low-income households benefited less from the house price upward trend, which contributed to increased income and wealth inequality, despite subsidised interest rates targeted to young low-income individuals for access to mortgage credit (Martins & Villanueva, 2006). On the financial assets side, in Portugal, as in other European countries, the richer households hold more financial assets (Santos & Teles, 2016), which allows them to benefit more from asset price booms.

Some of the middle and lower classes who were able to access credit and who were severely hit by the economic crisis, ended up losing their houses to the bank and had to find alternative housing in a narrow rental market. After the economic crisis, there was pressure for an increase in housing rents due to low house supply and increasing demand from foreign households and holiday home rental.

Thirdly, the increased political power of finance may have led to a reduction in wages and to poorer working conditions through several channels, notably the shareholder orientation in firms' management, which also causes a reduction in trade union power – these mechanisms will be developed below. To aggravate the situation, financialisation all over the world pressures for a retrenchment of the welfare state, with a reduction in social and pension benefits, increasing financial payments by households, and privatisation of public corporations. The idea of an asset-based welfare becomes more important, and individuals should own assets (financial, real estate and human capital) to accommodate difficulties, with the responsibility for covering risks moving from the state to the individual (Finlayson, 2009). In Portugal, we do not observe a reduction of social protection. Instead there is an increase in such expenditure during the period of financialisation (Rodrigues, Santos & Teles, 2018), which is associated with the late consolidation of the welfare state. Nevertheless, that does not mean that financialisation did not hamper, in some degree, the expansion of state intervention in social and connected areas. Some important examples in which such effects occurred are the increase of the share of total health expenditure supported by the private sector (mostly households) – from 29.52 per cent in 2000 to 33.35 per cent in 2017;[1] the emergence of private firms in the water provision system (Teles, 2015); and the favouring of private provision of housing (Santos, Serra & Teles, 2015) and of pensions (Rodrigues, Santos & Teles, 2018).

Finally, the effects of finance-dominated capitalism in Portugal are not restricted to the period of growth in finance, as they include the creation of conditions for subsequent crisis. The growth in the financial sector produced serious fragilities in the sector (low capital and liquidity ratios and a high concentration of credit in the real estate area – households, construction and real estate firms) and ultimately made the economy more vulnerable to financing in international markets (Barradas et al., 2018). Those fragilities contributed to the Portuguese sovereign debt crisis in 2011, which resulted in a severe austerity programme, negotiated with the Troika, aimed at internal devaluation (reduction in wages) and fiscal austerity, with cuts in social benefits and pensions, stalling of collective bargaining, and labour market reforms with adverse consequences for workers. The support of some banks (BPN, BANIF and BES) with public money, ultimately deepened the crisis.

Thus, for several reasons, the financialisation process is often associated with increasing income inequality, in terms of both functional and personal income distribution (Baiardi & Morana, 2018; Clarke, Xu & Zou, 2006; Hein, 2012, 2015). The former is related to the distribution of income between production factors (capital and labour) and the latter to the distribution of income among individuals. We will discuss each of these in turn. Both phenomena are of growing importance in contemporary societies due to their negative impacts in economic, social and political areas, as recent events have shown. Nevertheless, inequality issues have received little attention from mainstream economics. One notable exception is Piketty (2014), who argues that in the last century economic progress has not delineated a reduction in inequalities as predicted by the Kuznets curve. The average return of capital has been stable and higher than the average economic growth, indicating that capital owners are growing richer than the remaining population. Milanovic (2016) argues that in some industrialised countries there is a second Kuznets cycle of upward income inequality from 1980, due notably to globalisation and free movement of capital, technological change and rents from technological innovations, policy changes weakening the welfare state (the move from Keynesian to neo-liberal policies), and the movement of labour from manufacturing to services (which are more heterogeneous).

In this chapter we look at how the evolution of inequality in Portugal in the last years is related to financialisation. The second section analyses functional income distribution, looking at the wage share and rentier income. The third section focuses on personal income distribution and poverty. The fourth section approaches briefly other effects of financialisation and other factors explaining functional and personal income inequality and poverty. Finally, we present a broader discussion of the main conclusions.

## Functional income distribution

Functional income distribution relates to labour and profit shares, more specifically, the portions of the national income that are channelled to workers through wages and to capital owners through profits, respectively. Despite the theoretical and empirical suggestion by mainstream economics that labour income and profit shares should remain stable over time (Kaldor, 1961), decline in the former and the consequent rise in the latter have been common trends in the most advanced economies since the early 1980s (Dünhaupt, 2011; Lin & Tomaskovic-Devey, 2013; Stockhammer, 2012). Barradas (2019) stresses that this evolution was transversal to all EU countries, with the labour share being already less than 50 per cent of the national income in 12 European countries (Czech Republic, Greece, Lithuania, Hungary, Poland, Romania, Slovakia, Latvia, Norway, Ireland, Malta and Sweden).

From a theoretical point of view, the downward trend in the labour share implies a more unequal income distribution between workers and capital owners with several deleterious consequences, notably the rise of social tensions between workers and shareholders (Dünhaupt, 2011), the fall of aggregate demand in countries with a wage-led model (Dünhaupt, 2013),[2] the erosion of the financial sustainability of social security systems as they are typically financed by wages (Cichon et al., 2004), the rise of personal income inequality (Karanassou & Sala, 2013), and the heavy indebtedness of households to compensate for the fall in wages and to support consumption (Hein, 2012).

Some authors associate the downward trend of the labour income share with the financialisation processes occurring from the 1980s on, which produce a more unequal functional income distribution through three channels and various sub-channels (Hein, 2012, 2015).[3] The first channel is associated with a change in the sectoral composition of economies, which operates through two different (and independent) sub-channels: the increasing importance of the financial sector and the decreasing weight of the public sector. Indeed, the growth of the financial sector pressures for a reduction in wage share as this sector is more capital-intensive than the non-financial sector (Hein, 2012). The reduction of the public sector leads to a similar outcome because it has a smaller profit share than the private sector (Dünhaupt, 2013) and its trade union membership is higher.

The second channel acts through the paradigm of 'shareholder orientation' that leads to the rise in profit and dividend claims by shareholders. These demands create a pressure to cut wages and other benefits to workers, and to engage more in financial activities, which reinforce the growth of the financial sector (Crotty, 2005). Finally, the third channel involves the weakening of trade unions and workers' bargaining power, which operates through several different sub-channels, notably the aforementioned paradigm of 'shareholder orientation' in corporate governance and the increasing importance of finance (trade unions are weaker in the financial sector); see also Chapters 5 and 6 in this volume.

In addition to financialisation and the decline in unions' power, technological progress and globalisation have contributed to the fall in labour income share (Dünhaupt, 2013). Effectively, technological progress has been capital-augmenting since the 1980s, thereby implying a substitution of low-skilled and unskilled labour by new technologies.

Globalisation has also been responsible for a fall in labour income share in the developed countries. The argument is in line with the Hecksher-Ohlin model, which, using simplifying assumptions, concludes that globalisation raises the return of the factor that is relatively abundant (capital in developed countries) and lowers the return of the nonabundant factor (labour in developed countries). The increase in world labour supply due to the participation of China in world trade pressured for a decline of wages in developed countries. In addition, globalisation has contributed to a deterioration of the bargaining power of workers.

A relatively small body of empirical literature has emerged in recent years to provide an econometric assessment of the impact of financialisation on functional income distribution (Barradas, 2019; Barradas & Lagoa, 2017; Dünhaupt, 2013; Lin & Tomaskovic-Devey, 2013; Köhler, Guschanski & Stockhammer, 2018). Most of these empirical studies find statistical evidence supporting the theoretical claim that financialisation has been a driver of the fall in the labour income share.

In the Portuguese case, the indicator usually used to assess functional income distribution, namely the adjusted wage share (the ratio of compensation of employees to GDP),[4] had a downward path from the late 1970s. Figure 10.1 shows the wage share at market prices and factor cost; we focus on the latter because it assesses the distribution of national income between labour and capital without considering state intervention through indirect taxes and subsidies. Five main subperiods are observed in the overall trend during the last 60 years (Lagoa et al., 2014). From 1960, when Portugal joined the European Free Trade Association (EFTA), to the early 1970s, the wage share rose gradually due to the rapid industrialisation of the Portuguese economy. The Colonial War (1961–1974) also played a role by reducing the labour supply and increasing real wages.

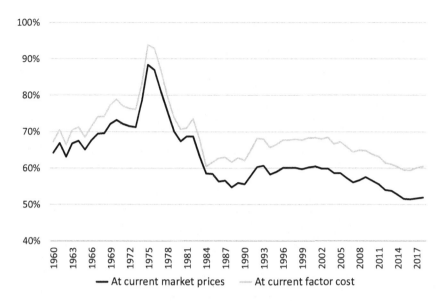

*Figure 10.1* Adjusted wage share as percentage of GDP
Note: adjusted for full-time equivalent employees, 2018 is a projection.
Source: AMECO

In the revolutionary period of 1974–1976, real wages went up sharply in comparison to labour productivity as a result of both the need to improve labour and social conditions and radical left-wing-oriented economic policies.

In the post-revolutionary period, the adjusted wage share registered a steep decline from 93.9 per cent in 1976 to 60.4 per cent in 1984. This was a period marked by international economic crises, rising external imbalances, and two adjustment programmes under the IMF (1977 and 1983), all forcing a drop in real wages. In contrast, between 1985 and 1992 the adjusted wage share increased to 68.3 per cent, reflecting Portugal's strong economic growth in this period due to its admission to the European Union in 1986. The positive effect of GDP growth on the wage share is explained by the low levels of unemployment and rapid wage growth occurring when the economy is expanding (Estrada & Valdeolivas, 2012). Yet, such a direct connection may not always exist due to wage rigidity and delayed employment changes by firms because of adjustment costs and uncertainty in the business cycle (Willis & Wroblewski, 2007).

Indeed, from the mid-1990s until 2003, the adjusted wage share remained stable even though an increase had been expected due to high GDP growth rates (until 2001). Besides wage and employment rigidities, this is probably explained by growth in credit and the financial sector, increasing financialisation of NFCs, the privatisation of public firms, and increasing integration in the international economy. As mentioned above, the growth of the financial sector, the financialisation of NFCs and the privatisation of public firms together reduced wage share. Integration in the global economy further pressured for lower wages due to imports from low-wage countries, delocalisation of firms, weakening of trade unions and penetration of international financial capital seeking short-term profits (Hein, 2012; Chapter 4 in this volume).

A downward trend of wage share began in 2003, continuing until 2016 when it reached the minimum of 59.3 per cent. Initially, this decline is explained by the slowdown of the Portuguese economy from 2002 onwards, which produced an increase in unemployment from 5 per cent in 2002 to 7.6 per cent in 2008. The Portuguese sovereign debt crisis and the consequent adjustment measures implemented from 2011 onwards continued the downward trend via wage cuts. After the crisis, namely between 2017 and 2018, there was a slight recovery of 1.1 p.p in the share of workers in income as a result of higher GDP and wage growth rates and a lower unemployment rate.

In short, the increasing importance of finance from 1995 until 2008 was accompanied by a decline in the wage share only from 2003 onwards. It should be mentioned that other phenomena contributed to the reduction in the wage share from 2003 to 2016, notably the sovereign debt crisis, the reduction in union power (Table 10.4), the increase in competition from abroad (Table 10.4) and technological progress (although this was relatively small: total factor productivity grew 0.38 per cent per year between 2003 and 2016 (data from AMECO).[5] The reduction in the wage share would probably be larger if the remuneration of top management were removed from compensations, as they are closer to profits than to employees' remunerations.

Barradas and Lagoa (2017) estimate an aggregate labour income share function for Portugal, including control variables (technological progress – total factor productivity; degree of openness of the economy; education; and the business cycle) and four other variables to capture the aforementioned channels linked to financialisation (size of the financial sector – value-added; government expenditure; shareholder orientation – interest and dividends paid by NFCs relative to Gross Value Added; and trade union density). They use annual data between 1978 and 2012 to estimate an Autoregressive Distributed Lag (ARDL) model.

They find that in the long term while government activity, trade union density and education exert a positive effect on labour income share, international trade has a negative impact. They argue that financialisation contributes indirectly to the decline in labour share by weakening trade unions and reducing public spending.

Finally, financialisation, by contributing to a decline of the labour income share, can explain the weak economic dynamism in Portugal between 2000 and 2013. Portugal is characterised by a wage-led model (Onaran & Obst, 2016), which means that the decrease of wages has a detrimental effect on private consumption that is not compensated for by the beneficial effects on investment and net exports.[6] This suggests that the hypothesised 'secular stagnation' in the era of financialisation could materialise, with consequent rise of inequalities and poverty in the future.

### Rentier income

If financialisation is at least in part responsible for the decline in the wage share observed in Portugal, then rentiers should be beneficiaries. To analyse the share of rentier income in the national income, as Dünhaupt (2011) did for Germany and the US, we start by noting that the net national income is:[7]

*Wages + (Operating Surplus) + (Indirect taxes) − Subsidies*

Property income is paid out of the operating surplus, and corresponds to:

*(distributed income of corporations) + Interests + Rents + (reinvested earnings of FDI) + (property income attributed to insurance policy holders)*

If there were no 'rest of the world', the sum of the net property income (received minus paid) of households, financial and non-financial corporations, and the government would be zero, as the income paid by one sector is received by another. For instance, when corporations pay dividends to households, there is an outflow from corporations (negative property income) and an inflow into households (positive property income), but for the sum of the two sectors the net property income is zero. Therefore, to obtain the rentier income we use the net property income of households only, as they are the recipients of the money paid by corporations and the government.[8] Thus, rentier income includes all the property income received by households (minus the one paid), including dividends distributed, interest and rents.

Rentier income is a component of the net national income, which is obtained by:

(Rentier income) + (Compensation of employees) + (Operating surplus/ mixed income of households) + (Primary income of government) + (Primary income of non-financial and financial corporations)

Primary income of non-financial and financial corporations is approximately the retained earnings of corporations. Using this formula, we can assess the evolution of the other elements of the national income in comparison with the rentier income, notably the compensation of employees and the retained earnings of corporations.

Analysing Figure 10.2, we observe that property income has not registered an upward trend; in fact, it only grew significantly between 1977 and 1985, due to the increase in deposit interest rates (which reached a historical maximum in 1984–1985). The high interest rates may also explain the strong decline in the

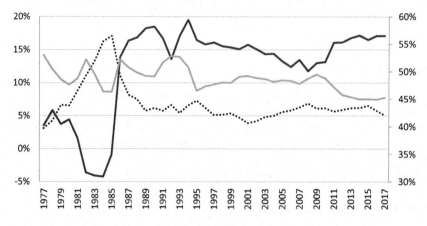

*Figure 10.2* Property income and its counterparts in proportion of gross national income

Source: INE up to 1994 and Eurostat from 1995

gross primary income of corporations over the period 1977–1986, which was actually negative in some years.

After a slight downward trend between 1995 and 2001, property income registered a gradual and slight increase between 2002 and 2008 (+2.7 p.p.). Employees' compensation rose from 1995 to 2008 and was accompanied by a decrease in the gross primary income of corporations. In 2010, the sovereign debt crisis led to a profound change: employees' compensation decreased and retained earnings increased, while rentier income remained broadly constant. The increase in retained earnings was a response to the difficulty in obtaining banking financing for investment or working capital.

A closer analysis of the components of rentier income shows that whereas rents (rents on land, excluding housing rents) are insignificant, property income of insurance policy holders is quite important, ranging from 0.9 to 2 per cent of national income since 1995 (Figure 10.3).[9] The two most important components of the rentier income – interest and dividends – had distinct evolutions. The interest share decreased from 1985 to 2010 in line with the fall in both interest rates and savings (directed to fixed income products).[10] From 2011 to 2015, there was an increase in interest received, partly explained by the rise in the interest rates of deposits and government securities, due to the European sovereign debt crisis. On the other hand, distributed dividends (by listed and non-listed companies) showed an upward trend from 1995 to 2007

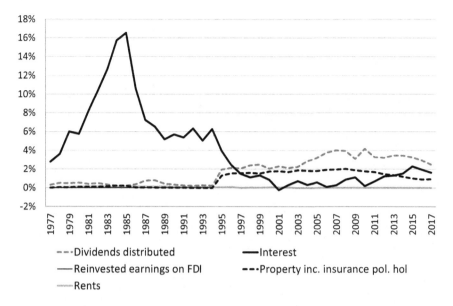

*Figure 10.3* Breakdown of primary income as percentage of gross national income
Source: INE up to 1994 and Eurostat from 1995

(+2.1 p.p.),[11] followed by a downward trend until 2017 (-1.5 p.p.), explained by the aforementioned increase in retained earnings in response to the reduction in banking financing to firms. Thus, we can conclude that, from 2002 to 2007, the rise in the property income of households is explained primarily by the increase in dividends.

It is interesting to analyse whether the share of property income in Portugal is very different from other developed countries. Dünhaupt (2011) computes the rentier share for Germany and the US using the net national income discounting the consumption of physical capital. Our data are not directly comparable to these data because we do not deduct the consumption of physical capital due to the lack of data before 1995. For comparative purposes, we recalculated the rentier income in proportion to the net national income from 1995.

Using the data in Dünhaupt (2011) for Germany, we observe that over the whole comparable period (1995–2008), the share of property income in Portugal was smaller than in Germany: in Portugal it reached a maximum of 8.6 per cent of net national income and in Germany it ranged between 10.5 and 17 per cent. In 2008, the indicator stood at around 17 per cent in Germany and 8.2 per cent in Portugal.[12] Property income was around 7 per cent in both Portugal and the US in 2006 – the US data are from Dünhaupt (2011).

## Personal income distribution and poverty

Turning to personal income distribution, mainstream economics emphasises that growth in finance reduces inequality (in this case, typically measured by Gini coefficient). This relationship is justified on the grounds that financial development stimulates economic growth, eases access of the poorer households to financial resources (typically through credit), which allows them to increase their investments in own business or in training and education, and mitigates the fall of purchasing power in periods of high inflation through access to non-fixed-rate financial resources (Shahbaz et al., 2015).

Panel data econometric studies by Clarke, Xu and Zou (2006) and Shahbaz et al. (2015) show that growth in finance (measured by credit to the private sector, liquid liabilities and stock market capitalisation as a share of GDP) reduces the Gini coefficient. However, Clarke, Xu and Zou (2006) also show that in many contexts, the growth in finance only benefits the richest and leaves poorer households financially excluded and with many difficulties in accessing credit and/or other financial resources. Financial institutions tend to operate on the intensive margin, channelling financial resources only to current clients and not looking for new ones (Baiardi & Morana, 2018). Indeed, some empirical studies that econometrically assessed the impact of financialisation, measured either by the proportion of Gross Value Added and employment of the financial sector (Assa, 2012) or by financial payments – interest and dividends – in percentage of corporate profits (Karanassou & Sala, 2013), concluded that financialisation increases inequality in personal income distribution.

In the Portuguese case, Antão et al. (2009) indicate that debts are asymmetrically distributed among families with a small fraction of middle- and upper-class families having a large proportion of overall debt. Likewise, Costa (2016) confirms that about 54 per cent of households in Portugal have no debt and that 80 per cent of total household debt is mortgage credit for acquiring a main residence. Thus, the advantages of sound use of credit were not at the disposal of the poorer households.

But, to the best of our knowledge, there is no empirical study on the finance–inequality nexus for the Portuguese economy, which is probably due to the lack of long historical data on the Gini coefficient.

In fact, as there is no comparable series for the Gini coefficient from 1980 onwards in Portugal, it is necessary to resort to several sources to obtain a complete picture of the whole period. Although different sources cannot be compared, they can be used to characterise the evolution of income inequality in the period for which they are available (Table 10.A1 includes a summary of inequality indicators' trends).

Between 1980 and 1990, the inequality of income measured by the Gini coefficient decreased slightly from 33 to 32 (Gouveia & Tavares, 1995). The evolution is the opposite from 1989 to 1994 with the Gini coefficient of total monetary income going from 32.9 to 35.9 (Rodrigues & Andrade, 2013).[13] This significant increase occurs despite the rise in the wage share (Figure 10.1) and high GDP growth rates (except in 1993 and 1994), indicating that this growth was unequally distributed, as shown by the sharp increase in wage inequality – see Rodrigues, Figueiras and Junqueira (2012). Besides the effect of the crisis of 1993, the increase in inequality may be the result of the liberalisation and privatisation of the financial sector, the disinflationary policy, the increase in international trade and declining union power (see Table 10.4 for the two last indicators). We have already explained above why the two last factors reduce wages, but the first two need additional explanation. Firstly, the liberalisation and privatisation of the financial sector lead to a considerable increase in credit (according to the data from the Bank of Portugal, total credit went from 49 per cent of GDP in 1989 to 56 per cent of GDP in 1993), reverting the negative trend of credit-to-GDP of the previous years. The access to credit tends to benefit more the better off (Clarke, Xu & Zou, 2006), thus contributing to income inequality, as explained in the introduction to this chapter. The privatisation of banks led also to changes in the sector: a widening of the wage distribution and an increase in profits concentrated in rich households.

Secondly, from the beginning of the nineties, the tradable goods sector was negatively affected by the disinflationary policy based on an exchange rate peg, which culminated in admission to the European Monetary System in 1992. Because of that policy there was a strong real appreciation of the currency, with negative impact on production, employment and wages of the tradable goods sector (see also Chapters 4 and 7 in this volume).

From 1995 onwards, data available from Eurostat show that household income inequality was roughly constant until 2001 (oscillating between 37 and 36),[14] while from 2001 to 2005 the Gini coefficient increased by 1.1 (Figure 10.4); however, this increase should be read with caution due to the break in the series in 2004 as a result of a different survey methodology.[15] But the use of a different survey does not seem enough to explain the increase in inequality (Rodrigues, Figueiras & Junqueira, 2012). From 2005 to 2010, income inequality decreased sharply (Figure 4.4), even though the behaviour of economic growth and unemployment was less favourable than in 1995–2001.[16]

In contrast with the downward trend in previous years, in 2011 and 2014, the Gini coefficient increased almost one point due to the detrimental effect of the sovereign debt crisis, as the unemployment rate reached a record of 16.2 per cent, in 2013, wages fell and social transfers were cut. The rise in inequality was not larger due to the increase in direct taxes (which reduce inequality due to their progressivity), as well as to the reduction in wage asymmetry (Rodrigues, Figueiras & Junqueira, 2016). From 2015 to 2017, there is a downward trend (drop of 1 in the Gini coefficient) explained by the improved economic outlook. Despite some oscillations, income inequality had a downward trend between 1995 and 2008 (-1.6), and this trend was even clearer for the longer period between 1995 and 2017 (-3.5).

*Figure 10.4* Gini coefficient of equivalised disposable income
Note: break in the time series in 2004.

Source: Eurostat

*Table 10.1* Inequality indicators

|                              | 1989 | 1994 | 1999 | 2005 | 2009 |
|------------------------------|------|------|------|------|------|
| Gini index (total income)    | 31.5 | 34.6 | 34.7 | 34.2 | 33.2 |
| Gini index (monetary income) | 32.9 | 35.9 | 36.7 | 37.3 | 36.4 |
| S90/S10 (monetary income)    | 8.8  | 10.5 | 10.8 | 11.0 | 10.1 |

Source: Rodrigues and Andrade (2013) based on Household Budget Surveys from INE

Rodrigues and Andrade (2013) is the only source that shows comparable data covering the period from 1989 to 2009 (Table 10.1). Unlike Eurostat, which uses the SILC survey (from 2004), these authors base their work on the Household Budget Survey (HBS) done by INE (Instituto Nacional de Estatística / Statistics Portugal). This survey has a larger sample and a slightly different definition of disposable income from that of the SILC survey. According to Rodrigues and Andrade (2013), the Gini coefficient of monetary income (the same used by Eurostat) grew from 32.9 in 1989 to approximately 36.4 in 2009, indicating a clear increase in personal inequality over the whole period. Between 1995 and 2009, the period for which we also have data from Eurostat, the two sources give different indications: while Eurostat shows a decline in inequality, Rodrigues and Andrade (2013) show a slight

*Table 10.2* Gini coefficient after and before social transfers

|  | 1995 | 2001 | 2004 | 2008 | 2013 | 2017 |
|---|---|---|---|---|---|---|
| Gini coefficient after and before social transfers | | | | | | |
| EU15/EA18★ | 31 | 29 | 30.7 | 30.5 | 30.7 | 30.4 |
| Portugal | 37 | 37 | 37.8 | 35.8 | 34.2 | 33.5 |
| Gini coefficient after and before social transfers | | | | | | |
| EA18 | – | – | 48.6 | 49.0 | 51.3 | 50.8 |
| Portugal | – | – | 50.8 | 50.2 | 55.9 | 58.2 |
| Gini coefficient of gross private wages | | | | | | |
| Portugal | 33.9 | 33.8 (2000) | 34.9 | 34.7 | – | – |

Source: Eurostat and Rodrigues, Figueiras and Junqueira (2012) for the Gini coefficient of wages
★ EU15 in 1995 and 2001, and EA18 from 2004.

increase. Looking at the period 1995–2009 in more detail, while the latter source confirms the increase in inequality reported by Eurostat between 2001 and 2005, it contradicts Eurostat data by indicating that 1995–2001 was also a period of increasing inequality.

When Rodrigues and Andrade (2013) use the Gini of total income,[17] they conclude that between 1994 and 2009 inequality decreased by 1.4. The indicator remained more or less constant between 1994 and 1999, and decreased thereafter.

Comparing the Gini coefficient with other European countries, Portugal had the highest Gini coefficient in the EU15 in 1995 (37 vs 31 for the EU15 average, respectively). More than 20 years later, in 2017, inequality had declined in Portugal (Gini coefficient of 33.5), but relatively speaking, the situation is the same with Portugal ranking as the third most unequal country in the EA18 (after Latvia and Spain). The higher levels of personal income inequality in Portugal are partially explained by the low levels of education of the population and the high wage premium for holders of higher education diplomas (Carmo & Cantante, 2015), along with the low efficacy and efficiency of redistributive policies implemented through the tax system and social transfers (Bronchi & Gomes-Santos, 2002; Rodrigues, Figueiras & Junqueira, 2012). Nevertheless, Portugal registered a similar decline in inequality to that observed in Europe between 1995 and 2008 (Table 10.2). It is during and after the crisis (2008–2017) that inequality in Portugal declined more than in the EA18 (-2.3 and -0.1, respectively).

In general, it is difficult to disentangle the effect of financialisation on inequality from the effect of the development and modernisation of Portugal. It can be argued that the decrease in inequality during the period of more intense financialisation (1995 to 2008) is explained by the increase in government social expenditure (Table 10.4). The main income redistribution policies in effect in that period included the income support allowance (Rendimento Social de Inserção) and the senior citizens pension supplement (Complemento Solidário para Idosos, introduced in 2005) (Carmo & Cantante, 2015).[18] But even when we look at the Gini coefficient before social transfers (pensions included in social transfers), there is a slight decrease in the indicator (-0.6) between 2004 and 2008 vis-à-vis a small increase in the EA18 (+0.4) (Table 10.2).[19] The decline is much greater after social transfers (-2), showing the relevance of social transfers in reducing income inequality. These transfers were especially important during the crisis of 2008–2013, increasing from 5.9 per cent of GDP in 2008 to 8.1 per cent in 2013. Over these years, and using the Gini coefficient before social transfers, Portugal experienced a greater increase in inequality than the EU18 (+5.7 and +2.3, respectively); however, the Gini coefficient after social transfers shows inequality declined more than in the EU18, as seen above.

Nevertheless, analysing the Gini coefficient before taxes and social transfers from OECD data,[20] we observe an increase in inequality in Portugal between 2004 and 2008, whereas there was a small decline in the EA12 (Table 10.3).[21] The evolution of this indicator between 2008 and 2013 is similar to the Eurostat Gini coefficient before social transfers (pensions included in social transfers). Overall, the data for Portugal show that the tax system was paramount in decreasing disposable income inequality.

It is relevant to consider whether we should use the Gini coefficient after or before taxes and social transfers to assess the impact of financialisation. On the one hand we must consider that state intervention by reducing inequality can mask the effect of market mechanisms.[22] On the other hand, financialisation implies a reduction in the state's role, as financial interests look for profit in the areas under control of the state and pressure for more liberal economic policies – all factors with negative implications for inequality. Therefore, the most

*Table 10.3* Gini coefficient before taxes and social transfers

|  | 2004 | 2008 | 2013 | 2015 |
| --- | --- | --- | --- | --- |
| Portugal |  |  |  |  |
| New income definition since 2012 |  |  | 55.2 | 53.6 |
| Income definition until 2011 | 50.6 | 52.7 | 56.3 |  |
| EA12* (simple average) |  |  |  |  |
| New income definition since 2012 |  |  | 50.9 | 49.6 |
| Income definition until 2011 | 48.8 | 48.1 | 51.2 |  |

Source: OECD. These data are also based on the EU Survey of Income and Living Conditions (EU SILC)

* Due to the lack of data, we considered the following fixed composition of 12 countries: Belgium, Estonia, Finland, Germany, Greece, Ireland, Italy, Latvia, Luxembourg, Portugal, Slovak Republic and Slovenia. Using the income definition until 2011, there were no data in 2013 for Germany or Finland, and for the new income definition there were no data available for Luxembourg.

sensible answer to the initial question is that we should look at the Gini coefficient both before and after social transfers and taxes, as we have done.

Wage inequality is relevant to analyse the distribution of income before state intervention with taxes and social policies. Looking at total monthly gain (*ganho mensal*) from Quadros de Pessoal (database of private earners), there is an increase in wage inequality between 1995 and 2008, notably in the period 2000 to 2005 (Rodrigues, Figueiras & Junqueira, 2012). This evolution is similar to that of the Gini coefficient after social transfers, except that the increase in wage inequality between 2000 and 2005 is more persistent.

It is difficult to measure the multiple dimensions of inequality using a single indicator such as the Gini coefficient, and it is well known this coefficient is more sensitive to the distribution of income in the middle of the distribution. As an alternative indicator, we use the ratio between the proportion of income of the tenth and first (the lowest) deciles (Indicator S90/S10), which is an important indicator to characterise the extremes of the distribution. Using that indicator, we conclude that the inequality between the richest and the poorest decreased from 14 in 1995 to 10 in 2017, but it increased from 2001 to 2004 (Figure 10.A1). Thus, the S90/S10 indicator confirms the overall picture drawn by the Gini coefficient.

To assess the evolution of the middle-income group, we now show the ratio between the deciles at the extremes and the middle decile, S90/S50 and S50/S10.[23] The population in the middle of the income distribution suffered a small loss of position vis-à-vis the richest group between 1995 and 2008 (S90/S50 increases 0.3), whereas the poorest group improved their position in relation to the middle-income population (S50/S10 declines 1.36) (Figure 10.A2). Likewise, Rodrigues, Figueiras and Junqueira (2012) show that the reduction in inequality from 1993 to 2009 was due to the improvement in the situation of the population in the lowest decile of the distribution, obtained through social policies directed to them, such as the income support allowance (Rendimento Social de Inserção) and the increase in both minimum pensions and child benefits. From 2008, there is an improvement in the position of the middle class vis-à-vis the richest and the poorest groups of the population.

Analysing the very rich group of the population (top 0.1 per cent) – the most benefited by financialisation – we observe a decline in the share of their income between 1977 and 1982, but this is followed by a sharp increase from 1989 to 2005 (Figure 10.A3). There are no data available for more recent years, and so we resort to the income held by the richest 1 per cent, which despite some oscillations, had a slight increase from 6.1 per cent in 2005 to 6.6 per cent in 2009.[24] In conclusion, especially from 1989 to 2005, there are indications of a changing economic system, increasingly financialised, favouring the richest of the rich. For a complete picture, let us now look at the other extreme of the distribution by analysing the poverty rate.

When analysing income inequality, the focus is on relative differences between households, without concern for poverty, that is, for the incapacity of some households for having a minimum income that ensures an ordinary living pattern (Cantillon, 2011). As in the case of personal income distribution, mainstream economics uses the same arguments to defend the claim that growth in the financial sector reduces poverty, which can occur through either a direct channel (access to more financial resources) or indirect channel (higher economic growth) (Bayar, 2017).

The negative relationship between finance and poverty (that is, the growth of the financial sector reduces poverty) is confirmed by several econometric studies for a variety of countries (Portugal not included) and time periods (Bayar, 2017; Beck, Demirgüç-Kunt & Levine, 2007).

Portugal is an interesting case because it has one of the highest levels of poverty in the EU, despite the downward trend in recent years. In what follows, we complement our previous analysis of inequality indicators with the at-risk-of-poverty rate after social transfers (referred to as 'poverty rate').[25]

In 1995, Portugal had the highest poverty rate in the EU15 (23 per cent vs 17 per cent for the EU15 average).[26] Between 1995 and 2008, Portugal's great effort to reduce poverty is reflected in a 4.5 p.p. decline in poverty compared with a 1 p.p. decline in the EU15/EA18 (Figure 10.5). This occurred in a context of low unemployment, notably between 1995 and 2001, and enhanced social policies directed to the poorest of the population (see section 'Personal income distribution and poverty' above); but concurrently some factors challenged the European Social Model in the early 2000s, notably globalisation and ageing population (Marques, Salavisa & Lagoa, 2015). In the crisis period,

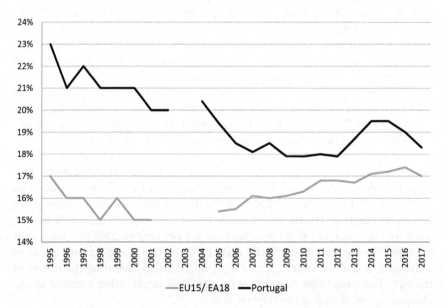

*Figure 10.5* At-risk-of-poverty rate
Note: EU15 until 2001 and EA18 thereafter.

Source: Eurostat

the poverty rate initially remained unchanged (2010–2012), before increasing considerably (1.6 p.p.) in 2013 and 2014, and finally decreasing again after the economic recovery (2016 and 2017). Notice that the increase in poverty between 2009 and 2014 was not larger because the median income used to define the threshold of poverty also declined during the crisis. However, the increase in poverty is much greater (6.3 p.p) if a fixed poverty line is used. (Rodrigues, Figueiras & Junqueira, 2016).

Despite the improvement, in 2016 Portugal was still one of the EA18 countries with the highest percentage of at-risk-of-poverty population (19 per cent), only exceeded by Greece, Spain, Italy, Latvia and Estonia. These data suggest that the economies of Southern countries generate more poverty than those of the rest of the EA18 (Hall & Soskice, 2001). In particular, the low levels of education of the Portuguese labour force, the over-specialisation in low-value-added industries (some segments of manufacturing, construction, real estate and, more recently, tourism), and the peripheral position in relation to the main European markets, are constraints that made the Portuguese economy more vulnerable during and after the crisis (Barradas et al., 2018; Chapters 3 and 4 in this volume). These limitations explain lower wages and higher labour precariousness, sustaining the phenomenon of the working poor, who do not have access to many social benefits and contribute to the high levels of inequality and poverty.

It is worth noting that even before social transfers (pensions not included in social transfers), the poverty rate in Portugal registered a decline from 27 per cent in 1995 to 24.9 per cent in 2008, which, as expected, is smaller than after social transfers.

In conclusion, in 1995, Portugal was one of the most unequal countries of the EU15 and had one of the highest poverty rates, but the situation has since improved. The high levels of inequality and poverty in Portugal are a structural characteristic that was already present before the growth in finance in the past decades. As such, it is hard to sustain the thesis that financialisation is responsible for the high levels of inequality and poverty. Nevertheless, there is evidence that financialisation produced an increase in personal income inequality in part of the period, and, as will be developed below, it may have also impeded processes of addressing the causes of inequality.

## Other effects of financialisation and other factors explaining personal income inequality and poverty

Financialisation may also affect income inequality by pressing for the decline in trade union power, as clarified in the section 'Functional income distribution' above. In Portugal, the union membership rate had a downward trend from 1978 onwards (Figure 10.6), and specifically in the period 1995 to 2008 (it decreased 5.9 p.p.). The reduction in union power cannot be attributed just to financialisation, not least of all because the biggest decrease in this indicator did not occur in the period of highest growth in finance-dominated capitalism

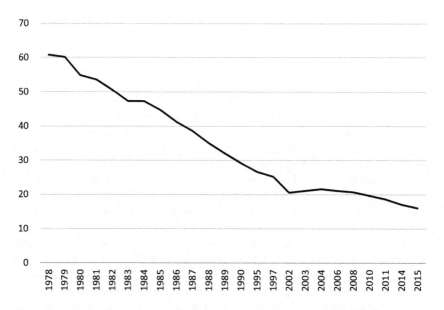

*Figure 10.6* Union membership rate (%)
Sources: 1979–2012: ICTWSS; 2014–15: Labour Force Statistics, OECD

but occurred instead in the period of deindustrialisation of the economy. Other factors, indirectly related to financialisation, contributed to the fall in union membership rates, such as the mentioned deindustrialisation of the economy, the reduction in the number of civil servants (notably between 2005 and 2012), privatisations, increase in the international mobility of firms, and the increase in the precariousness of labour relations, partially as a result of the liberalisation of the labour market (see Chapters 6 and 7 in this volume).[27]

The increase in competition from abroad, as measured by the greater openness of the Portuguese economy – up 14.57 p.p. from 1995 to 2008 (Table 10.4) – may also have contributed to the growth in income inequality. Given its trade specialisation, the Portuguese economy was especially hit by growing competition in trade and in attracting FDI from the emerging Asian economies and Eastern and Central European countries. The Portuguese productive system is over-specialised in sectors with low value-added per worker that face both strong international competition (from China and other economies) and a world demand with weak dynamism (Chapters 2, 3 and 4 in this volume). This problem is aggravated by the predominance of small- and medium-sized corporations, which compared to EA countries, occupy mostly low-skilled segments of the global value chains, which represents a constraint on innovation, productivity, higher wages and lower levels of inequality and poverty.

*Table 10.4* Inequality and poverty indicators and their determinants

|  | 1995 | 2001 | 2004 | 2008 | 2013 | 2017 |
|---|---|---|---|---|---|---|
| Gini index (%) ★ | 37 | 37 | 37.8 | 35.8 | 34.2 | 33.5 |
| Poverty rate (%) ★ | 23 | 20 | 20.4 | 18.5 | 18.7 | 18.3 |
| Unemployment rate (%) ★★ | 7.1 | 4 | 6.6 | 7.6 | 16.2 | 8.9 |
| Government expenditure in social security (%) ★★★ | 3.5 | 3.6 | 4.9 | 5.9 | 8.1 | 7.0 |
| Degree of openness of the economy (% GDP) ★★ | 62.63 | 68.56 | 66.80 | 77.20 | 81.9 | 82.09 (2016) |
| Secondary school enrolment (%) ★★ | 51.5 | 62.5 | 58.0 | 63.2 | 73.6 | 77.6 |
| Trade union density (%) ★★★★ | 25.4 | 22.4 | 24.4 | 20.5 | 17.0 (2014) | – |
|  | 1995–2001 | 2002–2004 | 2005–2008 | 2009–2013 | 2014–2017 |
| GDP growth (average of annual growth rate, %) ★★ | – | 3.52 | 0.56 | 1.25 | − 1.61 | 1.66 |

Source: ★ Eurostat, ★★ INE, Pordata, ★★★ INE, Bank of Portugal, Ministry of Finance, Pordata, ★★★★ ICTWSS and OECD in 2014

On the other hand, in addition to better redistributive policies described above, the improvement in educational levels, with the population holding secondary schooling degrees growing from 51.5 per cent in 1995 to 63.2 per cent in 2008 (Table 10.4), may also explain the overall decrease in personal income inequality registered between 1995 and 2008. A labour force with higher skills tends to have better employment prospects and wages (Lin & Tomaskovic-Devey, 2013).

## Discussion and conclusions

We started this work by acknowledging that a period of financialisation in Portugal between 1995 and 2008 was preceded by the privatisation and liberalisation of the financial system and was contemporaneous with the accession to the euro area. The goal of this chapter was to investigate whether, in that period, there was an increase in income inequality that can be attributed to financialisation, considering that the former is determined by a complex set of processes and structures.

Firstly, we observe that the development of financialisation between 1995 and 2008 was accompanied by a decline in wage share only from 2003 onwards, and by a growth of rentier income share between 2002 and 2008, basically due to an increase in dividends.

Personal disposable income inequality increased sharply in 1989–1994, before the strong growth in finance in 1995–2008. From 1995, there was an overall decline in income inequality, with a temporary increase only in 2001–2005. The downward trend in the poverty rate between 1995 and 2008 is even more impressive. In contrast, during the economic crisis of 2013–2014, poverty and inequality rose considerably – this can be seen as an indirect consequence of financialisation as the crisis was in part explained by this phenomenon.

Despite improvement in disposable income inequality and poverty rates, in 2016 Portugal was still one of the most unequal countries in the EU15 and had one of the highest poverty rates. Between 1995 and 2008, the reduction in inequality was achieved by improving the position of the poorest households, rather than by greater proximity of the position of the middle class to that of the richest. There was also a clear increase in the share of income held by top incomes (0.1 per cent) from 1989 to 2005. Another indicator pointing to a deterioration of income distribution is the increase in the Gini coefficient of income before taxes and social transfers over the period of 2004 to 2008.

In short, we do not find a generalised increase in both personal income inequality (after taxes and social transfers) and functional inequality in the period in which finance grew the most (1995–2008). However, three remarks need to be made. Firstly, financialisation may have had some negative effects on inequality because there was a rise in the Gini coefficient of disposable income between 2001 and 2005, an increase in the Gini coefficient of income before taxes and social transfers between 2004 and 2008, a rise in private wage inequality between 2000 and 2005, an increase in the rentier income share between 2002 and 2008, a substantial increase in the share of income held by top incomes from 1995 to 2005, and the middle class did not improve its position towards the high class.

Secondly, the impact of financialisation cannot be perceived by looking only at the contemporaneous and immediate modification of inequality and poverty indicators. The economic crisis in Portugal, which followed the growth in finance and is partially explained by it, led to a substantial increase in both functional and personal income inequality. And the effect of the economic crunch may even be more long-lasting, as the observed increase in public debt may limit economic growth (due to higher interest rates and less public investment) and reduce the fiscal space for more spending in the welfare state. Moreover, the crisis implied a large increase in unemployment, which due to the hysteresis effects will have long-term impact on unemployment, especially of the more vulnerable groups. The upgrade of the Portuguese growth model to one grounded on higher wages may also have been dampened by low investment, especially on R&D, during the crisis.

Another long-term effect of the crisis is the set of changes in pension rules during 2010–2014, such as the modification of the sustainability factor, the temporary suspension of early retirement and the temporary non-updating of pensions.[28] Through different mechanisms, these changes imply a reduction in future pensions, leading to worse living conditions of pensioners, who usually do not have enough savings to complement their pensions with private pension funds.

A third explanation for why we do not find a strong effect of financialisation on inequality rests on the fact that other factors hindered its increase in the period, notably the growing importance of social policies resulting from the late consolidation of the welfare state. The ability of financial interests to reduce social policies was limited by the population's demand for a degree of protection close to European standards. Thus, public policies using a variety of instruments directed to the poorest of the population avoided the deterioration of their income during the period of stronger financialisation.

A limitation of our analysis is that we focus on income inequality and poverty, yet inequality has other dimensions, such as inequality of wealth, opportunity, education, skills, health, life expectancy, welfare and happiness (Heshmati, 2004). In particular, we do not refer to inequality in wealth, a subject with little research in Portugal (Rodrigues et al., 2012), partially due to the lack of data. Nevertheless, financialisation increases wealth inequality, because mortgage credit to buy houses is more accessible to the richer households, which are also the ones that take more advantage of the rise in the prices of financial assets. Moreover, it accentuated the privatisation and commodification of housing, resulting in the decrease of an already small stock of social housing (Santos, Rodrigues & Teles, 2018).

The evolution of housing calls our attention because the indicators of inequality and poverty do not account for the cost of living. Individuals having the same income may have different living standards. For instance, tenants must support higher housing costs than homeowners. Moreover, the increase in the cost of consumption goods hits more individuals at the bottom of the income distribution, because they spend a larger proportion of their income in consumption. Likewise, the provision of public goods, such as health, social housing and education, is not taken into account by the indicators of poverty and inequality, as these latter only affect the disposable income purchasing power. When the degradation of public services, such as health and social housing, is taken into consideration, it is observed that it disproportionally affects more vulnerable groups such as women, single parent households and ethnic minorities (Chapter 8 in this volume).

Regarding inequality of opportunities, a usual indicator is the risk of poverty among young people, as their material conditions of living are less explained by choices and more by the opportunities available to them. At the end of the financialisation period, between 2007 and 2009, we observe an increase in poverty or social exclusion among children less than 18 years old in Portugal, from 26.9 per cent to 28.7 per cent – an increase above the average of the EU18.[29] The increase was even more dramatic during the crisis, between 2009 and 2013, reaching a high of 31.7 per cent. This is evidence that the financialisation process deepened the inequality of opportunities, especially by contributing decisively to a dynamic of crisis.

The reason why we do not observe an overall strong effect of financialisation on inequality may be linked to the specificities of the Portuguese economy, notably the small importance of financial markets, which determines a weaker shareholder orientation of corporate governance. Instead, the main impact of financialisation on personal income inequality has been through bank credit, not only due to its role in creating the sovereign debt crisis, but also due to different capacities of households in benefiting from credit to buy houses in the boom phase and to manage credit burden in the crisis period.

In conclusion, the Portuguese experience shows that the financialisation process has some direct and indirect effects on income inequality. As these effects are dependent on the country's socio-economic and institutional characteristics, the topic calls for studies that consider these elements. One of the greatest impacts of financialisation in Portugal is that it created the conditions for the financial crisis, which ultimately hit the poorest households more severely. Hence, public policies are required that appropriately regulate the financial sector to mitigate its negative impacts on income inequality, public services, labour market institutions and non-financial firms' behaviour.

## Acknowledgements

This chapter develops and elaborates the preliminary results published in Mamede, Lagoa, Leão and Barradas (2016). We thank the editors of the book (Ana C. Santos and Nuno Teles) and Ben Fine for comments that contributed to improving the chapter.

## Notes

1  Source: INE, PORDATA.
2  This is the case of the majority of countries in the OECD and EU (Onaran & Obst, 2016). The wage-led model, in opposition to the profit-led model, occurs in countries where the beneficial effects of higher wages on private consumption more than compensate for its prejudicial effects on investment and net exports, implying that an increase in wages raises aggregate demand.
3  It is worth noting that this author states that the three channels are not linked exclusively to financialisation but are also connected with neoliberalism. In fact, the literature on financialisation recognises that these two phenomena – financialisation and neoliberalism – emerge simultaneously and they are interrelated and dependent on each other (Van der Zwan, 2014, among others).
4  AMECO defines the adjusted wage share as [(Compensation of employees) / (GDP)] / [(Total full-time equivalent employment) / (Full-time equivalent employees)]. The adjustment factor corrects for part-time workers and for self-employment.
5  We do not analyse the role of sectoral composition on the overall wage share, but it may be an important factor. See Chapter 4 in this volume.
6  Although the concept of a wage-led model applies to the overall economy, the evolution of wages affects more the sectors that more intensively use low-wage labour.

7 The net national income includes property income and wages received (less paid) by the domestic economy vis-à-vis the rest of the world. This is particularly relevant for a small open economy like the Portuguese one.

8 In a different approach, Power, Epstein and Abrena (2003) define the rentier income as the profit of financial firms plus the interest income of the rest of the private economy. We opt not to use this definition of rentier income because it excludes dividend payments, an important component of the financialisation of corporations.

9 The break in 1995 results from a different data source.

10 Due to the heavy dependence on international financing from 1995, a large fraction of the interest paid by households, corporations and the government went to external entities.

11 This is in line with the upward trend of dividends paid by NFCs as a percentage of GOS between 1995 and 2008, referred to in the introduction to this chapter.

12 One factor contributing to that difference is the property of dwellings: whereas in Portugal dwellings are mostly owner-occupied, in Germany they are mostly rented by households. When the house is owner-occupied the imputed rental generates an operating surplus to the household that is not considered rentier income. But when the house is rented from a corporation, the operating surplus generated when distributed as dividends enters in the rentier income. In summary, rentier income in Germany may be higher than in Portugal due to rentals paid by households to corporations. Rents paid to other households do not contribute to that effect because they also produce operating surplus for other households.

13 Using disposable income by equivalised adult and based on the INE Household Budget Survey.

14 Eurostat data exclude non-monetary income. Disposable income includes market income (received from work and from investment and property) and social transfers in cash, including old-age pensions. Disposable income is obtained by deducting direct taxes from gross income.

15 The data on income distribution from Eurostat has a break in 2005 due to the use of a different survey. Between 1994 and 2001, inequality indicators were computed using the European Community Household Panel (ECHP) or the national databases (especially the Household Budget Surveys), and the European Statistics on Income and Living Conditions (EU-SILC) are used from 2001.

16 In the section 'Functional income distribution' above we describe some factors contributing to the stabilisation of income inequality in 1995–2001.

17 Total income includes monetary income plus consumption of own production, wages in kind, imputed rents of house owners, etc.

18 The Rendimento Social de Inserção and the Complemento Solidário para Idosos are two non-contributory benefits in cash paid by the social security system for poverty relief. The first is paid to individuals who live in a poverty situation and aims to help them to satisfy their basic needs. The second one is paid to older people (over 66 years and 5 months in 2019) who live with scarce resources (below 5,175.82 euros per year in 2019).

19 Eurostat has only released data for this indicator since 2004.

20 Eurostat does not publish this indicator.

21 OECD has only published this indicator since 2004.

22 Nevertheless, the better-off tend also to benefit more from state intervention, such as in the provision of higher education and of fiscal incentives for particular applications of household savings, such as pensions.

23 S50 is the share of income held by the fifth decile.
24 Data from Eurostat using equivalised income.
25 The poverty rate is the proportion of persons with an equivalised disposable income below 60 per cent of the national median equivalised disposable income after social transfers.
26 All EU and EA averages refer to weighted averages.
27 For a sectoral disaggregation of these effects, see Chapter 4 in this volume.
28 Besides these more long-lasting measures, there were also temporary cuts in pensions.
29 This indicator from Eurostat is available only from 2007.

# References

Antão, P., Boucinha, M., Farinha, L., Lacerda, A., Leal, A.C., & Ribeiro, N. (2009). Integração financeira, estruturas financeiras e as decisões das famílias e das empresas. In Banco de Portugal (ed.), *A economia portuguesa no contexto da integração económica, financeira e monetária*. Lisbon: Banco de Portugal.

Assa, J. (2012). Financialisation and its consequences: the OECD experience. *Finance Research, 1*(1), 35–39.

Baiardi, D., & Morana, C. (2018). Financial development and income distribution inequality in the euro area. *Economic Modelling, 70*, 40–55.

Barradas, R. (2019). Financialization and neoliberalism and the fall in the labor share: a panel data econometric analysis for the European Union countries. *Review of Radical Political Economics, 51*(3), 383–417.

Barradas, R., & Lagoa, S. (2017). Functional income distribution in Portugal: the role of financialization and other related determinants. *Society and Economy, 39*(2), 183–212.

Barradas, R., Lagoa, S., Leão, E., & Mamede, R.P. (2018). Financialization in the European periphery and the sovereign debt crisis: the Portuguese case. *Journal of Economic Issues, 52*(4), 1056–1083.

Bayar, Y. (2017). Financial Development and Poverty Reduction in Emerging Market Economies. *Panoeconomicus, 64*(5), 593–606.

Beck, T., Demirgüç-Kunt, A., & Levine, R. (2007). Finance, inequality and the poor. *Journal of Economic Growth, 12*(1), 27–49.

Bronchi, C., & Gomes-Santos, J. (2002). Reforming the tax system in Portugal (Working Papers 191/2002, December, 56). Pavia: Società Italiana di Economia Pubblica.

Cantillon, B. (2011). The paradox of the social investment state: growth, employment and poverty in the Lisbon era. *Journal of European Social Policy, 21*(5), 432–549.

Carmo, R.M., & Cantante, F. (2015). Desigualdades, redistribuição e o impacto do desemprego: tendências recentes e efeitos da crise económico-financeira. *Sociologia, Problemas e Práticas, 77*, 33–51.

Cichon, M., Wolfang S., van de Meerendonk, A., Hagemejer, K., Bertranou, F., & Plamondon, F. (2004). *Financing Social Protection*. Geneva: International Labor Office and International Social Security Association.

Cingolani, M. (2013). Finance capitalism: a look at the European financial accounts. *Panoeconomicus, 3*, 249–290.

Clarke, G., Xu, L.C, & Zou, H. (2006). Finance and income inequality: what do the data tell us? *Southern Economic Journal, 72*(3), 578–596.

Costa, S. (2016). Situação financeira das famílias em Portugal: uma análise com base nos dados do ISFF 2013. *Estudos Económicos, 2*(4), 15–59.

Crotty, J.R. (2005). The neoliberal paradox: the impact of destructive product market competition and impatient finance on nonfinancial corporations in the neo-liberal era. In G.A. Epstein (ed.), *Financialisation and the World Economy* (pp. 77–110). Cheltenham: Edward Elgar.

Dünhaupt, P. (2011). Financialization and the rentier income share – evidence from the USA and Germany. *International Review of Applied Economics, 26*(4), 465–487.

Dünhaupt, P. (2013). The effect of financialization on labor's share of income (Working Paper No. 17/2013). Berlin: Institute for International Political Economy.

Estrada, A., & Valdeolivas, E. (2012). The fall of the labour income share in advanced economies (Documentos Ocasionales No. 1209). Madrid: Banco de España.

Finlayson, A. (2009). Financialisation, financial literacy and asset-based welfare. *British Journal of Politics and International Relations, 11*, 400–421.

Gouveia, M., & Tavares, J. (1995). The distribution of household income and expend-iture in Portugal: 1980 and 1990. *Review of Income and Wealth, 41*(1), 1–17.

Hall, P., & Soskice, D. (2001). *Varieties of Capitalism: The Institutional Foundations of Comparative Advantage.* Oxford: Oxford University Press.

Hein, E. (2012). *The Macroeconomics of Finance-dominated Capitalism and Its Crisis.* Cheltenham: Edward Elgar.

Hein, E. (2015). Finance-dominated capitalism and re-distribution of income: a Kaleckian perspective. *Cambridge Journal of Economics, 39*(3), 907–934.

Heshmati, A. (2004). Inequalities and their measurement (IZA Discussion Paper No. 1219, July). Bonn: IZA.

Kaldor, M. (1961). Capital accumulation and economic growth. In F.A. Lutz (ed.), *The Theory of Capital.* London: Macmillan.

Karanassou, M., & Sala, H. (2013). Distributional consequences of capital accumu-lation, globalization and financialization in the US (Discussion Paper No. 7244). Bonn: Institute for the Study of Labor.

Köhler, K., Guschanski, A., & Stockhammer, E. (2018). The impact of financialization on the wage share: a theoretical clarification and empirical test (Economics Discussion Papers No. 1). London: Kingston University London.

Lagoa, S., Leão, E., Mamede, R.P., & Barradas, R. (2014). Financialisation and the finan-cial and economic crises: the case of Portugal (FESSUD Studies in Financial Systems No. 24). Leeds: FESSUD.

Lin, K-H., & Tomaskovic-Devey, D. (2013). Financialization and US income inequality, 1970–2008. *American Journal of Sociology, 118*(5), 1284–1329.

Mamede, R.P., Lagoa, S., Leão, E., & Barradas, R. (2016). The long boom and the early bust: the Portuguese economy in the era of financialisation. In E. Hein, D. Detzer & N. Dodig (eds.), *Financialisation and the Financial and Economic Crises: Country Studies.* Cheltenham: Edward Elgar.

Marques, P., Salavisa, I., & Lagoa, S. (2015). What are the best policies to fight poverty? Learning from the recent European experience. *Portuguese Journal of Social Sciences, 14*(2), 207–223.

Martins, N.C., & Villanueva, E. (2006). The impact of mortgage interest-rate subsidies on household borrowing. *Journal of Public Economics, 90*(8–9), 1601–1623.

Milanovic, B. (2016). *Global Inequality: A New Approach for the Age of Globalization.* Cambridge, MA: Harvard University Press.

Onaran, O., & Obst, T. (2016). Wage-led growth in the EU15 member-states: the effects of income distribution on growth, investment, trade balance, and inflation. *Cambridge Journal of Economics, 40*(6), 1517–1551.

Piketty, T. (2014). *Capital in the Twenty-First Century*. Cambridge, MA: Harvard University Press.

Power, D., Epstein, G., & Abrena, M. (2003). Trends in rentier incomes in OECD countries: estimates, data and methods (PERI Working Paper No. 58a). Amherst, MA: Politica Economy Research Institute.

Rodrigues, C.F., & Andrade, I. (2013). Growing inequalities and their impacts in Portugal (GINI Country Report for Portugal, January). Amsterdam: Amsterdam Institute for Advanced Labour Studies.

Rodrigues, C.F., Figueiras, R., & Junqueira, V. (2012). *Desigualdade económica em Portugal*. Lisbon: Fundação Francisco Manuel dos Santos.

Rodrigues, C.F., Figueiras, R., & Junqueira, V. (2016). *Desigualdade do rendimento e pobreza em Portugal – as consequências sociais do programa de ajustamento*. Lisbon: Fundação Francisco Manuel dos Santos.

Rodrigues, J., Santos, A.C., & Teles, N. (2016). Semi-peripheral financialisation: the case of Portugal. *Review of International Political Economy*, *23*(3), 480–510.

Rodrigues, J., Santos, A.C., & Teles, N. (2018). Financialisation of pensions in semi-peripheral Portugal. *Global Social Policy*, *18*(2),189–209.

Santos, A.C., Rodrigues, J., & Teles, N. (2018). Semi-peripheral financialisation and social reproduction: the case of Portugal. *New Political Economy*, *23*(4), 475–494.

Santos, A.C., Serra, N., & Teles, N. (2015). finance and housing provision in Portugal (FESSUD Working Paper Series No. 79). Leeds: FESSUD.

Santos, A.C., & Teles, N. (2016). Recent trends in household financial behaviour (FESSUD Working Paper Series No. 171). Leeds: FESSUD.

Shahbaz, M., Loganathan, N., Tiwari, A.K., & Sherafatian-Jahoromi, R. (2015). Financial development and income inequality: is there any financial Kuznets curve in Iran? *Social Indicators Research*, *124*(2), 357–382.

Stockhammer, E. (2012). Financialization, income distribution and the crisis. *Investigación Económica*, *71*(279), 39–70.

Teles, N. (2015). Financialisation and neoliberalism: the case of water provision in Portugal (FESSUD Working Paper Series No. 102). Leeds: FESSUD.

van der Zwan, N. (2014). Making sense of financialisation. *Socio-Economic Review*, 12(1), 99–129.

Willis, J.L., & Wroblewski, J. (2007). What happened to the gains from strong productivity growth? *Economic Review*, *92*(1), 5–23.

## *Appendix*

*Table 10.A1* Trends in inequality indicators

| *Gini coefficient* | | | | | |
|---|---|---|---|---|---|

| Longer Trends (1980–2017) | *1980–90* | *1989–94* | *1995–2008* | *2008–2017* | |
|---|---|---|---|---|---|
| | ↓ | ↑ | ↓ | ↓ | |
| | (GT 1995) | (RA 2013) | (Eurostat) 1995–2009 ↑ (RA 2013) | (Eurostat) | |
| Shorter trends (1995–2017) | 1995–2001 | 2001–05 | 2005–10 | 2010–14 | 2014–17 |
| Eurostat | → | ↑ | ↓ | ↑ | ↓ |
| | 1994–2001 | 2001–05 | 2005–09 | | |
| RA 2013 | ↑ | ↑ | ↓ | | |

| *S90/S10* | | | | | |
|---|---|---|---|---|---|

| | 1980–90 | 1989–94 | 1995–2008 | 2008–2017 | |
|---|---|---|---|---|---|
| Longer Trends (1980–2017) | ↓ | ↑ | ↓ | → | |
| | (GT 1995) | (RA 2013) | (Eurostat) | (Eurostat) | |
| Shorter trends (1995–2017) | 1995–2001 | 2001–04 | 2004–10 | 2010–14 | 2014–17 |
| Eurostat | ↓ | ↑ | ↓ | ↑ | ↓ |
| | 1994–99 | 1999–2005 | 2005–09 | | |
| RA, 2013 | ↑ | ↑ | ↓ | | |

Note: RA 2013 refers to Rodrigues and Andrade 2013, and GT 1995 refers to Gouveia and Tavares 1995.

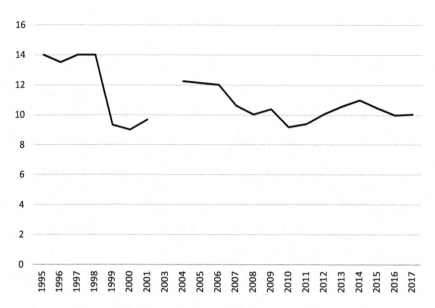

*Figure 10.A1* Indicator S90/S10, 1995–2017
Note: break in the time series in 2004.

Source: Eurostat

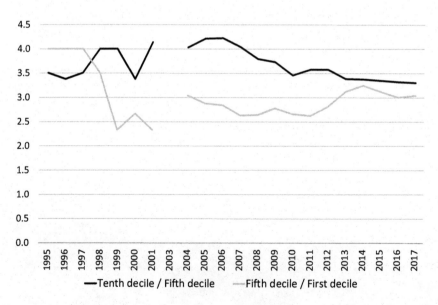

*Figure 10.A2* Indicators S50/S10 and S90/S50, 1995–2017
Source: computed data from Eurostat

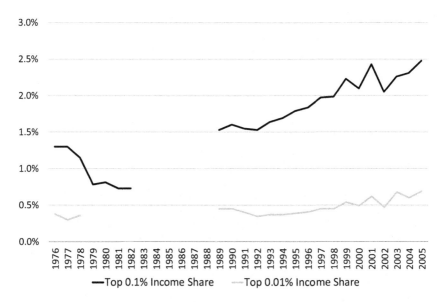

*Figure 10.A3* Income of the very rich population in proportion to total income
Source: The World Top Incomes Databases

# 11 The case for semi-peripheral financialisation

## Conclusion

*Ana Cordeiro Santos and Nuno Teles*

### Going beyond the Portuguese case study

This book has examined the context-specific attributes of financialisation processes in Portugal and of their impacts on the economy, labour relations and social reproduction, providing a comprehensive account of the recent evolution of this Southern European country.

Placed within the wider process of European integration and its financialised trajectory, the various chapters of this book have examined the recent evolution of the Portuguese economy, of particular sectors, and systems of social provision. They have also examined the recent evolution of labour relations and income distribution, offering a comprehensive critical analysis of various aspects of capital accumulation and social reproduction in the country. Taken together, they show how the country has gone through drastic transformations in the aftermath of the Global Financial Crisis (GFC), and, particularly, the euro crisis, resulting in the intensification of households' direct and indirect engagement with the global financial system in newly (re)formed domains of social reproduction.

Notwithstanding the interest in and of itself of the recent financialised path of the Portuguese economy, the contribution of this book goes beyond the provision of a comprehensive national case study. Taking the semi-peripheral character of the Portuguese economy as vantage point of analysis, this book also elaborates the concept of financialisation and puts forward a methodological framework for a comprehensive analysis of financialisation processes in other semi-peripheral countries.

A premise of this book is that financialisation must be understood as a process that interacts with others in specific circumstances, which requires considering historically given conditions and particular geographical contexts. This temporal-spatial contextualisation of the Portuguese financialisation proceeded in three parts. First, it examined the insertion of the economy in international financial markets, given that external (mostly European) forces have been driving financialisation in this semi-periphery, and the impacts on its economic structure. Second, it examined the impacts of the GFC and its derivation into a euro crisis leading to the request of official lending in 2011 to the Troika, comprised of the European Central Bank, the European Commission and the International Monetary Fund, and the associated austerity adjustment programme that had particularly harmful effects on employment and workers' protection. Third, it examined the varied and novel ways through which individuals and households have become increasingly dependent on the functioning of financial markets and associated interests via changes in relevant systems of provision, as in housing and water provision.

By bringing together these different angles and scales of analysis, the various contributions of this book put together show how the context-specific nature of semi-peripheral financialisation derives from the multiple and variegated ways through which finance interacts and impacts across different domains of economic and social reproduction. That financialisation is variegated is not a novel idea. However, financialisation studies started with the study of 'core' capitalist economies, such as the USA and the UK, then considered the most accomplished exemplars of financialisation with which others would converge. But as the field increasingly incorporates other geographies, it has revealed the variegated ways through which different political economies have become entangled with global finance with differentiated impacts. A central point of this book is, then, that the reach in geographical extent of the new case studies must not be perceived as simple add-ons to an already established literature, merely illustrating a common and convergent trajectory. These studies must be perceived instead as paramount contributions to a fairly recent, even if fast-growing, literature that advances the idea of variegated financialisation, ever more prevalent in the world economy with the rise of global finance and to which peripheral and semi-peripheral contexts are analytically most relevant.

## Variegation as a pinpoint for financialisation

Even if the term was first applied to the Anglo-American world, as mentioned, financialisation is increasingly perceived as a geographically and temporally heterogeneous process, benefiting from the subsequent growth of cross-country, and within-country, studies. Financialisation is deemed to be a 'variegated' process in order to be contrasted to the idea of mere 'variation' since this latter term 'implies their embeddedness in disconnected or static (national-) institutional types'. Financialisation processes are instead variegated, meaning that 'they are embedded within an uneven world system replete with inter-dependencies and linkages with no a priori scale but which is, at the same time, constituted by historically embedded, path-dependent and scale-bound/ -generative political economic institutions' (Ward, van Loon & Wijburg, 2019, p. 124). That is, the term 'variegation' is meant to underline the heterogeneous outcomes resulting from the reach of finance in particular territories, and the role of national institutional frameworks in shaping this reach in different political economies, as the way in which 'it unfolds within and impacts upon particular nations and regions is mediated by the institutions, politics, and culture of those nations and regions' (Brown, Spencer & Passarella, 2017, p. 67). This is why there are differences in the process of financialisation as it develops and is developed across diverse nation states and regions, and across diverse systems of provision, while recognising at the same time that there is a common process of financialisation connecting this diversity at a global level.

(Brown et al., 2017, p. 67).[1]

This is meant as constructive criticism of the Varieties of Capitalism literature that builds on a dichotomy between two ideal types, opposing the 'liberal market economy' to the 'coordinated market economy', the former corresponding to a stylised representation of the Anglo-American world while the latter is exemplified by Germany (Hall & Soskice, 2001). In a nutshell, the 'liberal market economy' is characterised by the predominance of market-based forms of organisation, liquid financial markets, deregulated labour markets with decentralised wage bargaining, and, thus, low levels of worker protection, intense competition in product markets, shareholder-oriented corporate governance regimes, and rapid innovation. The 'coordinated market economy' is instead deemed to be more heavily regulated, with a bank-based system providing patient capital, regulated product and labour markets, nationwide or industrywide collective bargaining, high levels of employment protection, a stakeholder-oriented model of corporate governance, and incremental, rather than radical, innovations. The narrow scope of these two polar ideal types led to the elaboration of new ones, such the social democratic and Mediterranean models of capitalism (e.g. Amable, 2003) to account for the higher levels of social protection via the welfare state and the solidarity component to wage-setting of the Scandinavian countries, and the lower levels of social protection and lower levels of skills and education in the Southern European (SE) countries, preventing the implementation of a high-wage and high-skills industrial strategy therein. More recently still, the model of dependent market economies has been advanced to account for the importance of foreign capital for the socioeconomic setup of East European countries (Nölke & Vliegenthart, 2009), or the state-led market economies more typical of large emerging economies (Nölke et al., 2015).

While these archetypes of contemporary capitalism have been decomposed into various and distinct parts (e.g. product markets, labour markets, the financial and the corporate sectors, social protection and the welfare state, education, and so forth), allowing for institutional variation within and across countries, the archetypal coherence at the national level was assumed and, thus, national states were understood as fitting into ideal types. The nations were thus 'the natural institutional containers within which macro-regulatory integrity is both accomplished historically and comprehended theoretically', informing a 'methodological nationalism' approach that conceives the world economy in terms of '[competing] national development models' and 'the relationship between neoliberalism and regulatory uneven development as being *national, territorial* and *bipolar*' (Brenner, Peck & Theodore, 2010, p. 187, emphasis in original).

The consideration that financialisation, as well as other systemic processes, interacts in context-specific ways with inherited institutional landscapes producing differentiation across places, territories and scales, has in turn inspired the examination of 'geographies of financialisation' with a view to overcoming the methodological nationalism of comparative institutional exercises (e.g. Engelen, Konings & Fernandez, 2010; French, Leyshon & Wainwright, 2011; Pike & Pollard; 2010).

Engelen, Konings and Fernandez (2010) argue that understanding variegated financialisation calls for comparative institutionalism aimed at the examination of different trajectories of financialisation in terms of the effects of the interaction between national institutional configurations and the dynamics of global finance as a process of mutual constitutive interaction. To this end, they propose the analysis of 'national institutional frameworks' to better understand the extent to which 'not every locality has been connected to the same degree and in the same way' (p. 54), giving due account of particular institutional frameworks that 'do not merely function to alter, resist, or mediate the effects of financialisation', but have instead 'a constitutive role to play in the mutual interaction between global markets and local financial changes' (p. 69), opposing the thesis of convergence and rejecting the dynamics of financial change as an homogenising process.

The geographical expansion of financialisation studies has shown how patterns of financialisation are constituted by processes of both global and local nature, entailing variegation not only between core countries and peripheries, but also across regions that share many characteristics, such as Latin America, and Eastern or Southern Europe, as addressed in this book. Such variegation is also visible at a more sectoral level, as in housing and real estate more broadly, where global institutional investors such as hedge and real estate funds increasingly interfere with national and local systems of housing provision, leading to housing crises in many cities around the world (e.g. Fernandez & Aalbers, 2016, 2019).

The typologies of capitalism fail to accommodate peripheral and semi-peripheral geographies of the Global South, leaving uncounted the range of agents and sites increasingly engaged with the international financial system. Furthermore, and more relevant for these geographies, they do not account for interdependences and power relations between (semi-)peripheral and core countries.

Notwithstanding the growing importance of global, international actors in leading financialisation processes, these should not be taken as a homogenising force across the globe. For one thing, their power relations vary across the globe. Moreover, regional institutions and interdependencies force their own variegation on the international scale that eludes what can sometimes be the overstated role of the two most relevant international institutions, such as the IMF and the World Bank, or the structural power of the United States, in shaping processes in other geographies. The outcomes depend on how such international organisations and power structures interact with the regional, national and local institutional contexts. In Europe, the institutional transformations led by EU institutions have had differentiated impacts in Eastern and Southern European countries, as well as within these two regions (Chapter 2 in this volume). The same goes for the EU core. Based on a comparative study of Germany, the Netherlands and the UK, Ward, van Loon and Wijburg (2019, p. 134) underline the role of 'common processes at supra-national scales', namely the 'monetarist, liberalising policies which, at the European scale, were institutionalised through the formation of the European Union and the Eurozone during the early 1990s'. But they also note that 'the extent and form of financialisation has been divergent across European countries', concluding that 'financialisation globalisation has not led to the universalisation of the liberal market economic structure' (pp. 124–125).

However, analyses of non-core geographies are still incipient and very much based on comparative cross-country exercises even if decomposed into smaller units, such as the corporation, the household and the state. International financial forces still require further attention, as well as unexamined geographies, such as the regions and semi-peripheral and peripheral countries. Based on such diagnosis, French, Leyshon and Wainwright (2011) urge for considering with more analytical seriousness the international financial system and other missing geographies or, in short, what they dub 'spacing financialisation' (p. 809). This would then require further work on political and economic power relations at a world scale and on the growing integration of the international and domestic financial systems.

We have endeavoured to make such a contribution with this edited book. Being a small, open economy, Portugal has been subjected to external pressure since the instauration of democracy in 1974, having intensified its economic and political interdependence with the centre of Europe and with the economies with which it is more deeply integrated, namely Spain. In this period, it was subjected to three external interventions with the involvement of the IMF (Chapter 2 in this volume). Nonetheless, the shape of financialisation in Portugal, as in the rest of SE, has been decisively influenced by the European institutions, particularly those leading the process of the creation of a single currency across a very heterogeneous region. Notwithstanding their differences, the single currency has locked these countries in a path divergent from the European core. This has been a financialised path, reflecting the uneven and combined character of the European integration process, and the evolving forms of financial subordination of this periphery towards the centre of Europe, whose paths have also been shaped by their powers of subordination.

As financialisation continues to be a fast-growing field of research, forging new links between global financial markets and regional, national and local spaces in new geographies, the political and economic power relations at the regional and world levels are increasingly brought to the fore (see e.g. Kaltenbrunner & Painceira, 2018, and references therein). This is in turn brings into the analysis the notion of semi-peripheral financialisation that we revisit in the next section.

## Revisiting the notion of semi-peripheral financialisation

The concept of semi-peripheral financialisation (Rodrigues, Santos & Teles, 2016) was originally advanced to account for the context-specific traits of the Portuguese case, attempting to give due account of both the commonalities with and differences from other processes in core and peripheral geographies. This relied on the dependency theory (Wallerstein, 1974), having as an analytical starting point the international insertion of the Portuguese economy in the world economy, and the differences in form and content relative to financialisation processes in core and peripheral economies. Following on previous work on the semi-peripheral position of the country (e.g. Santos, 1985; Reis, 1993), the term semi-periphery was used to convey two ideas. First, the intermediate position of the country in the world economy, i.e. a late industrialised country that is increasingly unable to compete with the European countries with which it is most closely integrated, favouring the growth of the more protected non-tradeable sector based on low-productivity activities and an unskilled low-waged workforce. Second, the institutional features of its financial system, which draws characteristics from both core and peripheral countries, having been shaped by the process of European integration and the more recent creation of the monetary union, resulting in the significant predominance of cross-border loanable-money capital relative to fictitious capital, i.e. on broader borrower–lender relationships rather than on the securitisation and securities markets more relevant in core countries (Chapter 1).

The concept of semi-peripheral financialisation also relied on more recent work on the experience of peripheral countries (Becker et al., 2010; Lapavitsas, 2013; Lapavitsas & Powell, 2014; Painceira, 2011; Powell, 2013), which underlined the 'subordinated' nature of financialisation processes in the periphery. Focusing on emergent economies, they argue that their subordinated nature stems from peripheral countries' mode of insertion into the financialised world economy requiring high interest rates to attract foreign capital so as to accumulate reserves of quasi-world money (e.g. dollars) to ensure participation in international trade and financial transactions. This often points to the accumulation of liquid assets denominated in a foreign currency, mostly US public debt securities, meaning that the periphery is actually financing the core. This in turn requires significant sterilisation operations to avoid inflationary pressures and exchange rate oscillations, implying the accumulation of national public securities by banks feeding the expansion of credit to the domestic market. That is, the subordinated integration of (semi-)peripheries into the international monetary and financial system has led to the rise of loanable-money capital in peripheral and semi-peripheral countries, mostly to households.

Based on the recent evolution of the Brazilian economy, Kaltenbrunner and Painceira (2018, p. 301) argue that this subordinated financialisation is exacerbating uneven development in emerging countries through two main mechanisms:

First, reserve accumulation implies a constant resource transfer from ECEs [emerging capitalist countries] to CCEs [core capitalist countries]. Whereas ECE central banks hold low-yielding, safe, and liquid CCE sovereign bonds, foreign capital flows generate substantial returns which are repatriated abroad [...]. At the same time, sterilisation operations lead to an increase in public debt, whose service negatively weighs on ECEs' fiscal capacity [...]. Second, the substitution of productive loans by household loans adversely affects capital accumulation, negatively weighing on ECEs' growth potential.

Financial crises accentuate these effects as they lead to a rise in the demand for assets denominated in a foreign currency, often due to reasons other than those pertaining to domestic economic conditions.

Fernandez and Aalbers (2019), in their cross-regional and cross-country empirical analysis, underline the effect of US and EU recent macroeconomic policies in Global South (GS) contexts. Particularly, they argue that 'loose monetary policies' led to 'a sharp rise in capital flows into select GS countries' (p. 7), mostly channelled to real estate. They also note the added layers of vulnerability thus created insofar as, once these policies end, 'these capital flows may reverse, leaving behind a stock of unpayable debt' (p. 8). This reinforces the notion of (semi-)peripheral financialisation and underlying processes of 'subordination' as financialisation in non-core geographies is by and large shaped by the integration of these geographies in hierarchical global monetary structures on terms and conditions they do not control.

Thus, the notion of 'subordinated financialisation' resonates with the ideas and the lexicon of dependency theories as it underlines asymmetric power relations that may manifest themselves at various scales in various geographies. It is important to stress that the term periphery or semi-periphery is not a mere geographical prefix, depicting an asymmetry in power relations between the North and South hemispheres. Portugal, placed in the North, may be closer to the core than to peripheral countries, sharing with the former more characteristics at the economic, social, cultural and political levels (cf. Chapter 13 in this volume). But as we have tried to argue in this book, Portugal is more aptly perceived as a periphery within Europe, or a semi-periphery in the world system, considering that it is more often than not an object rather than an agent of subordination.

We then reassert analytical role of the notion of semi-periphery that can be adequately applied to the countries of the Northern hemisphere that are vulnerable to asymmetric power relations at the world or regional level. In the present financialised neoliberal era, the subordinated type of integration in a hierarchical global monetary structure is a distinctive feature of the (semi-)peripheral condition. Such subordination stems from the impossibility of these countries borrowing in their domestic currencies, having instead to accumulate foreign exchange reserves, being vulnerable to sudden capital and exchange rate movements. If they are part of a single currency zone, which does not require the accumulation of foreign exchange, the subordination of the (semi-)peripheral position stems from the impossibility of borrowing in a currency which (semi-)peripheries issue and control, resulting in mounting economic and financial imbalances.

Within the EMU, countries' participation in global financial markets did not require high interest rates to attract international capital flows, nor the accumulation of reserves of quasi-world money to deal with inflation and exchange rate fluctuations. The single currency assured foreign investors and creditors of the repayment of debt by eliminating exchange rate risk and by the adoption of a macroeconomic policy devoted to the maintenance of low inflation. But like emerging capitalist economies, semi-peripheral financialisation was equally marked by dependence on international financial markets and the prevalence of loanable-money capital in the form of interbank loans. In the Portuguese case, the insertion of the economy in international financial circuits proceeded in particularly unfavourable terms due to an overvalued new currency that undermined the country's competitiveness. Even though the structural weaknesses of the country are not solely attributable to asymmetric power relations, the new currency together with the eased access to international financial markets stimulated the continuing rise of imports while harming the export sector. These difficulties have accentuated an uneven development within the region.

Focusing on the Portuguese experience, this book has shown how the extraordinary influx of financial flows accentuated the economic fragility of the country as the Portuguese economy continued to rely on traditional labour-intensive sectors, stimulating, from the 1990s on, the construction and real estate sectors (cf. Chapters 3 and 4 in this volume). This means that the unprecedentedly advantageous financial conditions, such as an almost unlimited access to hard currency and loanable-money capital at low interest rates, were not directed to overcome the structural weaknesses of the country but resulted in reduced productivity growth relative to wage and price increases. The absence of an autonomous monetary and exchange rate policy in the face of growing international competition exacerbated these structural weaknesses, manifested in a persistent and growing current account deficit and fuelling a record external debt to GDP.

However, these structural fragilities only became overtly critical when the GFC hit the eurozone, showing the extent to which financialisation in the periphery has deepened unevenness, notwithstanding differentiated institutional configurations across countries. Increasingly integrated into a highly hierarchical and asymmetric financial system, the recent evolution of SE was marked by the sovereign debt crisis when, in the wake of the GFC, and contrary to conventional financial market wisdom, these eurozone states were initially left on their own without ECB support. They were then unable to refinance themselves in the international markets upon which they had become dependent. The end of capital flows and consequent collapse of externally over-leveraged domestic banks added financial stress to the already vulnerable semi-peripheral states, culminating in the request for official loans to the Troika (comprised by the European Central Bank, the European Commission and the International Monetary Fund).

These official loans were used to impose particularly violent austerity measures in these economies, which downgraded their situation even further. The financial crisis, having turned into a sovereign debt crisis, thus placed SE countries in a worsened position, as states' efforts were increasingly devoted to the rescue of banks and thereby the solvency of external creditors. In Portugal, national banks benefited from various forms of public aid totalling 24 billion euros (BdP, 2019). The squeeze of the domestic sector produced by the freeze on public expenditure further undermined the role previously played by loanable-money capital in sustaining the domestic economy.

It is true that semi-peripheral SE countries did not have to keep high interest rates to attract foreign capital so as to be able to participate in the world economy. Interest rates have in fact decreased to historically unprecedented low values. Semi-peripheral SE countries did not have to accumulate foreign exchange reserves to protect themselves from balance-of-payment crises resulting from exchange rate fluctuations. However, they were as dependent on foreign financial institutions to finance themselves as peripheral countries have been. Thus, SE countries not only faced similar liquidity problems to those prevailing in emerging countries, they also lacked political autonomy to conduct monetary, exchange rate and fiscal policy, constraining the implementation of policies that could at least attempt to revert from their semi-peripheral condition.

The outcome of financialisation and of the financial crisis has been growing divergence across EU countries and growing unevenness, despite the low unemployment rates and the recent reduction of the extraordinarily high levels of income inequality (Chapter 10 in this volume). This unevenness is most clearly conveyed by the deterioration of the sectoral composition of the economy based on low-skilled labour and low wages (Chapters 3 and 4), the deterioration of labour protection (Chapters 6 and 7), and of democratic forms of work organisation within the firm (Chapter 5), as well as by the growing strains in various and essential systems of provision (Chapters 8 and 9; for a broader theoretical discussion, see also Chapter 12).

However, one should not mistake the stagnation and relative decline of European semi-peripheral economies for any kind of convergence with peripheral countries. If on the one hand, the euro crisis has shown the SE periphery the hierarchical power relations at the EU level (as exercised by the Eurogroup, and most vocally expressed by the then German finance minister Wolfgang Schäuble, who never hesitated to scornfully comment on the dire situation of the periphery, accused of 'living beyond their means'), on the other hand, the same crisis has shown the interdependence of EU economies. This was most visible in the change of monetary policy by the ECB after 2012. Threatened by Greece's possible departure from the euro, and its likely domino effect, the preservation of financial interests in the core forced a policy change, remarkably stated by the then ECB President, Mario Draghi, who assured that the ECB would do 'whatever it takes' to preserve the unity of the eurozone. The ECB then started a so-called quantitative easing programme, buying billions of euros of public and private bonds across the eurozone. This benefited the peripheral countries as the yields charged by international markets began to collapse. This bond-buying programme resulted in a renewed convergence of interest rates (close to zero) between core and periphery, making it easier for the periphery to pay back their loans, thus curbing political and popular pressure for public debt restructuring.

The effects were immediate. Indebted countries started benefiting from lower debt service payments, enabling the attenuation of austerity, and domestic economic agents benefited again from low interest rates. Moreover, in an environment of very low interest rates, the search for yield by financial agents favoured foreign investment in the SE periphery due to the devaluation of its assets during the crisis. As we have seen, SE became attractive to foreign investment, notably in the real estate sector which became the basis of economic recovery, as well as in the recently privatised sectors (Chapters 2, 8 and 9 in this volume).

However, the notion of semi-peripheral financialisation remains as relevant as ever. If prior to the crisis, the common currency assured creditors that indebted peripheral countries would pay back their debts, in the post-crisis period, the common currency assures foreign investors of the profitability of their investments. While this influx of capital seems to provide a temporal fix to the SE periphery, this means that in a not-too-distant future more resources will be transferred from national agents to foreigners. These outflows include the payment of public debt incurred to allegedly rescue the national bank system, but which has actually been used to promote the acquisition of cleaned-balance-sheet banks by foreign financial groups. They also include the transfer of dividends resulting from the increasing participation of foreign capital in the economy and social provisioning, in areas such as energy, transport, telecommunications, real estate and water. All in all, the same mechanisms of subordination are at play in SE, entailing a constant resource transfer to the core.

Not only is financialisation variegated due to the differentiated ways in which national institutional frameworks shape countries' insertion in global financial markets, financialisation also varies within countries. The analysis of different systems of provision shows just that. The analysis of housing, in particular, has shown how the growing presence of international financial agents in the real estate sector is having differentiated impacts on the two main metropolitan areas of the country. This is by and large an outcome of its dependence on foreign finance due to the structural weaknesses of the economy and its insertion in the EMU that jeopardises its fiscal capacity to conduct autonomous macroeconomic policy.

The qualitative transformations generated by the gradual substitution of domestic by foreign investment reinforce the idea that a new phase of peripheral financialisation in SE is emerging. This means not only that financialisation has intensified divergence between core and periphery within the EU, but also that this divergence has detrimental socio-spatial impacts for the underprivileged of the periphery, resulting in the loss of political power. Foreign proprietors and their representatives in turn exercise more and more influence on the control of national resources and mobilise against perceived threats to property devaluation, further reinforcing unevenness and subordination. The straitjacket of the EMU maintains the pressure on SE governments, ever more dependent on foreign investment under ever more exploitative conditions, thereby promoting further financialisation of the SE countries in novel ways.

Even though the quantitative easing policies are having detrimental impacts on the major cities of the globe, in both the Northern and Southern hemispheres, enhancing vulnerability everywhere, countries are not equally equipped to deal with these global pressures. The effects of these trends will be necessarily variegated and uneven, with more detrimental impacts on the peripheries and semi-peripheries of the world system. This is due to their subordinated position, increasingly driven by foreign capital and its interests, even if national agents that gravitate around this process also benefit, if not join in.

## Final notes

Although this book focused on the financialised context-specificity of the Portuguese case, it did so by highlighting the role of European integration and by considering the experiences of other core and peripheral countries, further elaborating the evolving notion of semi-peripheral financialisation. It attempted to show that the trajectory of the SE periphery cannot be fully grasped without consideration of the role of EU financial institutions, and of the European core countries that dominate them. By the same token, the recent financialised trajectory of core European countries cannot be fully understood without considering the instrumental role of the European periphery in the expansion of their financial interests. While this is increasingly emphasised in analysis of (semi-)peripheral contexts, it is still a fairly unexplored topic in the analysis of core countries, which still privileges the national scale over accounting for the inherently international nature of capitalist finance.

With this book we hope to contribute to further studies of relations of financialised subordination within the EU and beyond. We believe that this requires thorough examination of how financialisation has impacted on the sectoral composition of the economy, the organisation of the various systems of social provisioning, and on labour relations. It also offers a theoretical and methodological framework for such a study, integrating different scales of analysis, including international, national and local, and different objects of study, embracing the economy and its sectors, labour relations and realms of social reproduction. It is also meant as a modest contribution to fighting against relations of subordination and the human suffering that they cause in the most vulnerable parts of the world.

## Acknowledgements

This work received the financial support of the Portuguese Foundation for Science and Technology (FCT/MEC) through national funds, and of the

ERDF through the Competitiveness and Innovation Operational Program COMPETE 2020 (Project FINHABIT-PTDC/ATP-GEO/2362/2014-POCI-01-0145-FEDER-016869). The authors are grateful to Ben Fine and Manuel Aalbers for comments on previous versions of this chapter. All errors and omissions remain the responsibility of the authors.

## Note

1 This notion resembles and/or draws on earlier debates on 'uneven and combined development' as applied to the advancement of capitalist relations in pre-capitalist societies (e.g. Fernandez & Aalbers, 2016), or discussions on 'variegated neo-liberalism' understood as a more generic process (Brenner, Peck & Theodore, 2010). Some accounts, though, do link the various approaches, taking financialisation as the current stage of neoliberalism (Fine, 2012).

## References

Amable, B. (2003). *The Diversity of Modern Capitalism*. Oxford: Oxford University Press.

BdP (Banco de Portugal) (2019). Relatório extraordinário. 23 de maio de 2019. Retrieved from www.bportugal.pt/sites/default/files/anexos/pdf-boletim/relatorio_extraordinario_lei152019.pdf.

Becker, J., Jäger, J., Leubolt, B., & Weissenbacher, R. (2010). Peripheral financialization and vulnerability to crisis: a regulationist perspective. *Competition & Change, 14*(3–4), 225–247.

Brenner, N., Peck, J., & Theodore, N. (2010). Variegated neoliberalization: geographies, modalities, pathways. *Global Networks, 10*(2), 182–222.

Brown, A., Spencer, D.A., & Passarella, M.V. (2017). The extent and variegation of financialisation in Europe: a preliminary analysis. *Revista de Economía Mundial, 46*, 49–70.

Engelen, E., Konings, M., & Fernandez, R. (2010). Geographies of financialisation in disarray: the Dutch case in comparative perspective. *Economic Geography, 86*(1), 53–73.

Fernandez, R., & Aalbers, M.B. (2016). Financialization and housing: between globalization and varieties of capitalism. *Competition & Change, 20*(2), 71–88.

Fernandez, R., & Aalbers, M.B. (2019) Housing financialization in the Global South: in search of a comparative framework. *Housing Policy Debate*. Advance online publication available from www.tandfonline.com/doi/abs/10.1080/10511482.2019.1681491?journalCode=rhpd20.

Fine B. (2012). Neoliberalism in retrospect? It's financialisation, stupid. In C. Kyung-Sup, B. Fine & L. Weiss (eds.), *Developmental Politics in Transition* (International Political Economy Series) (pp. 51–69). New York: Palgrave Macmillan.

French, S., Leyshon, A., & Wainwright, T. (2011). Financializing space, spacing financialization. *Progress in Human Geography, 35*(6), 798–819.

Hall, P., & Soskice, D. (2001). *Varieties of Capitalism: The Institutional Foundations of Comparative Advantage*. Oxford: Oxford University Press.

Kaltenbrunner, A., & Painceira, J.P. (2018). Subordinated financial integration and financialisation in emerging capitalist economies: the Brazilian experience. *New Political Economy, 23*(3), 290–313.

Lapavitsas, C. (2013). *Profiting without Producing: How Finance Exploits Us All*. London: Verso.

Lapavitsas, C., & Powell, J. (2014). Financialisation varied: a comparative analysis of advanced economies. *Cambridge Journal of Regions, Economy and Society, 6*(3), 359–379.

Nölke, A., ten Brink, T., Claar, S., & May, C. (2015). Domestic structures, foreign economic policies and global economic order: implications from the rise of large emerging economies. *European Journal of International Relations, 21*(3), 538–567.

Nölke, A., & Vliegenthart, A. (2009). Enlarging the varieties of capitalism: the emergence of dependent market economies in East Central Europe. *World Politics*, 61(4), 670–702.

Painceira, J.P. (2011). Central banking in middle income countries in the course of financialisation: a study with special reference to Brazil and Korea. PhD thesis, SOAS, University of London.

Pike, A., & Pollard, J. (2010). Economic geographies of financialisation. *Economic Geography, 86*(1), 29–51.

Powell, J. (2013). Subordinate financialisation: a study of Mexico and its non-financial corporations. PhD thesis, SOAS, University of London.

Reis, J. (1993). Portugal: a heterogeneidade de uma economia semiperiférica. In Boaventura de Sousa Santos (ed.), *Portugal: um retrato singular* (pp. 133–161). Porto: Edições Afrontamento.

Rodrigues, J., Santos, A.C., & Teles, N. (2016). Semi-peripheral financialisation: the case of Portugal. *Review of International Political Economy, 23*(3), 480–510.

Santos, B.S. (1985). Estado e sociedade na semiperiferia do sistema mundial: o caso Português. Análise Social, *87–89*, 869–901.

Wallerstein, I. (1974). *Semi-peripheral Countries and the Contemporary World Crisis.* New York: Academic Press.

Ward, C., van Loon, J., & Wijburg, G. (2019). Neoliberal Europeanisation, variegated financialisation: common but divergent trajectories in the Netherlands, United Kingdom and Germany. *Tijdschrift voor Economische en Sociale Geografie, 110*, 123–137.

# Part 4

# Commentary

# 12 Framing social reproduction in the age of financialisation[1]

*Ben Fine*

## From economic to social reproduction?

The purpose of this note, at the expense of considerable self-indulgence, is to reflect on past work in which I have been involved. Much of this work, across apparently disparate topics, came together in the Fessud project on the effects of financialisation, but its thrust has been continued since and has been taken up by others.[2] The unifying theme across these endeavours has been to shed light on how the notion of social reproduction can be framed, especially but not exclusively in conditions of financialised neoliberalism – although these terms are themselves contentious, like social reproduction itself, whether coupled together or not. Only a skeleton and abstract/general outline are provided across a range of concepts that have been developed and applied in the literature cited, and much more besides is available. What is involved is necessarily a matter of methodology, concepts, theories as well as finessing both the abstract and the historically and socially specific at many different levels. The intention is to spark debate over the various elements involved that make up the approach, the approach as a whole, and whether and how it might be developed, refined, applied or rejected in whole or in part.

An appropriate starting point is with capitalist economic reproduction which forms a part of social reproduction but to which the latter is not reducible. This is easy to say but complex to address as will be seen. An initial choice, however, has to be made between treating economic and social reproduction as a dualism in which one interacts with the other or whether economic is part of social reproduction, the option chosen here on the grounds that economic is, indeed, part of social reproduction but, as both positions accept, does not fill it out, to whatever degree and in whatever ways it is determinant. But, starting with economic reproduction, I have summarised Marx's approach to it in the following diagram (Figure 12.1), first appearing in Fine (1975) and now available most recently in Fine and Saad-Filho (2016a). This diagram can be used to interpret the conditions for balance for simple, extended and expanded reproduction, and whether there is accumulation or not, and with or without transformations in value proportions (for example, whether the organic composition of capital does or does not grow with accumulation).

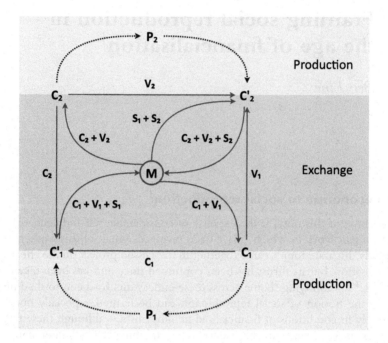

*Figure 12.1* Economic reproduction

The reproduction schema is, however, subject to contested interpretations whether, as in some sense, representing (a moving) equilibrium, a (false) presumption that sustained accumulation is impossible without Luxemburgian or underconsumptionist external sources of demand, or (as I suggest) a simple and momentary representation of structures, flows, and balances across money, commodities (as use values), and values, representing temporary resolutions of corresponding value relations (Fine, 2012), where in addition it is argued that, contrary to underconsumptionism, capitalism thrives by *expanding* the realm of non-commodity production rather than relying parasitically upon it (see later) until exhausted (as with Luxemburg on the role of non-capitalist formations as they are brought into capitalism's orbit on a world scale).

Whatever the ways within which it fits into interpretations of Marx's value theory, a number of important implications for social reproduction arise out of this representation of economic reproduction. First, economic reproduction appears to be self-contained (and sustained) in the production and circulation of (surplus) value, indicative of a number of structures such as those between production and circulation, and with the value of labour power as the precondition of production, and surplus value as its consequence – so that distributional relations, for example between wages and profits, are not appropriately seen as the division of a given cake arising out of production (in Ricardian or Sraffian fashion) but as the surplus generated in production on the basis of a wage that has already been paid in principle prior to the labour process. Second, though, the shifting boundaries of economic reproduction structurally create, or vacate, the space where the broader social reproduction is situated, without in any way specifying its form and content other than in being conditioned by, and compatible with, economic reproduction and its corresponding contradictory trajectory. Traditionally, this space is interpreted as the political and ideological superstructure, and as being filled out by the state and civil society, both of which are engaged in, but are not reducible to, value relations. As Ferguson (2016, p. 55) puts it:

> Capitalist social relations play such a pivotal role in shaping the means and processes by which people organise their lives outside of the specifically economic wage-labour/capital relationship because (i) the vast majority of people cannot access the means of producing their own subsistence except by selling their labour in the service of capital or other forms of market dependence; and (ii) capitalist profit and accumulation is crucially dependent on the availability of 'free' wage labourers for that exploitation.

Third, in this respect, the value and reproduction of labour power occupy a significant if far from exclusive position – the capitalist class, monetary and property relations, and many other elements are involved in social as opposed to economic reproduction. Focus on how labour power is reproduced has had the effect of narrowing down how social reproduction is understood in terms of the reproduction of workers alone, and often in their material and, occasionally, emotional lives in the sense of broader well-being. But *social* reproduction is much broader than confinement to the working class.

Even so, within Marxist value theory, the value of labour power has been interpreted and deployed in two different ways, although each draws upon Marx's notion that the purchase of labour power presumes rather than establishes how it brings about its reproduction, with this presumed otherwise to occur outside of economic reproduction (to complement what is capitalistically produced means of consumption). One definition of the value of labour power is in terms of physical subsistence, the wage bundle, or the so-called moral and historical elements that make up a customary standard of living, or (social) norm(s) as I will put it (since different items of the standard will have their own norms both in terms of what is delivered and how and to whom, a recurring theme in what follows). Yet, given the use values that comprise the value of labour power so interpreted, there would appear to be a corresponding value of labour power, the socially necessary labour time required to produce them.

As will soon be revealed, matters are not so simple. But, for the moment, consider the other way of defining the value of labour power, as simply a value magnitude, a quantum of labour time. In principle, this could correspond to a whole range of different physical wage bundles according to the customary consumption decisions of workers. At least in principle, the two different ways of approaching the value of labour power would appear to be compatible. Indeed, they are more or less interchangeable, especially in Ricardian/Sraffian analysis since the value of labour power is given by an equilibrium quantum of goods or equivalent quantum of labour (value).

## Interrogating the value of labour power

However, incompatibilities between the two definitions arise when we move beyond the static or momentary analysis associated with the simple reproduction schema. For, with accumulation over time, and corresponding productivity increase, the first definition of the value labour power as a fixed set of use values would mean a reduction in the value of labour power by the second definition since the labour time of production of the wage bundle would be reduced. Or, to put it the other way round, if the value of labour power by the second definition were applied, it would correspond to an increase in the customary standard of living (as more commodities could be purchased from a given value of labour power as commodities become cheaper).

Now, no doubt simplifying, according to Lebowitz (2006 & 2009), how this tension between the two definitions of the value of labour power is resolved in practice depends upon what he terms the degree of *separation*, by which he means the extent to which the working class is able to overcome its fragmentation across different sites of production and collaborate to appropriate the productivity increases for which they are responsible in terms of their production of (relative) surplus value. To a large extent, I agree that this an important factor but it seems to represent an unreasonable narrowing of how social reproduction is understood to just one aspect of economic reproduction if adding the element of class struggle at the point of (and across sites of) production. In this respect, there are two shortcomings – one is the failure to acknowledge other unspecified elements in the processes of establishing the value of labour power, and the other is methodological in locating these processes (or, at least, the only one considered) at the same level of abstraction as the creation of value itself, as a class relation of production (Fine, 2008, 2013).

This unduly abstract discussion can, however, be approached in different ways that avoid the niceties of value theory and its abstractions. On the one hand, as is apparent from questioning what is the value of labour power whilst its productivity is changing, the attempt is essentially being made to address exactly how it is that the moral and the historical elements of social norms in the value of labour power are established, or, indeed, what they are or how they are to be understood, rather than taking them as given (whether as a bundle of use values or as a quantum of value). There is nothing in the value relations attached to economic reproduction that allows us to answer this – we have to delve into the broader, as yet unspecified aspects of social reproduction that go beyond the degree of separation. Such considerations necessarily reside beyond the narrow confines of value relations as such within the scope of economic reproduction.

On the other hand, although labour as a class may enter the process of production with a given value of labour power reflecting established social norms, the latter are themselves complex in and of themselves and in how they are created and transformed. This is true across a number of dimensions. First, the value of labour power itself, across different workers within and across different occupations and sectors, let alone locations, will reflect different standards whether it be by virtue of skill or organisational strength or bargaining power. Such is the nature of labour markets and how they are structured and evolve over time (Fine, 1998). Second, there will be correspondingly different quantitative levels of consumption across the different use values that make up the value of labour power. Some will consume more and differently than others although this will inevitably reflect differences in access to purchasing power as well as (unspecified) cultures of consumption. Third, both quantitative and qualitative differences in such norms will differ from one use value to another, possibly relatively limited in case of washing machines within households in developed countries but more distinguishable in terms of the quantity and quality of holidays taken. Fourth, such differences will also be reflected in differences in forms of provision, whether housing be owner-occupied or (privately or socially) rented for example. Fifth, there will also be shifting norms over whether provision is through the (capitalist) market or not, with other forms of provision straddling or lying outside of the orbit of economic reproduction such as through domestic production or provision by the state, charity or otherwise. Thus, for Floyd (2016, pp. 79–80):

> the determination of the value of labour-power by the value of the means of subsistence it requires implies that the domestic household labour needed to transform those means of subsistence into labour-power adds no new value to that commodity. Within capital, these domestic activities are 'structurally made non-labour': in order for labour-power to have a value, the domestic labour that reproduces labour-power has to be dissociated from the circuit of value.

In this way, so-called domestic labour can be seen to be not only a vital component of social reproduction alongside health, care, education and so on, but also mutually to constitute the social norms associated with the value of labour power in which the content of each and the balance between them can shift as well as be transformed, as with commodification and de- and re-commodification. Thus, if in the equally applicable context of non-capitalist as opposed to domestic labour, Hall (2016, pp. 99–100) seeks a

> framework [that] makes space for other forms of labour that persist relationally with capitalist labour, but are not necessarily themselves capitalist: specifically, an engagement with non-capitalist subsistence labour and its location in relation to social reproduction and capitalist production.

Often this dualism between the capitalist and non-capitalist (often taken to be household) labour is seen as a trade-off between one another, for example in a crisis or in austerity, when the domestic labour compensates for lower wages. No doubt, this does happen but the approach adopted here sees the corresponding relationship between economic and social reproduction to be much more complex in a number of ways (see below).[3]

Sixth, as already indicated and readily overlooked even from the perspective of the enriched understanding of the value of labour power as based on social norms that straddle social reproduction, these norms are not defined nor determined simply by reference to the working class and its cultures. On the one hand, social norms attached to commodity consumption derive in part from the income available to spend which is closely correlated to, but not synonymous with, wages (as opposed to other forms of income and wealth). On the other hand, the formation and influence of norms from the household, civil society, and the state equally straddle class boundaries even if their levels and forms are heavily conditioned by class (as with owner-occupation, state versus private pension, access to the health service and education, and so on).

## Specifying social reproduction by SoPs and financialisation …

In short, the moral and historical elements in the value of labour power are complex and differentiated by who gets what and how, in the broader circumstances of social reproduction. The outcomes may be a value for labour power for economic reproduction but are not determined there. Furthermore, extrapolating from work on (private) consumption, beginning with Fine and Leopold (1993) and leading through Fine (2002) to Fine (2013), the differentiation in provisioning and evolving content of such social norms within social reproduction can be addressed through the system of provision (SoP) approach, in which how the elements in the value of labour power are defined and delivered is seen to be contingent upon specific, 'vertically' organised chains of structures, processes, relations, and agencies.[4] Thus, attention is drawn to pensions, housing, food, health systems, and so on, each with its modes of production and reproduction, and corresponding social norms that reflect both the value of labour power and the social as well as the economic reproduction in which it is embedded.

One key element in redefining the value of labour power, creating new norms in forms, and often levels, of delivery, is the processes of commodification and de- and re-commodification. This is, however, not a matter of either/or but how. Thus, decommodification can be the result of removing provision either to domestic or to state responsibility (as non-commodity producers), as well as being contingent upon developments expanding commodification (as in self-entertainment and even self-production through purchase and use of electronic devices). Thus, state provision in particular may massively expand markets for capitalist commodity production without being capitalist production itself nor, in and of itself, necessary to guarantee realisation as opposed to social reproduction.

Typically, in the post-war Keynesian boom, there was in the developed world a coincidence of growth in both commodified *and* non-commodified forms of provision, as with norms for consumer durables, expanding levels of consumption more generally, and the rise of the welfare state for health, education and different elements of social security and well-being, including pensions. Neoliberalism over the past three decades has meant that the value of labour power has been determined in different ways, and not just through class offensive, austerity and so on. Rather, as emphasised in Fine and Saad Filho (2016b), neoliberalism represents the contemporary stage of capitalism in which economic and social reproduction has become increasingly governed by financialisation both directly and indirectly, and see Fine (2014a, 2016a) for (neglect of) the relationship between social policy and financialisation.

What is meant by this is the increasing role of financialisation in both economic and social reproduction. First, observe, though, that I adopt a mean and lean definition of financialisation itself, drawing upon Marx's theory of interest-bearing capital, capital that is lent for the purposes of reaping rewards out of profitmaking capital (Fine, 2014b). This contrasts with more amorphous notions of financialisation that allow for the presence of more finance of any sort and its reflection in the ethos and institutions of contemporary life. This difference is not to deny the impact of such broader considerations but to seek to locate them analytically in relation to one another and to what has been raised before in this text, in particular how has financialisation impacted upon or through the value of labour power (and is this a useful way to proceed in addressing the relationships between financialisation and social reproduction).

Nonetheless, the direct impact of financialisation on social reproduction under neoliberalism has rightly been emphasised by reference to its shifting boundaries around economic reproduction, not least through privatisation of state provision to private capital which can then itself engage in what is termed financial engineering on the basis of the commodities provided – with UK water, for example, providing a stunning illustration, if itself differing from developments within health (Bayliss, 2016). But privatisation itself takes many different forms, ranging from denationalisation, through allowing private providers, to sub-contracting, PPPs and PPIs, and simply raising user charges. These themselves necessarily involve differentiated transformations in the corresponding SoPs, the norms with which they are associated (in both senses – differently distributed levels and forms of provision), and the scope for financialisation itself, narrowly interpreted.

## ...through CCFCC and periodisation ...

Analyses of consumption have tended both to limit it to the purchase of capitalistically produced commodities and to deplore neglect of the wider context upon which corresponding consumption and social reproduction depend.

To some extent, if not fully, such a dichotomy can be broached by unpicking what has been an unrefined understanding of commodity relations. In particular, distinctions can be drawn between commodification, commodity form, and commodity calculation, CCFCC (Bayliss, Fine & Robertson, 2017; Fine, 2017b; together with other contributions in the special issue in which these appear; and also Bayliss et al., 2020). Commodification, commodity form, and commodity calculation correspond, respectively, to fully established (private) capitalist production (although possibly regulated), the presence of charges and hence streams of revenue for whatever is provided (although not necessarily fully privatised capitalist production), and the absence of such revenue streams but the incorporation of practices dictated by some form of market logic or its substitute (as in the discourses and practices of New Public Management for which there is a mantra of market mimetics of quantify, Q, evaluate, E, and prioritise, P, a.k.a. cut through austerity, although these neoliberal imperatives can be challenged through alternative systems of QEP as in gendered macro, cost-benefit analyses or whatever). Both commodification and commodity form directly allow for financialisation, as narrowly interpreted here, since there are streams of revenues that can be securitised and traded on financial markets.

It is vital to acknowledge, however, that the shifting relations between economic and social reproduction are not unilinear nor even (back and forth) linear – the forward march of the market, or not, at the expense of the state as neoliberal ideology (and simplistic reference to Polanyian double movement) would have it. This can be seen in two overlapping ways. On the one hand, extension of CCFCC in social reproduction inevitably creates those who fall outside its orbit, as it were the hard to employ, house, educate, support with income, etc. This raises the question of the nature of social reproduction under financialised neoliberalism both where each of CCFCC does and does not prevail (the rolling back by, and rolling out of, the neoliberal state). It is neither a simple nor a uniform logic. At the same time, for example, that the privatisation of social reproduction is being pursued (i.e. its commodification), emphasis has also been placed upon the extent to which domestic labour, particularly of women, has become increasingly necessary to compensate for cuts in commodified forms for provision that accompany recession and austerity. Thus, as has especially been acknowledged in the feminist literature on social reproduction if not necessarily in this way, the extension of CCFCC to social reproduction tends to shift social to individualised forms of provision and to create added burdens on women in compensating in response to the withdrawal of sources of income and other forms of material support.

Understanding the value of labour power as part and parcel of social reproduction, then, involves acknowledging both the imperatives of capital accumulation and the variable ways in which these are realised. As Ferguson (2016, pp. 54–5) suggests:

> that our means of social reproduction are organised capitalistically –
> that workers have no direct or communal access to shelter, subsistence,

healthcare, and so on – sets definite limits on those changes ... To say that the social totality is a *capitalist* social totality is to suggest that the logic and imperatives of accumulation and production for profit over need – one specific set of social relations among many – dominate (in the sense of exerting pressures on and setting powerful limits to) all aspects of social reproduction.

However, such a discourse of limits only serves to raise the question not only of where those limits lie (and what form of specification can be placed upon them, quantitative or qualitative for example) but also what are the outcomes (and what determines them) within the imposed limits.

To some extent, an answer can be offered in historical as opposed to or, more exactly, in conjunction with, logical terms. A classic analysis is provided by Marx himself in his discussion of the transition from primary dependence on the production of relative as opposed to absolute surplus value. This can be interpreted in narrowly conceived value terms – whether to get more surplus value through extending the amount of labour time performed or through reducing the value of labour power directly or indirectly through productivity increase in the means of workers' consumption. But in terms of social reproduction, reduction in the value of labour power through production of relative surplus value is contingent on social legislation to protect the working-class family from over-exploitation (as female and child labour).

In this respect, there are a number of crucial implications. First, reinforcing the earlier point about how the value of labour power should be interpreted in terms of differentiated social norms within and across its different components, is that the value of labour power is very different in the (earlier) stage of capitalism dominated by the production of absolute surplus value in contrast with that (later) stage dominated by the production of relative surplus value. This is not simply a matter of more or less use of socially necessary labour time that makes up the value of the wage goods nor more or less use values that are provided. Rather, it concerns how labour is reproduced and how it engages as wage labour. This involves differences in what are the material and social elements that are provided, how, and for whom.[5] Furthermore, as Marx carefully notes, the reproduction of labour power is very different in these and in other respects, not least in who provides what amount of labour in constituting the commodity labour power and its reproduction, with changes in both whether and how work extends to women and children. The same applies to how potentially both working conditions and those outside of work (welfare more generally) are or are not subject to systematic control and/or provision. In short, with shift from predominance of absolute to relative surplus value, what is the value of labour power and how it is determined are both fundamentally transformed in relation to one another. This raises questions over what is provided as social norms to reproduce labour power, both across market and non-market forms, to whom and how, even if Marx's own analysis tends to be restricted to legislation to shorten the working day and to protect female and child labourers (as the social forms taken of reducing the value of labour power – underpinning the social reproduction of longer-lived, more productive labourers – as opposed to relying exclusively upon the productivity increase in wage goods as such that derives exclusively from increased productivity, or even product quality change, in economic reproduction).

More generally, then, the value of labour power, and the economic and social reproductions with which it is associated, are subject to broad and major transformations with the transitions between capitalist stages. Previously, for example, I have argued that three periods of capitalism can be identified, the competitive, monopoly and state monopoly periods, in which production of absolute and relative surplus value correspond, respectively, to the first two stages, and the third stage involves extensive state intervention in economic and social reproduction with corresponding implication for the capitalist family (as well as for welfare provision, demography, female labour market, and so on) (Fine, 1992). Social reproduction, and the value of labour power, are very different and very differently determined across these periods, not least as mass production/consumption and Keynesian welfarism are associated with the last stage – but see concluding observations for the neoliberal period.

Second, in major part, the determination of the what, how, for whom, and when, of transformations in the value of labour power is a consequence, not only of some remorseless capitalist logic, but of class and other forms of conflict. It is a matter of whose interests are represented and how. Even if there is some abstract interest of capital in making provision for a social reduction in the value of labour power by protecting and supporting the reproduction of its workforce, this still has to be brought about and, inevitably, will involve conflicts of interest between, for example, those capitals that remain dependent upon cruder forms of exploitation as opposed to those with higher levels of productivity. This means that progressive capitalists may support measures for social beyond economic reproduction, especially in response to, or when struggled for by, an organised working class and, potentially it should be added, progressively oriented or incorporated intermediate strata which can also benefit from universalist forms of provision.

In other words, for capitalist imperatives, 'the sense of exerting pressures on and setting powerful limits to' social reproduction is played out in practice through complex forms of (class) struggle and alliances. These cannot be appropriately reduced to (although they can be read as) the simple interplay between the (potentially fragmented interests) of capital and labour. Social reproduction inhabits the world of the family/household, civil society, and the state variously configured in relation to economic reproduction both logically and historically.

## ... to 10Cs and V[3]

Such considerations raise issues around, indeed make vital given the non-economic indeterminacies involved, what might be termed the material cultures of social reproduction and, in particular, what role ideational factors play in forming and transforming the social norms that underpin social provisioning, and how such factors interact with provisioning itself as well as broader economic and social developments and interests. How are such interests formed and pursued, and with what success and outcomes? Corresponding ideational factors are prominent in the literature – as with the rise of owner-occupation as the ideal form of housing tenancy, the decline of the male-earner model with rising female labour market participation, the individual responsibilisation of pension provision as an asset as opposed to collective provision for old age, the general viability and quality of state care and responsibility as opposed to self-reliance and familial burdens, and so on. Attached to the SoP approach in addressing the material cultures of provisioning has been developed a framing in terms of what is called the 10Cs: that such material cultures are Constructed, Construed, Conforming, Commodified, Contextual, Contradictory, Closed, Contested, Collective, and Chaotic (again see Bayliss, Fine & Robertson, 2017; and Fine, 2017b; together with other contributions in the special issue in which these appear; as well as Bayliss and Fine 2020; and Bayliss et al. (2020).

It may have escaped notice that one C not included here is Class. Surely class has a major influence on consumption and other norms associated with social reproduction, and the meanings and cultures associated with such norms? Indeed, class does run through such norms but it does not determine them. Individual consumption under capitalism is proximately determined by income and price, which clearly creates some divisions by class through income levels available, and which is why norms are differentiated within working-class consumption as well as between it and the norms for other classes and strata. Accordingly, and even more so in the case of the influence of non-economic factors on norms, as in political and social as opposed to economic citizenship, norms for social reproduction cannot be derived from class location alone – hospital access, owner-occupation, university attendance can straddle classes.

And the same applies to other socio-economic and socio-cultural categories, and their intersections, involving age, race, ethnicity, nationality, and gender. The latter in particular has been particularly and appropriately prominent in the understanding of social reproduction and the value of labour power, with varieties of approaches seeking to explain the continuing if shifting asymmetries across men and women in economic and social reproduction upon and through which gender relations are themselves (re)constructed (Sears, 2016; and Bhattacharya, 2017). But, as emphasised in case studies, how the corresponding structures, relations, processes and agencies work out in practice, across different aspects of social reproduction and across time and place, is far from uniform, not least because, for the current period for example, the incidence, impact and influence of financialisation are highly individually and mutually uneven. As a result, on a longer time horizon than contemporary capitalism, it follows that the SoP approach, drawing on a framing of provision through distinguishing CCFCC in practice, can serve to disentangle corresponding variegated outcomes. Under conditions of financialised neoliberalism, these inevitably exhibit considerable volatilities in both economic and social reproduction whether as a result of financialised crisis itself or the (austerity policy) responses to it. This leads to an emphasis upon the variegated, volatile vulnerabilities, $V^3$, of neoliberalism, with the separate aspects of social reproduction often being reconfigured with new norms subject to greater levels of stress and inequality. To some degree, this has been both recognised and exaggerated through reference to extremes, the 1 per cent as opposed to the unemployed or low-paid, deprived of, or subject to privatised, social provision and seeking to sustain consumption norms (and so changing their forms) through access to (exploitative) credit. The picture is, however, much more mixed across what is provided, how, and to or for whom.

Unsurprisingly, then, and itself a consequence of the nature of social repro-duction, one closely debated issue over the SoP approach is how to disentangle where one SoP ends and another one begins. Essentially, this reflects the much broader methodological issue of the relationship between abstract and/or more general analysis and the more concrete and specific. Focusing on the pension system, for example, as an integral system is not to disassociate it from the broader processes within which it is situated, its interaction with financialisation, labour markets, other elements of social policy, and so on. The answer to the question of what is one SoP as opposed to another, then, depends upon what question is being asked (for example, is it about retirement age, entitlements or gendered inequalities) and, in relation to that, inductive examination of inte-gral if differentiated and interdependent structures of provision, and how such structures are attached to corresponding processes, relations, and agencies. In effect, by posing social reproduction in terms of an enriched understanding of the value of labour power, the relationship between the general and the specific can be bridged. The way in which this has been framed here is by reference to the variegated, volatile vulnerabilities accompanying the shifting social norms that are attached to differentiated SoPs, that are themselves underpinned in financialised neoliberalism by the processes of CCFCC that themselves res-onate with the material cultures of provision understood through the 10Cs.[6] In doing so, social reproduction unambiguously engages consumption beyond what determines the value of labour power (working-class consumption) and other aspects than household economic reproduction. The new literature on social reproduction, with emphasis upon intersectionalities, does need to escape its origins in the aspects of reproduction beyond the economic (and hence the focus upon the household and domestic labour) as well as the differentiated consumption and work of the oppressed since all classes are involved relation-ally and structurally in social as in economic reproduction.[7]

## Concluding observations on policy/activism

It is commonplace to observe the austerity of financialised neoliberalism and the weakness and fragmentation of opposition, and even its perverse forms, raising the issue of how to strengthen and unite the case and movement for alternatives. Social reproduction does represent such an opportunity, in part because it impinges upon daily life, and it is an opportunity that is liable to expand in the coming period as neoliberalism seeks avenues for renewing accumulation that draws upon expanding the role in social reproduction of private capital in general and of finance in particular, even if tempered by austerity tendencies. This is all far from new, given privatisations in the past. But there are growing trends for more interventionism by the state to engage *financialised* capital in expanding provision of economic and social *infrastructure* (which might be shortened to the admittedly awkward *finnfrastructure!*) with PPPs, etc., to the fore. These initiatives open windows of opportunity in diverse ways to criticise their form and content (from hospital PPIs to railway reprivatisation as is occurring within the UK after continuing, failing attempts to privatise) and to build movements not only to oppose but to propose alternatives. For this to be successful and sustained, however, requires a keen eye to identify what is going on and to undertake corresponding research to expose it both on its own terms and, to a greater or lesser extent, by situating it relative to the conditions and politics and ideologies of economic and social reproduction.

In this respect, it is worth returning to the issue of how historically the current period of neoliberalism departs from the Keynesianism of the postwar boom. Significantly, for the latter, debate amongst progressives was pitched between reformism and revolution and, in particular, whether the continuing socialising tendencies of capitalism – as evident in large-scale globalised production and extensive state intervention in economic and social reproduction, including welfarism – could be sustained or not. In the event, both have proved unreliable as prospective grasps on the continuing socialisation of reproduction. For neither of these seems now to be in prospect and neoliberal ideology, to the contrary, in terms of its emphasis upon individuation and reliance upon the market, and socialisation of economic and social reproduction (and state intervention to promote it), has continued apace through the unanticipated process of financialisation that does itself underpin neoliberalism.

As Himmelweit (2016) has suggested, with what has been termed by others as the rolling back of the state, the prospects for collective provision in support of social reproduction in such circumstances seem to be bleak, with progressive policies squeezed between their national provision and the uninterest of both finance and global capital in supporting them directly (let alone facilitating them being funded by policy). From my perspective, this may be unduly homogenising (across countries and programmes), and even unduly pessimistic, and, without acknowledging the dynamism of neoliberalism itself, contingent upon extrapolating from the past trajectory of neoliberalism through its first two phases as well as the global crisis in which it has resulted, from which policies for austerity have derived. In the past, as emphasised by Himmelweit herself, the interests of individual capitalists in avoiding the costs of more progressive forms and levels of social reproduction have been overcome, not least through working-class pressure and more active negotiated engagements between capital and labour (see Fine, 2016b on the decline and redefinition of social compacting in the age of neoliberalism). There can be no doubt that both globalisation (of production) and financialisation transform the ways in which social policy and reproduction are realised and weaken the prospects of progressive interventions, not least because of the role of short-termism in returns that tend to characterise financialisation.

However, as is already emerging in the wake of the global crisis and its resistance to being remedied by the traditional policies attached to neoliberalism, a third phase of neoliberalism may be in prospect with the following characteristics: first is close integration between large-scale globally organised finance and industry; second is a renewal of state expenditure on economic and social infrastructure through active involvement of private finance; and third is a renewal of state intervention to promote such developments in tandem with one another. In short, the task ahead is liable not only to put the different elements of social reproduction upon the policy agenda but also to contest the differentiated policies that are already in place and in the processes of emerging as the 'tension that lies at the heart of capitalism between capital accumulation and sustainable forms of reproduction' progresses (Roberts, 2016 cited in Himmelweit, 2016). In summary, this is a tension that continues to unfold – rather than stagnating in the doldrums of financialised, crisis-induced austerity[8] – as well as being underpinned by the imperatives derived from economic reproduction that requires the production and accumulation of surplus value as well as social reproduction however much this may itself be subject to neglects and crises, $V^3$. In its prospective third phase, one avenue for neoliberalism to sustain accumulation is for the state to address social reproduction through extending and intensifying financialised forms of provision on a scale that goes far beyond what has already been experienced. As already emphasised, this is bound to take diverse forms and contents across the different aspects of social reproduction, as new social norms of what and how are transformed, with corresponding responses required in terms of scholarship, culture, and organised struggles for alternatives.

## Notes

1  This is a revised version of Fine (2017a).
2  Apart from fessud.org, see research programmes, for example, around https://environment.leeds.ac.uk/dir-record/research-projects/940/ibuild-infrastructure-business-models-valuation-and-innovation-for-local-delivery and https://lili.leeds.ac.uk.
3  See Winders and Smith (2018) for the increasingly complex ways in which social reproduction has been imagined.
4  For an overview of the SoP approach and how to operationalise it, see Bayliss and Fine (2020).
5  Thus, for example, it is surely no accident that the timing of legislation to protect labour from excessive work coincides with more effective legislation to prevent it from being poisoned by excessive adulteration of consumption goods!
6  For social reproduction as variegated, see Bakker and Gill (2019).
7  Significantly, for example, the wider take of the recent literature on social reproduction still tends to neglect shifting levels of support for the disabled (itself arguably

like pensions an element in the value of labour power) even though disability is at the forefront of neoliberalised austerity in policy form and content. For the UK, see Ryan (2019) covering poverty, work, independence, housing, women, and children.

8 Of course, a different view is taken by those who, setting aside the financialised accumulation of the past three decades, view the current conjuncture as one of having continually failed to have resolved the contradictions of the supposed over-accumulation of the post-war boom.

# References

Bakker, I. & Gill, S. (2019). Rethinking Power, Production, and Social Reproduction: Toward Variegated Social Reproduction. *Capital & Class*, *43*(4), 503–23.

Bayliss, K. (2016). The Financialisation of Health in England: Lessons from the Water Sector (FESSUD Working Paper Series No. 131). Leeds: FESSUD. Available from http://fessud.eu/wp-content/uploads/2015/03/Financilisation_Health_England_WorkingPaper131.pdf.

Bayliss, K., & Fine, B. (2020). *A Guide to the Systems of Provision Approach: Who Gets What, How and Why*. Basingstoke: Palgrave MacMillan, forthcoming.

Bayliss, K., Fine, B., & Robertson, M. (2017). Introduction to Special Issue on the Material Cultures of Financialisation. *New Political Economy*, *22*(4), 355–70. [Repr. in K. Bayliss, B. Fine & M. Robertson (eds.) (2018), *Material Cultures of Financialisation*. London: Routledge.]

Bayliss, K., Fine, B., Robertson, M., & Saad Filho, A. (2020). *Neoliberalism, Financialisation and Welfare: The Political Economy of Social Provision in the UK*. Cheltenham: Edward Elgar, forthcoming.

Bhattacharya, T. (ed.) (2017). *Social Reproduction Theory: Remapping Class, Recentering Oppression*. London: Pluto.

Ferguson, S. (2016). Intersectionality and Social-Reproduction Feminisms: Toward an Integrative Ontology. *Historical Materialism*, *24*(2), 38–60.

Fine, B. (2017a). A Note towards an Approach towards Social Reproduction. Unpublished manuscript. Available at http://iippe.org/wp-content/uploads/2018/12/sroverviewben.pdf.

Fine, B. (2017b). The Material and Culture of Financialisation. *New Political Economy*, *22*(4), 371–82. [Repr. in K. Bayliss, B. Fine & M. Robertson (eds) (2018), *Material Cultures of Financialisation*. London: Routledge.]

Fine, B. (2016a). The Systemic Failings in Framing Neo-Liberal Social Policy. In T. Subaset (ed.), *The Great Financial Meltdown: Systemic, Conjunctural or Policy Created?* (pp. 159–77). Cheltenham: Edward Elgar.

Fine, B. (2016b). Across Developmental State and Social Compacting: The Peculiar Case of South Africa (ISER Working Paper No. 2016/1). Grahamstown: Institute of Social and Economic Research, Rhodes University. Available at www.ru.ac.za/media/rhodesuniversity/content/iser/documents/ISER_Working_Paper_No._2016.01.pdf.

Fine, B. (2014a). The Continuing Enigmas of Social Policy (UNRISD Working Paper 2014-10, June). Geneva: United Nations Research Institute for Social Development. Available at www.unrisd.org/Fine.

Fine, B. (2014b). Financialisation from a Marxist Perspective. *International Journal of Political Economy*, *42*(4), 47–66.

Fine, B. (2013). Consumption Matters. *Ephemera*, *13*(2), 217–48. Available at www. ephemerajournal.org/contribution/consumption-matters.

Fine, B. (2012). Revisiting Rosa Luxemburg's Political Economy. *Critique*, *40*(3), 423–30.

Fine, B. (2008). Debating Lebowitz: Is Class Conflict the Moral and Historical Element in the Value of Labour Power? *Historical Materialism*, *16*(3), 105–14.

Fine, B. (2002). *The World of Consumption: The Cultural and Material Revisited*. London: Routledge.

Fine, B. (1998). *Labour Market Theory: A Constructive Reassessment*. London: Routledge. [Repr. in paperback, 2010.]

Fine, B. (1992). *Women's Employment and the Capitalist Family*. London: Routledge. [Repr. as Routledge Revival edn, 2011.]

Fine, B. (1975). The Circulation of Capital, Ideology and Crisis. *Bulletin of Conference of Socialist Economists*, *12*, 82–96.

Fine, B., & Saad-Filho, A. (2016a). *Marx's 'Capital'*. 6th edn. London: Pluto.

Fine, B., & Saad-Filho, A. (2016b). Thirteen Things You Need to Know about Neoliberalism. *Critical Sociology*, *43*(4–5), 685–706.

Fine, B., & Leopold, E. (1993). *The World of Consumption*. London: Routledge.

Floyd, K. (2016). Automatic Subjects: Gendered Labour and Abstract Life. *Historical Materialism*, *24*(2), 61–86.

Hall, R. (2016). Reproduction and Resistance: An Anti-colonial Contribution to Social-Reproduction Feminism. *Historical Materialism*, *24*(2), 87–110.

Himmelweit, S. (2016). Changing Norms of Social Reproduction in an Age of Austerity. Available at www.iippe.org//wp-content/uploads/2017/01/suegender.pdf.

Lebowitz, M. (2009). Trapped inside the Box? Five Questions for Ben Fine. *Historical Materialism*, *18*(1), 131–149.

Lebowitz, M. (2006). The Politics of Assumption, the Assumption of Politics. *Historical Materialism*, *14*(2), 29–47.

Roberts, A. (2016). Household Debt and the Financialization of Social Reproduction: Theorizing the UK Housing and Hunger Crises. *Research in Political Economy*, *31*, 135–64.

Ryan, F. (2019). *Crippled: Austerity and the Demonization of Disabled People*. London: Verso.

Sears, A. (2016). Situating Sexuality in Social Reproduction. *Historical Materialism*, *24*(2), 138–63.

Winders, J., & Smith, B. (2018). Social Reproduction and Capitalist Production: A Genealogy of Dominant Imaginaries. *Progress in Human Geography*, *43*(5), 871–89.

# 13 Peripheries and precarity

## Portugal, Lisbon and Europe

*Manuel B. Aalbers*

Is Portugal a semi-peripheral country? The answer to that question depends on your perspective. The editors of this book see Portugal as being at the periphery of the European Union (EU) and the eurozone (EZ), but from most of the Global South, Portugal would appear to be very close to the core of the global economy, perhaps at the semi-core. In both cases, however, the global position of Portugal is defined by its position vis-à-vis other European countries.

If the core of Europe is defined by what are commonly considered the non-Mediterranean parts of Western Europe, stretching from Ireland to Austria and from Norway and Iceland to Switzerland and France, there would be vast peripheries of Europe: the Mediterranean periphery that includes Portugal, the East-Central European periphery that includes former socialist states now included in the EU, and the further-East European periphery that includes former socialist states not (yet) included in the EU. In addition, countries that economically speaking appear to be at the core of Europe may actually not be part of the EU, such as Iceland, Norway, Switzerland, and now also the UK. Politically speaking, these countries are peripheral to the EU, in part because many EU regulations will apply to them as well; except for Switzerland they are part of the European Economic Area (EEA) and except for the UK they are part of the Schengen Information System (SIS). Portugal is not only in the EU and EZ but also in the EEA and the SIS. In other words, Portugal may as well constitute the core.

Yet, the inclusion of Portugal in the EZ oddly also may define it as peripheral as the monetary conditions of the EZ may favour richer EZ countries with higher GDP and employment figures, while potentially frustrating policies that would benefit countries with lower wages and lower employment, as the Greek/EU crisis has made so perceptibly clear. This book also explains very well how and why Portugal's inclusion in the EU/EZ contributes to shaping the country as part of Europe's periphery more than contributing to its inclusion in the core of Europe. To me, however, Portugal does not need to be either (semi-) core or (semi-) periphery. In a way, it is the tension between its mixed positionality – defined, shaped, and challenged by its different positions at different scales – that makes Portugal, along with other Mediterranean countries, such an interesting case.

Speaking of scales, there is another element that adds further tensions to the framing and analysis of Portugal as a semi-periphery. Core and periphery can be defined at different scales and Portugal is not only part of different cores and peripheries of the world, there are also cores and peripheries within the country. The Lisbon metropolitan area is the undisputed core of the country. On 3.3 per cent of the total area of Portugal, it accommodates 2.8 million people, which constitutes 27 per cent of the population. It also concentrates 32 per cent of national employment and contributes 36 to 45 per cent to the national GDP.[1]

In other words, when we speak of Portugal we may be speaking of a number of different realities, not just Lisbon metropolitan area versus the rest of the country, but one should also take into account the second largest metropolitan area, Porto, as well as other strong economic regions like the coastal zones of the Alentejo and Algarve compared to the North and Central regions as well as other parts of the Alentejo region.

It is worth noting that the Lisbon metropolitan area is not only the richest in Portugal but also well above the EU's average in terms of statistics like GDP per capita. Although the perception may sometimes appear to be different, Lisbon is an economic powerhouse, which scores higher in PricewaterhouseCoopers' *Global City GDP Rankings* than capital regions in core countries like Berlin and Brussels.[2] Likewise, the Brookings Institution's *Global City GDP* puts Lisbon higher than Dublin and Manchester.[3] Although these lists have their issues, the point is that it is not so easy to define Portugal's most populous region as (semi-) peripheral.

Books and papers that deal with specific places are often very good in explaining what makes these places unique, but they may not be as strong in explaining why and how these places are similar to other places. This edited volume contextualises the development of Portugal into a wider semi-peripheral trajectory of Southern Europe. But I would argue there is more scope for comparison. Many of the developments that are analysed in this volume are not unique to Southern Europe and may be witnessed in many core EU countries as well, e.g. austerity policies, the rise of the financialisation of rental housing or the casualisation (or perhaps 'Mediterraneanisation') of the labour market. For example, in the Netherlands – by all means a core country within the EU and the global economy – there are now almost 2 million people (out of 7.4 million workers) with a so-called 'flex contract'.[4] In addition, 1.1 million people are self-employed without any employees. This suggests some 40 per cent of Dutch workers are no longer on 'permanent' contracts. Perhaps Southern Europe is becoming more different from Northwestern Europe but, at the same time, Northwestern Europe is becoming more like Southern Europe in some ways. My point is not that there is more convergence than divergence but rather a call to complicate matters a bit when comparing developments in different parts of Europe.

The idea that the Portuguese trajectory may be less unique than one would appear to think and perhaps not simply a typical Mediterranean trajectory does not disqualify the analysis presented in this volume. To the contrary, it demonstrates the relevance of understanding the Portuguese case in order to make sense of broader developments in Europe and perhaps also elsewhere. Without claiming that Portugal is becoming like other countries or that Europe necessarily is becoming 'Mediterraneanised', Portugal can serve as a case of what happens when monetary policies are taken 'far from home' at a different scale with other interests at the centre, when unemployment hits an already fragile labour market, and when economic recovery by-and-large takes place on the back of tourism.

Like in Greece, but also Iceland and many other countries, tourism in Portugal has boomed since the economic crisis and recession, and government and those looking for employment alike welcome new jobs. But the new jobs tend to be poorly paid, insecure, and generally won't support a family. These jobs also tend to be concentrated in capital cities, like Lisbon, and other tourist hotspots like Porto and coastal zones. In other words, the tourism boom deepens the existing uneven development, with jobs being added to comparatively strong regions and few prospects of economic recovery in most of the rest of the country. This pushes the labour force to move towards the few regions that appear to recover well.

This faces the country with two additional – and related – problems. First, these are the regions with the highest housing costs. These regions not only have severe affordability problems, with most rental and owner-occupied housing priced out for lower-income groups, including new arrivals from other parts of the country as well as abroad; these regions also face an absolute housing shortage in the sense that not enough houses are available to meet the demand, thereby locking out part of the population. This is a paradox that is far from unique to Lisbon or Portugal and it also is not unique to the post-crisis era. This is a dynamic that is common to cities around the world and has been around for decades and possibly centuries.

The second problem enhances the first but is a more recent trend that is becoming visible in an increasing number of cities. It is the effect of tourism property being used to accommodate non-locals rather than locals (including jobseekers from elsewhere). This includes hotels and tourism facilities that are physically replacing (affordable) housing, but more recently it includes accommodation that is taken off the long-term housing market and converted into short-term rentals. Airbnb is the most widely discussed face of this phenomenon, but it extends much wider. The result is not only that the stock of (affordable) housing goes down but also that not only tourists but also locals are increasingly pushed into short-term rental contracts as well as that housing prices and rents increase much faster than income.

In other words, there is an emerging – or perhaps better: deepening – parallel between the labour and housing markets with an absolute shortage of supply of jobs and housing units coupled to a growing casualisation of conditions and contracts in both markets. The blossoming of part-time, poorly paid, and poorly protected labour happens alongside the rise in short-term, overpriced, and low-security housing. More informal markets are complementing both formal markets, although the border between formal and informal may be a fluid one. Mediterranean countries such as Portugal have a long history of informality in both their labour and housing markets, but whereas the decades running up to the global crisis and recession appeared to be one of increasing – but never full – formalisation, informal labour and housing have made a surprise comeback. Informal housing in this sense should not be limited to self-built housing in the peripheries of the cities but could be expanded to a range of housing 'solutions' that include the aforementioned short-term contracts that were not designed for residents, house-sharing, sub-letting, and overcrowding. Such conditions, in both housing and labour, are increasingly normalised.

I intended to avoid the label 'neoliberalism' in writing this reflection but this kind of normalisation of precarity, unaffordability, and generally poorer conditions appears to be one of the key dimensions of the post-crisis re-emerging – or reinforced – neoliberal order. Whereas pre-crisis neo-liberal discourse was premised on the idea of economic growth, labour and homeownership for all, post-crisis neoliberal discourse is premised on the idea that one should not complain about worsening conditions and should be content to have some sort of employment and some type of accommodation, no matter how insecure, poorly paid or over-priced.

Again, this development is not unique to Portugal. Millennials are told to skip the avocado toast and work harder but, no matter how hard they work, employment and accommodation remain insecure for a larger part of the population and for a longer period of life than was common in the decades preceding the global recession. TV series like *Friends*, *New Girl* and *Adulting* are widely mobilised to advertise a young lifestyle for people sharing housing far beyond their college years and well into their working lives. While a life of sharing, dating, brunching, and generational solidarity surely has its appeal and may actually help to further denormalise the suburban, heteronormative, family-centred homeownership ideal, it is not necessarily shaped by the free-choice paradigm of neoliberalism and mainstream economics.

By and large it is the lack of choice – and lack of security and lack of pur-chasing power – that shapes these fluid lifestyles. While the reality of shared living may appeal for some years and to some for longer periods, it is increas-ingly becoming a normalised condition, not only in global cities like New York and London, or in Mediterranean cities like Lisbon and Athens, but also in sec-ondary global cities in Europe's core such as Berlin and Amsterdam. At the same time demographers and economists complain about delayed and diminished childbearing, which are – at least in part – a consequence of not being able to afford a private residence or the required income security.

Portugal, like other Southern European countries – Greece in particular – shows that casualisation, precarity, and insecurity can be pushed further. In that sense, they present a lesson to other parts of Europe where such conditions are still emerging and could be pushed much further; and will be pushed much fur-ther if some national and European politicians get their chance. But at the same time, Portugal shows that it is possible to fight back with a different kind of politics. Although I would like to end my reflection on this more positive note, the case of Portugal also demonstrates how difficult it is to turn things around in the direction of more equity, security, and stability.

## Notes

1 See www.ine.pt and https://ec.europa.eu/eurostat.
2 https://pwc.blogs.com/files/global-city-gdp-rankings-2008-2025.pdf.
3 www.brookings.edu/research/global-metro-monitor.
4 www.cbs.nl/nl-nl/nieuws/2019/07/aantal-flexwerkers-in-15-jaar-met-drie-kwart-gegroeid.

# Index

Printed in the United States
by Baker & Taylor Publisher Services